LITERATURE AND THE CRIME AGAINST NATURE

LITERATURE AND THE CRIME AGAINST NATURE

Keith Sagar

CHAUCER PRESS
LONDON

Published by Chaucer Press
20 Bloomsbury Street, London WC1B 3JH

Copyright © Chaucer Press 2005

Cover design: Detail of: 'Animals in a Landscape', 1914
(oil on canvas) by Franz Marc (1880–1916) in
The Detroit Institute of Arts, USA,
gift of Robert H. Tannahill

A copy of the CIP data is available from the
British Library upon request

ISBN 1 904449 476

Typeset in Caslon by Rowland Phototypesetting Ltd.
Bury St Edmunds, Suffolk

I should like to dedicate this book to the many adult students with whom I have studied these texts over the last forty years.

ACKNOWLEDGEMENTS

Since this book contains so much of what I have spent my life working on, to acknowledge all my debts would need an autobiography. The extent of my indebtedness is broadly indicated by the length of the bibliography. Though a good deal of the bibliography consists of secondary and background material, it is the imaginative writers themselves who have provided most of the stimulus for my response to other writers.

I am very grateful to a number of friends who gave me contructive criticism of work in progress, particularly Ted Hughes, Peter Redgrove, Walter Stein, Michael and Alix Draper, Peter Hardwick, and Lindsay Clarke.

Chapter 6 was published in *Critical Survey* 7, i, 1995; some pages in chapter 12 derive from my essay 'The Originality of *Wuthering Heights*' in *The Art of Emily Brontë* (Vision Press 1976); chapter 15 was published in *The Cambridge Quarterly*, 27, i, 1998; some pages in chapter 17 derive from chapter 8 of *D.H. Lawrence: Life into Art (Penguin/Viking 1985)*, some from 'The Open Self and the Open Poem', *D.H.Lawrence Review*, 24, i, 1992, and some from 'Lawrence and the Resurrection of Pan' in *D.H. Lawrence: The Centre and the Circles*, ed. Peter Preston, University of Nottingham, 1992; and the final chapter was first published in *The Laughter of Foxes: A Study of Ted Hughes*, Liverpool University Press, 2000.

Such outrage done to nature as compels
The indignant power to justify herself;
Yea, to avenge her violated rights
For England's bane.

[William Wordsworth]

'Virtue,' said Marcus Aurelius, 'what is it, only a living and enthusiastic sympathy with Nature?' Perhaps indeed the efforts of the true poets, founders, religions, literatures, all ages, have been, and ever will be, our time and times to come, essentially the same – to bring people back from their persistent strayings and sickly abstractions, to the costless average, divine, original concrete.

[Walt Whitman]

The artist speaks to our capacity for delight and wonder, to the sense of mystery surrounding our lives; to our sense of pity, and beauty, and pain; to the latent feeling of fellowship with all creation.

[Joseph Conrad]

Yet even the truth into which Plato dies is a form of death, for when he separates the Eternal Ideas from Nature and shows them self-sustained he prepares the Christian desert and the Stoic suicide.

[W.B.Yeats]

The character of great works is exactly this: that in them the full presence of the inner world combines with and is reconciled to the full presence of the outer world. And in them we see that the laws of these two worlds are not contradictory at all; they are one all-inclusive system; they are laws that somehow we find it almost impossible to keep, laws that only the greatest artists are able to restate. They are the laws, simply, of human nature. And men have recognized all through history that the restating of these laws, in one medium or another, in great works of art, are the greatest human acts.

[Ted Hughes]

CONTENTS

FOREWORD

One of the many benefits of adult teaching is that one can teach more or less whatever is of most interest to oneself at the time, including foreign literature in translation; there are no examination syllabuses, and there is no need to repeat oneself. Consequently I found myself early in my career teaching a vast range of literature, and most of the authors I engaged with, however remote in time, and not necessarily poets, seemed to offer exciting connections with each other, and require to be thought about in the same context, the context of man's relationship with the non-human world.

In the early seventies I started teaching Greek literature in translation, and became through it more aware of the essentially religious nature of the whole poetic undertaking, and specifically the dedication of nearly all the imaginative art which interested me to Dionysos as against Apollo. The purpose of the greatest works of Greek poetry, whether mythic, epic or dramatic, seemed to be to warn man against that particular kind of pride the Greeks called *hubris*. And the primary symptom of *hubris* was man's belief that by virtue of his intelligence and technology he could stand apart from and above the natural world. Such works as the *Odyssey,* the Oedipus plays of Sophocles, and *The Bacchae*, seemed to me to have as their primary raison d'etre the need to warn civilization of the dangers, simultaneously inner and outer, psycho-spiritual, social, and global, of the crimes committed against Nature in its name. It was the function of the poet, then as always, to challenge and expose the dominant beliefs of his culture.

Aristophanes' *The Frogs* was performed at the Great Dionysia in 405, possibly the same festival at which *The Bacchae* was performed. And *The Frogs*, for all its knock-about comedy, is almost as tragic in its implications for Athens as *The Bacchae*. The idea of the play is that since the three great poets, Aeschylus, Sophocles and Euripides, were all now dead, the only hope for Athens was to send Dionysos down to Hades to bring back the greatest of them. When Dionysos gets there, the ghost of Euripides asks him what he wants a poet for. 'To save the city of course', he replies. The comedy lies entirely in the idea that a dead poet might be brought back, not at all in the idea that a poet might save the city. The absolute seriousness of that proposition marks the difference in the status of the poet in Athenian society from our own. The idea that a poet could save us if listened to would provoke almost universal laughter, not least among academics. Yet even then the saving wisdom of the tragic poet was not heeded. Both statesmen and people preferred, in Aristophanes' words, to 'sit at the feet of Socrates / Till they can't distinguish the wood from the trees / And tragedy goes to POT'. The poet shares, it seems, the curse of Cassandra. The gift of prophesy must be paid for by the fate of never being heeded. The elected leaders pursued their hubristic, blind, suicidal policies with the support of the majority of the electorate. The following year Athens fell. There followed the long decadence, and the rise of Rome.

The tragic poets had foreseen not only that, but that Athens was creating a template for all Western civilization, which would eventually succeed in spreading universal plague, spilling all germens, destroying the Sphinx, Pan, Dionysos, 'great creating Nature' herself.

I am thus entering a debate which has existed as long as civilization, about whether art is part of civilization's struggle to transcend or maintain itself independently of nature, or whether it operates in alliance with nature infiltrating and subverting civilization in the attempt to prevent it from cutting itself off from nature's sustaining energies and values – whether it is properly, in Nietzsche's terms, Apollonian or Dionysian. It is no longer possible to regard this debate as academic. It is now a matter of life and death.

The scope of my book was becoming more complex and topical as it was affected by my growing interest in ecology. I became more aware, like every sane person, of the gravity of what was being done to the environment, and of our ecological interdependence with the rest of life. I did not develop ecological theories and then go looking for literary works which could be interpreted as supporting those theories. My interest in ecology did not provide me with a means of interpreting, still less judging literature. I had no need of that. It simply alerted me to the fact that in work after work, works from many periods and cultures, chosen for many different reasons, the thinking and feeling of deep ecology (systemic, holistic and biocentric thinking), had been there all along, as if that were also the inevitable language of the imagination. I simply paid more attention to the central theme of much of the greatest literature, man's attempt to redefine himself in relation to Nature, the cosmos, the not-self in which he is such a small but crucial speck.

*　　*　　*

Other extra-literary reading of course fed into the process: the complete works of Jung and Joseph Campbell (especially *The Hero with a Thousand Faces*) for example, and such stimulating essays as Laing's *The Politics of Experience*, and Lorca's *Theory and Function of the Duende*. From these I learned that the imagination requires the opposite of hubris, an ego-death.

Trying to keep up with Ted Hughes remained my primary concern, and I saw that what I was in effect doing in much of my other work was exploring the way in which, according to Eliot's proposition that every new writer added to the tradition changes the tradition, Lawrence and Hughes had changed the way we needed to read almost all previous literature dealing with Nature. And since by Nature I now understood all man's understanding of and dealings with his own nature and everything beyond himself in the created universe, including his ideas of spirit, godhead and the sacred, that meant virtually all literature of any importance.

The works which strike home will be different for each of us. But some works have struck large numbers of readers particularly deeply, at different times and in different places and cultures. These are the classics, which every generation reinterprets and revalidates in terms of its own experience and problems. For there is nothing unique about our experience or new about our problems, except their urgency. Two thousand five hundred years ago the visionary writers saw the beginning of a process which would inevitably, ultimately, lead to our present predicament. But the existing classics cannot answer all our needs. As Eliot insisted, there must be a succession of new works both extending and changing the tradition. It is one of the most important functions of the contemporary writer to bring home to us what our deepest needs are. This awareness we can then translate into new demands made upon the literature of the past, and a revaluation of it in terms of its ability to meet them.

The classic status of recent work cannot be finally determined. But the critic must attempt to identify the contemporary classics in order to engage with them at their moment of maximum relevance and urgency. Perhaps one measure of the greatness of a recent or contemporary writer is precisely his or her ability to revitalize for us the great literature of the past, by providing us with the bearings by which we can understand and respond to it anew. The two twentieth-century writers who have most deeply affected my own reading of earlier literature have been Lawrence and Hughes.

By now I was taking every teaching opportunity and every window in my work on Lawrence and Hughes, to work on this book. But it was growing alarmingly. For every chapter I wrote two more were added to the list of those requiring to be written. I knew that I must start to find parameters which limited rather than extended the scope of the book. These came, as usual, by chance. In the mid-eighties I was asked to be the external examiner for a thesis at Exeter University by Nick Bishop, which was later published as *Re-Making Poetry: Ted Hughes and a New Critical Psychology*. What I gained most from this fine thesis was a sense of how a kind of hubris can express itself stylistically; how a certain rhetorical command of language is itself a way of reasserting the dominance of the ego, whatever the content.

But the most important breakthrough, which came at about the same time, was a result of looking, for some other purpose, at the notes I had taken at various talks and readings by Ted Hughes. I came across my notes on an unpublished talk he had given on the Eastern European poets at the Cheltenham Literature Festival in 1977, which I had not looked at since. He had said that he could never understand how critics could presume to pass judgement on literature, since it was the function of literature to pass judgement on its readers. It was obvious from other sources that Hughes believed literature earned the right to do this by first putting its own author in the dock for crimes against nature and his own nature, or complicity in such crimes. We are all, including writers, criminals; but the writer differs from the rest of us by pleading guilty and allowing himself to be tried and punished as a representative of the race, most of whose crimes and hubris he can find replicated in himself easily enough. Sometimes he manages to get himself, to a degree, corrected. It was from that time that I changed the title of the book to *Literature and the Crime Against Nature.*

By 'nature' I understand not only the physical environment, the earth with its climate and landscapes, its flora and fauna; not only the powers and processes, systems and relationships, which we now call the ecosystem; but also those psychological, moral and spiritual conditions which might be spoken of as consonant with or expressive of nature. The inner crime, the crime against our own nature, must precede any crimes against the environment. There is little surviving myth, folklore or imaginative literature which does not deal in some way with the nature of man in relation to whatever non-human powers he perceives as operating in the world. It is by such enquiry that the imagination seeks to understand the turmoil of history. Thus the oldest myths, stories and poems are always relevant to the most specific and urgent problems of any age. The story of the Trojan War is about any and every war; the Prometheus myth is about nuclear energy; the Tiresias myth is about genetic engineering; the Oedipus myth is about the disposal of toxic wastes . . .

But I am not concerned with the crime against nature simply as a theme, central and pervasive though it is. Imaginative literature speaks a different language from that of any other discourse, not only exploiting timbre and rhythm which, in Lawrence's phrase 'sound upon the plasm direct', but, most significantly, speaking the ancient language of symbol and metaphor, a language of connections, relationships, patterns, systems, wholes, as distinct from the language of analysis and dualism and atomization which is our normal modern speech. Thus even literature which is not directly about the crime against nature can contribute to changes in consciousness which are highly relevant to it. An awareness of these aspects of the experience of reading imaginative literature can transform that experience in the same way that scientific thought is being transformed by ecology and systems theory and religious thought by the new orientation towards the sacredness and blessings of creation.

We know that all mirrors held up to nature, even by scientists, are distorting mirrors. All descriptions of nature are coloured by attitudes, are partly descriptions of the contents of the writer's own psyche projected onto the receptive face of nature. For the scientist this might be a problem; but for the imaginative artist it is the whole point of his art, to strive for a vision which can unify the subjective and the objective, inner and outer:

❋   ❋   ❋

The character of great works is exactly this: that in them the full presence of the inner world combines with and is reconciled to the full presence of the outer world. And in them we see that the laws of these two worlds are not contradictory at all; they are one all-inclusive system; they are laws that somehow we find it almost impossible to keep, laws that only the greatest artists are able to restate. They are the laws, simply, of human nature. And men have recognized all through history that the restating of these laws, in one medium or another, in great works of art, are the greatest human acts. [Ted Hughes, *Winter Pollen*, 150–1]

There are broadly three possible attitudes to nature: first, that it is cruel, ugly, obscene, amoral – that life lived in accord with it would be 'nasty, brutish and short'; second, that it has its beauties and charms, but that these are irrelevant or seductive – a temptation away from truth or ultimate values, which are to be sought elsewhere; or third that, without turning a blind eye to anything in nature, it is still possible to find it sacred, and a source of permanent values. All these are, of course, represented in literature. The question is whether the creative imagination, by its very nature, tends towards one rather than another. Has it taken sides in the two-thousand-year battle between rational, civilized man and Nature? How relevant is great imaginative literature to the most urgent problems of the twenty-first century?

※　　※　　※

This book could have been published as early as about 1990; but that was about the worst moment, a time when the anti-literary forces within English studies had gained such power and influence that they were able to prevent the publication of almost any book which took literature seriously (and to prevent the promotion or even employment of lecturers who took it seriously). It languished for a decade unread except by friends, by several creative writers, and by some of the few academics (most notably Jonathan Bate) who were sympathetic to my approach. Then I put it on my website, and the fact that the essays were downloaded at the rate of about two hundred a day for a year or so, with plenty of positive feedback, encouraged me to look again at the possibility of book publication. There were by now plenty of signs that the tyranny of post-modern critical theory, 'cultural studies' and political correctness which had made English departments the laughing-stock of universities for the closing decades of the twentieth century was collapsing through sterility and in-breeding. It is time for criticism to take up the only task which can justify its existence, to serve imaginative writing, both its writers and its readers.

Reading works of imaginative literature has given me much of great value. I do not mean pleasure, which is a frequent but not essential by-product. Nor do I mean in the old sense 'enhancing the quality of life' by reading the right books. That is uncomfortably close to enhancing it by drinking the right wines. It has modified for the better my own consciousness; it has given me access to wisdom, vision and experience far beyond my own; it has fertilized my own creativity; it has shown me something of the survival gear the race will need to live in this world in the new millennium. Many others, I know, both from personal testimony and published work, have had similar experiences. Some readers need no intermediaries; others need a little help to gain access to these gifts. It seems to me that my career as teacher and writer on literature can be justified only to the extent that it has provided such help.

This attitude to literature is, of course, politically incorrect. It is accused of lacking any theoretical basis or discipline, of being elitist, and of being traditional (which is now synonymous with 'out-of-date'). These accusations assume that it is based on nothing more substantial than half-baked or unacknowledged theories or assumptions, or worse, that it is merely a statement of faith, unsupported and insupportable. It is, of course, text-based, and one of its 'incorrect' assumptions is that texts, especially those of the traditional canon, have any status, should command any respect. But what I am talking about is incontrovertible *fact*. If someone, without provocation, is savaged and mutilated by a dog, their subsequent statement that the dog is dangerous is not an assumption or opinion or theory or superstition, it is a fact – they have scars to prove it. If my imagination is fertilized by exposure to a work of literature, my subsequent statement that literature can fertilize the imagination of readers is similarly a fact, and I have poems to prove it. Unfortunately, not all the proofs are so tangible. In many cases there is no alternative to taking the reader through the texts implying continually, 'is this not so?'

Students for decades now have been discouraged on theoretical grounds from making such journeys. When, in Brecht's telling, Galileo asked the papal astronomers to look at the moons of Jupiter through his telescope they said that there was no point in doing so, since they could prove to him by disputation that the moons of Jupiter could not exist. 'Political correctness' can be equally obscurantist.

Post-modern critics have appropriated to themselves the authority formerly enjoyed by the writers of the traditional canon. Essential core reading is now a vast canon of post-critical theory, which leaves no time for the reading of imaginative works. Post-modern critical theorists are the self-appointed judges of literature; yet many lack, or fail to demonstrate, the basic ability even to read such literature.

I am not interested in engaging in any debate with post-modern critical theorists, or in advancing any opposing theories. It is impossible to engage in serious debate with those who argue (using language of course) that language has no purchase on reality. All theories, even those I subscribe to, get in the way of open and appropriate reading. What does interest me is any means by which we can make ourselves better, more perceptive, responsive and cooperative readers, more alert to what is there on the page. For this reason I shall not at this point say anything of the book's conclusions. The proof of the pudding is in the eating. My aim is to offer convincing readings – convincing to any open-minded readers, irrespective of their prior affiliations – of a wide range of major works of Western literature, ancient and modern. My hope is that the readings which follow, will, cumulatively, draw the reader towards certain general conclusions. Some of the conclusions to which I have been gradually driven by my reading and teaching of a great deal of literature from Homer to Hughes I shall set out in an Afterword.

1 REBELS AGAINST THE GODS: PROMETHEUS, ODYSSEUS, JOB

The Prometheus myth lays the groundplan of what is most central in all subsequent Western history and literature. Prometheus himself subsumes God and Lucifer, Adam and Christ.

In some versions of the myth, Prometheus (whose name means 'foresight'), a Titan, son of Earth herself, makes the first men. In others, men spring spontaneously from the earth, but Prometheus is the first and only god to make common cause with them, to assume responsibility for them (since they are utterly helpless), to take sides with them against a tyrannical god, to commit the first crimes on their behalf, and voluntarily to suffer the extreme of physical and mental torment in order to guarantee their survival and progress. The myth tells us nothing of his motives. He is unique among Greek gods in that he seems to have no *raison d'être* beyond his partnership with man. Most of his fellow Titans had been defeated by Zeus and the Olympian gods and subjected to terrible punishments. Prometheus' foresight had enabled him to predict the outcome and take sides with Zeus. He is equally able to see the even more terrible consequences for himself of his later single-handed rebellion against Zeus on behalf of man, yet accepts them, as if he had no choice. He seems to represent that which is indestructible in the human spirit – man's aspiration to raise himself above the condition of the brutes and become independent of both nature and the gods. If that spirit is an absolute, then it is also, for the Greeks, a *theos*, a god. Equally, he can be seen as an eternal image of the imperfection of man's nature, his greed, pride, violence, materialism, his blinkered intelligence. To try to put it more neutrally, as the myth does, he embodies man's inability to submit to the given conditions of his being, which always seem to man to constitute, in themselves, an injustice against him.

Ovid elaborates on Hesiod's account of Prometheus as creator of man:

> Though all the beasts
> Hang their heads from horizontal backbones
> And study the earth
> Beneath their feet, Prometheus
> Upended man into the vertical –
> So to comprehend balance.
> Then tipped up his chin
> So to widen his outlook on heaven.
>   [*Tales from Ovid,* 8]

Not only does this free man's hands to become tool-maker, weapon-maker and technician, it also makes man the 'godlike novelty' of all creation, the only creature capable, for good or ill, of looking beyond the earth and of aspiring to a condition of superiority to its conditions and processes. Thus

1

Prometheus planted in man the seeds of rebellion against the given conditions, nature's laws.

Prometheus' next significant act in relation to man was to slay an ox. According to Pliny he was the first ever to do so. His purpose, presumably, was to provide man with meat. Knowing that such a sacrilegious act would anger Zeus, he instituted sacrifice, whereby man might provide himself with meat and placate the gods simultaneously. Thus sacrifice was invented as a cover-up for sacrilege. So one-sided were Prometheus' sympathies, so irresistible his trickster nature, that he could not resist attempting to trick Zeus himself by hiding all the good meat in the stomach-sac, covering the bones with luscious fat, and then inviting Zeus to choose. Did he really expect all-seeing Zeus to be taken in? Zeus saw through the deception, but deliberately chose the bones in order to give himself an excuse to condemn man to misery or extinction by withholding fire, without which man's condition would be wretched, bestial and hopeless.

Prometheus had another trick up his sleeve. He stole a spark of fire from the gods concealed in a hollow fennel stalk, and gave it to man. The possession of the divine spark bestows on man his essential subsequent condition, combining the mortality of the beasts with the power of the gods. Zeus had withheld fire expressly so that man should die out. Therefore, Prometheus' theft is an act of salvation, and a protest against injustice. Man needed fire to keep himself warm, to cook his meat, to smelt iron to make utensils. A surviving fragment of Aeschylus' *Prometheus the Fire Kindler* is part of a lesson in smelting. But Prometheus foresaw that eventually the gift would enable man to do much more than this, to stand spiritually erect, to become independent and civilized. He taught man all his own skills: architecture, astronomy, mathematics, navigation, medicine, metallurgy, and other useful arts. As Aeschylus writes in *Prometheus Bound*:

> And fire has proved
> For men a teacher in every art, their grand resource.

The myth foretells man's appropriation of nature, of life itself, his creator, to his own purposes. The myth itself does not prejudge the issues. It neither validates nor condemns Prometheus. It is open to whatever interpretation writers who draw upon it choose to give it. The Promethean fire has been for some writers (Shelley, for example) man's glory, his unbreakable revolutionary spirit. Prometheus is the hero who lifted man out of the mud and gave him his humanity with its limitless potential. He bared his own breast to draw the wrath of Zeus upon himself, suffering pain and humiliation incalculable that man might be free, confident of ultimate victory. Not only Zeus, but all the other gods would die. The savage god's days are numbered unless he can arrive at some accommodation with man. Only Prometheus would live on, in man, to witness man's apotheosis.

Such an interpretation has become more difficult for us, witnesses as we are of the culmination. We are more likely to see the gift of fire as just as deceptive as Zeus' gift to men through Prometheus' brother Epimetheus of Pandora, described by Hesiod as 'an evil thing in which they may all be glad of heart while they embrace their own destruction'. Perhaps Zeus in his wisdom had better motives for withholding fire, and Prometheus worse motives for stealing it. Fire is the divine creative and destructive energy of the universe. The gift of fire puts into man's hands power which he is quite incapable of handling safely. It will not be long before he is forging weapons. The logical conclusion of the gift of fire, its contemporary equivalent, is nuclear power. Roszak reports that

> J. Robert Oppenheimer, witnessing the first test of a nuclear weapon, confessed to tasting sin. But he and all his colleagues knew from the beginning what lay waiting at the end of the project. And which was the stronger flavor, the sin, or the satisfaction of having stolen fire from the gods?
>
> [195]

Therefore, from another perspective, Prometheus, like all tricksters, gets it wrong. In trying to remedy what he takes to be God's mistakes, he makes things even worse. He commits, on man's behalf, the original sin, a theft of forbidden knowledge, the purpose of which and the punishment for which is to separate man from nature and from divinity, to encourage man to indulge in *hubris*, that Faustian pride which prompts him to become his own god, or to remake the gods in his own image. In *Frankenstein* Shelley's wife saw this as hubris taken to the point of suicidal insanity.

In teaching man sacrifice and the use of fire, Prometheus taught him to destroy both Fauna and Flora, in Kerenyi's words to 'strike wounds in the divine environment' [*Prometheus*, 53]. In this he is the exact opposite of Osiris:

> Osiris became the first king of Egypt and the creator of civilization, teaching his people the art of cultivation and the honouring of the gods, 'establishing justice throughout both banks of the Nile'. He taught the Egyptians how to plant wheat and barley, how to gather the fruit from the trees and to cultivate the vine, and before their time the races of the world had been but savages. When he travelled to teach other nations, Isis ruled vigilantly and peacefully in his absence.
>
> [Baring 228]

Mythically, it was Prometheus who determined that the Neolithic Golden Age should be violently replaced by the terrible Age of Bronze:

> Earth's natural plenty no longer sufficed.
> Man tore open the earth, and rummaged in her bowels.
> Precious ores the Creator had concealed
> As close to hell as possible

3

Were dug up – a new drug
For the criminal. So now iron comes
With its cruel ideas. And gold
With crueller. Combined they bring war –
War, insatiable for the one,
With bloody hands employing the other.
Now man lives only by plunder.
[*Tales from Ovid* 12]

Prometheus continues throughout his agony, crucified upon a crag, his liver pecked out daily by Zeus' vulture, to rail at Zeus. Zeus is identified with things as they are, eternality. Zeus fears change and is angered by any attempt to bring it about. Prometheus, for all his foresight, knows and foresees less than Zeus. He is distinguished from Zeus and almost all the other gods by his inability to accept things as they are, his assumption that permanent change – evolution, 'progress' – must be preferable. He is motivated partly by compassion for man, but also by Faustian pride, which blinds him to the long-term consequences. The would-be redeemer is himself in need of redemption, and that can be bought only by suffering:

I must be bowed by age-long pain and grief.
So only will my bonds be loosed.
[*Prometheus Unbound*]

Prometheus must undergo an ego-death. He must accept suffering as a necessary and permanent part of the human condition. Kerenyi interprets the wreath with which the delivered Prometheus is crowned as a

sign and token of release and redemption, of repentance and
reconciliation with Zeus, the symbol of a bond with the hard laws of a
luminous, rigidly established heaven consciously accepted by an eternally
restless being, a victim of injustice, a sufferer from his own darkness,
exposed to unendurable torments.   [127]

Given that only fragments survive of the first and third parts of Aeschylus' trilogy, such interpretations must remain speculative, but they are in accord with the most recent recycling of the myth in Ted Hughes' *Prometheus on his Crag*. Hughes' version also testifies to the validity of Nietzsche's account of the permanent relevance of the Prometheus myth:

The presupposition of the Prometheus myth is primitive man's belief in
the supreme value of fire as the true palladium of every rising civilization.
But for man to dispose of fire freely, and not receive it as a gift from
heaven in the kindling thunderbolt and the warming sunlight, seemed a
crime to thoughtful primitive man, a despoiling of divine nature. Thus the

original philosophical problem poses at once an insoluble conflict between men and the gods, which lies like a huge boulder at the gateway to every culture.   [*Birth*, 63]

❊   ❊   ❊

The original palladium was a protective statue of Pallas Athene (given to Troy by Zeus himself) which Odysseus stole. Odysseus, like Prometheus, was a clever trickster, and a robber and enemy of the gods. However, he differs from Prometheus in several important respects: first, he is entirely human and mortal; second, his actions are purely selfish; third, he is successful, winning, at last, (in Homer's telling), the admiration of Athene and the respect of men and gods.

In *Occidental Mythology* Joseph Campbell gives a lengthy interpretation of *The Odyssey* in terms of a spiritual quest and initiation in which Odysseus overcomes the psychically disabling divisions between male and female, life and death, culminating 'in a realization of an identity *in esse* of the individual (microcosm) and the universe (macrocosm)' [164]. That the adventure begins with a crime, the sacking of Ismarus, a particularly bloody crime with women as booty (which is all in a day's work for Odysseus), is not in dispute. Zeus responds to this with a tempest, which drives Odysseus' ships 'beyond the bounds of the known world'. But once Odysseus has entered the mythic realm, according to Campbell he can do no wrong. Campbell can describe the encounter with the Cyclops as 'self-divestiture' only by ignoring completely the last two and a half pages of the 'Cyclops' chapter, where Odysseus rashly reinvests himself with the full string of his names and titles and ensures the enmity of Poseidon himself. Odysseus is occasionally humiliated, but never humble. He is downcast, but shows no sign of the self-questioning which characterizes the Dark Night of the Soul (which Campbell would have us believe he enters). His encounters with Circe, Calypso, and Nausicaa represent, we are told, 'psychological adventures in the mythic realm of the archetypes of the soul, where the male must *experience* the import of the female before he can meet her perfectly in life' [164]. The most important of these females is Circe: 'The goddess who in her terrible aspect is the cannibal ogress of the Underworld was in her benign aspect the guide and guardian to that realm and, as such, the giver of immortal life' [171]. Campbell ends by contrasting Greece with India and the Judaic world. In the bible the dialogue between patriarchal and matriarchal thought is 'deliberately suppressed in favour exclusively of the male'. In India

the principle of masculine ego initiative was suppressed, even to the point of dissolving the will to individual life; whereas in Greece the masculine will and ego not only held their own, but prospered in a manner that at that time was unique in the world: not in the way of the compulsive 'I want' of childhood (which is the manner and concept of the ego normal to the Orient), but in the way of a self-responsible intelligence, released from both 'I want' and 'thou shalt', rationally regarding and responsibly judging the world of empirical facts, with the final aim not of serving gods but of developing and maturing man. For, as Karl Kerenyi has well put it: 'The Greek world is chiefly one of sunlight, though not the sun, but man, stands at its centre'.   [173–4]

It is strange that Campbell should here allow himself to be so carried away by the attractions of the emerging anthropocentric vision, for in his opening chapter he had expressed deep reservations about 'the warrior principle of the great deed of the individual who matters', 'the freely willing, historically effective hero':

> And yet, one cannot help feeling that there is something forced and finally unconvincing about all the manly moral attitudes of the shining righteous deedsmen, whether of the biblical or of the Greco-Roman schools; for, in revenge or compensation, the ultimate life, and therewith spiritual depth and interest, of the myths in which they figure continues to rest with the dark presences of the cursed yet gravid earth, which, though defeated and subdued, are with their powers never totally absorbed. A residue of mystery remains to them; and this, throughout the history of the West, has ever lurked within, and emanated from, the archaic symbols of the later, 'higher' systems – as though speaking silently, to say, 'But do you not hear the deeper song?'   [24–5]

Perhaps that deeper song is the song of the sirens, daughters of Earth, to which Odysseus must make himself deaf if he is to survive as hero.

All Campbell says about The Odyssey is, it seems to me, perfectly accurate, except the suggestion that Homer is wholly to be identified with his hero. As I read The Odyssey I can respond to Odysseus only as a parody of the quest hero, who undergoes all the archetypal initiations and psychic adventures only to emerge completely unchanged. He does not meet Penelope 'perfectly' on his return. He is still far from being in a mature and responsible frame of mind in relation to women or life in general. His ego remains, through-out, unquestioned, and very much a matter of 'I want'. His main concern is not that man should stand at the centre of the world, but that Odysseus should. He wins acknowledgement from the gods in the end not because he has found the right relationship between man and the universe, but because he is the first man to stand up to the gods and survive to tell the tale. That is an achievement, which commands some admiration, but not quite in Campbell's terms. And Homer's admiration is severely qualified. His Odysseus is both hero and anti-hero.

Far from becoming a self-responsible adult, Odysseus is locked into a permanently childish state. According to Philip Slater it is a type fostered not only by such heroic myths as The Iliad, but also by the pattern of Greek family life. When Slater writes 'He will feel that if he is not a great hero he is nothing, and pride and prestige become more important than love' [33], he is not speaking of Odysseus, but of the typical Athenian boy. When Slater describes what Freud calls the 'narcissistic type', he comes even closer to a description of Homer's Odysseus:

> The fatal charm of such persons lies in the illusion of independence they maintain – if others help them they perceive themselves not as receiving but as taking, by virtue of their cleverness at manipulating people. They do not in fact 'need' specific others, since they are concerned only with their personal survival and self-aggrandizement. Nor does conscience ever make cowards of them, for they have none. This emotional obliviousness to others, this seeming independence and self-love, endows them with considerable *mana* as leaders. [151]

Homer begins the story near the end so that most of it can be told by Odysseus himself. Odysseus tells the tale compulsively. He is single minded in his pursuit of name and fame. He begins his tale to Lord Alcinous: 'I am Odysseus, Laertes' son. The whole world talks of my stratagems, and my fame has reached the heavens'. He cannot bear the thought of his tale coming to an end. There must always be a yet unwritten sequel. His fame is only as bright as his last adventure. The happy homecoming is an ending to be deferred as long as possible, until that too becomes a violent adventure. There is heavy irony in Odysseus' frequent complaints that a harsh fate has kept him from his hearth so long. He voluntarily stays a year with Circe and eight with Calypso. He offers to stay a year with the Phaeacians. When he does finally reach home, we know that he will not stay there long.

The purpose of all the adventures is to tell others about them afterwards. His must be the story not of one hero among many, but of a hero to end all heroes. Unlike the other heroes of the Trojan War, he has no military exploits to boast of. He expects to be admired not for noble deeds, but for deceit and the sacking of many cities. And his enemies are not Trojans but monsters and gods. The childish formula is to accept a dare (usually of his own devising), to tell his story (how I won through; how much I suffered in the process, but how much more suffering I brought to others), to show his scar, to receive praise. He requires nothing more from life than its endless repetition.

One difficulty, which prevents some readers from recognizing the persistent irony of The Odyssey, is that they carry over to it the values of The Iliad. But even if Homer did write both epics, The Odyssey may well be twenty or thirty years later than The Iliad, and constitute an ironic commentary on the values of the earlier book. Those values are summed up by George Steiner:

> War and morality cry havoc, yet the centre holds. That centre is the affirmation that action of body and heroic spirit are in themselves a thing of beauty, that renown shall outweigh the passing terrors of death, and that no catastrophe, not even the fall of Troy, is final. [9]

The mature Homer may well have looked back on that youthful vision with a wry smile. It is the vision with which Odysseus attempts to console the shade of Achilles in the underworld, but Achilles gives him short shrift: 'My lord Odysseus, spare me your praise of Death. Put me on earth again, and I would rather be a serf in the house of some landless man, with little enough for himself to live on, than king of all these dead men that have done with life' [184].

Odysseus had been named by his grandfather Autolycus, whose own name meant Lone Wolf. Autolycus, proud of his pre-eminence as 'the most accomplished thief and liar of his day', hoped his grandson might inherit these qualities. The Rieu translation reads: 'In the course of my lifetime I have made enemies of many a man and woman up and down the wide world. So let this child be called Odysseus, "the victim of enmity"' [298]. This clearly makes no sense, and Dimock has demonstrated that it is a mistranslation. Autolycus uses the verb *odyssasthai*. What he is, in effect, saying, according to Dimock, is: 'I have odysseused many in my time, up and down the wide world, men and women both; therefore let his name be Odysseus' [Steiner 106]. It is clear that Odysseus is to be the perpetrator, not the victim. Dimock calls him Trouble-Bringer. The fictitious name he later invents for himself, Eperitus, means Quarrelman. He brings trouble to all he meets, not least to those closest to him.

Autolycus is an unscrupulous and ruthless self-made man. His morality is wholly that of success and the outward signs of success – the loot, the scars, the tall tales. The means are of no moral interest to him. His wish that Odysseus should follow in his footsteps is amply fulfilled. On his return to Ithaca Odysseus (disguised) says of himself:

> Indeed Odysseus would have been here long ago, had he not thought it
> the more profitable course to travel about in the pursuit of wealth – which
> shows that in business enterprise he is unsurpassed.   [295]

He proposes to make good 'the ravages that gang of profligates have made among my flocks' by ravaging himself.

Odysseus' name is inseparable from his scar, which he also owes to his grandfather, who introduced him to boarhunting. That first adventure had all the characteristics of the later ones. The young Odysseus goes looking for trouble. He pits himself against nature at its most dangerous and inhuman, a mighty boar. Later, loaded with gifts and displaying his scar, he returns home to tell the tale to his doting parents: 'They asked him about all his adventures, in particular how he had come by his scar, and Odysseus told them how in the course of the chase he had been gashed by a boar's tusk on the expedition to Parnassus with Autolycus' sons' [300].

Odysseus has two other tokens, a brooch, which depicts a dog throttling a fawn, and a soft gleaming shirt, which is attractive to women. He is the ruthless male predator, not least sexually. Women are like any other plunder.

He begins his story to King Alcinous with a casual reference to the sacking of Ismarus: 'I sacked this place and destroyed the men who held it. Their wives and the rich plunder that we took from the town we divided' [140]. This is a striking instance of the black comedy of *The Odyssey*. For only four pages earlier Homer had used the sack of another city, Troy, to provide a bitterly ironic, ludicrously inappropriate simile (a device frequently employed) for Odysseus' womanish weeping:

> He wept as a woman weeps when she throws her arms round the body of her beloved husband, fallen in battle before his city and his comrades, fighting to save his home-town and his children from disaster. She has found him gasping in the throes of death; she clings to him and lifts her voice in lamentation. but the enemy come up and belabour her back and shoulders with spears, as they lead her off into slavery and a life of miserable toil, with her cheeks wasted by her pitiful grief. Equally pitiful were the tears that now welled up in Odysseus' eyes. [136]

Here again *The Iliad* is stripped of all its glamour. The irony is in the distance between the moral sensibility of the narrator and that of his hero.

An equally striking example of the ironically inappropriate simile occurs when Odysseus is pondering what to do with the suitors' mistresses:

> Should he dash after them and put them all to death; or should he let them spend one last night in the arms of their profligate lovers? The thought made him snarl with repressed fury, like a bitch that snarls and shows fight as she takes her stand above her helpless puppies when a stranger comes by. So did Odysseus growl to himself in sheer revolt at these licentious ways. [304]

This absurd casting of Odysseus as female protector of the helpless throws into harsh relief his actual savagery, and the unnaturalness of his uncontrollable murderous revulsion against female sexuality.

It is appropriate that the story should begin with Calypso, whose name means 'engulfed'. To languish on an island in the middle of nowhere in absolute security, with a beautiful goddess who offers not only love but immortality would be for many an earthly paradise. For Odysseus it is misery. It denies him the possibility of that 'recognition' which is his *raison d'être*. The Lotus eaters (who have no names) are for him images of oblivion. And the Phaeacians are not much better, though their society corresponds to many a subsequent utopia. Their lives are trouble-free, being under the protection of Poseidon. They are at one with their environment. Women dominate in a peaceful, life-loving society. Such fame as they have is for sports and dancing. They try to evict Odysseus, but he represents the selfish element in human (or perhaps only male) nature, which sooner or later undermines all utopias. As a result of harbouring him, they are cut off from the sea on which their lives depend.

The sea is that which by its sheer size and unknowability threatens to overwhelm Odysseus. His greatest fear is death by drowning, a 'villainous death', which is to him what the casting ladle is to Peer Gynt, an obliteration of the ego. He would rather have died where the spears were flying at Troy 'and the Achaeans would have spread my fame abroad'. He is skilled in ship-building and seamanship. After centuries of hugging the coast, he is the first man to head for the horizon to confront and, if possible, master the unknown and the great powers of the natural world which pay no heed to human name and fame.

Polyphemus means 'much fame' and the mutilation of him, the son of Poseidon, promises that. Antiphates, on the other hand, means 'against re-nown', for in the encounter with him, Odysseus sends his men into danger while he sits safely on his ship. He regains his name when Circe recognizes him as Odysseus 'the man whom nothing defeats. . . . Royal son of Laertes, Odysseus of the nimble wits' [168].

It is similarly by refusing to accept a position of dependence, even upon those gods who seek to help him, that Odysseus wins their respect. He does not tell the truth to Athene: 'It had been on the tip of his tongue, but loyal as ever to his own crafty nature he contrived to keep it back'. It is Athene who must first abandon her reserve:

'What a cunning knave it would take,' she said, 'to beat you at your tricks! Even a god would be hard put to it. And so my stubborn friend, Odysseus the arch-deceiver, with his craving for intrigue, does not propose even in his own country to drop his sharp practice and the lying tales that he loves from the bottom of his heart. But no more of this: we are both adepts in chicane. For in the world of men you have no rival as a statesman and orator, while I am pre-eminent among the gods for invention and resource.' . . . 'How like you to be so wary!' said Athene. 'And that is why I cannot desert you in your misfortunes: you are so civilized, so intelligent, so self-possessed.'   [209–11]

Athene's admiration should not surprise us. She had invented the bridle and the chariot, built the first ship, and helped Odysseus build the wooden horse. It does not follow that Homer shares Athene's admiration. There is bitter irony once more in that a god should sanction Odysseus' behaviour as 'civ-ilized'.

The climax of *The Odyssey* is Odysseus' massacre (with a little help from his son Telemachus) of the suitors for Penelope, who for many years have been unwanted guests wasting his estate. In the massacre and its aftermath we are presented with atrocities all too similar to those which have characterized the flowering of 'civilization' in our own day. Odysseus finds out from his informers which of the suitors have behaved decently, then kills them with the rest. The twelve women who had fraternized with the suitors are rounded up:

Wailing bitterly, with the tears streaming down their cheeks, the women all arrived together. Their first task was to remove the bodies of the slain, which they laid under the portico of the walled courtyard, propping them one against the other. Odysseus himself took charge and hounded them on till they had finished their unwilling work. Next they washed down the tables and the beautiful chairs with sponges and water, after which Telemachus and the two herdsmen scraped the floor of the great hall with spades, while the maids removed the scrapings and got rid of them outside. Finally, when the whole house had been set in order, they took the women out of the building, and herded them between the round-house and the great courtyard wall in a narrow space from which there was no escape. Then Telemachus spoke. 'I swear I will not give a decent death,' he said, 'to women who have heaped dishonour on my head and on my mother's, and slept with members of this gang.' With that he took a hawser which had seen service on a blue-bowed ship, made one end fast to a high column in the portico, threw the other over the round-house, and pulled it taut at such a level as would keep their feet from touching earth. And then, like doves or long-winged thrushes caught in a net across the thicket where they came to roost, and meeting death where they had only looked for sleep, the women held their heads out in a row, and a noose was cast round each one's neck to dispatch them in the most miserable way. For a little while their feet kicked out, but not for long. Next Malanthius was dragged out across the court and through the gate. There with a sharp knife they sliced his nose and ears off; they ripped away his privy parts as raw meat for the dogs, and in their fury they lopped off his hands and feet. Then, after washing their own hands and feet, they went back indoors to Odysseus and the business was finished. [339–40]

The appallingly matter-of-fact tone and attention to detail only accentuates the outrage. And we leave Odysseus a few lines later 'overwhelmed by tender feelings' as the other women of the household shower him with affectionate kisses. All this was accomplished with the blessing and active help of Athene, the goddess of war, arts, crafts and intelligence, (in other words, of civilization), who had sprung from the head of Zeus, and who became the arch-enemy of the older nature-god Poseidon.

The Odyssey ends with Odysseus launching himself into another massacre, of his own rebellious subjects, before the gods themselves are forced to say 'enough is enough'.

Odysseus learns to survive in a world where mere prudence is useless, since the whims of the gods make life a lottery. Craft, opportunism, self-reliance, the calculated risk, ruthlessness, are the means. Never lower your guard or turn your back. Push your luck as far as it will go. Never give except in the expectation of getting back more. Write off the past immediately. Let others look after themselves. Odysseus demanding and getting his royal titles

11

from the gods has come a long way from the miserable victimized wretches Prometheus undertook to champion, but at a price. Individuation taken to these lengths is surely monstrous. The ego isolates itself behind its weapons and goes insane. He will ensure that his sons and grandsons, in Auden's words, have never heard

> Of any world where promises were kept
> Or one could weep because another wept.
> ['The Shield of Achilles']

And Odysseus is setting the pattern of heroic manhood which persists to this day.

*　　*　　*

The intelligent, self-reliant, violent man who thinks he can live without reference to the gods, dictating the terms of his own life, is the typical protagonist of Greek tragedy. And this form of pride, *hubris*, is the typical tragic flaw. The type was not limited to the Greek world. In Judaic myth the ancient heroes, the 'mighty men which were of old, men of renown' [*Genesis* 6:4], who filled the earth with violence, are the very men who cause God to regret having created man at all and to resolve to flush the earth clean of such men. But human pride cannot be so easily extinguished.

At the beginning of the Book of Job, Satan assumes (correctly) that, like himself, no man subjected to the tyranny of God will not rebel against it. Job is the opposite of Prometheus in the quiet and modest humility of his rebellion, and of Odysseus in that he responds to the amorality of God not by miming divine ruthlessness but by affirming a purely human morality of justice. No man could be further than Job from the egotism and freebooting pride of the heroes. Nor is he so foolish as to curse God to his face. But his very integrity demands that he should maintain his own ways before God. His pride is a pride in humanity itself, its understanding and morality, its righteousness. Job is as aware of the irresistible power of God as his comforters, but, unlike them, refuses to be entirely cowed by it. The comforters argue that man is a mere worm, but Job assigns him a lordly status: 'He hath stripped me of my glory, and taken the crown from my head' [19:9].

The comforters insist on a strict correlation between purity and prosperity. They insist that God never betrays the heart that loves him, that any evil which befalls man must be God's 'correction' of some fault, whether that fault is evident or not. But Job knows that his punishment is 'without cause'. His comforters deny him the right to plead 'not guilty'. Job can see that to plead 'not guilty' is equivalent to charging God with injustice (or at least with neglecting to consult his own omniscience), of claiming to be more righteous than God. He is fully aware of the enormity of that; yet he cannot avoid the conclusion that 'He destroyeth the perfect and the wicked', that there is no correlation whatever between the ways of God and man's standards of morality and justice. The question he must ask of God is 'seest thou as man seeth?'. And even if God does *not* see as man sees, Job will still maintain his own ways before him. To submit in silence would be spiritual death: 'for now, if I hold my tongue, I shall give up the ghost'.

The pattern Job seeks to impose on God is (as in *The Oresteia*) that of the court of law: 'O that one might plead for a man with God, as a man pleadeth for his neighbour!' [16:21]; 'Behold, I cry out of wrong, but I am not heard: I cry aloud, but there is no judgement' [19:7]. He wishes that heaven itself were a court of law, with God as both prosecutor and judge:

> Oh that I knew where I might find him! that I might come even to his
>   seat!
> I would order my cause before him, and fill my mouth with
>   arguments.
> I would know the words which he would answer me, and understand
>   what he would say unto me.
> Will he plead against me with his great power? No; but he would put
>   strength in me.
> There the righteous might dispute with him; so should I be delivered
>   for ever from my judge.   [23:3–7]

But since no redeemer yet stands on the earth, Job will have to conduct his own defence, and fears that God will answer him, if at all, in a voice of thunder, and 'the thunder of his power who can understand' [26:14].

These fears seem amply justified when God at last speaks. Far from answering Job he batters him with a series of rhetorical questions, mocking man's pretensions to understanding. The chief of the ways of this God is behemoth; and leviathan is 'king over all the children of pride' [41:34]. God seems not to know that the time will come when, acting in the spirit of Prometheus and Odysseus and the Ode to Man in *Antigone*, the children of pride will indeed fill the skin of leviathan with barbed irons [41:7].

Yet with a sudden unexplained volte-face, God turns in anger on the comforters, and praises Job for having 'spoken of me the thing that is right' [42:8]. The rebel, it seems, in spite of all God's bluster, has, simply by standing by his lights, triumphed: 'the Lord also accepted Job' [42:9]. He is rewarded with much wealth and length of days. According to Jung's *Answer to Job*, this is the moment when God realizes that man has developed a higher conscious-ness than his own, and first conceives the ambition to become man. It is the first stage in the process by which the God of creation becomes the God of sin and redemption and the divine sanction for humanistic moral values. Man's intellectual and moral development had brought him to a point where the old Nature god or gods no longer fulfilled the role he required of the godhead, which was now to validate the aspirations of men in an increasingly male-dominated and civilized society.

Robert Graves comments:

The result of envisaging this god of pure meditation, the Universal Mind still premised by the most reputable modern philosophers, and enthroning him above Nature as essential Truth and Goodness was not an altogether happy one. . . . The new God claimed to be dominant as Alpha and Omega, the Beginning and the End, pure Holiness, pure Good, pure Logic, able to exist without the aid of woman; but it was natural to identify him with one of the original rivals of the Theme and to ally the woman and the other rival [the devil] permanently against him. The outcome was philosophical dualism with all the tragi-comic woes attendant on spiritual dichotomy. If the True God, the God of the Logos, was pure thought, pure good, whence came evil and error? Two separate creations had to be assumed: the true spiritual Creation and the false material Creation.   [*Goddess*, 465]

This is very close to Jung's conclusion that when God becomes a god of goodness, love and light *only*, the dark side of god, which won't go away, becomes a terrible burden of sin and guilt, a terrible impulse to hatred and violence, in the human unconscious.

2 THE *ORESTEIA* AND THE SUPERANNUATION OF THE GODS

Almost all religions began as creation myths – the existence of the world had to be accounted for – and the gods were simply the elemental powers of the world, given the names of sun, moon and stars, earth and sea, wind and rain, and so on. The gods were Nature gods, and Nature herself was thought of as a female deity by analogy with living creatures, where the female brings forth. Man's relation to these gods was one of pure subservience and helplessness, doing whatever he could think of to placate them when they seemed angry and to win their benevolence. But as man mastered the techniques of agriculture and husbandry, came to understand some of the workings of Nature, or at least became habituated to them, came to feel that he was to some extent in control of the natural world, or insulated from it by living in cities, the links between the gods and nature became tenuous, and other functions began to be assigned to them. Men now had aspirations beyond mere survival, and wished to dignify these with divine sanctions. Man's intellectual and moral development had brought him to a watershed (the moment recorded in *The Book of Job*) where the old Nature god or gods no longer fulfilled the role he required of the godhead, which was now to validate the aspirations of men in an increasingly male-dominated and civilized society.

According to Robert Graves, the religious revolution of which *The Book of Job* is part, was initiated by Ezekiel (622–570 B.C.). In Persia Zoroaster (c.628-c.551 – an almost exact contemporary of Ezekiel) was instituting similar changes, converting a polytheistic nature-worship into a dualistic system of Good versus Evil, with a single male God, Ormazd or Mazda, a god of light, so that religion becomes a quest for enlightenment in a purely mental world, the real world of nature becoming a mere obstruction or distraction (what Graves calls 'the erroneous material universe'), and the female principle being correspondingly devalued. The male intellect deifies itself. Graves also argues that the changes initiated by Ezekiel were 'taken up by the Greek-speaking Jews of Egypt and borrowed from them by the Pythagoreans'. A specific manifestation of these changes in Greece was the founding in 592 of the Areopagus, which took justice out of the hands of archaic gods. Aeschylus was born only 67 years later.

In *The Oresteia* Aeschylus is attempting to encapsulate this whole process into the experiences of a single family. To do this he must foreshorten history to the extent of beginning with the Trojan war, which probably took place in the twelfth century B.C., and ending, after only a year or two of dramatic time, with the founding of the Areopagus in 592 B.C. Hamlet is torn apart because he has to undergo, in his own psyche, all the pressures of moving from the Middle Ages through the Reformation and Renaissance. The time is equally out of joint for Orestes who must suffer in his own fate the evolution of Greek society from barbarism and piracy to the beginning of the great age of Athenian civilization.

The *Oresteia* is our only surviving Greek trilogy. The first part, *The Agamemnon*, provides a template for many subsequent Greek tragedies. The pattern is almost always the same The hubristic male protagonist – Agamemnon, Creon, Oedipus, Jason, Hippolytus, Pentheus – is violently opposed to the values represented by Dionysos, or, behind him, the Great Goddess. He lives by the values of a patriarchal code, which begins as that of the warrior hero but is later to disguise itself as the voice of reason, law and order – of civilization itself. The hero's contempt for the goddess is dramatized as his victimization of actual women – in this case his wife and daughter and the conquered women of Troy. His offences reach a point where he loses his existential freedom, the possibility of redemption, and becomes a hostage to Necessity, a doomed man. This deed (the slaughter of Agamemnon's younger daughter Iphegenia in this play) starts a chain reaction, which devastates an entire family and nation. The agent of doom is usually one of the victimized women – Clytemnestra, Antigone, Medea, Phaedra, Agave – whose creative female energies, denied and persecuted, have turned destructive, dragonish.

❊   ❊   ❊

The Agamemnon, like several plays of Shakespeare's, communicates its deepest meaning through its imagery, some of which is lost in even the best translations.

Within a few lines the first chorus launches into an elaborate metaphor for the anger of Menelaus and his brother Agamemnon at the 'rape' of Helen.

> Then loud their warlike anger cried,
> As eagles cry, that wild with grief,
> On some steep, lonely mountain-side
> Above their robbed nest wheel and sail,
> Oaring the airy waves, and wail
> Their wasted toil, their watchful pride;
> Till some celestial deity,
> Zeus, Pan, Apollo, hears on high
> Their scream of wordless misery;
> And pitying their forlorn estate
> (Since air is Heaven's protectorate)
> Sends a swift fury to pursue
> Marauding guilt with vengeance due.
>
> [43]

Here Aeschylus, for heavy irony, borrows Homer's trick of the overelaborate and wholly inappropriate simile. The vultures scream because their nest has been robbed of their young. Menelaus and Agamemnon are not seeking revenge for slaughtered children; they scream because they are denied the opportunity to slay the innocent children of Troy. Agamemnon had merely lost a sister-in-law, and she had flown of her own accord. The chorus would like to cast

Agamemnon in the role of avenging eagle, but the imagery works against them. We know that his motive for going to Troy was not vengeance but robbery, pillage, rich pickings. The 'rape' of Helen was a heaven-sent excuse for the rape of Troy, in which so many Greek princes who cared nothing for Helen were glad to share. The image of a swift fury screaming for vengeance for murdered children does not fit Agamemnon but fits Clytemnestra perfectly. This speech is immediately preceded by her anticipatory cry of triumph from within the palace, and immediately followed by her first appearance at the doors. The original audience would know that when Agamemnon had killed her husband and forcibly married her, he had also slaughtered the child at her breast, and that, as we are shortly to be reminded, he had sacrificed their daughter Iphegenia to buy a favourable wind for the Greek fleet at Aulis. They would also know of the curse upon the house of Atreus. The horrible facts of it – Atreus, Agamemnon's father, had served his brother Thyestes with the flesh of his own children at a feast – work just below the surface of *Agamemnon* until the end, when Aegisthus tells the whole story, concluding: 'That deed gave birth to what you now see here, this death' [98].

The chorus shortly returns to the image of the two eagles, this time real ones, which had been seen by the army as it set out for Aulis:

> Two kings of birds, that seemed to bode
> Great fortune to the kings of that great fleet.
> Close to the palace, on spear-side of the road,
> One tawny-feathered, one white in the tail,
> Perched in full view, they ravenously tear
> The body of a pregnant hare
> Big with her burden, now a living prey
> In the last darkness of their unborn day. [45]

The prophet Calchas interprets the omen. The hare is Troy; the eagles the 'relentless pair' Agamemnon and Menelaus. But he warns them against arousing the enmity of Artemis by their savagery:

> For virgin Artemis, whom all revere,
> Hates with a deadly hate
> The swift-winged hounds of Zeus who swooped to assail
> Their helpless victim wild with fear
> Before her ripe hour came;
> Who dared to violate
> (So warning spoke the priest)
> The awe that parenthood must claim,
> As for some rite performed in heaven's name;
> Yes, Artemis abominates the eagles' feast! [46]

17

Calchas addresses Artemis as

> You who love the tender whelp
> Of the ravening lion, and care
> For the fresh-wild sucking young
> Of fox and rat and hind and hare
> [46]

He warns the brothers against transforming the lovely Artemis, Lady of the Wild Things, into what Fagles translates as a 'child-avenging Fury'. Since the ravening lion is clearly Agamemnon, her protection extends to Iphegenia, 'the tender whelp of the ravening lion', as well as to the as yet unborn young of Troy.

Calchas reveals that the North wind, which prevents the Hellene fleet from leaving Aulis Bay week after week, has been sent by Artemis. Why? Obviously because she knows what suffering of innocents there is bound to be when Agamemnon's army 'in time shall make King Priam's town their prey' [46]. Yet the remedy she offers Agamemnon – that she will stop thwarting him if he will slaughter his own child, Iphegenia – seems to be in violation of all she stands for. But it is not that she *wants* Agamemnon to kill his daughter, rather that she forces him to make an existential choice, to present to him in the starkest and most personal form the moral implications of what he proposes to do to Troy. As one might say to a pacifist, would you stand by and watch your own child murdered, so Artemis is saying to Agamemnon, 'Is this "vengeance", this punitive expedition, with its promise of rich spoils, for the recovery of an adulteress, really so important to you that it is worth the sacrifice of many innocent lives, that it is even worth the sacrifice of your own most loved daughter?' The gods can pose such questions not hypothetically, but in reality.

Agamemnon is fully aware of the horror of the act:

> What can I say?
> Disaster follows if I disobey;
> Surely yet worse disaster if I yield
> And slaughter my own child, my home's delight,
> In her young innocence, and stain my hand
> With blasphemous unnatural cruelty,
> Bathed in the blood I fathered! [49]

But it is not a matter of disobeying. It is a matter of making a free choice between this sacrifice or disbanding the fleet, abandoning his command, betraying the alliance, and earning 'the deserter's badge'. That he cannot contemplate. Within ten lines he has made his decision – 'a maid must bleed'. Up to this point he had been a free man; but with this decision he puts on 'the harness of Necessity', he wears 'the chains of those who lose Freedom and life to war and Fate', he becomes a man marked by the gods, doomed. And the nature of his doom is already hinted at in the image of harness, and the images of nets and meshes which follow. Clytemnestra, aided by the Furies, will weave her spiderweb of intrigue. Literally, she will wrap Agamemnon in a cleverly sewn bathrobe, 'a trap made like a gown', virtually a straight-jacket:

> I cast on him
> As one who catches fish, a vast voluminous net.
>   [90]

Clytemnestra is a mere agent, acting out of that Necessity whose harness Agamemnon put on when he elected to kill his daughter. That was an act of 'shameless self-willed infatuation', of 'blasphemy', even of madness. The eagle is so maddened by blood-lust that he plunders his own nest:

> Heedless of her tears,
> Her cries of 'Father!' and her maiden years,
> Her judges valued more
> Their glory and their war.   [50]

It is typical of the tight poetic organization of the play, its Shakespearean metaphorical coherence and density, that we should later be told that during the storm which wrecked the Greek fleet on its return from Troy: 'The sky was a mad shepherd tearing his own flock' [65]. This is the play's controlling image of unnaturalness.

Agamemnon is to be punished not simply for the murder of Iphigenia. That act was merely an extreme manifestation of Agamemnon's sickness, his dedication to the false male value-system of stiff-necked honour, courage in killing, holding life cheap, power and plunder. The play contains remarkably modern-sounding anti-war passages:

> They sent forth men to battle,
> But no such men return;
> And home, to claim their welcome,
> Come ashes in an urn.
> For War's a banker, flesh his gold.
> And back to waiting homes he sends
> Slag from the ore, a little dust
> To drain hot tears from hearts of friends;
> Good measure, safely stored and sealed
> In a convenient jar – the just
> Price for the man they sent away.   [58]

The sack of Troy had been as bad as Artemis feared. And Agamemnon boasts of it:

19

> We have made Troy pay
> For her proud rape a woman's price. The Argive beast,
> The lion rampant on all our shields, at dead of night
> Sprang from the womb of the horse to grind that city's bones,
> A ranked and ravening litter, that over wall and tower
> Leaping, licked royal blood till lust was surfeited.   [71]

Again the image of a womb unnaturally giving birth to death. Clytemnestra had expressed the hope that the victors would not profane the holy places in Troy, but the Herald's account indicates that the vengeance on Troy had been in every way disproportionate, and carried out in a spirit of indiscriminate blood-lust and gratuitous destruction, a spirit disqualifying the enterprise from any claim to be considered a holy war, performing the will of the gods:

> The Avenger's plough
> Passed over Troy, to split her towers, scar and subdue
> Her fields, raze the altars and temples of the gods,
> And from her fair soil extirpate her seed.   [61]

At this moment Agamemnon enters in his chariot, followed by another bearing the riches he has plundered, including the Trojan princess Cassandra. The chorus greets him with obsequious praise and reverence. In their eyes now, the whole enterprise has been justified by its success, the rights of women and children, the cost in corpses, all forgotten.

Clytemnestra spreads before Agamemnon a long carpet of crimson silk. His scruples about treading on it have more to do with his unwillingness to soil such precious stuff than with humility:

> It offends modesty, that I
> Should dare with unwashed feet to soil these costly rugs,
> Worth weight for weight of silver, spoiling my own house!
> But let that pass.   [75]

Clytemnestra knows the significance of that heart's purple:

> There is the sea – who shall exhaust the sea? – which teems
> With purple dye costly as silver, a dark stream
> For staining of fine stuffs, unceasingly renewed.
> This house has store of crimson, by Heaven's grace, enough
> For one outpouring.   [74]

A Greek audience would know the relevance of the sea, and why purple dye was so costly. It was produced by crushing alive millions of Murex snails. Again the image is of Nature violated for man's self-indulgence. Agamemnon's last words are: 'Treading on purple I will go into my house' [75].

There can be no doubt that Agamemnon deserves to die. As Clytemnestra says, he 'drains his own cursed cup to the last dregs'. And she has more justification than anyone to be the agent of his death:

Who with as slight compunction as men butcher sheep,
When his own fields were white with flocks, must sacrifice
His own child, and my own darling, whom my pain brought forth –
He killed her for a charm to stop the Thracian wind!   [92]

Almost the only image in the play of natural fertility is uttered by Clytemnestra in her description of the death-blow:

There spurted from him bloody foam in a fierce jet,
And spreading, spattered me with drops of crimson rain;
While I exulted as the sown cornfield exults
Drenched with the dew of heaven when buds burst forth in Spring.
                                                          [91]

It is as though the shedding of Agamemnon's blood cleanses the world and makes possible a resumption of the processes of fertility.

*   *   *

The Libation-Bearers, though it takes place only a few years after *Agamemnon*, belongs to a different world-age, when human moral sense comes to revolt against such a barbaric code. Orestes, returning home to find that his father has been butchered by his mother, seeks advice from Apollo, who has shown little sign of any highly developed moral sense in his dealings with Cassandra. He is told that he must kill his mother, or be hounded to madness by the Furies. This shows a complete misunderstanding by Apollo of the nature of the Furies, who are far more outraged by the murder of a mother than of a husband.

The Furies, strikingly, are not at all interested in Clytemnestra's crime, because they are agents of Nature, and Clytemnestra's crime is not seen by them as unnatural. Nor has she shed the blood of a blood-relative. It is Apollo, not the Furies, who insists that she must in turn be killed, for no better reason, it seems, than that she is a woman and cannot be allowed to get away with killing a man. The Furies have nothing to do with morality. Their function is anterior to it. They are concerned only to defend Nature, which cannot be separated from human nature, from violation. They are no more moral than phagocytes rushing to destroy pathogens. Yet a principle of Justice had been abstracted from their behaviour and given divine sanction – blood for blood – vengeance.

The Furies have not yet needed to appear. They are there, a 'bloody ravening pack', in case they are needed. Cassandra sees them. Clytemnestra has done their work for them, extirpating the guilt of Agamemnon. (Aegisthus

describes Agamemnon's body as 'tangled in a net the avenging Furies wove
... in the trap of Justice' [97–8].) When we see them at last, in the final
play, they are monstrous – women, but not women, though certainly female.
Gorgons, yet not quite Gorgons, something like Harpies

> but these
> Are wingless, black, utterly loathsome; their vile breath
> Vent in repulsive snoring; from their eyes distils
> A filthy rheum; their garb is wickedness to wear
> In sight of the gods' statues or in human homes.
> They are creatures of no race I ever saw; no land
> Could breed them and not bear the curse of God and man.
>
> [149]

In other words, they seem to be manifestations of everything unnatural and
evil; yet they are also 'Powers of the deep earth' and felt to be, in some way,
necessary. They are primeval nature spirits, chthonic divinities, unaffected
by all the wars in heaven and the advent of the Olympian gods. But why are
they so ugly and destructive? They are associated with plagues and barrenness, as Artemis is associated with fertility and health. Every Olympian deity
had his or her dark underworld counterpart or opposite. Every deity can be
turned into or replaced by its opposite if defiled. Up to the sacrifice of Iphigenia, Artemis is a major force in *The Oresteia*. Subsequently, she is never
heard of again. Her role as Nature goddess is taken over by her underworld
equivalents, the Furies. Nature once violated becomes in turn violent and
destructive. The behaviour of Agamemnon in killing his daughter (as in his
whole dedication to war and wealth) and of Orestes in killing his mother, is
unnatural. Each has to distort his own nature to perform such a deed. Each
thereby severs the umbilical cord which connects him with the sustaining and
creative forces of Nature. Orestes denies the right of these powers to determine
his life. He thrusts them down into the underworld of his own unconscious
where they coil, reptiles of the mind, poisoning the whole being and bringing
madness.

Orestes has to chose between two courses, both fatal. Apollo rashly
promises an immunity he cannot enforce. Once Orestes has obeyed Apollo,
killed his mother, and is being hounded by the Furies nonetheless, Apollo can
only advise him to seek the protection of Athene, famed for wisdom. And
suddenly, in *The Eumenides*, we find the whole drama turning away from the
tragic mode and beginning to deal with these intractable problems as though
they were fairly easily soluble after all, given Athene's sweet reasonableness.
The implacable Furies improbably agree to accept her arbitration. Athene will
form a jury of 'wisest citizens' and vest her judgement in them. She gives her
casting vote in advance to Orestes on the ground of 'male supremacy in all
things' and the relative dispensability of women. On that casting vote Orestes
is acquitted. The Furies make a few noises, but as soon as Athene offers them

an honoured and guaranteed place in the life of Athens, they graciously accept, turn into 'Friendly Goddesses', and give their blessing to the city in terms more appropriate to a fertility goddess:

> Fortune shall load her land with healthful gifts
> From her rich earth engendered
> By the sun's burning brightness.
>
> No ill wind
> Shall carry blight to make your fruit-trees fade;
> No bud-destroying canker
> Shall creep across your frontiers,
> Nor sterile sickness threaten your supply.
> May Pan give twin lambs to your thriving ewes
> In their expected season;
> And may the earth's rich produce
> Honour the generous Powers with grateful gifts.
> I pray that no untimely chance destroy
> Your young men in their pride;
> And let each lovely virgin, as a bride,
> Fulfil her life with joy.   [178]

Athene concludes 'Thus God and Fate are reconciled', and everyone, presumably, lives happily ever after.

Surely this won't do. It can't be that easy. The Furies are supposed to retire to their home beneath the ground and never raise their ugly heads again. As for crime, the jury system will take care of that. Not only are the Furies to be superannuated, so is Athene herself. She can become her own statue, a merely nominal presiding presence, since she identifies her own wisdom with that of 'wisest citizens'. The gods withdraw, leaving human reason to guide the future of Athens and of Western Civilization:

> Let your State
> Hold justice as her chiefest prize;
> And land and city shall be great
> And glorious in every part.
>   [180]

Thus the worship of Athene becomes the worship of Athens, the city, whose walls include man and exclude Nature, as an end in itself, an absolute, almost a god.

✳   ✳   ✳

Freud saw the importance of the ending of *The Oresteia* for the future of our civilization:

This turning from the mother to the father points in addition to a victory
of intellect – that is an advance in civilization, since maternity is proved
by the evidence of the senses while paternity is a hypothesis, based on an
inference and a premise. Taking sides in this way with a thought-process
in preference to a sense perception has proved to be a momentous step.

[*Moses*]

Lawrence, on the other hand, saw it as a disastrous step:

In Aeschylus, in the *Eumenides*, there is Apollo, Loxias, the Sun God,
Love, the prophet, the male: there are the Erinyes, daughters of primeval
Mother Night, representing here the female risen in retribution for some
crime against the flesh; and there is Pallas, unbegotten daughter of
Zeus, who is as the Holy Spirit in the Christian religion, the spirit of
wisdom.

Orestes is bidden by the male god, Apollo, to avenge the murder
of his father, Agamemnon, by his mother: that is, the male, murdered by
the female, must be avenged by the male. But Orestes is child of his
mother. He is in himself female. So that in himself the conscience, the
madness, the violated part of his own self, his own body, drives him to the
Furies. On the male side, he is right; on the female, wrong. But peace is
given at last by Pallas, the Arbitrator, the Spirit of wisdom.

And although Aeschylus in his consciousness makes the Furies
hideous, and Apollo supreme, yet, in his own self and in very fact, he
makes the Furies wonderful and noble, with their tremendous hymns, and
makes Apollo a trivial, sixth-form braggart and ranter.   [*Phoenix* 482]

Surely every reader must feel the decline in power and depth of insight from
play to play; and the plays seem different in kind as well as in quality. If the
Agamemnon and *The Eumenides* were extant, and their authorship unknown,
who would suppose them part of the same trilogy? *Agamemnon* is one of the
greatest plays of world literature. It seems engaged with its themes (and they
are deep far-reaching themes) at the fullest. Its highly poetic, that is metaphorical, language opens it up to the full play of Aeschylus' imagination, gives every
incident ramifications and resonances in all directions. The metaphorical
structure gives its own interpretation of events, an interpretation inherent
in the events and in human psychology, not imposed by Aeschylus to lead
to some resolution decided in advance. Indeed there is no resolution, only a
sense of awe. To move from *Agamemnon* to *The Libation-Bearers* is like
moving from a tragedy to a problem play, from *King Lear* to Ibsen's *Ghosts*.
It is a fine play, but relative to the *Agamemnon*, limited, two-dimensional. To
The Eumenides is a steeper drop, for surely it degrades what has led up to it
by imposing an artificial resolution in terms of the merest propaganda, as
though there were political or legalistic solutions to the problem of evil.

The decline is also evident in the status of the gods. The great female goddesses, even Earth herself, were rapidly declining in importance. Artemis, whom Aeschylus elsewhere calls 'Lady of the wild mountains' (Fragment 342), stands for the deepest natural bonds between human beings, which cannot be broken without the direst consequences not only for the individual and the family but also for the nation and the race – for Nature herself. By the third part of the trilogy, she has been quietly dislodged by her brother Apollo, whose first act as a new-born baby had been to slay the great female serpent Delphyne (whose name is connected with an old name for the womb). Tony Harrison records that 'there is an alternative version of the story of the peaceful transition of the shrine of Delphi from Gaia to Apollo as told, for example, in the *Oresteia*. In some stories Apollo bludgeoned his way into possessing what was once a female shrine' [*Trackers* xix]. Apollo, like Athene, a child of Zeus, belongs to the patriarchal age. He even denies, at Orestes' trial, that woman has a necessary or important role in childbearing (Artemis was the patroness of childbirth). Athene was a goddess born from Zeus' brain without the aid of woman. She employed in her rituals exclusively priests, not priestesses. All this is part of the process Slater calls 'dematrification'.

Athene represents a further development, when gods become merely personifications of human values, in this case reason and justice. Apollo graduated from cow-keeper and sun-god to the patron god of high culture and enlightenment. The Furies declined from being psychological realities, to bloodhounds of the law, to toothless retired aunts.

The assumption is that reason banishes or transforms evil, and that man's purpose is to make the world and the gods consonant with his own civilized ideals. Socrates and Plato were later to give an elaborate philosophical superstructure to this movement away from Nature and its incarnate gods towards the worship of mental concepts and abstractions and the pursuit of knowledge as the highest good. They helped to determine that Western Civilization should take the course it has taken, a course determined by dualism, rationalism and the arrogant male intellect, in despite of Nature. Nature, once Isis or Artemis Mother of the Gods, became evil, doomed to manifest her powers only destructively; for when God becomes a god of light *only*, the dark side of god, which won't go away, or be pensioned off, becomes a terrible burden of sin and guilt, a terrible impulse to hatred and violence in the human psyche. The Furies had been conned, and it did not take them long to find out.

✳   ✳   ✳

When the *Oresteia* was first performed, at the Great Dionysia of 458, the triumph of Apollo and his stooge Athene was not the end of the matter. Aeschylus was obliged to provide an epilogue (or antidote) in the form of a satyr play. If the purpose of the satyr plays was merely to release the tension of the tragedies, why could that function not have been performed by a comedy? And why were the tragic poets required to write satyr plays rather than the comic poets? And why was there no gap between the tragedies and the satyr play? The audience must have been nearing the end of its attention span. Clearly the satyrs were felt to bring into the same world as tragedy some essential missing element:

> In the satyr play, that spirit of celebration, held in the dark solution of tragedy, is precipitated into release, and a release into the worship of Dionysus who presided over the whole dramatic festival. . . . This journey back into the service of the presiding god seems to be paralleled by the release of the spirit back into the life of the senses at the end of the tragic journey. . . . The sensual relish for life and its affirmation must have been the spirit of the conclusion of the four plays. The satyrs are included in the wholeness of the tragic vision.   [*Trackers* xi]

Tony Harrison is here paraphrasing Nietzsche:

> The cultured Greek felt himself absorbed into the satyr chorus, and in the next development of Greek tragedy state and society, in fact all that separated man from man, gave way before an overwhelming sense of unity which led back into the heart of nature. The metaphysical solace (with which, I wish to say at once, all true tragedy sends us away) that, despite every phenomenal change, life is at bottom indestructibly joyful and powerful, was expressed most concretely in the chorus of satyrs, nature beings who dwell behind all civilization and preserve their identity through every change of generations and historical movement. With this chorus the profound Greek, so uniquely susceptible to the subtlest and deepest suffering, who had penetrated the destructive agencies of both nature and history, solaced himself. Though he had been in danger of craving a Buddhistic denial of the will, he was saved by art, and through art life reclaimed him.   [*The Birth of Tragedy*, 50–1]

Not one of Aeschylus' many satyr plays survives; but in the one surviving satyr play of Sophocles, the *Ichneutae* (or *Trackers*), Apollo comes off very badly in his 'transition from macho cowpoke to cultural impresario' (Harrison). How could Aeschylus have reconciled the Dionysian earthiness of the satyr play with the triumph of Apollo (or indeed the triumph of Apollo with the whole spirit of the Great Dionysia)? Apollo is the male will to power; intellect, formalism, idealism raised to an unquestionable absolute; the arch-enemy of Nature and the female; the bully. Nietzsche wrote:

> In opposition to all who would derive the arts from a single vital principle, I wish to keep before me those two artistic deities of the Greeks, Apollo and Dionysos. They represent to me, most vividly and concretely, two radically dissimilar realms of art. Apollo embodies the transcendent genius of the *principium individuationis*; through him alone it is possible

to achieve redemption in illusion. The mystical jubilation of Dionysos, on the other hand, breaks the spell of individuation and opens a path to the maternal womb of being.   [op.cit. 97]

3 THE CURSE OF THE SPHINX

The feline Sphinx roamed free as air and smiled
In the dry desert at those foolish men
Who saw not that her crafted Riddle's clue
Was merely Man, bare man, no Mystery.
But when they found it out they spilt her blood
For her presumption and her Monstrous shape.
Man named Himself and thus assumed the Power
Over his Questioner, till then his Fate –
After, his Slave and victim.
from 'The Fairy Melusine' by Christabel LaMotte
[A.S. Byatt, *Possession*, 292]

Sophocles was still in his twenties when he wrote *Antigone*, and Athens was still at the height of its power and glory. It is often assumed that his plays must therefore be underwriting the optimistic patriarchal rationalism of his time. Yet Melville claims that it is the function of the great imaginative writer at any time to say 'No! in thunder' to the most cherished and unquestioned beliefs and values of his culture, and this is precisely what Sophocles did in his plays if not in his public life. Athens was founded upon the Promethean values of reason, technology, the conquest of Nature, and independence from the gods (except such gods as Athene and Apollo who could be interpreted as giving divine sanction to the tyranny of the male intellect). Sophocles sees these values not as heroic and glorious but as leading to a spurious and hubristic kind of 'progress' which must in the long run prove disastrous.

Theatre for the Greeks was not an entertainment. Though the comedies and satyr plays were very entertaining, they were not only that, and the main business of each day of the Great Dionysia was the performance of a trilogy of tragedies. Nor was it, as we are often told, a way of enforcing civic solidarity. The Great Dionysia was a religious festival, the greatest of the year. It was an act of worship of Dionysos, god of wild things and nature's bounty, of women, and of irrational creativity. The function of the annual festival, presided over by the statue of Dionysus, was to keep alive deeper values than those expressed the rest of the year in the rhetoric of the politicians and administrators (who were no fools, and tried several times without success to put a stop to the Dionysia). Its function was metaphorically to break down the walls within which man attempted to pursue his autonomous life, and let in the disorderly energies of Nature.

There is a common critical vice of ascribing to authors views expressed by their characters. This vice is an ancient one. Both Pericles and Demosthenes were to quote Creon in *Antigone* as if Sophocles had intended the audience to approve his specious arguments, as the chorus does for most of the play. There is a convention that oracles and soothsayers always speak the truth, but not that choruses do. The chorus in *Antigone* is about as morally reliable as Polonius. These Theban elders are, from the start, morally obtuse. They do not question Creon's ruling that the body of Polynices be left unburied; for the dead and the living, they say, his will is law.

The play as a whole makes perfectly clear that Antigone is wholly in the right and Creon wholly in the wrong. That anyone at all should be 'left unburied, his corpse / carrion for the birds and dogs to tear / an obscenity' [68] (in Creon's own words) is an offence against the gods. Any man who seeks to pursue his enemy beyond death usurps the province of the gods. In *Ajax*, probably the earliest of Sophocles' extant plays, the same issue had already been dealt with unambiguously. Menelaus and Agamemnon order that Ajax should be left unburied. Teucer is completely vindicated in his defiance of them. What Creon has done is an act of moral and physical pollution, which might well cause an actual plague, but, in any case, rises stinking to the nostrils of the gods. It is a violation both of human morality and natural law.

It is not that Creon is evil, rather that he is one-dimensional. His high intelligence operates solely in the secular, political dimension – 'our country *is* our safety'. He believes that any opposition to him must be politically motivated. The chorus continues blindly to support Creon, the status quo, law and order, right up to the revelations of Teiresias late in the play.

The manly qualities particularly eulogized in the famous Ode on Man are mastery and cunning, the qualities of Prometheus and Odysseus. Indeed, the first example given is man's mastery of the sea. Man is defined as he who 'crossing the heaving grey sea, / driven on by the blasts of winter / on through breakers crashing left and right, / holds his steady course' [76]. The power of the sea is to be evoked later in the play with exactly the opposite meaning, as a symbol of the irresistible power of the divine curse:

> the ruin will never cease, cresting on and on
> from one generation on throughout the race –
> like a great mounting tide
> driven on by savage mountain gales
>   surging over the dead black depths
> rolling up from the bottom dark heaves of sand
> and the headlands, taking the storm's onslaught full-force,
> roar, and the low moaning
>   echoes on and on   [91]

or of Destiny itself:

> neither wealth nor armies
> towered walls nor ships
> black hulls lashed by the salt
> can save us from that force.
>   [108]

The second claim made for man is that 'the oldest of the gods he wears away – / the Earth, the immortal, the inexhaustible – / as his plows go back and forth, year in, year out'. He exhausts the only apparently inexhaustible mother by perpetual rape. By the time of Sophocles man had worn away the earth to such an extent that he was already well on the way to reducing a green and fertile land to the largely rocky desert Greece is today. Plato's Critias remembers a time when 'the country was unspoiled: its mountains were arable highlands and what is now stony fields was once good soil. . . . What now remains is like the skeleton of a sick man, all the fat and soft earth wasted away and only the bare framework of the land left'.

Next the Ode passes to man the hunter:

> And the blithe, lightheaded race of birds he snares,
> the tribes of savage beasts, the life that swarms the depths –
> > with one fling of his nets
> woven and coiled tight, he takes them all,
> man the skilled, the brilliant!   [76]

Yet only four pages later the sentry gives us a less anthropocentric point of view when he compares Antigone screaming over her brother's body to 'a bird come back to an empty nest / peering into its bed, and all the babies gone' [80]. And it is to be the unnatural behaviour of birds which prompts Teiresias to make the tests of sacrifice which reveal that the blight upon Thebes is Creon's doing.

Another of the supposed achievements of man is in 'training the stallion, clamping the yoke across / his shaggy neck'. But Creon is shortly to be proved wrong in his assertion that (speaking of Antigone) he has known 'spirited horses you can break with a light bit' [83]. Against the Ode's claim for the wonder of the use of language, the play sets Antigone's screams, her dumb resistance, her spit in the face of Creon . Against wind-swift thought, it sets the deeper motions of the heart. The chorus is later forced into a choice between Creon and Aphrodite. It chooses Creon, for Love is a madness:

> Love! –
> you wrench the minds of the righteous into outrage,
> swerve them to their ruin.   [101]

What Creon calls woman's law is the law of Love, not only the law of Aphrodite, but also of Zeus himself, the god of family love. Polynices is Creon's nephew. His denial of the sanctity of love and marriage ('You'd kill your own son's bride?' 'Absolutely: there are other fields for him to plow' [89]) and family bonds makes it appropriate that his punishment should be to lose both wife and son. As Teiresias says: 'this is violence / you have forced upon the heavens' [115].

The last achievement the Ode specifies is that man has 'the mood and mind for law that rules the city'. But we are soon to see that while Creon inhabits an exclusively human and male world of what passes for intelligence and civic values, Antigone is throughout associated with that which lies beyond the city walls, with what Segal calls 'the subjugated natural world', and with the gods, including the gods of night and the underworld. The chorus sides with Creon partly because he is male and Antigone female. Creon himself makes the most of that distinction. We must, he says, 'never let some woman triumph over us' [94]. What a man prays for, he says, is 'to produce good sons'. His imagery reveals that he would really like to reduce women to the status of slaves, or even beasts of burden. It needs Teiresias (a man who had known what it was to be a woman) to heal the split, to show that neither the psychic health of the individual nor the health of the state can be maintained cut off from what lies beyond and beneath the city, the one life we share with animals and gods.

The Ode to Man ends with the absurd hubristic claim for 'ready, resourceful man' that he is 'Never without resources'

> never an impasse as he marches on the future –
> only Death, from Death alone he will find no rescue
> but from desperate plagues he has plotted his escapes.
>
> [77]

Odysseus himself would hardly have dared to make such a claim. By the end of the play the chorus is to be suitably humbled:

> The mighty words of the proud are paid in full
> with mighty blows of fate, and at long last
> those blows will teach us wisdom.   [128]

And Creon, the embodiment, for the chorus, of all the virtues of man, is judged by the play, and, ultimately, by himself, to be the very nobody Odysseus was so determined not to be: 'I don't even exist – I'm no one. Nothing' [126].

The Ode is not, in fact, a portrait of ideal man, but of a false ideal, of outrageously, blindly arrogant man, and a portrait therefore of both Creon and Oedipus.

In the final ode of the play the chorus belatedly remembers that Thebes is the 'mother-city' of Dionysus, whom they invoke as the only remedy for the ills caused by man. The healing spirit for which they plead, the joyful renewal of nature's bounty, the participation of men and women in the cosmic dance, is manifest in the very language and rhythms of this ode, as though in anticipation of the full flowing of that spirit in *Oedipus at Colonus*:

> Lord of the dancing –
> dance, dance the constellations breathing fire!
> Great master of the voices of the night!

Child of Zeus, God's offspring, come, come forth!
Lord, king, dance with your nymphs, swirling, raving
arm-in-arm in frenzy through the night
   they dance you, Iacchus –
                  Dance, Dionysus
giver of all good things!   [119]

*   *   *

Oedipus, even more than Creon, exactly fits the picture of a paragon in the Ode to Man. Before his fall he is the man proclaimed by Protagoras as the measure of all things. He manifests precisely those qualities which were deemed at the time to be characteristic of Athenians, a 'will to action' (in Pericles' phrase), courage, adaptability, intelligence, public spirit, respect for law and order. Sophocles measures Oedipus and finds him wanting. Since Sophocles was himself a model Athenian, *Oedipus the King* has all the urgency and depth of self-interrogation. Sophocles found in Oedipus the perfect metaphor both for his own nature and for the most urgent issues of his time. We have inherited that nature and those issues.

The Oedipus mediated to us by tradition – the innocent man predestined by fate to inescapable horrors – is not the Oedipus of Sophocles, still less of the original myth. If we can shed such preconceptions, we must recognize that, though Oedipus himself frequently proclaims his innocence, Sophocles holds him fully responsible for his own fate. There is no play in which it is more true that character is fate. Sophocles does not, within the play, see the oracles as a problem in relation to free will. Apollo simply foresees what sort of man Oedipus will allow himself to become, what terrible dangers lie in the path of someone so perversely blind. Oedipus has always held his head too high to see the pitfalls:

Pride breeds the tyrant
violent pride, gorging, crammed to bursting
 with all that is overripe and rich with ruin –
clawing up to the heights, headlong pride
crashes down the abyss – sheer doom!
                [209]

Oedipus could not know that Laius and Jocasta were his parents, but one might have expected any man, let alone a man with such warnings behind him, not to be so rash and violent as to escalate a quarrel about priority at a crossroads into multiple murder, including the murder of a man old enough to be his father, not to think the oracle so easily cheated that he can blithely marry a woman old enough to be his mother. Oedipus is the perfect tragic hero because it is the nature of tragedy to ensure that the full price must be paid for every flaw, especially those flaws which might well pass as strengths in ordinary life.

The gods in Sophocles are not the savage sadists Oedipus believes them to be; and he seems to believe in gods at all only when looking for someone else to blame for his predicament. His hubris is most evident in his treatment of Teiresias (whom Creon in the *Antigone* has also insulted and threatened). He calls Teiresias 'this scheming quack, / this fortune-teller peddling lies, eyes peeled / for his own profit – seer blind in his craft!' [182]. Teiresias, he says, cannot harm anyone 'who sees the light'. Only the holy man, after long training in spiritual disciplines and rituals, can be allowed to know something of the secrets of earth and 'the dark and depth of human life' known to the gods. Oedipus presumes to solve all life's riddles by unaided mother-wit. He shares Jocasta's contempt for oracles and seercraft. The chorus knows that such scepticism is the thin end of the wedge: 'But if any man comes striding, high and mighty / in all he says and does . . . the gods, the gods go down' [210].

There would, nevertheless, be something disproportionate about Oedipus' fate if it were the result of nothing more than pride. Surely more is involved in the curse upon Thebes than the failure to punish the murderer of Laius. That is Creon's rather literal interpretation of the oracle's words: 'Drive the corruption from the land'. Other characters, both at the end of this play and in the *Oedipus at Colonus*, seem to find the incest more horrifying than the parricide.

And what of the Sphinx? Oedipus refers to the Sphinx as a 'chanting Fury'. The Furies, as we have seen, were not simply maneating monsters, but ancient powers of earth concerned to prevent or cleanse moral corruption. Why had Teiresias not acted against the Sphinx? Surely he could easily have solved its riddle? Oedipus boasts:

> *I* stopped the Sphinx! With no help from the birds,
> the flight of my own intelligence hit the mark.
>
> [182]

We remember the claims of the Ode to Man in *Antigone* that man's thought, 'quick as the wind' had the remedy for every ill. Perhaps even in his greatest triumph, the solving of the riddle of the Sphinx, Oedipus had, as in all else, been wide of the mark. The life of Oedipus has been a series of disasters. All his encounters – with the oracle, his father, his mother, Teiresias – he gets disastrously wrong, in ways predictable in terms of his character. Why should we think that this sequence of disasters has been interrupted by a perfectly successful encounter with the Sphinx?

At the beginning of the play Thebes is a Waste Land, a 'city of death, one long cortege':

> and the fruits of our famous earth, they will not ripen
> no and the women cannot scream their pangs to birth –
> screams for the Healer, children dead in the womb ...

so many deaths, numberless deaths on deaths, no end –
Thebes is dying . . .   [169]

The Athenian audience of 425 would not think of ancient Thebes, but of the
mysterious plague which only three years earlier had killed a third of the
population of Athens; of which Thucydides wrote: 'The bodies of the dying
were heaped one on top of the other, and half-dead creatures could be seen
staggering about in the streets'. Sophocles here lifts that raw horror onto the
mythic plane where it can be given meaning.

Something has happened to break Nature's moulds, all germens spill
at once. The cause of plagues was believed to be often a rotting corpse. If
Oedipus Tyrannos were part of a trilogy, the previous play in the trilogy must
have dealt with the killing of the Sphinx, and ended with the coming of the
plague. What had become of the Sphinx's body? Had Oedipus simply left her
where she fell, assuming that her question about the brief life of man ('What
goes on four legs in the morning, two at noon, and three in the evening?') had
died with her? Could the cause of the Theban plague have been the rotting
body of the Sphinx?

If we turn to Seneca's *Oedipus* we find that this is indeed so:

That subtle creature's dust now rises up
To fight against you. She, the accursed pest
Whom I destroyed, is now destroying Thebes!
                                        [213]

And in Ted Hughes' adaptation of Seneca's *Oedipus* these lines become:

yet she's not dead as if I'd never solved her riddle
she never died she changed I drove her off the rock
and the questions stopped but her rottenness is flying
her stench is a fog smothering us as if we were living inside her
    carcase   [19]

Thus Thebes suffers far more from the dead Sphinx than from the living.

And this is no archaic fantasy. It is an accurate forecast of such actions
as the burning of toxic waste to scatter dioxins over the grass which sheep
and cattle eat, infecting meat and milk. The poison seeps into the waters
under the earth (the very bloodstream of the goddess) and pollutes the whole
ecosystem, causing deaths, misbirths and sterility.

It is perfectly in keeping with Oedipus' character that he should have
killed Laius, but there seems to be nothing in his character to predispose him
to incest. Jocasta, however, would seem to agree with those psychologists who
claim that such a predisposition is common: 'Many a man before you, / in his
dreams, has shared his mother's bed' [215]. Sophocles shows little interest in
Oedipus the King in the specific psychological or religious implications of the

incest theme which is so central in the original myth, and so mysteriously connected to the slaying of the Sphinx, but may have done so in an earlier part of the trilogy. Lacking that, we can only look to the mythological sources for further information about the Sphinx.

The Oedipus myth seems to be a later variant of older myths such as that in which Apollo becomes oracular god of Delphi only after slaying the dragon of Earth, who ruled before him, as told in the Homeric 'Hymn to Apollo':

> Whoever went to meet the she-dragon,
> the day of death would carry him off,
> until the lord Apollo,
> who works from afar,
> let fly at her his strong arrow.
> Then, heavily, she lay there,
> racked with bitter pain,
> gasping for breath
> and rolling about on the ground.   [Baring 292]

Older still is the Babylonian creation myth, which describes the slaughter of the mother-goddess Tiamat by the young sun-god Marduk. That myth Campbell places in a line of development of creation myths which progressively spurns the female. First, the world was created by a goddess without consort, then by a goddess fecundated by a consort, then fashioned from the body of a goddess killed by a young warrior-god, then by the unaided power of a male god. Historically, Campbell speculates that this progression reflects 'the conquest of a local matriarchal order by invading patriarchal nomads, and their reshaping of the local lore of the productive earth to their own ends':

And we are going to find, throughout the following history of the orthodox patriarchal systems of the West, that the power of this goddess-mother of the world, whom we have here seen defamed, abused, insulted, and overthrown by her sons, is to remain as an ever-present threat to their castle of reason, which is founded upon a soil that they consider to be dead but is actually alive, breathing, and threatening to shift.

[*Occidental Mythology*, 80,86]

Why is the Sphinx so monstrous? Jung interprets the Sphinx as 'fear of the mother':

In the Oedipus legend the Sphinx is sent by Hera, who hates Thebes on account of the birth of Bacchus; because Oedipus conquers the Sphinx, which is nothing but fear of the mother, he must marry Jocasta, his mother, for the throne and the hand of the widowed queen of Thebes belonged to him who freed the land from the plague of the Sphinx. The

35

genealogy of the Sphinx is rich in allusions to the problem touched upon here. She is daughter of Echidna, a mixed being; a beautiful maiden above, a hideous serpent below. This double creature corresponds to the picture of the mother; above, the lovely, human and attractive half; below the horrible animal half, converted into a fear animal through the incest prohibition. [*Psychology*, 112–13]

In another version of the legend, the Sphinx had been sent to Thebes by Hera to punish Laius for introducing pederasty to mankind. By laying claim to sexual self-sufficiency, Laius had denied his dependence on the female, who, in response, turns monstrous and destructive. This fear of the mother, and hence of the female in all its manifestations, is a characteristic neurosis of the predominantly narcissistic and homosexual Greek male. This fear is expressed in fantasies of devouring female monsters, which are then projected onto any aspect of nature which he experiences as threatening to his ego and autonomy.

Nietzsche also links the solving of the riddle with the parricide and incest:

How should man force nature to yield up her secrets but by successfully resisting her, that is to say, by unnatural acts? This is the recognition I find expressed in the terrible triad of Oedipean fates: the same man who solved the riddle of nature (the ambiguous Sphinx) must also, as murderer of his father and husband of his mother, break the consecrated tables of the natural order. It is as though the myth whispered to us that wisdom . . . is an unnatural crime, and that whoever, in pride of knowledge, hurls nature into the abyss of destruction, must himself experience nature's disintegration. [*Birth*, 61]

In the mythic realm, the killing of the father and breaking of the incest taboo with the mother may be heroic acts, stages in the process of individuation and rebirth. As Joseph Campbell puts it:

The mystical marriage with the Queen goddess of this world represents the hero's total mastery of life. . . . And the testings of the hero, which were preliminary to his ultimate experience and deed, were symbolical of those crises of realization by means of which his consciousness came to be amplified and made capable of enduring full possession of the mother-destroyer, his inevitable bride. [*Hero*, 120–21]

But in order for this to happen, the acts must be performed in full consciousness, or the full implications must be consciously accepted subsequently.

By deficient eyes she is reduced to inferior states, by the evil eye of ignorance she is spellbound to banality and ugliness. But she is redeemed by the eyes of understanding. The hero who can take her as she is, without undue commotion but with the kindness and assurance she requires is potentially the king, the incarnate god of the created world. [116]

Oedipus is emphatically not that hero. He cannot see Nature other than as the Sphinx's maw. He understands nothing. His approach is with the maximum of commotion and minimum of kindness. His blindness is not the blindness of Teiresias, the price to be paid for inner vision. It represents a refusal to see what, at the denouement, is being thrust in his face.

Hughes, in his adaptation of Seneca, does not merely link the Sphinx and the mother but fuses them. 'Song for a Phallus' is Hughes' savagely comic retelling of the story. Here Oedipus works on the principle of what you don't understand, kill:

> Oedipus took an axe and split
> > The Sphinx from top to bottom
> The answers aren't in me, he cried
> > Maybe your guts have got 'em.
> Mamma Mamma

The answer indeed emerges from the Sphinx in the form of his own mother. But Oedipus is ruthless, crazed in his determination to smash his way out of the darkness, the cycle of birth, death and eternal recurrence represented by the mother:

> He split his Mammy like a melon
> > He was drenched with gore
> He found himself curled up inside
> > As if he had never been bore.
> Mamma Mamma

Hughes' Crow makes all the mistakes of Oedipal or Socratic man, but he learns; he undergoes a psychic death and resurrection (in *Cave Birds*). He and his victim (mother and bride) with infinite care, kindness and assurance, bring each other to perfection. At the point where he has at last paid in full, has become capable of seeing her as she is, 'she gives him his eyes' ['Bride and Groom'].

The archetypal image remains the same. The interpretation of it varies according to ideological prejudice or conditioning. There is, for example, the image of a male and female being on either side of a flourishing tree. Associated with the female is a serpent. In Neolithic times the image was interpreted as the Great Goddess, Mother of All Things, through whom the life force (the serpent) becomes the fertile world (Tree of Life). Chief among her creations is the male, who now, as her consort, honours and balances her. The same image appearing in Judeo-Christian culture is interpreted as sinful Eve being seduced by the evil serpent to taste the forbidden fruit and betray her consort, thus spoiling the perfect world which had sprung from the mind of God. So, too, the image of a man sitting deep in thought before a beautiful maiden with the body of a winged lion was probably once interpreted as man receiving from the goddess an oracular revelation of her triple nature. Later it became Oedipus solving the riddle of the terrible Sphinx, thereby annihilating it.

Oedipus calls the Sphinx a 'Dog-faced Witch', but the chorus refers to her as the 'winged maiden'. If we can discount the distortions of Oedipus' 'evil eye of ignorance' and the equally deficient vision of that whole culture of which he is representative, we see the Sphinx on her mountain, virginal and maternal, beautiful and terrible, combining bird, lion and woman, as unmistakably an incarnation of the archetypal Great Goddess. Jung called her 'the great nocturnal goddess, the veiled Sphinx', Graves 'the winged moon-goddess of Thebes'. Jane Harrison described her as a soothsayer, who answered riddles as well as asked them, 'the oracular beast of the earth-oracle', which perhaps explains why Teiresias had been reluctant to act against her.

Peter Redgrove draws attention to an Attic cup which depicts Oedipus sitting deep in thought in front of the earth-oracle, the Sphinx on her column. She has a lion body, but is also 'a lovely attentive maiden' [*Black Goddess*, xxviii]. She is a symbol of the union of opposites, the earthly and the divine, body and spirit, instinct and intelligence, male and female, ugliness and beauty. Redgrove writes:

> If Oedipus had been aware of the duty he owed to forces greater than
> himself, the tragedy would not have occurred and the city would have
> been free of pestilence. But then he would have been the priest-king of an
> earlier rule. The ignorance of Oedipus ushered in the plagues of our
> superbly empty-clever modern age, full of disasters unconsciously invited.
>
> [xiv]

The Sphinx threw herself into the sea. Redgrove interprets this as a descent into the unconscious where she 'still operates in our lives as both curse and blessing. Moreover, the unconscious mind is no mere lumber-room of childhood errors and traumata but a living, breathing, sensing, perfumed, luminous Sphinx' [xxx].

The Sphinx, then, is the female, the Earth mother seen by civilized man as a threat and a monstrosity. He seeks to unriddle her mysteries, to replace her with the rule of his own unaided cunning and will. The Sphinx's riddle Oedipus solved was not really very difficult, Christmas cracker stuff, unless we take, as Oedipus did not, its deeper symbolic meaning. I cannot improve on Segal's account:

> The riddle that both exalts and defeats Oedipus has to do with the
> anomalous position of man in the natural world. Not only has he evolved
> from the four-footed beasts to his unique two feet, but, thanks to his use

of tools, he alone possesses that strange third foot. That third foot, however, can kill as well as support a lamed gait. Oedipus uses his staff both to kill his father, who is also the king, and to assert his own authority as king. . . . In Oedipus' hands 'the third foot' contains the ambiguity of man's civilizing power and his destructive capacity: *homo faber* is also *homo necans*.

[Segal, 216]

In Hughes' words 'he pounded and hacked at her / With numbers and equations and laws / Which he invented and called truth' ['Revenge Fable']. Modern man is still Oedipal man. Like a genetic engineer he plucks out the heart of her mystery: 'With tweezers of number / He picks the gluey heart out of an inaudibly squeaking cell –' ['Crow's Account of St. George'].

The serpent was, for the ancient Greeks, an exoteric symbol of *zoë*, undifferentiated life. But there was also a deeper symbol, which was esoteric, forbidden knowledge. The heart of Nature's mystery was symbolized for them by the double helix of a pair of entwined mating serpents. Teiresias, before he became a seer, had been the prototype of the genetic scientist, probing this secret. His punishment, like that of Oedipus, was blindness (a condition of inner sight) and to become for a while a woman, thus correcting the imbalance of his psyche.

Hughes sees the story of Oedipus and the Sphinx as very similar to the story of St. George and the dragon in that it 'sets up as an ideal pattern for any dealing with unpleasant or irrational experience, the complete suppression of the terror. In other words it is the symbolic story of creating a neurosis'. This suppression of the terror, whether projected as devil, dragon or Sphinx, 'in fact suppresses imagination and suppresses vital natural life'. In Hughes' poem 'Crow's Account of St. George', the hero, like Heracles, sees monsters everywhere, goes mad, and slaughters his own wife and children, in accordance with Nietzsche's saying 'He who fights with monsters should be careful lest he thereby becomes a monster' [*Beyond Good and Evil*, Apothegm 146]. The real challenge to the hero is to find a way of negotiating with the dragon, thereby including it in the world.

The real riddle for Oedipus was how to relate to the Sphinx, that is, to Nature. To that she is herself, in her fusion of all the opposites, the answer. It is, in part, the problem of mortality. Her solution is the acceptance of death as a condition of renewal. Thebes seeks the hero who will free it from death. That riddle Oedipus got disastrously wrong. He attempted not to solve it but to unpick it, separating out the two halves of the goddess. The acceptable, safe, tameable, human part becomes Jocasta, the rest, the unacceptable, the inhuman, is the nightmarish, monstrous Sphinx, who can then be simply obliterated. But the destruction of the Sphinx brings the real horror, death without renewal.

Oedipus' assumption that there are no questions Nature can ask to which Man is not the answer drove her over the cliff. The suicide of the Sphinx is a symbol of the death of essential connections in the human spirit. Oedipus is triumphant and rewarded, but at the cost of plague, horror, exile and blindness.

* * *

In the myth before Sophocles, Oedipus is hounded to death at last by the female guardian spirits of Nature, the Furies, cousins of the Sphinx. Why, in *Oedipus at Colonus*, did Sophocles change the story so radically, making the sacred grove of the Furies at Colonus into a sanctuary for Oedipus the holy man, and the place of his apotheosis? Oedipus, like Lear, is given a second chance, and gets it right.

Though the Oedipus of this play remains the old Oedipus, aggressive and unbending in his relations with men like Creon and his own sons, who still inhabit the world of power-politics, he claims that suffering has taught him the great lesson of acceptance. He is now a man at one with his fate, content to 'brood on the old prophesies, stored / in the depths of all my being, / that Apollo has fulfilled for me at last' [310]. He has come to terms with his own death, secure in the knowledge that 'only the gods can never age, / the gods can never die' [322]. The young Oedipus had approached a foreign city as hubristic hero and saviour, bringing, in the event, disaster. Old Oedipus approaches a foreign city as outcast and suppliant, bringing salvation.

More specifically, he accepts the Furies. Had he now approached them in the same spirit in which he had approached that 'chanting Fury' the Sphinx, he would have attempted to outwit and destroy them, to evade his own death and free Athens from the curse of these 'Terrible Ones'. He would have seen them as Orestes saw them, as simply monstrous, the unacceptable face of Nature. But his vision has been cleansed by suffering. He no longer projects the contents of a sick psyche onto the face of Nature. There is no longer that disastrous split down the middle of his psyche between acceptable and unacceptable. He asks their awesome names so that he can pray to these 'Daughters of Earth, Daughters of the Darkness' [285], and is told that these 'Terrible Goddesses' are called 'the Ones who watch the world, the Kindly Ones'. He later prays to them as 'you sweet daughters born of primeval Darkness' [290].

This fusion of opposites is no longer a problem for Oedipus. This is the true solving of the true riddle. Perhaps in this new spirit of Dionysian acceptance and wholeness, he might have prayed to the awesome Sphinx, acknowledging that there is no answer to the riddle of birth and death. And perhaps the Sphinx, accepted, would have shown him her kindly face.

The Sphinx stood in relation to Thebes as the Furies to Athens, a focus and personification of the spirit of the surrounding countryside on which the city depends. What had the Thebans done to earn the enmity of the Sphinx before the arrival of Oedipus? I have already mentioned the introduction of pederasty by Laius. More likely to have concerned Sophocles was his similarity to his son, quick to anger, determined to thwart the oracle, even, in his case, at the cost of murdering his child. But it may well be that not only the ruler but the whole of Thebes had offended in ways prefigured in the Ode to Man in *Antigone*. It is a consistent story of male violence from the founding of the city out of the teeth of the slaughtered serpent, through the crimes of Pentheus against Dionysus, his Bacchantes and all the women of Thebes, the crimes of Oedipus, the crimes of the warring brothers Polyneices and Eteocles, to the murderous misogyny of Creon.

The great Ode of *Oedipus at Colonus* is an Ode to Life, to Nature and its gods and goddesses at their most beneficent. Colonus, the chorus claims, is 'the noblest home on earth', a place where man lives at one with his environment. At the centre, the source, is the 'sacred wood ... where the Reveler Dionysus strides the earth forever' [326]. Here the narcissus is the 'crown of the Great Goddesses / Mother and Daughter dying / into life from the dawn of time'. Here are springs that never fail, 'the fountainhead ... quickening life forever, fresh each day – / life rising up with the river's pure tide / flowing over the plains, the swelling breast of earth'. It is the home also of the Muses and of Aphrodite. This land is famous for the 'grey-leafed olive, mother, nurse of children, / perennial generations growing in her arms', under the 'eternal eyes of Guardian Zeus' and great Athene. Famous too for its horses, horses not broken by men, but by Poseidon 'lord god of the sea-lanes'. It is Poseidon's ship, not man's, which mounts the white manes of the sea. There is not a trace of hubris in this Ode. All the pride and power and glory is credited to mother earth and the great Nature gods. And Nature, in response, yields all sane men could ask. The imagery unifies city, cultivated land and wild untouched nature, as it also unifies Olympian and chthonic deities. It is one with the movement of the whole play towards the unification of the human world in history and individual experience with the divine mysteries.

In contrast to his ready and blasting answer, which was death to the Sphinx, Oedipus approaches the sacred grove with tentative questions. In contrast to his brandishing of language as an all-powerful weapon, he enters it in silence. This deep silence leaves room for the voice of the god to be heard, gently but firmly calling on the hesitant Oedipus (Oedipus who had rushed so rashly into every previous encounter with the divine), to hurry.

The death of Oedipus has much in common with initiation into the Eleusinian mysteries. He is lead where none may follow by Hermes, the Escort of the Dead, and Persephone, Queen of the Dead. But the Mysteries are not of death, but of rebirth, a transformation exactly the opposite of that in *The Bacchae*, from destruction and terror into creation and kindness. From the violation of the mother Demeter springs the lovely maiden, the Kore (Persephone), and from the violation of the daughter springs the lusty son Dionysos. According to one version of the myth, it was Dionysos himself who had sent the sphinx to Thebes, that city of pride and violence. The very founding of Thebes had been in despite of Nature. Cadmus had slain a serpent, guardian of the waters and sacred to Ares. The sown teeth of that serpent had produced a race so belligerent that most of them quickly killed each other. (Pentheus was the son of one of the survivors.) Now Oedipus repays that ancient debt.

It is apt that the bringer of sterility to Thebes on the sacred mountain of the Sphinx should spend his last moments 'near a hill sacred to Demeter Euchloos, protectress of what springs green from the earth' [Segal, 371]. This is where Apollo the Healer has brought Oedipus at the end of his painful wanderings, granting him at last a vision of the atonement he had rejected in his pride. But it is more than a vision. Oedipus is to be himself a Healer, his grave a guarantee of the victory of Athens over Thebes. Theseus cannot at first see that Athens has any need of Oedipus, since there is no likelihood of war with Thebes. But Oedipus reminds him that no man can see what the future holds, that no amount of intelligence, goodwill, liberal-humanism, can lift an individual or a state out of the turmoil of history, independent of the operations of non-human powers. For wholeness, Athens needs to acknowledge Oedipus, a permanent reminder of the danger of self-sufficiency. Athens needed Oedipus as Arthur's court needed the green girdle, as Prospero needed Caliban.

Oedipus in his death leaves no polluting corpse. The power to which he finds access at last, and of which he becomes himself a transmitter, is a power which stems only from a proper contact with the unknown. Such healing as the artist can offer his countrymen, Sophocles offered in *Oedipus at Colonus*. The image of blind Oedipus, who stumbled when he saw, confidently leading his daughters to the sacred grove of the Eumenides where he is to become himself one of the invisible powers and presences he had formerly mocked is a wonderful image of healing. There is no longer any crippling division between the human and divine, between Olympian and chthonic gods, between intelligence and prophetic vision, between male and female, between civilization and Nature.

When Sophocles wrote this play, Athens was in desperate straits, within two years of finally losing, through insane hubris, the long and crippling war against Sparta. But by the time the play was performed, Athens had fallen and its great age was over.

4 NATURE STRIKES BACK: *THE BACCHAE*

Euripides was born in 480 B.C., the year of the battle of Salamis, which established Athens as the leading city-state in all Greece for half a century. Aeschylus, aged fifty-five, fought in the battle, and the sixteen-year-old Sophocles danced in the victory procession. Euripides became the darling of the sophisticates and rationalists, showing scant respect for the gods. At the age of seventy-two he left a war-torn, besieged, disillusioned Athens for voluntary exile in the wilds of Macedonia. There he wrote his last testament, *The Bacchae*, repudiating most of what he and Athens had stood for. Sophocles and Euripides died in the same year, 406 B.C., two years before the final defeat of Athens by Sparta in the Peloponnesian War. Euripides was seventy-four, Sophocles ninety. The last known work of each dramatist, written close to the end, was very different from what had gone before, but in quite different ways. Whereas Sophocles evoked the time of Theseus, the legendary founder of Athens, as a healing reminder of a time when the city flourished in a proper relationship with Dionysos and all the gods and goddesses, Euripides lashed, in the figure of Pentheus, (even more savagely than Sophocles had lashed Creon and Oedipus) the man of intelligence and civic virtue who repudiated Dionysos. He prophesied that the god who could join all in one, would, repudiated, simply manifest his power negatively, joining all 'in one destruction' [223].

The drama festival in Athens was held in the temple of Dionysos, presided over by his statue and dedicated to him. In this play, Euripides was returning to the roots of drama itself, which had grown from the rites of Dionysos.

✳   ✳   ✳

The play opens with the god himself addressing the audience: 'I am Dionysos, son of Zeus.' He has come from the east, disguised as a mortal man, with a band of his female followers, to Thebes, (the home of his mother Semele), now ruled by his cousin Pentheus. His purpose in coming is clearly stated:

> Thebes must learn, unwilling though she is, that my Bacchic revels are something beyond her present understanding; and . . . this Pentheus is a fighter against God – he defies me, excludes me from libations, never names me in prayer. Therefore I will demonstrate to him, and to all Thebes, that I am a god. [182]

We are not concerned here with gods as immortal overgrown children, squabbling amongst themselves and seducing or persecuting human beings. In claiming to be a god Dionysos is claiming that what he stands for is an absolute – that is something humanity cannot afford to deny or fail to respect without an inevitable collapse into madness and destruction. A god is a power, an energy-source, necessary to all life, but which can be so mishandled by man in his arrogance that it blows up in his face.

When Dionysos claims to have plagued the women of Thebes with madness – 'driven them all frantic out of doors; now their home is the mountains, and their wits are gone' [182], this is a symbolic way of dramatizing and objectifying the fact that to deny a god is the same thing as to go mad. Teiresias, who can be assumed always to speak the truth, calls Pentheus, for the same reason 'perverse' and 'raving mad'. Dionysos, despite (or indeed, as we shall see, because of) his association with ecstasy, is even more firmly associated, in this play, with sanity: 'The things one ought to know most of all, those things I know' [202]. Agave, when, at the end, she recovers her sanity, says: 'I am justly punished; for in pride I blasphemed the god Dionysos, and did not understand the things I ought to have understood'. What Agave and Pentheus ought to have understood is whatever is represented in the play by 'my Bacchic revels'.

We must make a clear distinction between the two groups of women now dressed alike and both performing Bacchic rites in the mountains. One group consists of, as it were, the professionals – full-time Bacchantes who have followed Dionysos from the east and are adepts in his mysteries. Dionysos calls them 'my holy band of revellers'. They speak throughout the play a language of perfect sanity and wholeness, the wholeness of a god who is simultaneously Olympian and chthonic, male and female, civilized and wild, Greek and barbarian. Their character is established in the first Chorus:

> Blest is the happy man
> Who knows the mysteries the gods ordain,
> And sanctifies his life,
> Joins soul with soul in mystic unity,
> And, by due ritual made more pure,
> Enters the ecstasy of mountain solitudes.
>
> O Thebes, old nurse that cradled Semele,
> Be ivy-garlanded, burst into flower
> With wreaths of lush bright-berried bryony,
> Bring sprays of fir, green branches torn from oaks,
> Fill soul and flesh with Bacchus' mystic power;
> Fringe and bedeck your dappled fawnskin cloaks
> With woolly tufts and locks of purest white.
> There's a brute wildness in the fennel-wands –
> Reverence it well.
>
> O what delight is in the mountains!
> There the celebrant, wrapped in his sacred fawnskin,
> Flings himself on the ground surrendered;
> While the swift-footed company streams on;
> There he hunts for blood, and rapturously

Eats the raw flesh of the slaughtered goat,
Hurrying on to the Phrygian or Lydian mountain heights.
Possessed, ecstatic, he leads their happy cries;
The earth flows with milk, flows with wine,
Flows with nectar of bees;
The air is thick with a scent of Syrian myrrh.

And, like a foal with its mother at pasture,
Runs and leaps for joy every daughter of Bacchus.

[183/6]

This is obviously a description of a holy communion. The purpose of the rituals is to enable a celebrant to become one with the god, to take the power of god into her own body: 'Fill soul and flesh with Bacchus' mystic power.' It is an act of atonement between humanity and the whole non-human creation, the 'brute wildness' of the mountains and their flora and fauna. The processes of nature are themselves a joyful dance in which the celebrant seeks to be caught up. This can only be achieved by the surrender of the self-contained hubristic ego, the total surrender to the god in each of us, who can only manifest himself when we are 'made pure', 'sanctified', reverential towards the universal mother, the earth. The celebrant, at one with nature, skips for sheer joy like a foal with its mother. The earth responds by flowing with milk, wine and honey. The grape is an image both of the earth bursting with sweetness and of the intoxication of atonement with the god, the ecstasy of escape from the perverse tyrannical ego which tells us that we have no need of gods, that we are ourselves the lords of the earth.

The Bacchantes are female because women are the guardians of the magical power; their flesh is filled with it; the rites are not only celebrations of the earth's fertility, but also of their own, which promotes that of the earth. Women are needed to act as intermediaries between men and the power of the god, to which most men are closed, seeing it, if at all, as a threat to their own self-sufficiency. Women must mediate between man and Nature and between man and his own anima, both of which he is likely to fear and persecute.

There is in the choric odes of *The Bacchae* something very suggestive of Crete. In Crete, which had not suffered the Kurgan invasions of the fifth, fourth and third millennia, the Neolithic spirit of atonement with Nature through the Great Goddess had survived into the second millenium:

In Crete artists did not give substance to the world of the dead through an abstract of the world of the living, nor did they immortalize proud deeds or state a humble claim for divine attention in the temples of the gods. Here and here alone (in contrast to Egypt and the Near East) the human bid for timelessness was disregarded in the most complete acceptance of the grace of life the world has ever known. For life means movement and the beauty of movement was woven into the intricate web of living forms which we call 'scenes of nature'; was revealed in human bodies acting their serious games, inspired by a transcendent presence, acting in freedom and restraint, unpurposeful as cyclic time itself.

[H.A. Groenewegen-Frankfort, 186]

Something of the same spirit was to be found in Etruscan culture, which was collapsing under the heel of Rome at the very moment *The Bacchae* was being written. The Romans justified their campaign against Etruria in much the same high moral terms as Pentheus uses against the Bacchantes, with accusations of sexual corruption. Lawrence writes:

Those pure, clean-living, sweet-souled Romans, who smashed nation after nation and crushed the free soul in people after people, . . . said the Etruscans were vicious.

[*Mornings* 98]

Cretan and Etruscan culture both differed from Athenian and Roman in the equal partnership of men and women in all aspects of life.

The most famous of the 'serious games' of the Cretans were the bull-dances, where young men and women expressed in astonishing grace and agility their oneness with the powers symbolized by the bull and its horns, which had long been symbols of the life-force of the goddess. Later these symbols were particularly associated with Artemis (whose name is Cretan) and with Dionysos. But the energies locked into the horns of the bull are potentially destructive energies, savage in self-defence. Rejection of the god transforms the life-energies into powers of death and destruction.

The maddened Theban women, the second group, look, to begin with, like real Bacchantes, but they are not. The real Bacchantes have freely chosen the hard disciplines of their mysteries and rituals, and are always in control of the energies they release. The Theban women know not what they do. The adjectives used to describe the two groups of women do not overlap. The true Bacchantes are ecstatic, rapturous, delirious, possessed, frenzied, joyful, holy, sacred, mysterious, mystic, pure, surrendered . . . The Theban women are riotous, stung, maddened, frantic, raving . . . When at the end, the Bacchantes see what Agave and her sisters have done in their madness, they are utterly horrified.

The religion of Dionysos is not just for young women. If what he represents is an absolute, it will be equally necessary for the sanity of men. Even the oldest and highest men were expected to participate. Teiresias and Cadmus enter to make clear to us what that means. Beating time with a thyrsus can make them forget their age: 'The god will guide us there, and without weariness' [187]. Any man failing to do all in his power to exalt this god, is, says Teiresias, perverse.

Now there enters just such a man – Pentheus. Pentheus reveals himself at once as a rash and violent man. He dismisses Dionysos as 'an upstart god'.

He savours completely untrue salacious accounts of the behaviour of the women:

> They tell me . . . the women go creeping off this way and that to lonely places and there give themselves to lecherous men, under the excuse that they are Maenad priestesses; though in their ritual Aphrodite comes before Bacchus. [188]

He says that he will 'hunt out' his mother and her sisters. Pentheus is to have recourse very often to imagery of hunting, which associates him with his cousin Actaeon. Indeed, Cadmus reminds him of that story:

> Remember Actaeon – his tragic end; he boasted, out in these valleys, that he was a better hunter than Artemis, and was torn to pieces and devoured by the very hounds he had bred. Don't invite the same fate! [191]

Of course Pentheus does invite and suffer exactly the same fate – he is torn to pieces by destructive powers he has himself called into being. He attempts to mobilize an army to slaughter the women. This threat transforms them into an army, which slaughters him.

Pentheus shares the common Athenian assumption that women belong at home. The rites of Dionysos afforded Athenian women their only opportunity to leave both home and city, and for that reason were opposed by Athenian men, who dared not, however, go so far as to forbid them. Pentheus, the tyrant and sceptic, sees no reason not to forbid them. There would have been much sympathy for Pentheus among the original audience when he threatens to send the Bacchantes to the slave market 'or retain them in my own household to work at the looms; that will keep their hands from drumming on tambourines! [197]'. Those Theban women who will not remain at home must be imprisoned. If they escape the city, defined as the area within which his authority (standing for all male, rational, civilized authority) holds, they must be killed.

> Pentheus' idealized image of himself rests on his image of the social order that he sees himself as leading and upholding: a warrior society of obedient, disciplined male citizens ready to form hoplite ranks and protect the enclosed, walled space of the city in which the women are safely shut in and secured. [Segal 1982, 190]

Pentheus has made the city into a fortress for keeping Nature out. He fears not only the god but the mountains themselves (which in his madness he threatens to uproot with his own hands). Anything unconfined, unrepressed, must be wicked. His hounding of the women is in the same spirit in which Francis Bacon was to advocate in Shakespeare's time that Nature herself should be 'hounded in her wandering'.

Pentheus gloats on the violence he will have an excuse to perpetrate on the 'Oriental magician or conjuror' posing as a priest of Dionysos, when he catches him. First he proposes to behead him, then hang him, then have him stoned to death. Teiresias tries to reason with him:

> You rely on force; but it is not force that governs human affairs. If you think otherwise – beware of mistaking your perverse opinion for wisdom. Welcome Dionysos to Thebes; pour libations to him, garland your head and celebrate his rites. Dionysos will not compel women to control their lusts. Self-control in all things depends on our own natures. This is a fact you should consider; for a chaste-minded woman will come to no harm in the rites of Bacchus . . . Your mind is most pitifully diseased; and there is no medicine that can heal you. [191]

Pentheus immediately turns his violent urges against the more immediately accessible Teiresias, a venerable holy man, seer:

> Go immediately to the place of augury where Teiresias practices, smash it with crowbars, knock down the walls, turn everything upside down, fling out his holy fripperies to the winds. [192]

Pentheus' hatred of religion obviously extends far beyond Dionysos. For the Greeks, almost the worst of sins was hubris, that extreme form of pride which makes a man spurn the gods, and take powers of life and death arbitrarily into his own hands. The Chorus draws the obvious conclusion:

> To know much is not to be wise.
> Pride more than mortal hastens life to its end;
> And they who in pride pretend
> Beyond man's limit, will lose what lay
> Close to their hand and sure.
> I count it madness, and know no cure can mend
> The evil man and his evil way
>
> Dionysos, son of Zeus, delights in banquets;
> And his dear love is Peace, giver of wealth,
> Saviour of young men's lives – a goddess rare!
> His enemy is the man who has no care
> To pass his years in happiness and health,
> His days in quiet and his nights in joy,
> Watchful to keep aloof both mind and heart
> From men whose pride claims more than mortals may.
> [193/4]

Pentheus, like Agamemnon and Oedipus, is a tragic hero in the special sense that all heroism is tragic, since any claim to 'heroic independence from the changes, cycles, and mortality of nature' [Segal 1982, 305] is disallowed and terribly punished in tragedy. The chorus speaks of any pretender to such heroism when it says:

> See! With contempt of right, with a reckless rage
> To combat your and your mother's mysteries, Bacchus,
> With maniac fury out he goes, stark mad,
> For a trial of strength against *your* invincible arm!
> The sober and humble heart
> That accords the gods their due without carp or cavil,
> And knows that his days are as dust, shall live untouched.
>
> [213]

Pentheus seeks to 'turn everything upside down'. At their first confrontation, Dionysos says to him:

> I am sane, you are mad.
> You do not know what life you live, or what you do, or who you are.
>
> [197]

This seems to me to be the crux of the play. To worship Dionysos is merely a dramatic and imaginative way of saying to be sane, to know what life you live, and who you are. The arrogance of Pentheus, which has become the arrogance of our entire civilization, is simply a lack of self-knowledge, a lack of the knowledge that the self is nothing apart from the rest of life. When Pentheus throws Dionysos into a dark prison he is thrusting that essential life-knowledge down into the depths of his own unconscious, denying it utterly. When, a few minutes later, his palace crumbles to pieces, it is the life-energies, which he has converted within himself to seething anger, breaking down the hard shell of his monstrous ego. He has transformed himself into a 'Brute with bloody jaws agape, / God-defying, gross and grim'. The Chorus, terrified that they are about to be violated, pray to Dionysos: 'Touch this murderous man, / And bring his violence to an end!' [198].

Dionysos is extremely patient and gentle with Pentheus, reasoning with him, presenting him with impartial objective evidence, for Pentheus claims to be the champion of reason. But Pentheus is deaf to rational argument. His reasons are merely rationalizations of his perverse and violent desires.

The herdsman comes to bring Pentheus an eyewitness account of the behaviour of the Theban women in the mountains:

> They lay just as they had thrown themselves on the ground, – but with
> modesty in their posture; they were not drunk with wine, as you told us,
> or with music of flutes; nor was there any love-making there in the

loveliness of the woods. Snakes licked their cheeks. Some suckled young gazelles or wolf-cubs. And one of them took her thyrsus and struck it on the rocks; and from the rock there gushed a spring of limpid water; another struck her wand down into the earth, and there the god made a fountain of wine spring up; and any who wanted milk had only to scratch the earth with the tip of her fingers, and there was the white stream flowing for her to drink; and from the ivy-bound thyrsus a sweet ooze of honey dripped. Oh! if you could have been there and seen all this, you would have entreated with prayers this god whom now you accuse. [202–3]

The god is virtually laying on miracles in a desperate last-ditch attempt to save Pentheus from himself. He is blind to them. Nature is ugly when we see it ugly (Pentheus) and beautiful when we see it beautiful (Shepherd). Its ugliness is imprinted on Pentheus' mind before he sees it. Therefore he cannot see *it,* only project his own perverse images upon it. He is essentially mad.

Next the god shows him what happens when the power which makes such miracles is switched to its destructive manifestations, as it is when the women are ambushed and hunted. Suddenly, like going mad, everything is turned upside down and becomes horrific. The women had been like wild creatures leading the unfallen life of joy in the woods and mountains, like the fawn later described by the Chorus:

> O for the joy of a fawn at play
> In the fragrant meadow's green delight,
> Who has leapt out free from the woven snare,
> Away from the terror of chase and flight,
> And the huntsman's shout, and the straining pack,
> And skims the sand by the river's brim
> With the speed of wind in each aching limb,
> To the blessed lonely forest where
> The soil's unmarked by a human track,
> And leaves hang thick and the shades are dim.
>
> [208]

Men are forever hunting down the equivalent of this fawn within themselves, their own capacity for love and innocence and naturalness. But in the psyche the hunter shall be hunted. The persecuted animal self, or feminine self, or god within, becomes itself a huge hound and turns on us. Agave cries: 'Oh, my swift hounds, we are being hunted by these men.' They turn on their attackers, who are put to flight, but the destructive energies released and rampant now turn equally upon the innocent, as they do in all wars:

So we fled, and escaped being torn to pieces by these possessed women. But our cattle were feeding there on the fresh grass; and the Bacchae attacked them, with their bare hands. You could see Agave take up a bellowing young heifer with full udders, and hold it by the legs with her two arms stretched wide. Others were tearing our cows limb from limb, and you could see perhaps some ribs or a cleft hoof being tossed high and low; and pieces of bloody flesh hung dripping on the pine-branches. [204]

This image of obscene violence prefigures the death of Pentheus, and is intended as a warning to him. His response is to threaten to kill his own mother and her sisters – 'slaughtered as they deserve in the glens of Cithaeron'. There is nothing more Dionysos can do to save him.

> Slow, yet unfailing, move the Powers
> Of heaven with the moving hours.
> When mind runs mad, dishonours God,
> And worships self and senseless pride,
> Then Law eternal wields the rod.
> Still Heaven hunts down the impious man,
> Though divine subtlety may hide
> Time's creeping foot.   [209]

Pentheus has himself transformed Dionysos ('most gentle to mankind') into 'a god of terror irresistible' [208]. All Dionysos has to do to let Pentheus destroy himself, is to hypnotize him into a state in which he acts out all his secret desires: 'Come, perverse man, greedy for sights you should not see, impatient for deeds you should not do – Pentheus! [210]' Pentheus is the typical Puritan nursing unacted desires, secretly lusting to do deeds for which he would slaughter others. It needs the merest nudge from Dionysos to trigger what Jung calls enantiodromia, a sudden psychic transformation whereby the whole psyche, having become intolerably one-sided, turns upside down and becomes its own opposite. So the fiercely puritanical and anti-feminine Pentheus suddenly becomes a voyeur and transvestite.

> In Pentheus' hierarchical view women, beasts, barbarians, maenads are analogous: all require repression by the discipline of the polis. . . . In putting on the maenads' 'female garb' he moves from male to female. By putting on the 'robe of Eastern linen' he becomes barbarian instead of Greek. In wearing the 'fawn's dappled skin', he confirms his place in the wild rather than the city.   [Segal 1982, 120–1]

The same fate, a transformation into his own opposite, befalls Cadmus at the end of the play. At the founding of Thebes Cadmus needed water from a sacred spring for lustrations to Athene, and killed the serpent which guarded it. He sowed the serpent's teeth, and the first Thebans, including Pentheus' father, were murderous warriors who sprung from them. The combination of serpent and water suggests the Great Goddess herself, so that Cadmus' act prefigures Oedipus' slaughter of the sphinx. Dionysos prophesies that Cadmus the serpent-slayer will himself become a serpent and Cadmus the founder of a great city will become the leader of barbarian hordes sacking the cities of Greece.

When Pentheus reaches the mountain he cannot believe the testimony of his own eyes, since the behaviour of the women does not correspond to his preconceptions. Once again the Maenads and the women of the city are behaving with perfect decorum:

> Some of them were twining with fresh leaves a thyrsus that had lost its
> ivy; others, like foals let loose from the painted yokes, were singing holy
> songs to each other in turn.   [215]

But Pentheus is determined to see 'their shameful behaviour', and his spying on them in that spirit again throws the switch which transforms them. The women whose creative energies have been systematically repressed and have turned destructive, cannot control those energies when the god releases them:

> Agave was foaming at the mouth, her eyes were rolling wildly. She was
> not in her right mind; she was under the power of Dionysos; and she
> would not listen to [Pentheus]. She gripped his right arm between wrist
> and elbow; she set her foot against his ribs; and she tore his arm off by
> the shoulder.   [216]

They tear off Pentheus' head and play ball with it.

Cadmus draws the obvious moral from the story:

> If there be any man who derides the unseen world, let him consider the
> death of Pentheus, and acknowledge the gods.   [223]

❊   ❊   ❊

Euripides saw with amazing clarity the madness, the suicidal folly and the blasphemy of it. Pentheus is the new man, claiming self-sufficiency, claiming to have no need of anything beyond his own intelligence. Pentheus has slivered and disbranched himself from his material sap [*King Lear* IV ii 34–5], severed the 'strandentwining cable of all flesh' [Joyce, *Ulysses* 34] which connects all of us back to the first mother. Dionysos appears in the play as a new god, but is in fact the oldest of gods, Nature herself, renewed. Some of his cult titles were: Power in the Tree, Blossom Bringer, Fruit Bringer, and Abundance of Life. In the play, Dionysos remains in his dark prison for only a few minutes. Those minutes encapsulate twenty-four centuries from that day to this. For Pentheus is the modern consciousness, ourselves, almost any of our legislators, businessmen, academics, busy despiritualizing the world for all he is worth in the name of reason, order, the 'standard of living', progress.

Euripides told us very early the price we should have to pay for such 'civilization' – in war, crime, mental and emotional breakdown, pollution. But we have gone on insisting that the world, nature, our own bodies and feelings, are there to do what we like with, to exploit and degrade and disfigure and suppress . . . Is it now too late to reverse the direction of all those centuries and honour Dionysos, whatever name we choose to give him now? According to E.R. Dodds:

> His domain is not only the liquid fire in the grape, but the sap thrusting in a young tree, the blood pounding in the veins of a young animal, all the mysterious and uncontrollable tides that ebb and flow in the life of nature. . . . To resist Dionysos is to repress the elemental in one's own nature; the punishment is the sudden complete collapse of the inward dykes when the elemental breaks through perforce and civilization vanishes.
>
> [273]

5 SIR GAWAIN AND THE GREEN GIRDLE

At the beginning of the Christian era, voices were heard off the coasts of
Greece, out to sea, on the Mediterranean, wailing: 'Pan is dead! Great Pan
is dead!'   [D.H. Lawrence, 'Pan in America']

Progress is indeed nothing else than the giving up of the female gender by
changing into the male, since the female gender is material, passive,
corporeal and sense-perceptible, while the male is active, rational,
incorporeal and more akin to mind and thought.   [Philo, 1st century AD]

Shield him from the dipped glance, flying in half light, that tangles the heels,
The grooved kiss that swamps the eyes with darkness.
Bring him to the ruled slab, the octaves of order,
The law and mercy of number.   [Ted Hughes, 'Gog']

The horned god, the Lord of Life, was not dead, but beginning his long exile
in the underworld, transformed by the early Christians into the Lord of Evil.
So too the Mediterranean serpent goddess, the Great Goddess of abundant
life, dressed, perhaps, in scarlet to symbolize her magical menstrual blood,
became the Scarlet Woman, a witch and a whore. Anath became Anathema.
Her serpent, symbol of undifferentiated life, of the power of life to renew itself,
and of phallic potency, must have his head crushed under the Christian heel.
The tree of life bears no longer the golden apple which is man's passport to
paradise, but only the poison apple of sin and self-consciousness which ensures
his eviction from it, his separation from nature and the sacred.

But the early Christian fathers knew that pagan beliefs and rituals and
images which had become part of the lives of cultures and communities over
thousands of years could not be eliminated overnight by edict. Some have
survived even to this day: Easter eggs, maypoles, May Queens, Yule logs,
Christmas trees, holly and mistletoe . . . They knew that many of these images
were what Jung was to call archetypes, deeply rooted in the racial unconscious.
To attempt to eliminate them all would be to drive them underground and
add to the energies of the many existing heresies. Therefore an effort was
made to retain all those rituals and images which could be sufficiently Chris-
tianized (the slaughter and rebirth of the god) or desexualized (the goddess in
the role of Divine Virgin). The birthday of Christ, for example, was moved
from its actual date in September to coincide with the existing pagan Yule,
the feast of the midwinter solstice.

Some images were more easily accommodated than others. The
Church must have agonized long over what to do with blatant fertility images
such as the Lance and the Cup:

54

But Lance and Cup (or Vase) were in truth connected together in a symbolic relation long ages before the institution of Christianity, or the birth of Celtic tradition. They are sex symbols of immemorial antiquity and world-wide diffusion, the Lance, or Spear, representing the Male, the Cup, or Vase, the Female, reproductive energy. [Weston, 75]

In Christian symbolism, the Spear became the spear which pierced Christ's side on the cross, and the Cup became the vessel which caught his blood (and/ or the dish of the Last Supper), the Holy Grail. The sword also became the sword of the questing or crusading Christian knight, riding out, perhaps, against the very serpent, now a dragon, which had coiled round the tree of life beside the Great Goddess (now a mere distressed maiden needing to be rescued from it). But these images retained too much of their former potency to be easily or totally transformed. Even in the hands of clerical writers such as the monk or clerk who wrote the *Queste del Saint Graal* the pagan elements and resonances could not be eliminated. For other writers these elements may have been the main attraction of the Arthurian material. Campbell goes so far as to say that 'the adventures, largely magical, are of the magic rather of poetry than of traditional religion, not so much miracles of God as signs of an unfolding dimension of nature':

The main purpose of the monk's *Queste del Saint Graal* was to check the trend of this reawakening to nature, reverse its current, and translate the Grail, the cornucopia of the lord of life, into a symbol no longer of nature's earthly grace, but of the supernatural – leaving nature, man, history, and all womankind except baptized nuns, to the Devil.

[*Creative Mythology* 566]

The *Queste* uses Gawain to point the inadequacy of the courtly ideals judged from a purely spiritual perspective. The unknown author of *Sir Gawain and the Green Knight* also finds them inadequate, but his perspective is very different.

❊   ❊   ❊

The *Gawain* poet, like any great imaginative writer, is capable of transcending the conventions of his time (the late fourteenth century), and of transforming mere emblems and allegories into symbols and myths; the difference being that symbols and myths do not depend on the reader having some conventional key to interpretation, but, as deep psychological and racial realities, are capable of communicating their essential meanings to any imaginatively open readers at any time.

In a way, the whole point of the story is that the Pentangle does have a specific simple allegorical meaning, which the poet spells out for us, but for that very reason cannot function as a complete code of conduct, since real life cannot be reduced to codes and concepts but will continually throw up situations which fall through the gaps between them or cannot be aligned simultaneously with all five points of the pentangle. The green girdle has no such precise meaning. Gawain does not know what it is, and neither do we, but that does not stop us responding to its manifold suggestiveness (and I use that word advisedly). Similarly, what Arthur's court stands for is clearly and simply spelled out at the beginning of the poem, but what Bertilak's Hautdesert stands for is ambiguous in the extreme. What the Virgin Mary, patroness of the Round Table, stands for is clear and simple, but what Morgan le Fay, patroness of Hautdesert stands for is shrouded in mystery. The poem dramatizes the conflict between man's attempt to live by imposing on life a grid of abstract codified values, and nature's determination that he should not. In this instance nature refuses to lie in man's Procrustean bed, and it is man himself who is, comically, in danger of losing his head.

The medieval Arthurian romances have, I suggest, three conflicting elements within them. Two of these are chivalry and Christianity, and these are overt. No serious writer could be unaware of the difficulty, if not impossibility, of fusing these two codes of values, as Arthur's Round Table claimed to do; and the strain generated by the attempt is a major part of the attraction of the material. The values of chivalry were essentially worldly, and many of them were strongly disapproved of by the church. For example, tournaments were banned by the Council of Clermont in 1130 as patently homicidal; and courtly love was of course seen by the church as simple adultery. Honour itself was mere vainglory in the eyes of the church.

The whole Arthurian venture was based on the doubtful premise that it was possible to combine the courtly chivalric virtues and the specifically Christian virtues, which meant that the Arthurian knight was obliged to combine humility with the pursuit of glory, and chastity with courtly love! In one hand he carried the shield of meek Christian virtues, in the other the sword of aggressive masculine worldliness. The collapse of the Round Table can be attributed to these inward divisions; and in *Sir Gawain and the Green Knight* they are the source of much of the poem's irony and wry comedy.

But there is a third, usually covert component, a component most of the Arthurian writers were, at least at the conscious level, unaware of, and that is a third value-system deriving from much older, pagan sources which themselves had derived from the natural world and its powers and processes. Already by the time of the romances this system of the ancient world had disintegrated, its myths reduced to folk-tales, its rituals to games, and its symbols to superstitions. This third element could not be excluded, since both chivalry and Christianity had evolved from it, and carried the traces not far below the surface. There is an unbroken line of descent, for example, from Heracles to Cuchulain to Gawain. And Christ was the last of a long line of crucified and resurrected man-gods. All his predecessors were fertility gods. The Green Knight virtually tells Gawain this when he reminds him that not only Arthur's blood flows in his veins, but also Morgan le Fay's, who was his aunt.

But there were at least two writers of medieval Arthurian romances who were not unaware of the pagan roots of both chivalry and Christianity, and who drew upon these half-submerged meanings in order to mount a searching critique of the Arthurian ideal of the Christian knight. They are Wolfram von Eschenbach in his *Parzival* and the unknown author of *Sir Gawain and the Green Knight*. I am not suggesting that these writers were pagans or anti-Christian; rather that they were disturbed by the extreme narrowness of orthodox Christian spirituality, its dualism, its unnecessary exclusiveness, particularly in relation to nature and the female, its bloody militancy. The retelling of Arthurian romances was one of the few methods available without danger of persecution of offering an alternative vision, a vision of wholeness rather than of impossible and ultimately undesirable perfection.

*   *   *

Why does *Sir Gawain and the Green Knight* begin with the fall of Troy? Clearly we are intended to see a parallel between Troy and Camelot. But *all* civilizations and high enterprises are relatively short-lived and doomed sooner or later to collapse. To claim immunity either from internal weakness or from the inevitable processes of 'war and woe and wonder' is hubristic. The 'bliss' of Arthur's company in its 'prime' is doomed to destruction through treachery and blunder and pride, had, indeed, as every reader knew, already long ago collapsed in precisely that way, the whole story having now passed into 'the lore of the land'. This introduction gives the poem not only a vast temporal perspective, but also the character of a cautionary tale. We are invited to begin by asking what in Arthur's court was vulnerable to these pressures from within and without. Though no mention is made of Helen, it cannot escape our attention that both Troy and the Round Table fell because of the adultery of a beautiful married woman, and this is precisely the temptation to which Gawain is to be exposed. The citadel of high masculine ideals is vulnerable not only to male treachery but also, since it is not a monastery or priesthood, to sexuality itself.

It is not just that the Arthurian code fails to take into account man's propensity to sin, that there will be a Mordred and a Lancelot in any group of a hundred men, and that there will be something of Mordred and Lancelot in every man; it excludes much more than that. In its preoccupation with armed conflict and the pursuit of the distant ideal it ignores and devalues the feminine in all its manifestations, including actual women. The women of Camelot are purely decorative. We hear nothing of children in any of the romances.

The third stanza, though it describes the knights as 'acknowledging Christ', gives otherwise a picture of heedless mirth and earthly delights and secular pleasure-seeking at Camelot non-stop for fifteen days, and it is still only New Year's Day. In fact in the whole poem we hear of no other activities at Camelot than feasting and revelry. The fourth stanza describes the luxury of the court, and of Guinevere in particular. Arthur himself, we are told, takes life lightly, is even a bit childish. His youth is clearly related to the youth of the year. Though the holiday tournaments at Camelot are merely jolly tussles, we are reminded of the real homicidal nature of jousting by Arthur's wish that some stranger might challenge one of his knights 'to join with him in jousting, in jeopardy to lay / Life against life'. The many references to Arthur's strength and nobility contrast somewhat with the picture of him 'trifling time with talk', and waiting passively for some adventure or 'momentous marvel' to come to him.

The feast is served, 'such freight of full dishes', twelve for every pair, that there is scarcely room on the tables. There is surely some irony in the line 'For all will acknowledge that ample was served'. But before the feast can begin, the handsome yet fearsome figure of the gigantic Green Knight rides on his green horse into the hall. He is by no means sinister or wild. His clothing and accoutrements are rich and comely, embellished with jewels and gold (treasures of the earth transformed into works of symbolic art). All the fabric is embroidered and metal embossed with birds and flies in green and gold. One is reminded of Walt Whitman, speaking for the earth itself: 'I am stucco'd with animals and birds all over'. His horse's mane, tail and forelock are all plaited and ornamented, suggesting, as in the combination of colours, green and gold, a perfect blend of nature and art: nature and art working in harmony to produce images of richness and harnessed power. This power seems irresistible, yet is here manifested peacefully, since the Green Knight wears no armour and bears no shield or spear. In one hand he carries a holly-bob, a pagan symbol of the preservation of life, in the other a huge axe, symbol, in any eyes, of fell destruction – life and death in perfect balance.

When the Green Knight asks which is Arthur, the whole assembly is 'daunted' and 'dared not reply'. This is something their elaborate code of behaviour gives them no help with, and without it, they are at a loss. The code is applicable only within the artificial circle of courtly life. That circle has now been shattered by the eruption into it of a figure straight out of what they would have regarded as Pagan superstition, the Green Man, who is soon to demonstrate his characteristic magic, the ability to regenerate himself.

The Green Knight declares that he has come in peace, wishing for no peril or conflict, merely to propose some 'good sport' with this cream of chivalry. Arthur, apparently, has not listened to a word he has been saying, and replies:

> If deadly duel's your whim,
> We'll fail you not in fight.

Arthur behaves here with the mindless conditioned reflex of the knight – if you don't understand it, try to destroy it, and ask questions later, if at all. Asking the right questions is a very important theme in the Arthurian tales. At Arthur's court we see a denial of real feelings in the name of the code. Parzival, in Wolfram, does not ask Anfortas if his terrible wound hurts – he pretends not to notice it. Similarly Arthur 'let no semblance be seen' of his surprise at the Green Knight's appearance and behaviour, and does not ask him for any explanation. This slavery to the seemly can work against his declared dedication to 'truth'. Sir Gawain later asks the Green Knight's name, as part of the formula of combat. Apart from that, no-one asks him anything. The obvious questions, what sort of being are you? how do you come to be green? are conspicuously not asked. Nor, later, how can you live without your head?

The 'game' the Green Knight proposes is that one of Arthur's knights should chop off his head, and agree to allow his own head to be struck off in a year's time by the Green Knight. If the Green Knight is mortal, this is murder, if not, suicide, yet Arthur unquestioningly accepts, exposing his youngest knight, Gawain. It is, as the Green Knight himself says, 'madly rash'. And Camelot itself comes round to the opinion a year later that 'It would have been wiser to have worked more warily', and that Gawain had been virtually sacrificed out of mere 'arrogance'. The Round Table is lured by its own code into putting itself at the mercy of supernatural forces mere chivalry is helpless against. Gawain decapitates the Green Knight, who picks up his head and rides away, the head calling back to Gawain not to forget their appointment in a year's time at the Green Chapel. Yet after the Green Knight's departure, the court simply resumes its feasting, with 'double portions of each dainty'.

Part Two begins with a wonderfully detailed description of the passing of the seasons, and there is no mistaking the seasonal significance of the Green Knight when, in spring, the fields and groves are described as 'garbed in green'. In autumn 'leaves are lashed loose from the trees and lie on the ground', like the head of the Green Knight.

The outside world does not play according to the rules of Camelot, which, as Gawain moves further from it, riding north in search of the Green Chapel, comes to seem more and more childish. Though Gawain is not going to fight, he goes, unlike the Green Knight, in full armour and elaborately caparisoned in resplendent chivalric gear, as if that could do him any good either against the pangs of winter or against the Green Knight. Gawain is said to be the best of Arthur's knights, yet being a worthy member of the Round Table seems to commit him to a perpetual performance, trying to work out what is the most fitting or seemly thing for him to do or say in any situation, regardless of his actual feelings. He is always, as we would say, projecting an image.

When Lawrence is looking for an image of self-conscious men who dare not risk themselves in relation to their own unknown selves, or woman, or the non-human world, he finds an image exactly like Gawain here:

They go forth, panoplied in their own idea of themselves. Whatever they do, they perform it all in the full armour of their own idea of themselves. Their unknown bodily self is never for one moment unsheathed. . . . not for one moment does he risk himself under the strange snake-infested bushes of her [woman's] extraordinary Paradise. He is afraid. He becomes extraordinarily clever and agile in his self-conscious panoply. With his mind he can dart about among the emotions as if he really felt something.

[*Phoenix II*, 620–1]

In addition to the physical paraphernalia of chivalry, Gawain also draws to the full upon the spiritual resources of Christianity. He attends Mass, prays, and makes offerings. His colours are red and gold. The covers of his visor are embroidered with parrots, turtle-doves and true-love-knots, all emblems of courtly love. But it is his shield, which most fully symbolizes the values of Christian knighthood in which he and the whole court put their trust. On the outside is depicted the Pentangle, on the inside the Virgin Mary. Two whole stanzas are devoted to the Pentangle. It is a five-pointed star drawn in such a way as to constitute an Endless Knot. It is five times five. First, he is faultless in his five wits; second, his five fingers never fail him; third, his trust is in the five wounds of Christ; fourth, his prowess depends upon the five pure joys of Mary; fifth are the five virtues – liberality, fellowship, continence, courtesy and piety. It will be seen that these virtues are a strange mixture of the courtly and the Christian. The incompatibility of continence and courtesy is to be a particular problem for Gawain. These five interlocking fives are believed to be in themselves an impenetrable spiritual shield. But if the knot should be broken at any point, the efficacy of the whole is shattered. It is this Pentangle as much as Gawain himself, which is to be put to the test. Since the Pentangle is intended to be a talisman against ill-health or injury or demons, what need of the protective magic of the green girdle?

'At every bank or beach' Gawain is confronted by foul and fierce foes. He leaves a trail of corpses behind him:

> He had death-struggles with dragons, did battle with wolves,
> Warred with wild trolls that dwelt among the crags,
> Battled with bulls and bears and boars at other times,
> And ogres that panted after him on the high fells.

Why is every creature he meets, natural or supernatural, his enemy? Insofar as this is a psychic journey into the hinterland of the soul Gawain is projecting his fears of nature onto the face of nature, transforming it into something invariably threatening and monstrous (as Adonis is to look upon the lovely face of Venus and see only the fangs of Hecate and the boar). Ted Hughes chose these lines as his epigraph for *Wodwo*. Gawain is one name for the 'blood-crossed Knight, the Holy Warrior, hooded with iron':

> The rider of iron, on the horse shod with vaginas of iron,
> Gallops over the womb that makes no claim, that is of stone.
> His weapons glitter under the lights of heaven.
> He follows his compass, the lance-blade, the gunsight, out

Against the fanged grail and tireless mouth
Whose cry breaks his sleep
Whose coil is under his ribs
Whose smile is in the belly of woman
Whose satiation is in the grave.   ['Gog']

That is one way to encounter the world. The other, according to Hughes, is the way of the wodwo, open, sensitive, exploratory, flexible, aware of the other unknowable beings, and the unknowable depths of the self, ready to negotiate with whatever happens to be out there. It is also the way of the child:

It is also still very much the naked process of apprehension, far less conditioned than ours, far more fluid and alert, far closer to the real laws of its real nature. It is a new beginning, coming to circumstances afresh. It is still lost in the honest amoebic struggle to fit itself to the mysteries.
[*Children as Writers* v]

The warring little worries Gawain – 'worse was the winter'. The enemy he rides out against is Nature herself. 'So in peril and pain, in parlous plight' Gawain prays for shelter and a place to hear High Mass on Christmas Day. Immediately his prayer seems to be answered, as he comes upon 'the comeliest castle' he has ever seen. 'It shimmered and shone' like a mirage, as perhaps it was, conjured up by Morgan le Fay. 'By chance', he finds the entrance at the first attempt. He is expected. The porter tells him, before announcing his arrival, that he may stay as long as he likes. Though Gawain arrives fully armed, in contrast to the arrival of the Green Knight at Camelot, he is greeted with the most ceremonious respect and hospitality. They tell him to treat the place as his own. His host, Sir Bertilak, is a man of 'stupendous size', with a bushy beard and a jocular outspokenness, but none of this rings a bell for Gawain. He is still living in the world of appearances. All his wariness is put off with his armour when he thinks, after his ordeals in the great unknown, that he is back in the world to which he belongs, that of luxurious courtliness. Gawain is 'set up' as a paragon of courtly virtues, particularly by the two ladies of the castle – one the image of youth and beauty, excelling even Guinevere, the other of age and ugliness. Together they form a composite image of the goddess in her bright and dark, attractive and repulsive, aspects – Venus and Hecate.

There is surely some irony in the discrepancy between the opening of stanza xx, where we are told that on Christmas Day 'Ecstasy wells in all hearts for His sake', and the continuation, where Gawain and the lady find their 'solace and satisfaction' in 'dalliance':

Each soul its solace found,
And the two were enthralled with theirs.

Such lines remind us that we are dealing here with a great comic poem, in which the pretensions of Arthur's knights are deflated not only in the action of the story, but in the play of such tongue-in-cheek irony as this.

Gawain says he must allow himself at least three more days to search for the Green Chapel, but the castellan tells him it is but two miles away, so Gawain may stay until New Year's Day. The castellan intends to spend the three days hunting, but orders Gawain to spend them resting in preparation for his confrontation. He proposes that, at the end of each day, they should play a game of exchanging what each has gained that day. Vivid descriptions of the hunt alternate with those of the equally ruthless pursuit of Gawain by the lady. As much attention is given to the butchery of the deer as to the hunting of them. Davenport describes these scenes as 'a brilliantly precise demonstration of the real nature of knightly occupation in the late Middle Ages, a knightly life which has little in common with that romantic picture of knighthood which the lady keeps urging on Gawain'. On the first day she creeps into Gawain's bedchamber before he is up, and offers herself to him, hoping, no doubt, to catch him off his guard. She comes close to blasphemy:

> But as I love that Lord, the Celestial Ruler,
> I have wholly in my hand what all desire
> Through His grace.

Gawain courteously parries her advances until, upon leaving, she questions whether such a courteous knight as Gawain could have stayed so long with a lady 'Without craving a kiss in courtesy'. Gawain, challenged on this sensitive point – his pride in his reputation for perfect courtesy, in whatever is 'becoming to a knight', consents.

The delicacy and squeamishness of Gawain in his comic dilemma, pretending to be asleep while the lady gets into bed with him, is forcibly contrasted with the unsparing detail of the butchery at the hunt – Gawain trying desperately to refine sex into courtesy while the poet reduces the delicate sensitive hinds to their basic blood, bowels and bones. There is a comic discrepancy between the mounds of meat the castellan gives Gawain at the end of the day and the coy kiss Gawain gives him in return.

On the second day, while the castellan and his men pursue a particularly savage boar, the lady accuses Gawain of lacking the true ardour of courtly love. Again Gawain talks himself out of giving her more than a kiss. On the third day she comes to Gawain topless, and presses him so hotly that 'he felt forced / Either to allow her love or blaguardly rebuff her'. He cannot contemplate the former, not so much because of his commitment to chastity as because it would involve him in betrayal of his host. He chooses to rebuff her. She has, however, one last temptation. She tries to persuade him to accept at least a love-token from her – her green girdle, which, she says, has the property of protecting its wearer against anyone who tries to kill him. This, it strikes

Gawain, would be 'a splendid stratagem to escape being slain' by the Green Knight, and he accepts it. This lapse in faith, in accordance with the indivisibility of the Pentangle, leads Gawain into several other faults: betrayal of his contract with the castellan to exchange winnings (he does not mention the girdle), and concealment of his fault from his confessor next morning. He emerges from confession 'so pure / That doomsday should have been declared the day after'. This is gallows humour, since the following day is literally Gawain's doomsday. It is hypocritical of Gawain to go to confession at all, since he intends to put his reliance not on being in a state of grace, or on the Pentangle, but on the green girdle.

There is a strong contrast between Gawain's departure from Camelot, with its emphasis on his shield with its Pentangle and image of the Virgin Mary, and his departure from Hautdesert, when there is no mention of either, all his faith being now pinned to the green girdle: 'For his own good, Gawain did not forget that!'

His guide, obviously under instructions from the castellan to undermine Gawain's courage as much as possible, gives him a fearful warning of what awaits him at the Green Chapel, a warning simultaneously comic (as we see Gawain blench) and a deeply serious reminder of the irresistibility and indiscriminateness of death itself:

> You cannot counter his blow,
> It strikes so sudden and sore.

Morgan knows that sex and death are the two chinks in Gawain's armour, as they are in the whole Arthurian enterprise. The guide undermines Gawain's residual faith in the saving power of Christ by specifying that many of the victims of the 'grim man' have been churchmen.

The setting of the Green Chapel is nature at its most 'savage and wild'. The Chapel itself is pre-Christian, a 'fairy mound', filling Gawain with superstitious dread:

> 'At such might Satan be seen
> Saying matins at midnight. . . .
> It is the most evil holy place I ever entered.'

Gawain has been tricked into a contract which, by its very terms, ensures that he has no physical defence. In fact, his helmet, the symbol of that defence, must be removed, and the most vulnerable spot, the nape of the neck, exposed to the biggest and sharpest axe he has ever seen. He shows a realistic scepticism when the moment comes, about the efficacy of either grace or girdle:

> Not again
> Shall I flinch as I did before,

> But if my head pitch to the plain,
> It's off for evermore.

The Green Knight makes clear what is at stake:

> May the high knighthood which Arthur conferred
> Preserve you and save your neck, if it so avail you!

The third swing slightly nicks Gawain's neck, breaking the skin and producing a merely symbolic shower of blood on the snow. Of this moment Penelope Shuttle and Peter Redgrove (in an as-yet-unpublished additional chapter for *The Wise Wound*) write:

> In Middle English, the poetry shows a free and easy relationship to
> nature, which often wears a loving aspect. Not always or immediately,
> though: Sir Gawayne has to bleed on the day of the Circumcision of Jesus
> under the fearful axe of the great figure of fertility, the Green Knight, and
> it has been said that this poem is the remnant of a liturgy of initiation of
> men into female fertility mysteries: becoming a feeling-being by shedding
> of his own blood peaceably. The axe is moon-shaped, like the Cretan
> labrys, and Gawayne was made to bleed, like Dracula's victims, in the
> neck. As Francis Berry says, in his *Penguin Guide to Literature* essay on
> Gawayne, one must waste a little blood to win fertility, and this has
> always been the theme of fertility rites. In the nape of the Knight's neck,
> in this case, which, in possession cults like Voodoo, is where the divine
> horsemen ride.

The girdle is a blatantly sexual image. In the diseased Puritan imagination it marks the boundary between heaven and hell, between the bright and beautiful aspect of woman and her rank satanic sexuality. In Lear's words:

> But to the girdle so the gods inhabit
> The rest is all the fiend's. There's stench, corruption.

At Hautdesert the girdle is a rich ornament, effortlessly accommodated as a rudimentary life-symbol in a virtually matriarchal household. At Camelot sex can only operate destructively (as in Troy), destroying the Round Table from within. The Round Table excludes all the girdle includes. The girdle, as Shuttle and Redgrove point out in *The Wise Wound*, symbolizes not only sex, but also the womb and the magical creativity of woman:

> She has the first original magic in her, which is that without her there
> would be no persons to consider magic; and that in her cycle is a nature
> that rhythmically dies to be reborn again in blood and through a descent
> into the underworld, a process which has been recorded in myths and

rituals all over the world, and distorted into surrogate myths in which it is the man, hero, not the woman, hera, who bleeds and resurrects. But this may be the woman's gift to the man, to show him how to sacrifice and return, and he has forgotten the giver. [220]

Moreover, the Pentangle itself, like the Grail, had been appropriated as a Christian symbol from pagan fertility magic. It had originally symbolized woman's 'whole pentagram nature, her witch-nature, her magic'. Shuttle and Redgrove quote Kenneth Grant:

Five was the primal number of woman as the genetrix long before the stellar seven and the lunar twenty-eight. For five days woman was engulfed in darkness and eclipsed; from her issued the deluge that primitive man rightly identified as the substance which would later congeal and flesh forth progeny. Blood was recognized as liquid flesh and the female expressed (through the number five) her nubility, which was the archetypal *nobility* because the only known lineage was of the blood of the mother alone. The male's role in the procreative process was at that time unknown. The five-day eclipse was the seal of woman's nobility, the nobility that wears the scarlet mantle of nature herself, the one unimpeachable rubric of her sovereignty. And because she was seen to renew life upon earth woman was likened to the goddess in the sky, who renewed herself through celestial cycles as a type of resurrection, a return to unity and ultimate perfection in the heaven and the hells. The number five thus became the seal of authority in the world of spirits; it was represented by the pentagram or five-pointed star, still used by magicians for establishing contact with and controlling transmundane entities. The origins of the magical pentagram can thus be traced to the first observed facts of elemental nature. [206]

The Green Knight reveals that he is also Sir Bertilak, and that the old woman at Hautdesert was 'Morgan the goddess' who had sent him to Camelot to 'put to the proof the great pride' of the Round Table. She is confident in her power. She warns the Round Table of the danger of pride, the inadequacy of its values, the need to acknowledge the nobility of woman and the power of her magic, which is also the nobility and power of the natural world. She reasserts her title to the Pentangle. She offers to heal the split, which will destroy the Round Table. She shows Gawain 'how to sacrifice and return', bearing with him as token of her 'original magic' the green girdle. Her method of healing is exactly what would be recommended by modern psychology. In Hughes' words:

A mentally sick person is sick, says the theory, because there is something in his mind which he refuses to face, which he has by some means or other cut himself off from and which he represses into the cellars of his mind, down into the nervous system where it plays havoc. And this devil of suppressed life stops making trouble the moment he is acknowledged, the moment he is welcomed into conscious life and given some shape where he can play out his energy in an active part of the personality.   [*Children's Literature* 58]

The archetypal quest hero rides out into the unknown, which is both the animal world and the spirit world, natural and supernatural. There he endures exposure, privations, horrors, perils and conflicts. He confronts monsters, often female, undergoes an ego-death, but returns at last transformed, reconstituted in alignment with the way things are, bearing a healing gift or vision for his people. But *Sir Gawain and the Green Knight* is a mock quest. Gawain completely misinterprets his adventure. As soon as he realizes that he is not going to die, he reverts to the posture of the knight 'audacious in arms' and 'bloodily resolute', essentially unchanged. Sir Bertilak compliments him: he has done as well as could be expected, his performance only slightly tarnished by his acceptance of the girdle:

> But here your faith failed you, you flagged somewhat, sir,
> Yet it was not for a well-wrought thing, nor for wooing either,
> But for love of your life, which is less blameworthy.

Gawain's judgement on himself is much more severe, since he is still applying the impossible standards of the Pentangle. Sir Bertilak succeeds in persuading him to keep the girdle as a 'perfect token' of the whole adventure when he is once again 'in company with paragons of princes'. This is heavily ironic, since the girdle is a token of precisely the ways in which Arthur's knights are not, and could not in the nature of things ever be, the 'paragons' they think themselves, of what Lawrence calls 'man's irremediable being in sensuality' [*Studies* 396]. Their claim depends on leaving too much out of account – the claims of the feminine, including the feminine side of their own natures and of wild nature with its irresistible seasonal processes. Christmas itself, for example, is an appropriation of the pagan festival of the mid-winter solstice. Gawain admits that the great Christian heroes – Adam, Solomon, Samson and David – could not cope with women. Gawain learns the wrong lesson, simply blaming the wiles of women for his own incompleteness. The green girdle he regards simply as a token of the wiles, not of the incompleteness. Thus the Round Table learns nothing from his failed quest, and proceeds blithely on its way to destruction.

✢   ✢   ✢

In Malory, Arthur has a dream which reveals the sexual abyss full of reptiles of the mind which lies beneath all the high ideals and 'noble felyship' of the round table (even as they are embodied in that 'hede of al Crysten knyghtes' Sir Launcelot):

And the kynge thought there was undir hym, farre from hym, an hydeous depe blak watir, and therein was all maner of serpentis and wormes and wylde bestis fowle and orryble. And suddeynly the kynge thought that the whyle turned up-so-downe, and he felle amonge the serpentes, and every beste toke hym by a lymme.

The great goddess, frustrated and rejected yet again, is transformed into a witch.

In other Gawain stories, it seems that Gawain has learned from, allowed himself to be corrected by, the adventure with the Green Knight. In 'The Weddynge of Sir Gawen and Dame Ragnell', Arthur's life is saved when a Loathly Lady, with a boar's tusks and snout, tells him the answer to the riddle (about the nature of woman) on which his life depends. But her price is Gawain for her husband. This time Gawain gets it right. By accepting the Loathly Lady, by dropping his insistence that only the beautiful and chaste is worthy of respect and love, by putting himself unreservedly in her hands, he is able to transform her into her true radiantly beautiful self. Similarly, Wolfram's Parzival is able to find the Grail only under instruction (in compassion) from Cundrie, a foul, tusked and snouted sorceress.

The Grail maidens bear, in addition to the Grail itself, 'two silver knives, like crescent moons . . . like the tusks or horns of all moon-animals, signifying the full career of the moon's phases' [Shuttle 118, 202]. With these they draw hot poison from the sick king's wound.

These images of an enchanted woman with the tusks of a boar go back to the moon-goddess and Queen of Hell, Persephone, one of whose shapes was a boar. Persephone fought with Venus for Adonis, and killed him when he refused her, or had him killed by her male counterpart, Ares or Apollo, as a boar. But his death was only the prelude to his resurrection and apotheosis. The consort of the goddess is killed in order to be reborn as her divine child.

Birth itself is woman's secret magic. Jean Markale calls the Grail 'the uterus of the mother goddess' [Shuttle 203]. Shuttle and Redgrove call it 'the "goblet" full of blood, the menstruation that contains many redeeming secrets' [119]. It has the power to 'make the Wasteland bloom' [17].

What is the Grail then, but the inexhaustible vessel, the source of life continuously coming into being, energy pouring into creation, energy as creation, the unquenchable fountain of eternal being? [Baring 654]

6 SHAKESPEARE'S MARRIAGE OF HEAVEN AND HELL: *A MIDSUMMER NIGHT'S DREAM* AND *THE MERRY WIVES OF WINDSOR*

The Romans celebrated the midsummer solstice with a Saturnalia, where young people drank wine in flower-wreathed boats. Frazer writes in *The Golden Bough*:

> In modern Europe, the great Midsummer festival has been above all a festival of lovers and of fire; one of its principal features is the pairing of sweethearts. . . . And many omens of love and marriage are drawn from the flowers which bloom at this mystic season. It is the time of the roses and of love. Yet the innocence and beauty of such festivals in modern times ought not to blind us to the likelihood that in earlier days they were marked by coarser features, which were probably of the essence of the rites. [202]

This is Frazer's way of saying that they began as fertility rites. If we are to believe the Puritan opponents of such rites, the 'coarser features' were much in evidence in Shakespeare's time. The church, in its attempt to extirpate paganism, realized in its wisdom that Nature was too big to be abolished; that if all forms of nature-worship were banned, it would simply go underground and escape the control of the church altogether (which happened under James I). Therefore certain days were set aside when such rites might be tolerated. The principal occasions were May, Whitsuntide, Mid-summer's Eve, and the Winter Revels, including Twelfth Night. But to the Puritans these were abominations. In 1583 Phillip Stubbes wrote:

> Against May, Whitsuntide, or other time all the young men and maids, old men and wives, run gadding over night to the woods, groves, hills, and mountains, where they spend all the night in pleasant pastimes. . . . And no marvel, for there is a great Lord present among them, as superintendent and Lord over their pastimes and sports, namely, Satan, prince of hell. But the chiefest jewel they bring from thence is their Maypole, which they bring home with great veneration, as thus: They have twenty or forty yoke of oxen, every oxe having a sweet nose-gay of flowers placed on the tip of his horns, and these oxen draw home this Maypole (this stinking idol, rather) which is covered all over with flowers and herbs, bound round about with strings, from the top to the bottom, and sometime painted with variable colours, with two or three hundred men, women and children following it with great devotion. And being reared up with handkerchiefs and flags hovering on the top, they strew the ground round about it, set up summer halls, bowers and arbors hard by it. And then fall they to dance about it, like as the heathen people did

at the dedication of the Idols, whereof this is a perfect pattern, or rather the thing itself. I have heard it credibly reported (and that *viva voce*) by men of great gravity and reputation, that of forty, three-score, or a hundred maids going to the wood over night, there have been scarcely the third part of them returned home again undefiled. These be the fruits which these accursed pastimes bring forth.

[quoted by C.L. Barber, *Shakespeare's Festive Comedy*, 21–2]

These are just the assumptions Pentheus had made about the pastimes of those who had followed Dionysus to the woods and mountains.

Stubbes is quite right. The maypole is a survival of pagan tree-worship. Despite it name it was (and still is in Sweden) more frequently erected on midsummer's eve than in May. The tree-spirit was one of many woodland deities whose marriage to produce the regeneration and growth in spring and summer was thought to be aided by representing it in the choosing of a May King and Queen, a Whitsun Bride and Bridegroom, and by such literal coupling as appalled Stubbes. Frazer writes:

We may assume with a high degree of probability that the profligacy which notoriously attended these ceremonies was at one time not an accidental excess but an essential part of the rites, and that in the opinion of those who performed them the marriage of trees and plants could not be fertile without the real union of the human sexes. . . . Some rites which are still, or were till lately, kept up in Europe can be reasonably explained only as stunted relics of a similar practice. [178–9]

The poets were normally opposed to the Puritans in their response to these rites. A few years before *A Midsummer Night's Dream*, Thomas Nashe wrote, in *Summer's Last Will and Testament*:

From the town to the grove
Two and two let us rove
A Maying, a playing:
Love hath no gainsaying.

And a few years after it Shakespeare wrote:

Between the acres of the rye,
    With a hey and a ho and a hey nonino,
These pretty country folks would lie,
    In spring-time, the only pretty ring-time . . .

All Shakespeare's comedies are attacks on the Puritans, and *A Midsummer Night's Dream* is the most thoroughgoing of them all.

The actual fairy folk were probably the remnants of pagan tribes which

69

had fled to the fastnesses of forests and mountains. They had kept up their pagan rites, including the worship of the horned god, who was the god of the animals, Pan to the Greeks, Cernunnos to the Romans. In England the horned god had many names including Herne the Hunter, Nick, Puck (from the Welsh *Boucca*, meaning 'God') and Robin Goodfellow. The church, of course, called him Satan, and those who continued to worship him witches. Fairies, according to the church, were evil spirits. Though Chaucer's Wife of Bath claims that the friars had purged England of fairies:

> Blessing the halls, the chambers, kitchens, bowers,
> Cities and boroughs, castles, courts and towers,
> Thorpes, barns and stables, outhouses and dairies,
> And that's the reason why there are no fairies.

these beliefs and rites lingered on into Shakespeare's time and beyond in the form of folklore and superstition, to the horror of the Puritans. In 1584 Reginald Scot mocked such superstitions in *The discovery of witchcraft*:

> These bugs speciallie are spied and feared of sicke folke, children, women, and cowards, which through weaknesse of mind and bodie, are shaken with vaine dreames and continuall feare. . . . But in our childhood our mothers maids have so . . . fraied us with bull beggars, spirits, witches, urchins, elves, hags, fairies, satyrs, pans, faunes, sylens, kit with the cansticke, tritons, centaurs, dwarfes, giants, imps, calcars, conjurors, nymphes, changlings, *Incubus*, Robin good-fellowe, the spoorne, the mare, the man in the oke, the hell waine, the fierdrake, the puckle, Tom thombe, hob goblin, Tom tumbler, boneles, and such other bugs, that we are afraid of our owne shadowes: in so much as some never feare the divell, but in a darke night. [*A Midsummer Night's Dream* 147]

However, even such a hostile witness admits that Robin Good-fellow was not entirely a hob-goblin to inspire fear. In return for a bowl of milk he would (so said the 'grandams maides') grind malt or mustard, or sweep the house at midnight.

In the frenzy of witch-hunting initiated by James I, attitudes to Puck hardened. In *Robin Goodfellow, his mad pranks and merry gests*, a pamphlet published in 1639,

> Robin is depicted as an ithyphallic god of the witches with young ram's horns sprouting from his forehead, ram's legs, a witches' besom over his left shoulder, a lighted candle in his right hand. Behind him in a ring dance a coven of men and women witches in Puritan costume, a black dog adores him, a musician plays a trumpet, an owl flies overhead.
> [Graves, *Goddess*, 396]

Shakespeare's Puck is the same Trickster and shape-changer of the popular imagination, but he is not in the least satanic. He does no harm beyond 'mad pranks and merry gests'. He claims to be glad when his mistakes cause 'jangling', but: 'Those that Hobgoblin call you, and sweet Puck, / You do their work, and they shall have good luck' [II i 40–1].

Similarly, Shakespeare goes out of his way to remove all sense of evil or threat from his fairies. Oberon's attitude to humans is from the start benevolent. And when Puck seems to fear the approach of dawn, as if he were indeed an urchin or goblin such as those Prospero employs to pinch Caliban, which may work only at night, Oberon assures him that 'we are spirits of another sort'. Although the night is their element, and they run from the presence of the sun, they do so by choice, having nothing to fear, as evil spirits have, from its 'fair blessed beams'. They are, specifically, 'triple Hecate's team' – not, that is, Hecate the goddess of witchcraft, but the Great Goddess who is queen of the realms of earth and heaven, as well as of the underworld. Even as goddess of the underworld, of winter and death, she is Proserpina who will be miraculously renewed every spring.

These fairies are throughout closely associated with the wood and its flora and fauna. This, together with their preoccupation with marriage, makes them clearly, in Barber's words 'tutelary spirits of fertility' [137]. A Midsummer Night's Dream is Shakespeare's attempt to reclaim this world of fairy as necessary to human health and wholeness.

Shakespeare may have gone too far in the direction of prettifying and miniaturizing the fairies to a degree unknown up to that time, in order to counteract any doubts and fears about them in his audience. This play alone (or the long tradition of sentimental productions of it) is largely responsible for our modern view of fairies as tiny charming winged gossamer creatures. Shakespeare can hardly have intended that, since there were no more actors then than now capable of creeping into an acorn. In countries where Shakespeare is less of an influence, fairies are not like that at all. If his purpose in this play is as anti-Christian and subversive of conventional belief as I take it to be, he may have found it necessary to make most of his fairies as far removed as possible from the hobgoblins of Puritan nightmares, so that Robin Goodfellow and even Hecate can be smuggled in with them.

Shakespeare was not interested in the actual existence of fairies, but in their symbolic potential. What they, as spirits who took over the world at night, symbolized for him was the contents of the inner dark, the unconscious, repressed by day, but taking over the sleeper in dreams. Joseph Campbell speaks of 'the realm that we enter in sleep' as 'the internal world', 'the everlasting realm that is within', 'the infantile unconscious':

We carry it within ourselves forever. All the ogres and secret helpers of our nursery are there, all the magic of childhood. And more important, all the life-potentialities that we never managed to bring to adult realization, those other portions of ourself, are there; for such golden seeds do not die. If only a portion of that lost totality could be dredged up into the light of day, we should experience a marvellous expansion of our powers, a vivid renewal of life. . . . The first work of the hero is to retreat from the world scene of secondary effects to those causal zones of the psyche where the difficulties really reside, and there to clarify the difficulties, eradicate them in his own case and break through to the undistorted, direct experience and assimilation of what C.G. Jung has called 'the archetypal images'.

[*Hero*, 17]

It is the function of Shakespearean comedy to fertilize those golden seeds; not only to show us but to give us a renewal of life. Those 'causal zones of the psyche' he symbolizes in *A Midsummer Night's Dream* by the triple imagery of dream, darkness and wood, all of them teeming with archetypal images, which are images so deeply rooted in the racial unconscious that they recur in dreams, visions and imaginative art in all times and cultures. One such archetype is the horned god.

Jung describes dreams as 'pure nature; they show us the unvarnished natural truth, and are therefore fitted, as nothing else is, to give us back an attitude that accords with our basic human nature when our consciousness has strayed too far from its foundations and run into an impasse':

We have known for a long time that there is a biological relationship between the unconscious processes and the activity of the conscious mind. This relationship can best be described as a compensation, which means that any deficiency in consciousness – such as exaggeration, one-sidedness, or lack of a function – is suitably supplemented by an unconscious process. . . . If such a compensatory move of the unconscious is not integrated into consciousness in an individual, it leads to a neurosis or even to a psychosis.

[Jung 10, 218–20]

When this deficiency is in a king, the consequences reverberate throughout his kingdom, with dire results in both histories and tragedies. But it is the nature of Shakespearean comedy that the deficiency is never disabling, that integration can and does take place, (which is the happy ending), symbolized by marriage, music and dance.

At the beginning of the play all seems concord until Egeus enters, 'full of vexation'. Love now appears not as a cause of marriage but of discord – a polarization between the irrational fantasy and doting which Egeus takes Hermia's love for Lysander to be, and the rational determination of his own judgement. This vexation immediately drives a wedge into the apparent harmony, for Theseus feels himself obliged to side with Egeus and the 'sharp Athenian law', while Hippolyta clearly sympathizes with Hermia. Egeus is only behaving as a cussed old father might be expected to behave. We might reasonably expect Theseus to know better. We might expect him, four days before his nuptials, and having just declared his intention to 'turn melancholy forth to funerals', to be well disposed to young lovers. Egeus seems totally oblivious of the claims of love. His objection to Lysander's wooing is that it took the usual form of wooing, that is, it played on Hermia's heart and 'fancy' rather than her reason. The songs Lysander has sung at her window by moonlight are to Egeus the equivalent of witchcraft. Already we have a whiff of the difficulty the Athenians have in coping with whatever belongs to the female, or to the night, or to the natural world. Egeus is a walking embodiment of Athenian law and 'the ancient privilege of Athens', which is patriarchal and cruel. That law sets male judgement above female feelings. Hermia says that she does not know 'by what power' she is made bold to refuse. The rest of the play defines that power and sets it up in opposition to the sterile and arbitrary legal power which governs Athens.

Theseus does offer Hermia an alternative to death: to 'abjure For ever the society of men', to become a nun. He goes through the motions of praising the vocation of the nun as 'thrice-blessed'; but everything else he says of it presents it as barren, cold, fruitless and inhuman:

> But earthlier happy is the rose distill'd
> Than that which, withering on the virgin thorn,
> Grows, lives, and dies, in single blessedness.

By the time we reach the word 'blessedness' it has been drained of all possible meaning, an empty gesture towards a lifeless, unnatural spirituality Theseus has no real belief in. Indeed the power to bless is shortly to be handed over to the fairies.

The cold fruitlessness of 'single blessedness' is exactly the opposite of what the rites of May and Mid-summer seek to guarantee – an access of warm fruitfulness. They seek to promote and bless coupling, love and marriage, not barren singleness.

Theseus has the opportunity to nip discord in the bud. To the dismay of Hippolyta he does not take it, but pleads helplessness in the face of the law, as though it were an absolute. As Harold Brooks puts it: 'The inescapable fact about love and reason in the *Dream* is that when the human love-conflict is first presented for judgement, reason has its chance to solve it, if unaided reason can; and it cannot, even to the satisfaction of the judge himself' [Arden cxxxvi]. Bottom shows himself wiser than Theseus when he says: 'Reason and love keep little company together nowadays. The more the pity, that some honest neighbours will not make them friends'. Theseus postpones final judgement. Hermia and Lysander seize that time to flee to the woods, and so the whole discordant action of the play is precipitated. The faults requiring to be corrected are small, which makes it all the more inexcusable (and comic) that matters are allowed to get out of hand.

Love without reason is just as much of a deficiency and imbalance as reason without love. It is the doting which causes Helena to betray her friend and her self-respect. It is the unreasoning love of Titania for her changeling boy, and later, in concentrated overdose, for an ass.

All the forms of deficiency or imbalance among the human characters are presented as, in varying degrees, unnatural. It was unnatural for Hippolyta to devote herself to a military life, as for Theseus to gain her by force of arms. This they both now recognize; but Theseus cannot see the relevance of what he has learned to the problem before him. The unnaturalness of a father suing for his daughter's death is blatant enough. Demetrius' rejection of the woman who loves him (and of his own love for her) in favour of one who hates him is unnatural. It is unnatural of Helena to love him the more the more he spurns her. Perhaps we should see (given the parallel of Titania) Hermia's insistence that Lysander sleep further off as mildly unnatural (especially on a night sacred to love). It is the distance between them which causes Puck's mistake and Lysander's subsequent unnatural behaviour.

Demetrius says at the end that he has come to his 'natural taste'. The movement of the whole play is the restoration, through the agency of the fairies, of all things unnatural (whether by folly or mischance) to their true nature. The woods are not a place of licence. They have their own deities and sanctities and morality (different though these may be from those of organized religion). Here unnatural is evil.

Oberon and Titania are, above all, the spirits who promote and bless coupling. Oberon's presence near Athens is accounted for by his desire to give joy and prosperity to Theseus' and Hippolyta's bed. Yet the first thing Titania tells us is 'I have forsworn his bed'. Oberon and Titania are the equivalent on the dream plane of Theseus and Hippolyta. Each is behaving unnaturally. There would be nothing wrong with Titania's attachment to the 'little change-ling boy' and his dead mother, were those attachments not exaggerated to the point where Oberon is displaced entirely from her affections and the marital bed. Oberon, on the other hand, rides roughshod over her sympathetic and maternal feelings, and overreacts by trying to deprive her of the boy altogether. No honest neighbour being on hand to mediate, their tiff escalates to under-mine their essential function.

Oberon, like Theseus, seeks to compel love by force. He does so again, even with benevolent intention, when he uses the rough magic of love-in-idleness, derived from Cupid's poisoned arrow. It is important that the love-juice should be rubbed on the eyes of a sleeper rather than drunk. This makes it more external, by-passing judgement. It is only, in concentrated overdose, what happens with any love at first sight which has nothing more to it than what the eyes can register. As Cressida is to say, 'The error of our eye directs our mind. . . . Minds sway'd by eyes are full of turpitude'. The too-much-love which is doting has to be cancelled by the antidote of too little which is virginity (Diane's bud). Oberon betrays his own essential nature as preserver of the natural by forcing on Titania the most unnatural love he can think of:

What thou seest when thou dost wake,
Do it for thy true love take;
Love and languish for his sake.
Be it ounce, or cat, or bear,
Pard, or boar with bristled hair,
In thy eye that shall appear
When thou wak'st, it is thy dear.
Wake when some vile thing is near.
[II ii 26–33]

On the dream plane of imaginative magnification, Titania is much more than a surrogate mother. She is the very goddess of motherhood and all nature's riches. Every mother or pregnant woman is a votress of her order. But every mother, like the goddess herself, requires a consort. The changeling boy has been stolen from its father, and becomes in turn a substitute for a husband. Oberon's jealousy further disturbs the delicate balance of the natural order, releases a plague of Theban proportions (Seneca's *Oedipus* was Shakespeare's main source for this passage), and reenacts the fall:

Therefore the winds, piping to us in vain,
As in revenge have suck'd up from the sea
Contagious fogs; which, falling in the land,
Hath every pelting river made so proud
That they have overborne their continents. . . .
The fold stands empty in the drowned field,
And crows are fatted with the murrion flock. . . .
The human mortals want their winter cheer:
No night is now with hymn or carol blest.
Therefore the moon, the governess of floods,
Pale in her anger, washes all the air,
That rheumatic diseases do abound.
And thorough this distemperature we see
The seasons alter: hoary-headed frosts
Fall in the fresh lap of the crimson rose;
And on old Hiems' thin and icy crown,
An odorous chaplet of sweet summer buds
Is, as in mockery, set; the spring, the summer,
The chiding autumn, angry winter, change
Their wonted liveries; and the mazed world,
By their increase, now knows not which is which.
And this same progeny of evils comes
From our debate, from our dissension;
We are their parents and original.

Although six of the characters spend a good deal of time asleep, only one of them actually dreams (when Hermia dreams that a serpent ate her heart away while Lysander sat smiling). All the other many references to dreams in the play are not to real dreams at all. They are metaphors, like wood, night and fairies, for the altered state of consciousness in which mere reason relaxes its grip and allows other powers and modes of perception to flood in, for those 'causal zones of the psyche' peopled by archetypal images, for, in a word, imagination. Lovers might have the experience, but, not being poets, miss the meaning. The main action of the lovers is framed by the repeated statement of their ignorance of the nature of the power they experience, Hermia's 'I know not by what power' in the first act, and Demetrius' 'I wot not by what power' in the fourth. As soon as they awaken, the experience seems to them cloudy, 'undistinguishable', 'everything seems double'. But they have enjoyed its benefits whether they understand it or not, and Shakespeare the poet has found archetypal images, objective correlatives to make all clear to the audience. The lovers enter the woods in flight, fear, anger and dotage. They return to Athens transfigured, made one with nature and their own natures. What has transfigured them is remembered as no more than 'the fierce vexation of a dream', but the privileged audience knows they have not dreamed it, that they had entered a deeper reality than 'the world of secondary effects', the spirit world, the Dream Time, where all has been corrected and atoned.

Oberon's word 'vexation' marks the end of the process necessitated by Egeus' entry, 'full of vexation' at the beginning. Shakespeare was throughout his life fascinated by alchemy. His last hero, Prospero, is an alchemist. The alchemist sought in his laboratory to correct the imbalance of matter. He used, like the poet, marriage (the chymical marriage, or coniunctio) as an image of the perfect union, fusion of opposites, which he sought. Shakespeare in the laboratory of the spirit often used terms from alchemy as images. 'Vexation' is one such term, a dangerous but necessary stage in the great work where the mixture had to be violently agitated. So here, the deficiencies and imbalances in the communal psyche of Athens, which threatened to spoil Theseus' nuptials, are put through the 'fierce vexation' of exposure to the world beyond rationality, as if that psyche were being violently stirred to exorcise its self-generated demons. As Barber puts it:

The teeming metamorphoses which we encounter are placed, in this way, in a medium and in a moment where the perceived structure of the outer world breaks down, where the body and its environment interpenetrate in unaccustomed ways, so that the seeming separateness and stability of identity is lost. [135]

When Oberon strikes the lovers 'more dead than common sleep', he prepares the way for their awakening to parallel the renewal of earth after the death-like sleep of winter. To sleep on the cold earth and awaken revitalized is a common feature of May rites throughout Europe. Oberon can exercise this power only because he and his queen are now themselves 'new in amity'.

The beginning of the last act returns us to Athens and Theseus, who immediately dismisses what the lovers have said and the audience witnessed as untrue, 'antique fables' and 'fairy toys'. Theseus claims that 'cool reason' comprehends everything, that love is a matter of 'seething brains' and 'shaping fantasies', that, since all are dominated by 'imagination', there is no difference between 'the lunatic, the lover, and the poet'. In other words, love and poetry, being non-literal and beyond reason, are forms of madness. That he should mock the poet's capacity to move freely between earth and heaven implies that for him heaven itself is no more than 'airy nothing'. He has allowed his reason to block off his access to the world of imagination, fearing that to relax strict control is to invite confusion. In so doing he has held feeling at arms length, consigning it to the unreal world of dream and the dangerous world of night. It is Theseus who, for the lovers, 'hath turned a heaven into a hell'.

Theseus' reference to 'fairy toys' is gratuitous, since the lovers can have told him nothing of fairies – they saw none. One human did see the fairies. Again Bully Bottom is the standard by which Theseus, for all his rank and urbanity, is found wanting. If only he or Peter Quince were enough of a poet, they could turn Bottom's dream into a 'gracious' ballad to counterbalance the death of Thisbe.

They are not, but Shakespeare is. The poet is someone who can enter the Dream Time while fully awake, and bring its contents into consciousness and expression, usually as story or drama. This activity is commonly dismissed by the exclusively rational as so irrational as to be crazy.

Hippolyta gently but totally refutes Theseus, making, in fact, Coleridge's distinction between imagination and fancy, and telling us what the whole play is about:

> But all the story of the night told over,
> And all their minds transfigur'd so together,
> More witnesseth than fancy's images,
> And grows to something of great constancy;
> But howsoever, strange and admirable.

That 'something of great constancy' is, within the terms of this play, the wholeness of nature. The idea of the wholeness of nature was anathema to the Puritans. Ted Hughes writes:

> The idea of nature as a single organism is not new. It was man's first great thought, the basic intuition of most primitive theologies. Since Christianity hardened into Protestantism, we can follow its underground heretical life, leagued with everything occult, spiritualistic, devilish, over-emotional, bestial, mystical, feminine, crazy, revolutionary, and poetic. [WP132]

Shakespeare reclaims and renews them all.

Theseus at this point drops his argument, and speaks to the lovers from the heart:

> Here come the lovers, full of joy and mirth.
> Joy, gentle friends, joy and fresh days of love
> Accompany your hearts.

He calls for mirth and revels, rejects offerings on the subjects of war, rage and mourning, and chooses the love story of Pyramus and Thisbe.

The unnaturalness, the gross artificiality and absurdity of *Pyramus and Thisbe* is compounded by the incompetence of the rude mechanicals. Yet, though they violate all the proprieties of art and courtly behaviour, their instinctive naturalness and goodwill overrides objections such as those of the Master of the Revels, eliminates the class divide, and humanizes the courtiers. The couples receive a blessing from Peter Quince and his team as well as from the fairies.

The declared purpose of the entertainment is to 'ease the anguish' of 'this long age of three hours / Between our after-supper and bed-time'. When the Bergamask is over it is almost midnight, and even the sceptical Theseus in his excited anticipation drops his rational guard: 'Lovers, to bed; 'tis almost fairy time'. He speaks truer than he knows, for a moment later Puck enters to prepare the way for 'the King and Queen of Fairies, with all their Train'. They come to bless the bride-beds, the couples themselves, their unborn children, the palace, Athens. Their holy water is 'field-dew consecrate', and their deity is the triple Hecate, who embodies in one indivisible goddess the world, the underworld, and the heavens. Her power extends over day and night, city and country, waking and dreaming. When she is welcomed, she brings concord, healing, a blessing on house and city. In the words of Graham Bradshaw, 'although Theseus does not believe in fairies, he needs, and receives, their blessing'. They are the powers we live or are lived by.

Nature is herself a poet, an imaginative artist whose manuscripts cannot but contain the occasional blot, whose creations are not without unnatural accidents – the mole, hare-lip or birthmark. These the fairies try to protect the unborn young against.

In Oberon's final speech we can no longer miss what has been steadily accumulated throughout the play – Shakespeare's arrogation of Christian terminology for his fairies. All Christianity's strongest words are there – grace, hallowed, consecrated, and, innumerable times, blessed – all usurped on behalf of pagan deities and nature spirits which nearly every Christian of the time would have thought satanic and sought charms to protect the house against:

> Saint Francis and Saint Benedight,
> Bless this house from wicked wight,
> From the nightmare and the goblin

That is hight Goodfellow Robin;
Keep it from all evil spirits,
Fairies, weasels, rats, and ferrets;
From curfew time
To the next prime.   [Murray 40]

And this fear of and hostility to nature is not restricted to Christians or to benighted centuries long ago. In *The Myth of the Goddess* Baring and Cashford write:

> Nature is no longer experienced as source but as adversary, and darkness is no longer a mode of divine being, as it was in the lunar cycles, but a mode of being devoid of divinity and actively hostile, devouring of light, clarity and order. The only place where the voice of the old order breaks through, though so disguised as to be barely recognizable, is where the inspiration of poetry re-animates the old mythic images.

In *A Midsummer Night's Dream* that voice is unmistakable: Shakespeare brings about no less than a marriage of heaven and hell.

* * *

Pagan rites are again in evidence in *The Merry Wives of Windsor*, but much closer to home, not in the woods near the Athens of antiquity, but in Windsor Forest close to a community of solid bourgeois Elizabethan citizens.

Falstaff is seen by the whole community as a threat to the order on which it depends, as the embodiment of riot, vice, in particular the deadly sin of lechery. In spite of the comic context, the words used of him – 'corrupted', 'tainted', 'unclean' – are very strong. He is the old Adam to be castigated and cast out. Almost, he is the devil himself. The pre-Christian horned god, known to the Romans as Cernunnos, 'lord of the animals', god of the chase, appears in British folklore as Herne the Hunter. This god was still worshipped by the witches of Shakespeare's time. But apart from the witches, knowledge of such cults had become for the average Elizabethan almost as shadowy as our own knowledge of the significance of such pagan rituals as still survive, our maypoles, bonfires, holly and ivy. Ford has an irrational hatred of witches, though he admits to knowing nothing of their practices. They are, he says, 'beyond our element'. That Falstaff should be disguised as the witch of Brainford is a parody of the shape-shifting powers of the witches and their god. The name of Herne the Hunter meant almost as little to the Pages and Fords of Shakespeare's day as it does to us:

The superstitious idle-headed eld
Receiv'd, and did deliver to our age,
This tale of Herne the hunter for a truth.

Yet his oak in Windsor Forest still seemed a fearful place to them, to be avoided after dark:

> Why, yet there want not many that do fear
> In deep of night to walk by this Herne's oak.

When the tree finally fell, two hundred years later, it must have been something more than mere antiquity which caused its wood to be made into curios, some of which survive to this day. One of them belonged to Ted Hughes, the author of *Gaudete*, in which a man who is part oak and part fertility god, a lecherous seducer of the village wives, throws their husbands into a panic and is hunted down by them, killed and burned.

Why should Shakespeare drag Herne the Hunter and all that hazy pagan folklore into so casual a comedy as *The Merry Wives*? Within the shallow materialistic world of Windsor, Falstaff comes to seem a representative, however degraded, of the fertility god himself. He sees himself as a scapegoat persecuted by Puritans: 'This is enough to be the decay of lust and late-walking through the realm'. He invokes, at the climax, 'omnipotent love', 'that in some respects makes a beast a man; in some other, a man a beast'. He has indeed become a beast – 'a Windsor stag, and the fattest, I think, i' th' forest' – but simultaneously a god shape-shifting for love: 'When gods have hot backs, what shall poor men do?' His frank sexuality ('My doe with the black scut') is much to be preferred to the puritanical violence Parson Evans schools the children in:

> Fie on sinful fantasy,
> Fie on lust and luxury! . . .
> Pinch him, and burn him, and turn him about,
> Till candles and starlight and moonshine be out.

Had Evans the power of Prospero and real hobgoblins at his disposal, Falstaff would no doubt have been as tormented as Caliban.

The 'public sport' which the merry wives improvise to exorcise Sir John is clearly based on, made up of vestiges from, ancient rituals whose original meaning has been quite forgotten. Falstaff is told to come to Herne's oak at night 'disguised like Herne, with huge horns on his head'. Their children, dressed as fairies, will then 'pinch him sound, And burn him with their tapers'. The original fairies were probably an ancient race, worshippers of the horned god. Herne is, according to Graves, closely associated with Hermes, who was Hecate's messenger and lover. Fairies had not, for Shakespeare, quite lost their association with the triple Hecate, but for the merry wives they have already declined into the gossamer creatures of children's stories. The pinching may be a dim memory of the fate of the hunter-god – to be torn apart by his hounds. It may also remind us of the pinching of Caliban by sprites. Caliban's mother Sycorax is identified by Graves with triple Hecate. The real fairies might well have danced round the horned god, dressed in white and green, 'with rounds of waxen tapers on their heads' (as in surviving Scandinavian rituals). They may well have burned him – to death, but not as an act of moral cleansing; rather, on the contrary, as a guarantee of his rebirth the following year rejuvenated and revitalized in order to be able to resume his role as fertility god. This is the opposite of Mistress Page, who, intending to 'dis-horn the spirit', is proposing a symbolic castration.

Falstaff's venery is also to be preferred to the cold materialistic calculation of those who triumph over him. Their 'virtue' and 'scruple' is devalued by the mutual deception of Page and his wife over the marriage of their daughter. Guarding her own honour so scrupulously, Mistress Page does not scruple to try to sell her daughter:

> You would have married her most shamefully,
> Where there was no proportion held in love.

Ford admits that money buys lands, not wives. And Page concedes that 'What cannot be eschew'd must be embrac'd'.

Falstaff, like the green girdle, is precisely that which cannot be eschewed from a full and balanced life. 'Banish plump Jack and banish all the world', he had said to Prince Hal. And here, this being a comedy, he is not banished. The union of Anne and Fenton under Herne's oak vindicates him. The distinction between love and lust dissolves in laughter. He is welcomed back into the human community:

> Master Fenton,
> Heaven give you many, many merry days!
> Good husband, let us every one go home
> And laugh this sport o'er by a country fire,
> Sir John and all.

7 SHAKESPEARE 2 – THE CRIME AGAINST VENUS

The history of Western civilization can be written as the story of the disastrous consequences of dualism. Dualism began in the ancient world as a philosophical and religious idea which gradually filtered into general consciousness and into language to the point where, from the Renaissance onwards, it became almost impossible for educated Europeans to think in any but a dualistic way. Dualism is the belief that everything in life can be divided into two opposing principles or constituents; but basically that matter and spirit are independent entities yoked together in life in violation of the essential nature of each. About two thousand five hundred years ago, a remarkable change took place in man's concept of the gods, the movement towards monotheism, a single male godhead existing independently of the created universe as pure spirit. In its most extreme form this leads to the universal dichotomy of God on one side and the world, the flesh and the devil on the other. Dualism sunders god and nature. It also sunders male and female, encouraging man to frame concepts of militant heroism which ride roughshod over the female in all its manifestations. And it sunders mind from body.

Dualism might not have been so disastrous had it not so often involved value judgements. That is, one of the artificially separated components is usually labelled good and to be fostered, the other bad, to be eliminated or suppressed. Thus man wages war against his own wholeness and the wholeness of his world, in the attempt to impose his own will, vain aspirations and blinkered vision on the world.

In the Middle Ages these beliefs were expressed in elaborate systems and hierarchies such as the Great Chain of Being. This envisaged the whole of creation as a chain each link of which was a species or class of objects. The chain descended from the throne of god, passed through all the heavenly orders – seraphs, cherubs, thrones, denominations, virtues, powers, principalities, archangels and angels to man, and then down through the beasts, birds, reptiles, fishes, plants and minerals, ending at the lowest stone. The image of links in a chain implied that each species shared properties or attributes with those above and below it.

The position of man in the great chain was critical, since that link alone had to hold together the heavenly and earthly, spiritual and material creations. And every individual man had to find a way of coping with the division of his being between faculties he shared with the angels, his reason and judgement, and those he shared with the beasts, his appetites, instincts and passions, and, of course, his mortality. Such a man is primed for tragedy.

Awareness of this problem and the stating of it in these terms had remained constant for over two thousand years, from Pythagoras through the Platonists and neo-Platonists to such Renaissance thinkers as Pico della Mirandola and Giordano Bruno, who was in England in 1583–5, where he met or influenced Raleigh, Marlowe, Sidney and John Dee (the original of Prospero).

Never was the problem more acutely felt and widely discussed than in Elizabethan England. Two very different views were held about how man should attempt to solve the riddle of his own divided nature. The more common was to assume that the chain was also a ladder, and that the duty of man was to climb as high as possible. An Elizabethan formulation of this idea was the translation of Romei's *Courtier's Academy* published in 1598 (two years or so before *Hamlet*):

> It is in our power to live like a plant, living creature, like a man, and lastly like an angel; for if a man addict himself only to feeding and nourishment he becometh a plant, if to things sensual he is a brute beast, if to things reasonable and civil he groweth a celestial creature; but if he exalt the beautiful gift of his mind to things invisible and divine he transformeth himself into an angel and, to conclude, becometh the son of God.
>
> [Tillyard, *The Elizabethan World Picture*, 75]

But others held that if God had wanted us to be angels, he would have created us angels in the first place; that to aspire above the place allotted to us in the scheme of things was to fall into the sin of pride; that the unique challenge to man was to accept and attempt to reconcile within him the opposing forces, to achieve a balance and harmony of his faculties. Theologians and moralists tended towards the first party, poets towards the second.

*   *   *

Shakespeare, throughout his works, accuses himself of every offence man is capable of, including, centrally, the crime against Nature. I do not say only that he accuses his characters, because Shakespeare's major characters are not invented to castigate human vices and follies (in the manner of Ben Jonson); they are projections from the depths of his own psyche. Shakespeare's universality stems not from his knowledge of all types and conditions of men (though that he no doubt had), but from his knowledge of himself and his ability to probe, imaginatively, even the unacknowledged parts of himself. It is not a 'negative capability', committing himself to neither side, but the very positive capability of committing himself to both. He suffers with those who suffer, but he is also the cause of that suffering. His psyche is the battle-ground on which all conflicts (but primarily the sexual and the religious) are waged. As in all great imaginative art, his works are (as Hughes expresses it) a perpetual search for truer metaphors for his own nature. And that nature happened to be more complex, more all-embracing, more honest, and more receptive to 'the age and body of the time, his form and pressure', than any other of which we have record. Thus all the plays are, in a sense, history plays.

But just as Greek tragedy was both a record of a crisis in the history of Athens and in human consciousness, and also an embodiment of permanent truths about the human condition, equally relevant after two and a half millennia, so Shakespeare also dramatizes the persistent polarization of the male psyche. As Hughes puts it:

> At one pole is the rational ego, controlling the man's behaviour according to the needs and demands of a self-controlled society. At the other is the totality of this individual's natural, biological and instinctual life. . . . From the point of view of the rational ego this totality appears to be female, and since it incorporates not only the divine source of his being, the feminine component of his own biological make-up, as well as the paranormal faculties and mysteries outside his rational ego, and seems to him in many respects continuous with external nature, he calls it the Goddess. Obviously, this is only a manner of speaking, or of thinking, but it is one that has imposed itself on man throughout his history.
>
> [*Shakespeare*, 513]

The hero's crime is the rejection of this Goddess. It is a crime not only against her and himself, but against humanity, since she is the source of life:

> It is the sin which every tragic hero commits, and it can be described as a failure of understanding, that alienation from the 'understanding heart' which . . . has to be exposed, condemned, punished, corrected, and eventually redeemed. [231]

*　　*　　*

What was to become by 1600 a tempest of the mind, the crucible of the tragedies, started out in 1592 as a sophisticated conceit to please a patron, a daringly erotic best-seller. But even when he wanted to, Shakespeare was incapable of writing superficially. He could no more keep his deepest concerns out of *Venus and Adonis* than he could keep Herne the Hunter out of *The Merry Wives of Windsor* or the morose Jaques out of *As You Like It*.

The story of *Venus and Adonis* is very simple and could be very quickly told. Venus, goddess of Love woos Adonis, a beautiful mortal. He resists, being disgusted by what he calls 'lust'. Venus tries everything, but fails to prevent him leaving her to go hunting. Later, having a premonition of disaster, she goes in search of him and finds his body savaged by a boar. He is transformed into a purple flower which she plucks and puts between her breasts. Nothing else happens. But Shakespeare elaborates this story to the tune of 1194 lines. Given his extreme economy and concentration in both the sonnets and the plays, why this prolixity? The simple story, chosen consciously, perhaps, as a witty cautionary tale to persuade the young Southampton, to whom it is dedicated, not to resist marriage (the theme also of the first seventeen sonnets), seems to have engaged with much larger and deeper issues which forced Shakespeare to dwell with fascination on its details and implications. Such fascination was justified, since this myth was to provide, as it were, a paradigm for all his mature work. It enabled him to combine, at the level where imagination finds its metaphors, his own most personal problems (his exile from Stratford and his family, his unrequited love for both a man and a woman, their betrayal of him, his covert Catholicism in an officially and repressively Protestant age) with the problems, the seething repressed energies, of Elizabeth's reign, energies which she contained with a reign of terror, but which were later to erupt in regicide and civil war. The fact that Shakespeare returned obsessively to this theme and these images throughout his career suggests that he had, almost accidentally, tapped a source of disturbing conflict in his age and in himself. Venus is the great goddess treated as a witch and a whore by the Puritans. She is also the voice of his own misused anima calling to the creative imagination for redress.

The first thing we are told about Adonis is that 'hunting he loved, but love he laughed to scorn'. The pagan Goddess invites him to come 'where never serpent hisses', but Adonis inhabits a fallen world where her unabashed sexuality causes him to burn with shame, not desire. Venus, 'having no defects', cannot understand the basis of his rejection. She is herself Nature ('My beauty as the spring doth yearly grow'). Her body is a landscape with mountains, dales and pleasant fountains

> Sweet bottom-grass, and high delightful plain,
> Round rising hillocks, brakes obscure and rough

where Adonis like a deer may safely graze. Therefore, in her terms, his rejection of her is unnatural. She marshals exactly the arguments Shakespeare deployed in the early sonnets to persuade Southampton to marry. She accuses him of being sick with self-love, narcissistic, and parasitic upon the natural world:

> Things growing to themselves are growth's abuse.
>   Seeds spring from seeds, and beauty breedeth beauty.
>   Thou wast begot; to get it is thy duty.

> Upon the earth's increase why shouldst thou feed
> Unless the earth with thy increase be fed?
> By law of nature thou art bound to breed,
> That thine may live when thou thyself art dead.

In the third sonnet Shakespeare asks his patron:

> Or who is he so fond will be the tomb
> Of his self-love to stop posterity?

And the next sonnet expands on this:

> Unthrifty loveliness, why dost thou spend
> Upon thyself thy beauty's legacy?
> Nature's bequest gives nothing but doth lend,
> And being frank she lends to those are free.

Shakespeare here comes perilously close to saying that to be thus in love with oneself ('having traffic with thyself alone') is to prefer masturbation to the unconditional offering of the self to the other which is love as Venus embodies it.

This theme is graphically illustrated in the incident of Adonis' horse which, as he goes to mount him, sees 'a breeding jennet, lusty, young, and proud'. Unlike his master, the courser needs no invitation, but

> Breaketh his rein, and to her straight goes he.

> Imperiously he leaps, he neighs, he bounds,
> And now his woven girths he breaks asunder;
> The bearing earth with his hard hoof he wounds,
> Whose hollow womb resounds like heaven's thunder;
> The iron bit he crusheth 'tween his teeth,
> Controlling what he was controlled with.

Once free, the horse ceases to be violent and begins to behave with 'gentle majesty and modest pride'. The violence transfers itself to the rider, whose 'angry stir' the horse completely ignores:

> He sees his love, and nothing else he sees,
> For nothing else with his proud sight agrees.

Pride seems to be the key, what Hopkins calls 'This pride of prime's enjoyment':

> Round-hoofed, short-jointed, fetlocks shag and long,
> Broad breast, full eye, small head, and nostril wide,
> High crest, short ears, straight legs and passing strong,
> Thin mane, thick tail, broad buttock, tender hide:
> Look what a horse should have he did not lack,
> Save a proud rider on so proud a back.

The very language here rears and curvets. It needs no caparisons or trappings. A mere Whitman-like listing of the horse's physical attributes is enough. And indeed there is a remarkably similar passage in 'Song of Myself', except that Whitman provides his horse with a worthy rider:

A gigantic beauty of a stallion, fresh and responsive to my caresses,
Head high in the forehead, wide between the ears,
Limbs glossy and supple, tail dusting the ground,
Eyes full of sparkling wickedness, ears finely cut, flexibly moving.
His nostrils dilate as my heels embrace him,
His well-built limbs tremble with pleasure as we race around and return.
I but use you a minute, then I resign you, stallion,
Why do I need your paces when I myself out-gallop them?
Even as I stand or sit passing faster than you.

What, then, is lacking in Adonis, what curbs his proud manhood, what iron bit controls him? It is impossible to use such metaphors without remembering the famous passage in Plato's *Phaedrus* where the driver of a chariot (will or ego) has to deal with a recalcitrant horse (desire or libido), which, through his puritan spectacles, he can see only as ugly: 'crooked, lumbering, ill-made; stiff-necked, short-throated, snub-nosed; his coat is black and his eyes a bloodshot grey; wantonness and boastfulness are his companions, and he is hairy-eared and deaf, hardly controllable even with whip and goad'. When this horse tries to take the bit between its teeth, and rush forward prancing towards the object of its desire, 'the driver . . . falls back like a racing charioteer at the barrier, and with a still more violent backward pull jerks the bit from between the teeth of the lustful horse, drenches his abusive tongue and jaws with blood, and forcing his legs and haunches against the ground reduces him to torment. Finally, after several repetitions of this treatment, the wicked horse abandons his lustful ways; meekly now he executes the wishes of his driver.' What I mean by calling this attitude puritanical is clear, I think, from a passage a few pages earlier in the *Phaedrus*: 'Pure was the light and pure were we from the pollution of the walking sepulchre which we call a body, to which we are bound like an oyster to its shell'.

Adonis is blind to the beauty of his stallion, and gives it no chance to respond to his caresses. He seeks to subdue its nature entirely to his purposes (which are to escape from Venus and to go hunting). He is equally blind to the beauty of Venus, since he cannot see the love which declares and offers itself as anything but lust. The imagery Shakespeare chooses to describe Adonis' rejection of her would be absurdly hyperbolic were he merely embroidering the romantic cliché that 'looks kill love'. What he is actually doing, as surely as with the images of storm and savage beasts in *King Lear*, is presaging the chaos which follows when Nature herself is violated:

Like a red morn that ever yet betokened
Wrack to the seaman, tempest to the field . . .
Or as the wolf doth grin before he barketh,
Or as a berry breaks before it staineth,
  Or like the deadly bullet of a gun,
  His meaning struck her ere his words begun.

87

Adonis, by his rejection, is releasing destructive energies into the world. As he sees Venus tempting him to the sin of lust, she becomes, in his eyes, not Venus the Queen of Heaven but the foul witch Hecate, the Queen of Hell:

> For by this black-faced night, desire's foul nurse,
> Your treatise makes me like you worse and worse.

Venus approves the behaviour of Adonis' horse, saying that deep desire should have no bounds. But Adonis replies:

> I know not love,' quoth he, 'nor will not know it,
> Unless it be a boar, and then I'll chase it.

By thus treating love as a boar, a foul and dangerous thing to be fought and killed, Adonis begins the process of converting Love (Venus) into a boar. For the first half of the poem Venus has been pleading and softly feminine, but now a transformation begins. Just as Dionysus, in his feminine aspect, spends half *The Bacchae* trying to win over Pentheus with gentle persuasion, but is at last transformed by Pentheus' own violent rejection into his opposite, male and murderous, the bull, so Adonis forces Venus to become more and more predatory, actually converts her love into ravening lust:

> Now quick desire hath caught the yielding prey,
> And glutton-like she feeds, yet never filleth.
> Her lips are conquerors, his lips obey,
> Paying what ransom the insulter willeth;
>   Whose vulture thought doth pitch the price so high
>   That she will draw his lips' rich treasure dry.
>
> And having felt the sweetness of the spoil,
> With blindfold fury she begins to forage;
> Her face doth reek and smoke, her blood doth boil,
> And careless lust stirs up a desperate courage,
>   Planting oblivion, beating reason back,
>   Forgetting shame's pure blush and honor's wrack.

By attempting to separate out 'pure' love, which is completely subservient to reason, shame and honour, from the totality of love Venus had originally offered him, Adonis splits Venus into the trembling, heartsick woman who warns him so graphically against the boar, and the boar itself. He speaks to her like Hamlet to his mother:

> Call it not love, for Love to heaven is fled
> Since sweating Lust on earth usurped his name.

But, as with Hamlet, his definition of lust leaves no room for love in bodily terms.

Venus is clearly Nature, and Nature is not divisible. In her loving phase, she associates herself with timid and vulnerable creatures. If Adonis must hunt, she says, let him hunt creatures which cannot harm him, the hare, for example. But Venus can describe the hunting of a hare only from the point of view of the hare. She 'goes into a hare With sorrow and sighs and mickle care', but Adonis is unmoved by the sufferings of poor Wat. Again, she goes into 'a milch doe, whose swelling dugs do ache, Hasting to feed her fawn'. And again into a snail, 'whose tender horns being hit Shrinks backward in his shelly cave with pain'. Adonis drives her back in pain into the darkness, the underworld, from which she emerges frothing at the mouth. She warns him in the clearest terms that to choose the boar is to choose death (which Venus calls 'divorce of love') in preference to life, to commit suicide. In rabid defence of his self-sufficiency he strikes out at all forms of love, including sympathy, the ability to suffer with those that suffer; he strikes at the feminine in all its forms – woman, Nature, his own anima. Richard of Gloucester's words would not be out of place in his mouth:

> And that word 'love', which greybeards call divine,
> Be resident in men like one another,
> And not in me! I am myself alone.

(Richard's totem is the boar.) And when he swears by 'black-faced night, desire's foul nurse' he is on the way to transforming himself into a Tarquin or a MacBeth. The extreme, frigid, love-denying, life-denying puritanism of an Angelo is the perfect breeding ground for the boar, the murderous tyrant.

Adonis escapes from Venus, preferring the boar-hunt; but he is no match for this boar. Finding the mangled body of Adonis, Venus in her distraction cannot distinguish between herself and the boar:

> If he did see his face, why then I know
> He thought to kiss him, and hath killed him so.

> 'Tis true, 'tis true! thus was Adonis slain:
> He ran upon the boar with his sharp spear,
> Who did not whet his teeth at him again,
> But by a kiss thought to persuade him there;
>   And nuzzling in his flank, the loving swine
>   Sheathed unaware the tusk in his soft groin.

It is a just reversal, since Adonis, terrified by the thought of the soft groin of Venus, is keen enough to plunge his spear into the living body of Nature. Venus then stains her own face with Adonis' blood.

She means, at the end, to 'immure herself and not be seen'. Love goes underground, and becomes, instead of a source of joy and harmony and fertility, a cause of suffering, discord, 'war and dire events'. All this would be absurdly disproportionate if it were a consequence of one young man desiring 'to grow unto himself'. But clearly much more than that is involved. Adonis may begin as Southampton, but he rapidly becomes a part of Shakespeare also, a part of those who were shaping English history at that time, and a part of each of us. He represents the Protestant attempt to degrade the Queen of Heaven to the Great Whore, but also the perennial male rejection and desacralization of Nature in the name of some perfection or abstraction assumed to be accessible only to the detached male intellect.

The character of Adonis we are to meet again and again in the mature works. In middle age he is called Angelo, and is still attempting to freeze out unconditional love in the form of Mariana. In later life he is called Prospero, now devoting his most potent Art to excluding Venus from the magic circle of his isle. In between, there will be the tragedies, where love, as Venus prophesies, will always be attended by jealousy and betrayal:

> It shall be fickle, false, and full of fraud;
> Bud and be blasted, in a breathing while;
> The bottom poison, and the top o'erstrawed
> With sweets that shall the truest sight beguile.
> The strongest body shall it make most weak,
> Strike the wise dumb, and teach the fool to speak.

*   *   *

It was to be some years before the truth of Venus' prophesies was brought home to Shakespeare. In the meantime, he was quick to see the potential of his theme for comedy.

Faust. What is the end of study, let me know?

Meph. Why, that to know which else we should not know.

Faust. Things hid and barr'd, you mean, from common sense?

Meph. Ay, that is study's god-like recompense.

Faust. Come on, then; I will swear to study so,
To know the thing I am forbid to know.

I wonder how many readers will have been taken in by this. These lines are not, in fact, a conversation between Faustus and Mephistophilis from Marlowe's *Doctor Faustus* (1592), but between Berowne and the King of Navarre from Shakespeare's *Love's Labour's Lost* (1593). I have transposed them to the apparently very different context of Marlowe's play in order to suggest that, though Shakespeare's mode is very light, his theme is not so distant from Marlowe's. Marlowe was, in fact, a member of the very 'school of night' to which the King later refers as wearing 'the badge of hell', the heretical 'Schoole of Atheism' whose chief patron, Sir Walter Raleigh, had been disgraced in 1592. Shakespeare's patron, Southampton, was a member of Essex' rival faction. We can get a whiff of the spirit of the School of Night from a poem which Peele addressed to another member of it, the Earl of Northumberland, in 1593, the very year in which *Doctor Faustus* had its first public performance, Marlowe was murdered, and Shakespeare wrote *Love's Labour's Lost*:

> Familiar with the stars and zodiac,
> To whom the heaven lies open as her book;
> By whose directions undeceivable,
> Leaving our schoolmen's vulgar trodden paths,
> And following the ancient reverend steps
> Of Trismegistus and Pythagoras,
> Through uncouth ways and unaccessible,
> Dost pass into the spacious pleasant fields
> Of divine science and philosophy;
> From whence beholding the deformities
> Of common errors, and world's vanity,
> Dost here enjoy the sacred sweet content
> That baser souls, not knowing, not affect.

Love's Labour's Lost opens with the King of Navarre inviting three other noble young men, Berowne, Longaville and Dumaine, to join him in living, for three years, a monastic life devoted to study. There is no suggestion that their studies are likely to lead them towards atheism or the black arts, but there is a strong suggestion that all such academies, such withdrawals from the world into the life of the mind, are fraught with danger. When such behaviour is no more than the passing fancy of affected and inexperienced youth, it is no great matter, or matter for comic resolution. But it had been a serious matter for Raleigh, and was to be so for the Duke in *Measure for Measure* and for Prospero. Navarre's desire for eternal fame, and for the 'god-like recompense' of the study of 'things hid and barr'd' is not so far from Faustus' lines:

> O, what a world of profit and delight,
> Of power, of honour, of omnipotence,
> Is promis'd to the studious artisan!
>
> . . .
>
> A sound magician is a demi-god;
> Here tire, my brains, to get a deity!

The danger is of that *hubris* which drives a man, in straining for an unnatural and unattainable god-like perfection, to spurn or neglect his proper sphere, the life of the body in time and in the world. Man's unique place in the Great Chain of Being, half beast, half angel, gave him two options. He could either strive to exterminate the beast in himself and become god-like, perfect himself in opposition to Nature (including his own god-given nature); or he could seek to reconcile the warring elements (as the alchemists did), converting duality, the terrible dual vision of tragedy, by acceptance into mutuality, interdependence, harmony, symbolized by marriage. And this is the pattern of all the festive comedies.

The young men commit themselves to strict abstinence in a parody of puritanical legalism – 'Out late edict shall strongly stand in force', – swearing to keep 'those statutes / That are recorded in this schedule here'. They are making war against their own affections, vowing to die to love. If the soul is that part of the self which loves, then, in subscribing their names, they are, like Faustus, signing their souls away. Of course we know from the play's title, and from the tone of the opening, that they are not on the road to damnation (or if they are, we know that they will not get far along it), but they are in danger of errors which, without the conventions of comedy, and without the saving intervention of strong women (in collusion with the old Adam in Berowne), could have been more serious. But they are, underneath their privileged affectations, normal young men, merely carried away by a passing fashionable enthusiasm. Their commitment to their oath is very shallow. Berowne is a little more mature, realistic and sensible than the others. His irrepressible common-sense undermines the whole enterprise from the outset. He can't take 'that angel knowledge' seriously. He knows the value of book-learning:

> Small have continual plodders ever won
> Save base authority from others' books.

He knows that the attempt to deny their own affections is doomed:

> For every man with his affects is born
> Not by might master'd, but by special grace.

Moreover, he knows that it is perverse to attempt to defeat the seasonal nature of Nature and of man's life within it:

> At Christmas I no more desire a rose
> Than wish a snow in May's new-fangled shows,
> But like of each thing that in season grows.

In spite of these reservations, he takes his oath in the spirit of making up a team for a game. But it is a game which involves sealing off the four from the rest of the human race.

It is, after all, not a play about Berowne. None of the comedies are plays about individuals locked within their own characters, as all the tragedies are (and the satirical comedies of Jonson or Molière); they are about communities where people determine their own and each other's lives. There is the scene where poor constable Dull has not spoken a word, nor understood one neither, but is, in the last line, drawn into the festivities: 'I'll make one in a dance, or so.' Despite the focus on marriage, love is not, in these plays, merely sexual love, but the whole network of sympathies and dependencies which knit together a human community, and weave human beings into the wider patterns of the non-human world.

No sooner have the four young men taken their oaths, including the oath 'not to see a woman in that term', than the pressures of 'necessity' – that is, of real life – force them to break it. The Princess of France arrives:

> We must perforce dispense with this decree.
> She must lie here on mere necessity.

That force, as Berowne is quick to point out, is the force which decrees, far more strongly than any king, that life cannot go forward without feelings and relationships:

> Necessity will make us all forsworn
> Three thousand times within this three years' space.

In the same speech in which Boyet describes the king in terms of perfection, he describes the Princess in terms of completeness and the prodigality of Nature. When the king tells her that he would be breaking his oath to admit her to his court, she says: ''Tis deadly sin to keep that oath'. She is aware that what the young men are doing is not only silly and impractical, but would, were they to carry it through, lead to the deadly sin of Pride. For the idea that perfection could be achieved in isolation from women and from the world at large, is hubristic in the extreme. Of course, this being the kind of play it is, the king and his three courtiers immediately fall in love with the Princess and her three attendants.

As we near the end of the play, our heroes have far to go if they are to prove themselves worthy of the hands of these ladies. Can their love survive outside the summer holiday climate? Could it survive in the winter world, the world where people actually die? The love the young men profess must be given the test of time, and of exposure to some deprivation far from the self-indulgence of the court. If a year of 'frosts and fasts, hard lodging and thin weeds' does not nip the hothouse blossoms of their love, they will be accepted. For shallow and false reasons they had sought to repudiate love for the sake of the monastic life; now they must endure the monastic life for the sake of love. Another year is 'too long for a play', so the play must end without the usual multiple marriages, but not without a potent affirmation of community, and of human life in harmony with the life of nature and the passing seasons.

The play ends with one of Shakespeare's finest songs. Nothing could be further from the artifice of the opening. In its homely simplicity, naturalness, realism, in its movement from spring to winter, it contains that whole 'gross world' and its 'baser slaves' that the four had vowed to die to, and measures the distance they have yet to travel to their hoped-for atonement.

✻   ✻   ✻

If I am to avoid the temptation to write at book length on Shakespeare, I must restrict myself to little more than jottings on some of the ways in which the theme of the crime against nature surfaces in several of the tragedies and problem plays prior to Shakespeare's final frontal assault on it in *The Winter's Tale* and *The Tempest*.

When, in 1600, Shakespeare moved into his tragic mode, licking his wounds from his own recent encounter with Hecate ('Who art as black as hell, as dark as night'), the *Venus and Adonis* paradigm revealed its tragic potential. The earlier male protagonists of this phase, Hamlet, Troilus, Angelo, Othello, are all variants or developments of Adonis. All, in their pride, idealism, lack of self-knowledge, commit the crime against woman, against Nature, and against their own best selves.

Though Claudius is the overt villain in *Hamlet*, what interests Shakespeare is Hamlet's crime, the unconscious crime of an apparently noble mind. In his first soliloquy, before he knows anything of the murder of his father, Hamlet is already suicidal: 'this flesh' is too soiled to live; not only his flesh, but all flesh is 'rank and gross'. He is later to say that the earth, which had seemed to him a 'goodly frame' has become 'a sterile promontory', and its noblest work, man, a mere 'quintessence of dust'.

Hamlet, formerly 'the expectancy and rose of the fair state' has swung to a position of extreme disgust without ever passing through the middle ground, where the good things of life are valued for what they are. In this soliloquy there are no wholesome brothers, no roses of May, nothing but rank weeds, canker and blight. What is the point of pulling out the fattest weed in such a garden?

Shakespeare goes out of his way to make the point that Hamlet's loathing of and rejection of his mother has nothing to do with his father's murder; but also implies that it has little to do with his uncle either. Hamlet's father claims that he had died with all his imperfections on his head. Yet for Hamlet he is the perfect man, and his perfection had impressed itself on the young Hamlet's mind as expressing a kind of love which did not descend to bodies, which spurned the physical with a god-like purity:

> So excellent a king, that was to this
> Hyperion to a satyr, so loving to my mother
> That he might not beteem the winds of heaven
> Visit her face too roughly.

In this he is contrasted not only with his bestial brother, but also with his all-too-physical wife: 'Why, she would hang on him / As if increase of appetite had grown / By what it fed on'.

Joseph Campbell recognizes this as a recurring type in myth, literature and real life:

> The crux of the difficulty lies in the fact that our conscious view of what life ought to be seldom corresponds to what life really is. Generally we refuse to admit within ourselves or within our friends, the fullness of that pushing, self-protective, malodorous, carnivorous, lecherous fever which is the very nature of the organic cell. . . . But when it suddenly dawns on us, or is forced to our attention, that everything we think or do is necessarily tainted with the odor of the flesh, then, not uncommonly, there is experienced a moment of revulsion: life, the acts of life, the organs of life, become intolerable to the pure, the pure, pure soul.
>
> [*Hero* 121–2]

The young idealist would clearly have subscribed to the views of Pico della Mirandola:

> Neither heavenly nor earthly . . . thou canst grow downward into the lower natures which are brutes. Thou canst again grow upward from thy soul's reason into the higher natures which are divine.

'A beast that wants discourse of reason' would have mourned longer than his mother. Yet he is flesh of her flesh. It is not only the image of his mother and his uncle making love over the nasty sty which sickens him. He is clearly almost as horrified by the thought of any sexual or physical contact between his parents. Sexuality itself is the problem, within the larger problem of physicality and mortality.

Once an extreme idealism is confronted with a reality which it cannot accommodate, it is suddenly replaced by its opposite, an equally extreme cynicism. Thus Hamlet sees only two possibilities for Ophelia; either she remains in the pestilent rank world to breed more sinners or she enters a nunnery. Here in Hamlet's mind is first adumbrated the division of the world into nunnery and brothel which becomes the Vienna of *Measure for Measure*.

* * *

The earliest sonnets are all assaults on time, alternative strategies to ensure that 'beauty's rose might never die' [1]. 'Devouring time' [19] is imagined as doing to beauty what the boar did to Adonis – 'And dig deep trenches in thy beauty's field' [2]. Later there is a growing recognition that only the infatuation 'in lovers' eyes' can evade the reality of 'sluttish time' [55]. 'So true a fool is love' [57] that he lives in a dream, impervious to proofs. In his desperation and self-abasement in the later sonnets Shakespeare offers as a definition of love that it does not 'alter when it alteration finds' [116].

'The Phoenix and the Turtle', probably written about 1600, is Shakespeare's valediction to 'love and constancy' – 'Truth and Beauty buried be'. When he had believed his love to be absolute and eternal he could allow time to 'burn the long-lived phoenix in her blood' [19] in the assurance that renewed love would rise from the ashes. Now

> Beauty, truth, and rarity,
> Grace in all simplicity,
> Here enclosed, in cinders lie.
>
> Death is now the phoenix' nest,
> And the turtle's loyal breast
> To eternity doth rest,
>
> Leaving no posterity.

There is no hint of bitterness in 'The Phoenix and the Turtle', only the deepest sadness and regret for the irrecoverable. But by the time we come to *Troilus and Cressida* in 1602, bitterness floods in with the recognition that what has been lost was never more than absurd idealism. Shakespeare now puts many of the words he had himself spoken in all earnestness in the sonnets into the mouth of Troilus, but perhaps the most telling are given to Cressida:

> Time, force and death,
> Do to this body what extremes you can;
> But the strong base and building of my love
> Is as the very centre of the earth,
> Drawing all things to it.   [IV ii 104–8]

By putting such words into the mouth of Cressida Shakespeare ruthlessly castigates his earlier Troilus-self. Troilus' inevitable disillusionment is his own: 'Never did young man fancy / With so eternal and so fix'd a soul' [V ii 164–5]. 'Lust in action' may be an 'expense of spirit in a waste of shame' [129], but so is its opposite, the attempt to purify sexual love to the point where it becomes a sanctifying absolute. For this Shakespeare now sees as no more than the ego using up all its faith and energies in a fruitless battle with 'time, force and death', a battle, that is, with 'Nature, sovereign mistress over wrack' [126], repudiating her in pursuit of the elixir of immortality, 'love's thrice-repured nectar' [III ii 20]. Shakespeare's desire that there should be 'no more dying' [146] is ultimately no different from Beckett's that there should be 'no more nature' [*Endgame*].

Troilus is a particularly clear example of the danger of an idealism which does not spurn woman and the life of the body, but exalts and refines them in an attempt to transcend time, chance and death. Adolescent, hot-house sexuality, requiring no value in the object beyond what the lover invests it with, is required to provide absolutes worthy the devotion of life and faith. Such a 'winnowed purity in love' does, in effect, spurn the real woman and the real possibilities of sexual fulfilment. It can lead only to disillusion, which causes a swing to its opposite, a cynicism or nihilism which denies value to all women and all life in time. In reaction Troilus transforms himself into his opposite, an agent of death and ruin, dealing 'mad and fantastic execution'. His model is Mars 'inflam'd with Venus'. The possessive lust which inflamed Mars was such as to transform him into the boar which savaged Adonis. By his insistence that love should be eternal, even in the form of an adolescent 'fancy' for a sexy stranger, Troilus has provoked the goddess to 'inflame' him with a madness which is both murderous and suicidal.

Troilus' 'love', purified out of all grounding in the world of substance, corresponds to the equally empty and sterile 'honour' in the name of which Troy fights and falls. Yet the dishonourable cynical pragmatism of the Greeks is even worse. In this play there appears to be no safe passage between the dangerous shores of will and judgement, no middle ground on which the life of substance and process can flourish. For Shakespeare's expression of the fullness of life is always, elsewhere, in terms of Nature's fruitfulness and bounty. The play leaves us in an unreclaimed waste land with putrefying corpses, like Thebes after the slaughter of the Sphinx, or like the world after the last holocaust:

> What's past and what's to come is strew'd with husks
> And formless ruin of oblivion.

*   *   *

Troilus and Othello are both idealists who violate love as effectively by putting it on an absurdly high pedestal as by rejecting it. Troilus was unlucky in his choice of woman, but even a Desdemona could not have given him 'such a winnow'd purity in love' as he demanded.

When Desdemona is forced to make a public declaration of her love for Othello, she does so in frankly sexual terms. Her heart's 'subdued even to the utmost pleasure of my lord'. She loves the Moor, she says, 'to live with him', so that, were she to be left behind when he goes to Cyprus 'The rites for which I love him are bereft me'. 'Rites' can only mean full marital intercourse. It is an admirably mature, sane, normal, declaration.

Othello turns a deaf ear to it, and unconsciously repudiates her, claiming that he is not interested in her body, that he is too old for sexual love. He begs that Desdemona should be allowed to go with him

> Not to comply with heat, the young affects
> In me defunct, and proper satisfaction,

> But to be free and bounteous of her mind;
> . . . no, when light-wing'd toys,
> And feather'd Cupid, foils with wanton dullness
> My speculative and active instruments,
> That my disports corrupt and taint my business,
> Let housewives make a skillet of my helm.

That for which Desdemona has consecrated her soul and fortunes, sexual love, is dismissed by Othello as something which would corrupt and taint his reputation. It is later revealed that he is, in fact, obsessed with her 'sweet body', 'that whiter skin of hers than snow', but to admit such feelings to himself would undermine his self-esteem and the image of whiter-than-white he seeks to project. I imagine Othello when we first see him dressed in dazzling white. He probably employs a better tailor than any of the Venetian grandees. His whole life effort has been to repudiate everything he and the world associated with blackness – his passions, his kinship with the whole animal creation. To acknowledge this part of himself would be to see himself as Iago sees him – the 'lascivious Moor'. To betray this part of himself, the part Coleridge was to call the 'natural man', is to repudiate Venus.

Thus Shakespeare is at pains to reveal to us that just as Hamlet was incomplete, tainted in his mind, before the Ghost undermined him, so Othello is not 'all-in-all sufficient' before Iago begins his work. He is already dry tinder awaiting the spark Iago supplies. He is a mature version of Adonis or Troilus for whom if love cannot be an absolute outside time it might as well be as Iago defines it 'merely a lust of the blood', in which case it can be left to goats and monkeys. The goddess, as always, once denied, appears in her ugly and destructive aspects, the only aspects in which Iago has ever seen her. Iago is but the externalization of what is left in Othello's psyche when his attempt to exclude the goddess altogether fails.

If there were no envious and calumniating Iago to push the pedestal into the ditch, envious and calumniating time would do it sooner or later. Othello half realizes that only death can preserve perfection:

> If it were now to die,
> 'Twere now to be most happy, for I fear
> My soul hath her content so absolute,
> That not another comfort like to this
> Succeeds in unknown fate.

Desdemona is disturbed by this:

> The heavens forbid
> But that our loves and comforts should increase,
> Even as our days do grow.

But the absolute content Othello strains for is by definition outside time, and therefore outside the world of process, the natural world where things increase and grow, and die in due season.

Othello's unconscious is a stormy sea he has never learned to navigate. His disciplined military life and apparently complete acculturization to Venetian civilization have so far successfully protected him from exposure to it. Iago senses that the veneer is thin; that his task is simply to lift a corner of it, and Othello will entirely lose his sufficiency:

> My blood begins my safer guides to rule,
> And passion having my best judgement collied
> Assays to lead the way.   [II.iii.196–8]

Having failed to preserve his image of Desdemona as angel, Othello relegates her first to the bestial, then, still lower, to the mineral. Her human body and beauty is something his mind cannot cope with. To escape the intolerable attraction of warm flesh and balmy breath (divorced from any knowledge of or interest in Desdemona beyond her beauty) he tries to convert it imaginatively into the cold and hard forms of non-human beauty which do not engage his passions, snow, monumental alabaster, chrysolite, pearl. All these are lifeless ('cold, cold, my girl'). It is safer, for his self-esteem, to kill her first and love her after.

Othello is the opposite of Hamlet's definition of the just man. Because his blood and judgement are so ill commingled, he becomes a pipe for Iago's finger to play what stop he please. By trying to overrule his natural passion he converts it into a demon and becomes its slave. In defence of male 'reputation' he kills the thing he loves, and with it his own soul.

✲   ✲   ✲

The three characters in the whole of Shakespeare who make the most stringent efforts to banish Sir John, and with him the goddess, are Adonis, Angelo and Prospero. And of these by far the most fanatical is Angelo in *Measure for Measure*.

At the beginning of the play we are led to believe that both the Duke and Angelo have lived monkish lives, in obscurity and seclusion, studying to frame theories of human nature and of government. The Duke has long had the opportunity to put his theories into practice, but has been unable to do so. He ends up with strict laws which he cannot bring himself to enforce. The result is that the law loses all respect and liberty breeds licence. Vienna has become a 'permissive' society (he uses the very word). Frazer reports that in many cultures the attempt by the priest-king to excercise spiritual and temporal powers simultaneously proved so burdensome that 'they sank under its weight into spiritless creatures, cloistered recluses, from whose nerveless fingers the reins of government slipped into the firmer grasp of men who were often content to wield the reality of sovereignty without its name'. The Duke is in not quite so bad a case, but the split in him is projected onto Viennese life with its polarized and life-denying extremes of convent and stews.

The Duke regards his own leniency as a vice rather than a virtue, and prefers Angelo as someone more likely to have the courage of his own convictions, as a man apparently without sin, whose own life could stand up to the most searching judgement. Angelo's severity is approved not only by the Duke but also by Escalus and others, including, however grudgingly, even Lucio.

But it is typical of the manifold ambiguities of this play that the Duke's motives should be mixed. His admiration for Angelo is from the first qualified by a slight suspicion that he might be too good to be true, a 'seemer' most likely to reveal his true colours when corrupted by absolute power. In a sense he is conducting an experiment to see whether harsh laws and harsher punishments, rigidly enforced, will in fact produce a better life in the common-wealth. The experiment shows that too much restraint is as damaging to the state as too much liberty, and more damaging to those who enforce it.

Within this framework of the problem of Justice, the real interest of the play lies in the delineation of two characters, Angelo and Isabella, in the way in which Shakespeare puts the conspicuous virtue of each under such pressure that it breaks open to reveal something ugly and destructive lurking unacknowledged beneath it, from which it has derived its extreme severity. The psychology is strikingly modern, and still shocking to those who believe in Victorian moral values. It fleshes out Blake's proverb of Hell 'Sooner murder an infant in its cradle than nurse unacted desires'.

In Angelo this is worked out in a fairly obvious and mechanical way. It is implied in his very name, surely a spiritually pretentious and unnatural name for a man:

> They say this Angelo was not made by man and woman,
> after this downright way of creation.

Montaigne knew these victims of moral hubris: 'They want to get out of them-selves and escape from the man. That is madness: instead of changing into angels, they change into beasts'. The man who denies his kinship with human-ity and nurses the spiritual ambition to be like an angel is in the way to overreach himself, fall, and become, instead, a devil.

When Angelo finds himself attracted by Isabella, what is to prevent him simply declaring his love for her? He is the kind of man she admires. If he freely pardoned her brother he would stand in her good grace. But for him love and lust have become separated as good and evil. When, in his desire for Isabella, he is forced to recognize his own humanity, he can only recognize it as sinful lust. Wilson Knight describes this very well:

> Sexual desire has long been anathema to him, so his warped idealism
> forbids any healthy love. Good and evil change places in his mind, since

100

this passion is immediately recognized as good, yet, by every one of his stock judgements, condemned as evil. The Devil becomes a 'good angel'. And this wholesale reversion leaves Angelo in sorry plight now: he has no moral values left. Since sex has been synonymous with foulness in his mind, this new love, reft from the start of moral sanction in a man who 'scarce confesses that his blood flows', becomes swiftly a devouring and curbless lust.

[*The Wheel of Fire* 87–8]

There is also a very pertinent passage by Ted Hughes about Adonis, which is even more apt for Angelo:

The boar that demolished Adonis was, in other words, his own repressed lust – crazed and bestialized by being separated from his intelligence and denied. The Venus which he refused became a demon and supplanted his consciousness. The frigid puritan, with a single terrible click, becomes a sexual maniac – a destroyer of innocence and virtue, a violator of the heavenly soul, of the very thing he formerly served and adored. . . . This metamorphosis is triggered by a simple and one might think academic factor: namely, Adonis's Calvinist spectacles, which divide nature, and especially love, the creative force of nature, into abstract good and physical evil. Nature's attempts to recombine, first in love, then in whatever rebuffed love turns into, and the puritan determination that she shall not recombine under any circumstances, are the power-house and torture-chamber of the Complete Works. And the vital twist, the mysterious chemical change that converts the resisting high-minded puritan to the being of murder and madness, is that occult crossover of Nature's maddened force – like a demon – into the brain that had rejected her.

[WP 114]

There is no fundamental critical disagreement about Angelo; but Isabella is another matter. For centuries she was regarded as one of Shakespeare's most pure and noble heroines; and there are still critics who find her wholly admirable. In terms of plot she is set against Angelo and suffers much at his hands. But it seems to me that in terms of the deeper meanings of the play she is essentially his female counterpart. Both are puritans dedicated to unusually harsh disciplines. Her seeming, screened by her youth and innocence and habit of a nun, is much less obvious than Angelo's, and less melodramatically revealed; but revealed it certainly is, if we are alive to the implications of the lines she speaks. She knows herself as little as Angelo knows himself, and is also deficient in common humanity.

Isabella's first appearance in the play is inauspicious. For we find that she is so far from accepting her own sexuality that she is about to enter a nunnery where she will never again speak to a man but with covered face and in the presence of the prioress. She gives no moral or spiritual reasons for this. The first thing she says is that the rules of the strict order of St.Clare are not strict enough for her. Her desire for 'a more strict restraint' upon the sisters parallels Angelo's desire for stricter laws and law-enforcement in Vienna – and the previous scene had ended with the Duke's expression of his doubts about the genuineness of that.

Of course there are vast differences between Isabella and Angelo. He is a mature victimizer, she a young and innocent victim. The text does not specify her age, but the most theatrically effective of many Isabellas I have seen was the youngest. We can focus the issue by asking where Isabella lives, and with whom. There is no mention of home or parents for her or Claudio. Indeed, there do not seem to be any ordinary houses in Vienna. When Pompey says that all the houses in the suburbs must be plucked down, he means bawdy houses; and it seems that, apart from the public buildings, ducal palace and gaol, there are only two kinds of houses, religious houses and bawdy houses. Even Mariana's moated grange is at Saint Luke's, a religious establishment, and moated as if to keep out the corruption of the city. We must assume that Isabella's parents are dead. Perhaps she has been living with Claudio; but he has left, or is about to leave to live with Juliet. Pompey claims that if the brothels were closed it would be necessary to 'geld and spay all the youth of the city'. Claudio and Juliet try to live in terms of normal sexual love. Claudio is condemned to death for it, and Juliet imprisoned along with the whores. It is not surprising that a passionate but high-minded and inexperienced girl such as Isabella should in such a moral environment equate her integrity with her chastity, and, feeling that she is obliged to choose between a pure life within the nunnery and a corrupt life out of it, unhesitatingly chooses the former. Nevertheless, the play judges that her decision is deeply mistaken. In her desire to protect herself against corruption she rejects not only sex, but all intercourse with men and most forms of intercourse with women; she rejects the world, including love, and, in doing so, compromises her own full humanity.

Angelo did not recognize himself to be a man. Isabella is immediately presented to us as aspiring to be something more than a woman, 'a thing enskied and sainted', an 'immortal spirit'. She succeeds only in being something less than a woman. In the dichotomy the play sets up between nunnery and brothel, it is Mistress Overdone, a bawd, who exemplifies womanly compassion and Christian charity by taking in Lucio's bastard. Can we imagine Isabella doing as much for her brother's child? (Mariana has to give her another lesson in compassion at the end.) The sterility of the life to which she aspires is underlined by the imagery of richness and fertility in which Lucio describes to her her brother's 'sin':

> Your brother and his lover have embraced;
> As those that feed grow full, as blossoming time
> That from the seedness the bare fallow brings
> To teeming foison, even so her plenteous womb
> Expresses his full tilth and husbandry.

It is the Provost, a man distinguished by a mature and balanced humanity, who describes Claudio as 'more fit to do another such offence, than die for this'. Claudio is a very ordinary young man, concerned not with abstract morality, but with living and loving. Yet Isabella is persuaded, very reluctantly, to intervene on her brother's behalf, not because a palpable and cruel injustice is about to be performed, but solely because Claudio happens to be her brother. Had it been any other man she would have concurred with Angelo's handling of the case. That is why she is so cold for so long and needs so much prompting.

When Isabella comes to plead for Claudio she never asks what harm he has done, or why his offence should be a capital one (as do not only Lucio, but also Escalus and the Provost). On the contrary, she claims that it is

> a vice that most I do abhor,
> And most desire should meet the blow of justice.

Why should she abhor the lovemaking of a young man and his fiancée so much if not in fear of her own sexuality – for the same reason, that is, that she wishes to enter a nunnery?

Just as Angelo's puritanism ensured that sex could only present itself to him in perverse forms, so Isabella's also diverts her sexuality from its normal course. There is a kind of perverted sexuality in the language she uses when Angelo makes his proposition – what Leavis calls 'a kind of sensuality of martyrdom':

> Were I under the terms of death,
> Th'impression of keen whips I'd wear as rubies,
> And strip myself to death as to a bed
> That longing have been sick for, ere I'd yield
> My body up to shame.

She feels that her integrity is dependent on her 'honour', a term she never questions, and which she confuses with her chastity. She is in no doubt that her chastity weighs more than her brother's life:

> Then, Isabel live chaste, and brother die:
> More than our brother is our chastity.

How can those who admire Isabella justify that vicious line? It is a product of sheer panic. She is under extreme pressure, but her total moral collapse in the name of morality calls that morality in question. And there is worse to come. When Claudio suggests that a sin done in charity, to save a life, is no sin but a virtue (and he is theologically impeccable), she becomes as ruthless as Angelo in defence of her puritanical self-esteem:

> Might but my bending down
> Reprieve thee from thy fate, it should proceed.
> I'll pray a thousand prayers for thy death;
> No word to save thee.

Yet she has no objection to the plan to let another woman make the same sacrifice on her behalf. The Duke has already told Juliet that sorrow which is merely for the shame sin brings 'is always toward ourselves, not heaven'. He speaks in the same vein as many Elizabethan moralists, such as Tyndale, who was very hard on Lucrece, another woman who placed an absolute value on chastity:

> She sought her own glory in her chastity and not god's. When she had lost her chastity, then she counted herself most abominable in the sight of all men, and for very pain and thought which she had, not that she had displeased god, but that she had lost her honour, slew herself. Look how great her glory and rejoicing therein, and much despised she them that were otherwise, and pitied them not, which pride god more abhorreth than the whoredom of any whore.

But it is not against such vehemence that we are required, within the play, to measure Isabella, rather against Mariana. Mariana has a very low profile in the play, but we should not allow that to obscure her centrality. Whereas Isabella chooses to enter a nunnery, Mariana is forced into exile and isolation at her moated grange. Vienna cannot accommodate someone who refuses to accept its division of body from spirit, sex from love. Mariana has no compunction about making love to a man to whom she is not yet married, and the Duke not only sanctions but sets up the act. Mariana corresponds to Venus, a woman of candid sexuality defined entirely by her unconditional love for a man who rejects her, taking him to her bosom in the end after he has undergone a symbolic death and resurrection. Mariana represents, in almost token form, the values embodied much more explicitly and richly in Helena in *All's Well that Ends Well*. Her simple plea for Angelo's life has all the total commitment in love and charity which was lacking in Isabella's plea to Angelo. When Isabella sinks to her knees beside her and speaks in like terms, she recovers her humanity, and that, in the terms of this play, is the only redemption.

✳   ✳   ✳

Hamlet will not step in blood without much scanning of the metaphysical dangers: 'And shall I couple hell?' Macbeth, the bloody soldier, does not lack resolution, but has the opposite imbalance:

> Strange things I have in head, that will to hand,
> Which must be acted, ere they may be scann'd.
> [III iv 138–9]

Macbeth has already, before the play begins, coupled hell by marrying Lady Macbeth. Marriage, which should be a creative and procreative bond, is, for Macbeth, his alliance with evil. Specifically, it represents his choice to reject the claims of love, pity and humanity, in favour of reputation, a reputation for valour which requires him to be as bloodthirsty as Pyrrhus:

> For brave Macbeth (well he deserves that name),
> Disdaining Fortune, with his brandish'd steel,
> Which smok'd with bloody execution,
> Like Valour's minion, carv'd out his passage,
> Till he fac'd the slave;
> Which ne'er shook hands, nor bade farewell to him,
> Till he unseam'd him from the nave to th' chops,
> And fix't his head upon our battlements.
> [I ii 16–22]

Macdonwald is described as

> Worthy to be a rebel, for to that
> The multiplying villainies of nature
> Do swarm upon him.   [I ii 10–12]

Macbeth himself is soon to learn what villainies multiply once mercy has been cast out. What Macbeth tries to stifle in himself is no less than his humanity, his soul, the essential feminine component in his psyche. And that violated component turns ugly and sits on his shoulder like an ape. It is Lady Macbeth. It is also Hecate in her ugliest guise, as Queen of Night and Hell. When Lady Macbeth invokes the 'murth'ring ministers' she is simply translating into an extreme form, ritualized as witchcraft, the unnatural values by which Macbeth already lives:

> And fill me, from the crown to the toe, top-full
> Of direst cruelty! make thick my blood,
> Stop up th'access and passage to remorse;
> That no compunctious visitings of Nature
> Shake my fell purpose, nor keep peace between
> Th'effect and it!   [I v 42–7]

In the language of Duncan and Banquo natural values are expressed in a natural imagery conspicuously absent from Macbeth's speeches. Dunsinane itself is fair:

> This guest of summer,
> The temple-haunting martlet, does approve,

By his loved mansionry, that the heaven's breath
Smells wooingly here   [I vi 3–6]

and is associated by Duncan and Banquo with all things natural and creative:

> no jutty, frieze,
> Buttress, nor coign of vantage, but this bird
> Hath made his pendent bed, and procreant cradle.
> [I vi 6–8]

But this fair is turned foul by Lady Macbeth:

> The raven himself is hoarse,
> That croaks the fatal entrance of Duncan
> Under my battlements.   [I v 38–40]

When his knife enters Duncan Macbeth makes indeed a 'breach in nature', severing a triple bond, the bond of kinsman, subject and host. The unnatural act troubles the whole natural world, as though 'Night's black agents' had flooded through the breach, overthrowing all natural law:

> And Duncan's horses (a thing most strange and certain)
> Beauteous and swift, the minions of their race,
> Turn'd wild in nature, broke their stalls, flung out,
> Contending 'gainst obedience, as they would make
> War with mankind.
> 'Tis said, they eat each other.   [II iv 14–18]

But even more important is the bond of common humanity:

> Come, seeling Night,
> Scarf up the tender eye of pitiful Day,
> And, with thy bloody and invisible hand,
> Cancel, and tear to pieces, that great bond
> Which keeps me pale!
> [III ii 46–9]

Like Goneril Macbeth disbranches himself from his material sap, and consequently withers: 'my way of life / Is fall'n into the sere, the yellow leaf'. This is exactly what the witches had set out to do: to drain him of the 'milk of human kindness':

> I'll drain him dry as hay:
> Sleep shall neither night nor day

Hang upon his penthouse lid
He shall live a man forbid.
[I iii 18–21]

The more giant-like his tyranny, the more dwarfish his spirit.

Though Macbeth says, with Richard of Gloucester 'evil be thou my good', unlike Richard, he retains a clear sense of the distinction, of the value of the 'Good things of Day' to which he must relinquish his claim:

And that which should accompany old age,
As honour, love, obedience, troops of friends,
I must not look to have.   [V iii 24–6]

Grace itself is defined in similar homely terms:

by the help of these (with Him above
To ratify the work), we may again
Give to our tables meat, sleep to our nights,
Free from our feasts and banquets bloody knives,
Do faithful homage, and receive free honours,
All which we pine for now.   · [III vi 32–7]

Macbeth is fully aware of the destructive potential of the forces he conjures up to serve his ambition, of the risks he is taking with the whole future of the world:

though the treasure
Of Nature's germens tumble all together,
Even till destruction sicken, answer me.
[IV i 58–60]

But what makes him a tragic figure as Richard is not is that word 'treasure', a word from the vocabulary of Cordelia, not Lady Macbeth. It is no mere butcher who is so fully aware of the price he is paying: 'and mine eternal jewel / Given to the common enemy of man'.

Macbeth's ambition is not simply to wear the golden round himself, but to defeat time by founding a dynasty, an infinite succession of future kings. To do this, he must, of course, have a child; but in terms of the controlling symbolism of the play, their potential child is exactly what the Macbeths have killed. In dedicating herself to evil, Lady Macbeth calls the spirits to unsex her and take her milk for gall. Both the Macbeths associate pity with 'a naked new-born babe', Lady Macbeth with her own babe, which she would cheerfully pluck from her breast and dash the brains out. However many children she may have had, she is, poetically, barren. And this imagery is later to erupt into the plot with the slaughter of all Macduff's pretty ones.

Far from defeating time, Macbeth has given himself as hostage to it:

To-morrow, and to-morrow, and to-morrow,
Creeps on this petty pace from day to day,
To the last syllable of recorded time.
[V v 19–21]

and the child he has ripped from the womb returns in the form of Macduff to put the rabid boar out of its misery.

         ❖   ❖   ❖

Cleopatra is Shakespeare's first attempt to present the Goddess undivided. The division is entirely in Antony, for whom she is simultaneously the source of life and the destruction of all the (Roman) qualities by which he has hitherto defined himself and his manhood, so that, with Cleopatra, he 'is and is not Antony'. Of all Shakespeare's tragic heroes, Antony is the one who tries hardest to accept Venus in her totality, to respond appropriately to her unconditional love. But the division of the play between Egypt and Rome corresponds to the deep split which ultimately destroys him. Whenever he is in Egypt, his Roman self pulls at him, and when he is in Rome he longs to return to Egypt where his heart is. In Egypt Antony is valued as lover and gourmet and drinker in a context of peaceful conviviality. In Rome he is valued for his ability to withstand deprivation in a military context.

All values are aligned along this Rome/Egypt axis. Egypt is associated with pleasure, sport, holiday, excess, extravagance, intoxication, conviviality, the heart, and the life of the senses; Rome with pain, business, duty, discipline, austerity, care, factiousness, the head, and the life of calculation. It seems no compromise is possible; each of the opposites demands total commitment; each can be satisfied only at the expense of the other. Again it is a matter of negotiating 'the dangerous shores of will and judgement', or bestriding them like a colossus; but the chasm is too wide, even for Antony.

Rome makes its absolute demands, to which the Roman Antony responds: 'I have not kept my square, but that to come / Shall all be done by the rule' [II iii 6–7]. Rome is the world of the selfish, the realistic, the invulnerable, the public; its stage is history. Egypt is the world of generosity, imagination, timelessness; a world contained in the privacy of Cleopatra's bedroom. But Cleopatra has no sooner said: 'Eternity was in our lips, and eyes, / Bliss in our brows' bent' than Antony interrupts with: 'The strong necessity of time commands / Our services awhile' [I iii 35–43].

Translated into sets, costumes and imagery, these opposites become the ground-pattern of the play's meanings. Egypt is a place of mystery, strangeness, infinite possibilities; Rome of that which is fixed, known, predictable, calculable. The Nile is the source of all life forms, but the Tiber is merely a river on which to launch warships. Rome is aggressively male, Egypt seductively female. Antony in Egypt is seen from Rome as effeminate. Cleopatra appeals to (in both senses) and corresponds with a part of Antony, his anima, the feminine, sensitive, loving, creative side of his nature; a side utterly scorned by the values of Rome, values we have inherited.

Rome is a secular civilization (at least as Shakespeare presents it), without roots, and dedicated to conquering others. It had moved far from the nature- and fertility-religion still practiced in Egypt, where the annual renewal of life depended on that great serpent-mother, the Nile. Wilson Knight gives a long list of birds and aquatic creatures mentioned in Egypt, suggesting the iterrelatedness and sacredness of all forms of life.[*Imperial Theme* 228]. The only non-human creature associated with the Romans is the war-horse – Nature subdued and disciplined to human destructive purposes. Egypt is associated with water and fruitfulness, Rome with land and sterility. In Egypt Antony is valued for his phallus, in Rome for his sword.

Antony cannot rid himself of Caesar, yet is continually thwarted and crossed by him. It is not, in Antony, as in Hamlet, that the opposing elements cancel each other out, producing stalemate, inaction. Rather, Antony oscillates between them, like a ship at the mercy of the tides, alternating between actions motivated by his Roman self (his military triumphs) and his 'Egyptian' self (his sensual riots). He cannot long be satisfied with either the Roman or the Egyptian definition of himself. Each denies and violates half of him. When Rome comes to Egypt in the form of his alter ego Caesar, he has to attempt to be general and lover, Roman and Egyptian, simultaneously. For one glorious moment it seems that he has succeeded:

> Lord of lords,
> O infinite virtue, com'st thou smiling from
> The world's great snare uncaught?
> [IV viii 16–18]

But not even Antony is capable of infinite virtue.

Antony calls Cleopatra 'my serpent of old Nile'. This should not be registered as a mere tease about her wiliness. It is an image which reverberates throughout the play, and becomes part of a whole pattern of related images. It is from this pattern of images, as in all Shakespeare's mature plays, that the deepest meanings of the play, the symbolic or mythic meanings, emerge.

Of all the symbols of ancient Egyptian mythology, the serpent is perhaps the most common and important. At the beginning of the world, the Primordial Snake held all subsequent creation in its folds. It was identified with the Great Goddess, mother of all things. In Egyptian hieroglyphic script the sign for goddess was a rearing cobra. Having neither arms nor legs, the snake seemed to belong not to the animal world, but to a world primeval, even further from the human world. Serpents lived in the dark earth and the depths of the water. They symbolized the energies and dark forces working below the world of appearances. They were worshipped as Water Gods and fertility spirits. The Nile itself, on which the fertility of Egypt depended, was itself a great winding serpent. They were thought to possess the secrets of a lost ancient wisdom. But as gods came to displace goddesses, as Osiris became more important than Isis and became a city rather than an agricultural god, the uncanny forces symbolized by the snake came to be more feared than revered.

The symbolic significance of serpents is much the same in other mythologies. The snake is probably the oldest, commonest and most potent of all theriomorphic images. It is found in Neolithic cultures, where it is also identified with the goddess. The snake is a symbol of vitality and fertility – of life flowing serpentine within all living things, the waters under the earth, the sap of plants, the blood of animals. The snake's ability to renew itself by sloughing its skin suggested the annual renewal of the earth itself. To the early Greeks these limbless, featureless, rapid, vital strips of animate earth or zigzags of the energy of the universe, were not just symbols of but embodiments of *zoë*, raw, undifferentiated life. The snake was sacred to Dionysos, and to Asklepios, god of healing and renewal.

There was also a deeper serpent symbolism which was esoteric, forbidden knowledge. Persephone, in some versions of the myth of her annual descent into the underworld, became a serpent as a bride for the Great Serpent Hades, so that the coupling of serpents came to symbolize the power of life to renew itself. Thus the heart of Nature's mystery was symbolized for the Greeks by the double helix of a pair of entwined mating serpents.

The snake was so closely associated with the goddess that when, throughout Europe and the Near East, worship of the goddess was overthrown by the emerging patriarchal religions, the snake inevitably went down with her. Marduk slaughtered the serpent-goddess Tiamat. The great female goddesses, even Earth herself, were rapidly declining in importance.

When the role of the male in procreation became known, the shape of the snake and its ability to erect itself suggested the fertilizing phallus of the goddess' consort. Thus when the goddess herself ceased to be depicted as a serpent, the serpent continued to be depicted alongside her. But in later ages such images came to be reinterpreted, according to ideological prejudice or conditioning, often with exactly the opposite meaning. There is, for example, the image of a male and female being on either side of a flourishing tree. Associated with the female is a serpent. Originally, the image was interpreted as the Great Goddess, Mother of All Things, through whom the life force (the serpent) becomes the fertile world (Tree of Life). Chief among her creations is the male, who now, as her consort, honours and balances her. The same image appearing in Judeo-Christian culture is interpreted as sinful Eve being seduced by the evil serpent to taste the forbidden fruit and betray her consort, thus spoiling the perfect world which had sprung from the mind of God.

The serpent is the first to receive Yahweh's curse: 'Upon thy belly shalt thou go, and dust shalt thou eat all the days of thy life . . .' (Gen. 3:14). No longer is he to be the ever-rising sap of the Tree of Life, supreme among all others; now he is cursed above cattle and every beast of the field. His former vertical posture, as it would seem in the light of later developments, has been appropriated. . . . [A] serpent of brass stood in the temple of Jerusalem, together with the Asherah, or image of the Mother Goddess, for about 200 years, until King Hezekiah 'did what was right in the sight of the Lord' (2 Kgs. 18:3).   [Baring 500]

The snake is now the Universal Enemy and, through the woman, the origin of all evil.

At the time of Cleopatra, the Goddess had already been dethroned and degraded in Europe and much of the near East, but not yet in Egypt. Nowhere had the process of dematrification gone further than in Rome, a patriarchal society dedicated to the masculine and militaristic virtues of conquest, domination, discipline, efficiency, and every kind of rigidity. To such an extent were all things feminine repressed, including the feminine element in the male psyche, that love was reduced to either the legalistic, in which form it became part of the economic and political structure, or the erotic, in which form it was part of the warrior hero's permitted relaxation, like heavy drinking. Actual women are thus allowed only two roles, either dutiful wife or exciting whore. All conception of the sacred wholeness of the goddess as source of life and death was lost. Octavius would put the goddess in a cage as a public entertainment.

Shakespeare probably knew little of Egyptian mythology. His immediate source, Plutarch, gives barely a hint of it. Yet it was not necessary for Shakespeare to know any mythology in order to make effective and mythologically accurate use in *Antony and Cleopatra* of serpent imagery and such related images as water and mud, for these images are archetypes, that is to say, images which have always occurred with much the same charge of meaning, in widely different cultures, independently of time and place, in dreams, visions, drug-induced hallucinations, and in the imaginations of poets. Serpents, for example, are so common in myths because they are an essential part of the symbolic language of the human psyche. And what they symbolize is life-giving female energies suppressed by the hubristic male intellect into the cellars of the mind, there to turn at last poisonous and destructive in response to rejection and persecution.

In the opening lines Antony's 'dotage' is expressed in terms of Mars disarmed by Venus. Mars stands for the absoluteness of manhood as defined in military terms, and Venus for the absoluteness of womanhood and the claims of love. Each needs the other, and each destroys the other. As Cleopatra triumphs, the god Hercules leaves Antony, and leaves him broken. Nothing in Roman mythology can put him together again, restore his integrity. He dies in disgrace and in error, bungling even his suicide. Cleopatra is , finally, very like Venus at the end of *Venus and Adonis*. The man she loves has been unable to meet the demands of her love. His betrayal of her draws out the destructive side of her nature, turns her serpent power to poison. But I am clearly not describing here the end of the play as we have it; rather, how the play might have ended had it been written in the spirit of *Troilus and Cressida.*

Cleopatra is Venus only in fancy dress, as a tribute to Antony and the mythology he is familiar with. Her real mythic significance emerges from her native Egyptian mythology, where she is, as she herself claims, Isis, mother of the gods, and wife of the god-king fertility hero Osiris, whose fate is to be torn apart, then reintegrated through her. But the Romans no longer recognized the absolute divinity of the great goddess; in their consciousness, as in the Judaic and the Christian, she had become the great whore. In their terms, Cleopatra is no more than a gypsy and a strumpet. Sylvia B. Perera writes:

> Most of the powers once held by the goddesses have lost their connection to women's life: the embodied, playful, passionately erotic feminine; the powerful, independent, self-willed feminine; and the ambitious, regal, many-sided feminine. . . . Thus constricted, the joy of the feminine has been denigrated as mere frivolity, her joyful lust demeaned as whorishness, or sentimentalized and maternalized, her vitality channelled into duty and obedience.

Cleopatra is the magical doorway into life. Wilson Knight says of her:

> In Shakespeare woman is both the divine ideal and the origin of evil: because she is more eternal than man, more mysterious, the mysterious origin of life. On that dualism the past agonies revolve. Woman, rather than man, is the creative essence, the one harmony, from which man is separated, to which he aspires. On her ultimate serenity and sweetness, not denying but overswamping her evil, depends the sanity of religion, and the universal beauty. [op.cit.316–17]

Though we, like Shakespeare, must find heart more attractive than head, Egypt more attractive than Rome, Cleopatra than Caesar, Shakespeare by no means devalues Antony's military exploits, nor does he always glamorize his erotic life. It is glamorous, almost divine in its excess, but it is also, simultaneously, reducible to a matter of drunkenness and gaudy nights. Antony himself, at his lowest point, utters the play's strongest condemnation of it:

> the wise gods seal our eyes;
> In our own filth dip our clear judgements; make us
> Adore our errors; laugh at's, while we strut
> To our confusion. [III xiii 112–15]

In *Troilus and Cressida* that would have been the last word, but it is not here. In spite of the worst that can be said against it, there is also a sense, which grows throughout the play, in which Cleopatra mysteriously redeems what to Roman consciousness is most vile:

> For vilest things
> Become themselves in her, that the holy priests
> Bless her, when she is riggish.
>
> [II ii 238–40]

Joyful lust is sacred.

After his death, Cleopatra is able to substitute for the torn Antony a regenerate man embodying the wholeness he never achieved in life, a man whose capacity for fullness and joy in life integrates human life with that of the non-human world and triumphs over death:

> For his bounty,
> There was no winter in't: an autumn 'twas
> That grew the more by reaping: his delights
> Were dolphin-like, they show'd his back above
> The element they lived in.   [V ii 86–90]

We now recognize over a hundred elements. In Shakespeare's day there were, and had been since the early Greeks, only four, earth, air, fire and water. Earth and water were regarded as gross elements which bound the nature of man to that of beasts. Air and fire were refined and linked man's composition to that of the spirits. The orthodox attitude, supported by Christianity, was that men should disown and suppress their grosser elements and do all they could to express only the finer. But there were those, including Shakespeare, who believed that man's task was rather to achieve a balance, a harmony of the potentially discordant elements of which he was composed; and that to fail to do so was to give oneself as a hostage to fate.

To the male intellect which aspires to a life all air and fire (that is renown and conquest), earth and water, the dominion of the serpent, are spurned as mere mud from which men have painfully dragged themselves (rising above women in the process), and Antony's lapse is a disgusting slide back into man's first slime. But Cleopatra looks back on Antony in his brief moment of perfect balance as a dolphin, simultaneously a creature of air and water.

Life is no longer in this play seen as a doomed battle against 'injurious time' and oblivion. Shakespeare's understanding of Egyptian religion, or the meaning with which he invests it for the purposes of this play, is very close to the meaning of Etruscan religion as Lawrence deduced it from the tomb-paintings:

In the tombs we see it; throes of wonder and vivid feeling throbbing over death. Man moves naked and glowing through the universe. Then comes death: he dives into the sea, he departs into the underworld. . . . But the sea the people knew. The dolphin leaps in and out of it suddenly, as a creature that suddenly exists, out of nowhere. He was not: and lo! there he is! The dolphin which gives up the sea's rainbows only when he dies. Out he leaps; then, with a head-dive, back again he plunges into the sea. He is so much alive, he is like the phallus carrying the fiery spark of procreation down into the wet darkness of the womb. The diver does the same, carrying like a phallus his small hot spark into the deeps of death. And the sea will give up her dead like dolphins that leap out and have the rainbow within them.   [*Mornings* 150–1]

Thus the sea gave up the dead Osiris to Isis in search.

Historically, the Romans did accuse the life-loving Etruscans of sexual viciousness. The Romans aspired to clear judgements in their doomed masculine pursuit of perfection. In Egypt nothing is clear, everything muddied, for their life is complete and does not disown its miraculous origins in the slime:

> The higher Nilus swells,
> The more it promises: as it ebbs, the seedsman
> Upon the slime and ooze scatters his grain,
> And shortly comes to harvest.   [II vii 20–3]

This is the context in which Cleopatra envisages her death, as preferable to life in Rome:

>   Rather a ditch in Egypt
> Be gentle grave unto me, rather in Nilus' mud
> Lay me stark-nak'd, and let the water-flies
> Blow me into abhorring.   [V ii 57–60]

Cleopatra here becomes the Black Goddess, as in Peter Redgrove's poem 'The Idea of Entropy at Maenporth Beach', where 'the mud spatters with rich seed and raging pollens' as the white woman enters black mud for earth's blessing. And the abhorrent crawling things, as the Ancient Mariner was to discover, are also sacred.

As in all tragedy the ending is a mixture of positive and negative elements. In terms of that part of our consciousness (and Shakespeare's) which regards death as final, we might say that no creative marriage has been possible in life between the mighty opposites of Rome and Egypt. Cleopatra, the Divine Mother, puts to her breast not a baby but an asp. Instead of milk flowing from her breast poison flows into it. Yet death cannot negate what the play has in human terms affirmed: that, in the last analysis, living one's life, participating in the life-processes of eating and drinking and making love and having children and relating to other people and to the non-human world in a spirit of joy is more important than any amount of power and conquest and male self-glorification; that to uphold such values is not simply play or childishness or effeminacy, but requires a total commitment, a willingness to sacrifice a great deal for it, and the final recognition that death is not a defeat and an ending, but another of nature's sacred processes; that participation in it can be a triumph and a blessing.

Having committed themselves to each other, and to a 'better life' in death, Antony and Cleopatra, like Lear and Cordelia in prison, are lifted into an almost godlike spiritual condition (symbolized by Cleopatra lifting the dying Antony to the top of her monument), from which vantage point it can be seen that Caesar is paltry, 'an ass unpolicied', and all things political are dwarfed into insignificance.

By the time we reach the ending the reader sensitive to the imagery has been conditioned to recognize also a mythic plane of meaning on which death is by no means final. Antony calls to Cleopatra to stay for him:

> Where souls do couch on flowers, we'll hand in hand,
> And with our sprightly port make the ghosts gaze:
> Dido, and her Aeneas, shall want troops
> And all the haunt be ours.   [IV xiv 50–4]

Unconsciously, Antony reunites the abandoned queen with her betrayer in the Elysian Fields, where Aeneas is given a second chance to accept Dido's unconditional love. 'I will be a bridegroom in my death' [IV xiv 100] is taken up by Cleopatra: 'Husband, I come: / Now to that name, my courage prove my title!' [V ii 286–7]. She claims the title not only of bride, but also of mother: : 'Dost thou not see my baby at my breast, / That sucks the nurse asleep?' [V ii 308–9]. (One of the several Egyptian serpent-headed goddesses, Renenet, was the goddess of suckling.) Behind the final tableau stands Isis giving new life to the dead Osiris and giving birth to his son Horus who will grow to be the renewed Osiris. The Goddess is able at last to achieve her completeness assuming those aspects denied her by Rome, and, until now, by Antony – Divine Mother and Sacred Bride.

Hughes traces in detail Antony's role as Osiris to Cleopatra's Isis. Here is his account of the ending:

> What now remains, for this Osirian Antony, is for him to free himself,
> wholly and finally, from that obsolete Herculean Roman Antony, and
> emerge as his true self, the universal love god, consort of the Goddess of
> Complete Being, in so far as that can be incarnated in the body of the
> middle-aged Roman warrior, lover of a middle-aged, reckless, fearful
> queen . . . While the drama portrays the self-destruction of the great
> Roman Antony on the tragic plane, it becomes, on the transcendental
> plane, a theophany, the liberation of Antony's Osirian Divine Love nature,

under the 'magical' influence of the completeness of Cleopatra's. The play
. . . begins with the love god fully formed but unacknowledged, trapped
within the self-ignorant, military Herculean *bon viveur*, who is still
confidently wrestling for political control of the Roman world. It ends
with the crushed, empty armour of the former Herculean warrior, like an
empty chrysalis, while the liberated love god, like an iridescent new
winged being, lies in the lap of the Goddess, his love 'total and
unconditional', reunited beyond life and death (in the high tomb) with
the adoring Goddess.   [*Shakespeare* 316–7]

This image may seem less far-fetched when we think of Coriolanus dying in
his belated attempt to emerge from the armoured chrysalis in which his
mother has locked him, (she had no doubt tought him, as she now teaches
his son, to mammock gilded butterflies); of the emergence of life from a coffin
in *Pericles*; and from a stone statue in *The Winter's Tale*.

8 SHAKESPEARE 3 – THE CRIME AGAINST CALIBAN

In 1608 Shakespeare's company acquired a second theatre, the Blackfriars, and his subsequent plays were perhaps written for it (though *The Winter's Tale* was first performed at the Globe). It gave him the opportunity to write for a more intimate and judicious audience than the audience at the Globe with its 'barren quantity of spectators'. It seems that he welcomed the chance to abandon all forms of realism (including psychological realism) in favour of mythic or folk-tale structures to carry meanings almost entirely poetic. The first two experiments in the new mode, *Pericles* and *Cymbeline*, were not entirely successful; but Shakespeare's persistence with it paid rich dividends in *The Winter's Tale* and *The Tempest*.

A great deal of the meaning is carried by the imagery. For example, there is the recurring image of physical contact between male and female. It is exactly such contact between Hermione and Polyxenes which triggers Leontes' psychic explosion. The mere taking of hands his disordered imagination extends to 'leaning cheek to cheek', 'meeting noses' and 'hanging about his neck'. This last phrase reminds us of the difficulty Hamlet had with his mother's physicality and sexuality even in relation to his father ('Why, she would hang on him / As if increase of appetite had grown / By what it fed on'). Against this sickness the play invites us to set Perdita's innocent venery ('No, like a bank, for love to lie and play on') and the mature advice of Leontes' courtiers:

> What holier than, for royalty's repair,
> For present comfort and for future good,
> To bless the bed of majesty again
> With a sweet fellow to't.   [V i 29–32]

The final reconciliation of Leontes and Hermione has no hint that at their age the hey-day in the blood is tame and young affects defunct:

> She embraces him!
> She hangs about his neck!
>   [V iii 111–2]

Leontes commits the primal crime against Nature, against the woman who has given him total unconditional love, and against his own anima ('the wrong I did myself'), that is his capacity for love, forgiveness and acceptance. The wronged female part of himself is objectified in his daughter, who is, in Mahood's words, 'returned by Apollo to the education of Nature'. At their reunion Leontes greets her, before he knows she is his daughter, with the auspicious words: 'Welcome hither / As is the spring to th'earth'. His crime is yet another variant of the hubristic male aspiration to transcend body, time and process.

In the folk-tale mode it is no longer necessary, as it was in tragedy, that everything must be paid for, or at least that it should be paid for by intolerable suffering, total breakdown, and death. The restoration of Lear by his daughter is a precious moment when fatal time is intersected by the timelessness and joy of acceptance; but it soon resumes its sway, and the survivors are hardly confident of their power to redeem it. Lear's progress from rash majesty to madness to humble joy occupies a few weeks. The same progress in Leontes, translated to the unhurried time-span of folk-tale, lasts sixteen years.

Shakespeare's main source for *The Winter's Tale* was Greene's *Pandosto*, whose subtitle was *The Triumph of Time*. In early Shakespeare such a phrase could only have signified the triumph of time over life, youth, beauty, value. But at the very centre of this play Time the Destroyer (tragedy) turns his hourglass and becomes Time the Revealer, the Healer, the Restorer and the Begetter (comedy). The turning of the hour-glass is but a visual enactment, a spelling out and underlining of what the old shepherd had said a few lines earlier: 'thou met'st with things dying, I with things new-born'. Birth, growth and maturity are as much the work of time as decay and death. Time had earlier been jolted into its destructive mode by Leontes' headlong acceleration of normal time, giving it no possibility of operating in any other way.

The triumph of time in this play is to return that which has been violated by man to normality, health, sanity:

> Time is allowed an authentic scope, evident alike in the 'wrinkled' face of Hermione (against the human wish to arrest time in a remembered perfection) and in the grief which Time will not assuage . . . But time has allowed a new generation to grow to maturity; time has taught patience and acceptance.
> [Lawlor 301]

Thus time itself functions as a bestower of grace. When the artificial gap between body and spirit is closed, life needs no straining for grace beyond itself. Every common act, speaking, singing, dancing, buying, selling, giving, praying, 'ordering your affairs', radiates spirit:

> Each your doing,
> So singular in each particular,
> Crowns what you are doing, in the present deeds,
> That all your acts are queens.   [IV iv 143–6]

In 'Easter 1916' Yeats shows how the 'casual comedy' of ordinary life can be transfigured by tragedy and lifted out of time, but simultaneously turned to stone. Here Shakespeare shows how tragedy can be transcended by comedy. Stone becomes flesh, participates once more in the flow of life.

Tragedy is largely subjective – a projection onto Nature and the world of the diseased or defective psyche of the protagonist. Comedy is temporal, communal and seasonal; all that cornucopia of rich human and natural values celebrated in the sheepshearing.

The world of the sheepshearing is no Eden or Arcady. Perdita distributes 'flowers of winter' as well as summer. The shepherd's wife is dead, but vividly present in his memory, 'her face o' fire / With labour, and the thing she took to quench it'. And an important part of the new-born life of the second half of the play is Autolycus. For the new life is not always 'gracious'; it can be wayward and anarchic. Mahood speaks of 'the folly of regarding everything in Nature as subject to moral judgement'. In the first half of the play 'blood' had meant 'lust' as it did for Othello:

> Now, in Autolycus's song about 'the red blood reigns in the winters pale',
> it represents a passion as natural and inevitable as the sap that rises in
> spring, to be accepted as philosophically as the old shepherd endures the
> ways of 'these boylde-braines of nineteene, and two and twenty'.
> Autolycus is an English coney-catcher, and his daffodil and doxy belong
> less to the classical Arcadia than to Herrick's Devonshire, where
> Christianity has absorbed much of an older cult, and if there is a Puritan
> he too sings psalms to hornpipes. According to Blake's paradox, the
> return of spiritual vision by which what now seemed finite and corrupt
> would appear infinite and holy was to be accompanied by 'an
> improvement of sensual enjoyment'; and such enjoyment is felt
> throughout the scenes in Bohemia.   [224]

Autolycus represents the roguish element which will always escape the rules, which will pop up again however often it is knocked down, which laughs at the posturing hero; what the Greeks acknowledged in their satyr plays, what the citizens of Windsor acknowledged in Sir John, what Prospero will have to learn to acknowledge in Caliban.

❖   ❖   ❖

Shakespeare's last play can be read as a metaphor (in poetry, magic, music and masque) for his own nature, the elements of which are divided into a cast of characters both natural and spiritual, a last supreme attempt to impose a resolution upon those conflicts which had fuelled all the great works.

Miranda's first speech is a strong condemnation of Prospero for using his Art to cause the shipwreck she has just witnessed :

> Had I been any god of power, I would
> Have sunk the sea within the earth, or ere
> It should the good ship so have swallow'd, and
> The fraughting souls within her.
>   (I ii. 10–13)

119

She is moved entirely by sympathy for the victims: 'O, I have suffered / With those that I saw suffer!' (5–6). Prospero comforts her with the assurance that there is 'not so much perdition as an hair / Betid to any creature in the vessel' (29–30), and we normally assume at this point that the 'virtue of compassion' is as strong in Prospero as in his daughter, and that the wreck is but the first of the trials which the evildoers must undergo for their own eventual redemption. An actor of serene dignity such as Gielgud would already by this point have convinced us, as much by his bearing, stage-presence and distinguished cadences as by what he actually says, that Prospero is a god-like being, totally in control of himself and everyone else, operating, like the Duke in *Measure for Measure* 'like power Divine' upon the lesser mortals around him. This was for centuries the traditional and orthodox reading of the play. But Prospero does not have to be like that. In Ninagawa's 1988 production Haruhiko Jo played Prospero with such smouldering hatred that one felt that he had preserved his enemies from the wreck only to prolong their suffering and to stage a confrontation before executing his final revenge. And this reading is, I suggest, more faithful to the text.

There is no character in Shakespeare more frequently identified with Shakespeare himself than Prospero. Perhaps Prospero is the most thinly-disguised appearance of the dramatist in his plays. But to say that Prospero *is* Shakespeare is not to exculpate him. Angelo was also Shakespeare. Is Prospero as white as he himself believes? What are his motives? Is his attempt to redeem Nature successful, or even, in the last analysis, desirable? What I want to do here is to outline some of the points which can be made against Prospero and in favour of Caliban; to ask to what extent Prospero fits the identikit of the criminal which we have derived from the earlier works.

In his introduction to the 1954 Arden edition (from which all my quotations are taken), Frank Kermode offers a summary of what he takes to be the play's central theme:

> The main opposition is between the worlds of Prospero's Art, and
> Caliban's Nature. Caliban is the core of the play; like the shepherd in
> formal pastoral, he is the natural man against whom the cultivated man is
> measured. But we are not offered a comparison between a primitive
> innocence in nature and a sophisticated decadence, any more than we
> are in *Comus*. Caliban represents (at present we must over-simplify)
> nature without benefit of nurture; Nature, opposed to an Art which is
> man's power over the created world and over himself; nature divorced
> from grace, or the senses without the mind. He differs from Iago and
> Edmund in that he is a 'naturalist' by nature, without access to the art
> that makes love out of lust; the restraints of temperance he cannot, in his
> bestiality, know; to the beauty of the nurtured he opposes a monstrous
> ugliness; ignorant of gentleness and humanity, he is a savage and capable
> of all ill; he is born to slavery, not to freedom, of a vile and not a noble

union; and his parents represent an evil natural magic which is the
antithesis of Prospero's benevolent Art.   [xxiv–xxv]

Prospero has been practicing magic for decades before the start of the
play: for what purpose? Until the ship carrying his enemies is accidentally
brought within his sphere, his operations have no bearing on the loss of his
dukedom, which, in any case, he had half-surrendered for their sake. Our
information about Prospero's magical activities prior to the beginning of the
play comes largely from the speech in which he renounces his Art [V i 33–57].
This famous speech, beginning 'Ye elves of hills, brooks, standing lakes, and
groves', derives directly from a passage in Ovid's *Metamorphoses* spoken by
the black witch Medea. The same passage was put by Middleton into the mouth
of Hecate in a play called *The Witch*. Kermode claims that 'only those elements
which are consistent with "white" magic are taken over for Prospero' (149).
This is not so:

> graves at my command
> Have wak'd their sleepers, op'd, and let 'em forth
> By my so potent Art.

What had been his benevolent purpose in raising the dead? There is not a
hint of benevolence in the entire speech. Dimming the sun, calling forth
mutinous winds, setting 'roaring war' between sea and sky, shaking the promontory, plucking up great trees, is doing violence upon the natural order,
exercising power for its own sake, or for the sake of playing god: 'and rifted
Jove's stout oak with his own bolt'. Nor is it true, as Kermode says, that
Prospero, unlike Sycorax who worked with demons, works only with higher
intelligences. The elves are 'demi-puppets'; and to persecute Caliban Prospero
employs goblins which are allowed to be active only in the hours of darkness.
    What has Prospero done with his twelve years on the island? Parasitic
on Caliban's knowledge of 'the qualities o' th'isle', he retires to his cell (having
one subject to whom can be left the provision of physical necessities) and
lives much as he had done before. The island exists for Prospero only as a
place of exile and a source of nature-spirits which can be coerced into serving
his purposes. He seeks total domination over nature and natural processes.
He has continued his studies in both 'rough' (i.e. black) magic, and in the
refined magic of alchemy (a not unusual combination which had helped to get
alchemy a bad name) developing both into a potent Art. But there is nothing
on the island on which he can exercise his potency, nothing more important
for his spirits to do but pinch Caliban. He would like to be able to use his
black magic to punish his enemies, but they are beyond his sphere of influence.
And his alchemical project is stalled for lack of a suitable partner for his
daughter in the *coniunctio*, the chymical wedding which must be the next
stage of the work. Meanwhile he has neglected his daughter, or, as he would

say, in care of her has kept her in ignorance of the world beyond the island, seeing no way of preserving her purity in a wicked world but the combination of her ignorance and his protective magic.

Prospero seems to have cultivated magic for the purpose of becoming, in Miranda's words, a 'god of power', and that magic is as black as Faust's or Sycorax's unless the power is sought from the first for purely benevolent purposes. Benevolent towards whom? Towards his enemies? There is no suggestion that Prospero had dreamed that he would ever see them again; and when he does, his attitude to them shows no trace of benevolence until the fifth act. Towards Miranda? He has protected her from Caliban, but could probably have done that without magic. He selects Ferdinand (who is totally unknown to him) as her husband out of pure political expediency, and overrides their true feelings by having Ariel bewitch them:

> At the first sight
> They have chang'd eyes. Delicate Ariel,
> I'll set thee free for this.   [I ii 443–5]

Towards Ariel? He releases Ariel from the cloven pine only on condition that Ariel serve him, against his true nature, and threatens to do to Ariel again what Sycorax had done if he so much as murmurs against his servitude. According to Caliban all the lesser spirits hate Prospero as much as he does.

Towards Caliban Prospero had originally behaved with a show of 'human care' and 'nurture', but with the same assumption of superiority which had been rationalized as benevolence by the colonists in the New World, who, calling the natives savages because their religion was not Christianity, their civilization unlike European civilization, their language not English or Spanish, their dress and appearance and customs outlandish, denied them full humanity, freedom, and any title to their own lands, and exported them to England, dead or alive, to be exhibited at fairs. The possibility was debated that the Red Indians might not be human at all, but humanoid monsters created as slaves for humanity.

The isle was indeed Caliban's. He retains an affinity with it never matched by Prospero, who quits it as soon as he is able. Caliban's 'gabble' was presumably able to refer to the bigger light that burns by day and the lesser that burns by night if not to say 'sun' and 'moon'. There is a comic contrast between the brutish Caliban's ineligibility as a mate for Miranda, and the cultural appropriateness of Ferdinand's response to her first words to him: 'My language! heavens!'. Because Caliban does not behave in accordance with Prospero's puritanical code of honour, he is denied all human rights, enslaved and persecuted. Prospero does not kill him or even drive him away. He cannot do without him:

> We cannot miss him: he does make our fire,
> Fetch in our wood, and serves in offices
> That profit us.   [I ii 313–15]

Visiting Caliban, provoking and reviling and tormenting him, seems to constitute a form of entertainment for Prospero, like bear-baiting.

Kermode defines Art as 'man's power over the created world and over himself'. We are no longer as likely as in 1954 to find what man has done to the created world and to himself over the 3000 years of his domination as something to be proud of, and are perhaps more likely to admire Caliban's sensitive response to and adaptation to the natural environment. There is nothing exclusively contemporary about taking the side of the native against the colonizer. In our awareness of the destructiveness of Western colonialism we are only returning to ideas which were commonplace in the sixteenth century. Reports from the New World differed widely in their descriptions of the Indians; to some they were demons or savage beasts, to others unfallen man. In his essay 'On the Caniballs' (translated by Florio in 1603) Montaigne argued that 'there is nothing in that nation, that is either barbarous or savage, unlesse men call that barbarisme which is not common to them', and that even if there were genuine barbarism, this was nothing in comparison with the barbarism of those who presumed to 'civilize' them.

Shakespeare himself in his earlier works (all of which deal with the art/nature conflict) had usually taken the side of Nature, from *Venus and Adonis* to *The Winter's Tale*, where Perdita rejects Polixenes' argument that art, itself a product of nature, can improve on nature. Perdita's reverence for 'great creating nature' echoes Montaigne's for 'our great and puissant mother Nature', and her rejection of 'our carnations and streak'd gillivors' as 'nature's bastards' is a paraphrase of his argument in defence of the natives of the New World:

> They are even savage, as we call those fruits wilde, which nature of her selfe, and of her ordinarie progresse hath produced: whereas indeed, they are those which our selves have altered by our artificiall devices, and diverted from their common order, we should rather term savage. In those are the true and most profitable vertues, and naturall properties most lively and vigorous, which in these we have bastardized, applying them to the pleasure of our corrupted taste. . . . There is no reason, arte should gaine the point of honour of our great and puissant mother Nature. We have so much by our inventions, surcharged the beauties and riches of hir workes, that we have altogether over-choaked hir: yet where-ever hir puritie shineth, she makes our vaine, and frivolous enterprises wonderfully ashamed.

The art to which Perdita refers is cultivation, whereas Prospero's Art (always with the capital) is supernatural, occult, and implies a spurning of the merely natural and earthy. Caliban represents the dark side of Nature, which Prospero seeks to exorcise, and of human nature, which he condemns in others but refuses to acknowledge in himself.

Certainly Caliban is brutish. He is also presented as both physically and morally ugly. This ugliness is usually assumed to derive from his evil parentage, but there is much to suggest that Caliban turns ugly, as Heathcliff does, in response to rejection and persecution.

The very name of Caliban, an anagram of canibal (Shakespeare's spelling of cannibal), and close to Cariban – a native of the West Indies – must have alerted many of Shakespeare's audience to the relevance of Montaigne's much-discussed essay, and the whole topical debate on the morality of colonialism. But Caliban is not simply an American Indian. He is also very much in the tradition of the wodwo, or wild man of the woods, so familiar in English art and folklore of the thirteenth and fourteenth centuries. (One tapestry depicts a wodwo abducting a woman from a castle.) One of Shakespeare's earliest editors, Malone, in his edition of 1790, wrote that Caliban's dress, 'which doubtless was originally prescribed by the poet himself and has been continued, I believe, since his time, is a large bear skin, or the skin of some other animal; and he is usually represented with long shaggy hair'. This tradition is still alive in the theatre.

The wodwo was itself a descendent of the satyr, with whom Caliban has much in common. The satyr had abundant hair and beard, broad nose, large pointed ears, horse tail, hooves, and large, permanently erect phallus. He represented natural as opposed to civilized man, everything man shares with the beasts. His characteristics were naive curiosity and credulousness, acquisitiveness, lust, drunkenness, lying, boasting and cowardice. He was completely gross and amoral. Yet every Greek tragedian competing in the Great Dionysia was obliged to follow his three tragedies with a satyr play. Neither in the satyr plays nor elsewhere was the satyr presented with disgust. Rather the satyr plays seem to have been celebrations of the life of the body at its most basic as a way of balancing the tragic vision with its relentless progress through suffering towards death. In the words of Tony Harrison:

> This journey back into the service of the presiding god [Dionysus] seems
> to be paralleled by the release of the spirit back into the life of the senses
> at the end of the tragic journey. . . . The sensual relish for life and its
> affirmation must have been the spirit of the conclusion of the four plays.
> The satyrs are included in the wholeness of the tragic vision. they are not
> forgotten or forced out by pseudo 'refinement'.   [*Trackers* xi]

In *The Trackers of Oxyrhyncus*, Harrison's completion of a fragmentary satyr play by Sophocles, Silenus, the leader of the satyrs, tells a story of such Apollonian 'refinement'. Marsyas, a satyr, found a flute and learned to play it so well that he competed against Apollo's lyre. Apollo had him flayed alive for his presumption. Perhaps there is here a deeply submerged link between Caliban's surprising responsiveness to music and the cramps and pinchings to which Prospero subjects him:

124

'How can *he* be a virtuoso on the flute?
Look at the hoofs on him. He's half a brute!'
His one and only flaw. He showed that flutes
sound just as beautiful when breathed into by 'brutes'.
It confounded the categories of high and low
when Caliban could outplay Prospero.

[*Trackers* 64]

By Shakespeare's time the tragic and comic visions had been wholly separated out by dualism, the satyrs permanently excluded from the world of Apollonian high culture. The animal man had to be converted into 'civilized' man, exterminated, or enslaved, whether in the colonies or in the individual psyche. Shakespeare had to rediscover the language of wholeness, even at the cost of relinquishing the high ground of his own rhetorical mastery in the great anthology pieces. The Othello music is discredited; the silence of Cordelia vindicated. Perdita repudiates art itself as the rape of nature. Once Apollo is silenced, the satyrs re-emerge from their darkness.

Prospero's style throughout is lofty and rhetorical, rising at times to a godlike perspective:

The cloud-capp'd towers, the gorgeous palaces,
The solemn temples, the great globe itself,
Yea, all which it inherit, shall dissolve,
And, like this insubstantial pageant faded,
Leave not a rack behind. We are such stuff
As dreams are made on; and our little life
Is rounded with a sleep.   [IV i 152–8]

It has no truck with the ordinary traffic of life, the casual comedy. Preoccupied with his insubstantial pageant he quite forgets the substantial plot against him (as he had earlier, preoccupied with higher things, failed to detect his brother's plot against him). His style is literary and self-conscious. It does not stoop to the details of life in the body and the natural world. Not only log-bearing, but living itself (if living is a delicate awareness of and subtle relatedness to the rest of life) can be left to his servant Caliban.

In comparison, Caliban's verse (and it is significant that, unlike the other 'low' characters, he almost always speaks verse) is virtually without style:

I prithee let me bring thee where crabs grow;
And I with my long nails will dig thee pig-nuts;
Show thee a jay's nest, and instruct thee how
To snare the nimble marmoset. I'll bring thee
To clustering filberts, and sometimes I'll get thee
Young scamels from the rock.   [II ii 180–5]

Wilson Knight comments:

> Whether as spirit-powers or as their ordinary selves, he is one with
> earth's creatures; 'all the qualities o' th' isle' come to us unmediated by
> any particular 'style' of expression; or we might say we have the
> perfection of style in its apparent absence. In Caliban's words we shall
> find a close-up of nature, and this apparent closeness seems to be unique
> in Shakespeare's nature poetry. He has always a vast resource at his
> disposal. There are nature-spirits in *A Midsummer Night's Dream* and
> there is Perdita's flower dialogue in *The Winter's Tale*. His tragedies have
> elemental tempests, and references to fierce animals, lion, bear, wolf and
> boar. There is pretty nearly every sort of nature, located or atmospheric,
> in reference or setting; but all are, in the comparison I am now making,
> used for literary or dramatic purpose, and so in a way distanced. Even the
> stallion in *Venus and Adonis*, the boar and hunted hare, yes, and the
> wonderful snail, might be called descriptive triumphs and are to that
> extent lacking in spontaneity. I am thinking on the lines of Tolstoy's final
> tenets, wherein he repudiated all artistic sophistication. Caliban's nature
> has an actuality beyond the literary; he speaks as one embedded in it, as
> sophisticated man cannot be.   [*Dimensions* 113–4]

Wilson Knight compares this kind of consciousness with that of the American
Indian, of which Shakespeare had (with the help of Montaigne) got an inkling
from the first reports:

> There was normally no hunting for pleasure and no wanton destruction of
> arboreal life. In human affairs they could both inflict and endure
> suffering; they seem to have been unique among races in acceptance,
> without sentimentality, of the conditions of incarnate life, both its
> wonders and its agonies. Caliban's words breath natural kinship,
> sympathy and understanding; but also mastery, through man's place in
> the created scheme.   [116]

Prospero does take pleasure in hunting, and, like some of the settlers, in
hunting men. He turns his spirits into hounds and sets them gleefully on
Caliban. Their names are telling: 'Fury, Fury! There, Tyrant, there!' [IV i 260].
It is hardly surprising that, with such a master, Caliban should turn vicious
and long to 'batter his skull, or paunch him with a stake, / Or cut his wezand'.

✣ ✣ ✣

I have used the word 'puritanical' of Prospero, and should like to return to
that; to look, for example, at the speech in which Prospero warns Ferdinand
not to anticipate the marriage ceremony. It is not the warning itself which is
noteworthy so much as the unnecessary extremity of the language, the hys-
teria almost, with which he expresses his horror at the unsanctified act:

If thou dost break her virgin-knot before
All sanctimonious ceremonies may
With full and holy rite be minister'd,
No sweet aspersion shall the heavens let fall
To make this contract grow; but barren hate,
Sour-ey'd disdain and discord shall bestrew
The union of your bed with weeds so loathly
That you shall hate it both.   [IV i 15–22]

As if that were not already too much, Prospero returns obsessively to the matter a few lines later, in lines which echo Hamlet's to his mother:

do not give dalliance
Too much the rein: the strongest oaths are straw
To th' fire i' th' blood: be more abstemious,
Or else, good night your vow!   [IV i 51–4]

This provokes Ferdinand to a ridiculous response:

The white cold virgin snow upon my heart
Abates the ardour of my liver. [IV i 55–6]

Unusually, sexuality has had little overt role in this play. But Prospero's determination that it should not rear its ugly head shows that it is a problem for him. He fears Venus as though she were Sycorax. He wants to refine Nature to bring it into alignment with arbitrary and exclusive human values. Or, insofar as his art is alchemical, the island is the crucible in which, now that the missing element, the groom, has become available, he prepares a chymical wedding. One particle of impurity would wreck the whole experiment, now nearing its goal. The experiment requires a very low temperature. The wedding is hedged about with vows, prohibitions, ceremonies. If sexuality is to be magically transformed into spirituality, courtship must be as circumscribed and codified as a game of chess.

Prospero sets up, as it were, a replay of *Venus and Adonis*, carefully rigged by magic to produce the opposite outcome. Venus is excluded, prohibited, replaced by Diana. The natural man in Ferdinand is put in a straight-jacket of prohibitions which almost stops his blood flowing. The result is a wooden tableau of contrived harmony which we cannot imagine surviving transplantation to the real world. To preserve such purity outside his laboratory, in Naples or Milan, he would have to geld and spay all the youth of the city.

There immediately follows the masque, performed by spirits pretending to be goddesses, 'temperate nymphs' and 'sunburn'd sicklemen'. The most important of the 'goddesses' is Ceres, goddess of *cultivated* nature, of husbandry. She returns to the same theme. Since Prospero must have written the script, or be unconsciously feeding the spirits their lines, he is elevating his obsession into a magic ritual. Ceres says that she has forsworn the 'scandal'd company' of Venus and her son, since they helped 'dusky Dis', king of the underworld, to drag down to his kingdom her daughter Proserpina or Persephone. Iris reassures her that Venus and Cupid have been successfully excluded from these rites:

> Here thought they to have done
> Some wanton charm upon this man and maid,
> Whose vows are, that no bed-right shall be paid
> Till Hymen's torch be lighted: but in vain.   [IV i 94–7]

This scenario repeats a pattern from the main body of the play, where Prospero's daughter has been threatened with rape, where he sets himself against a mother and son (Sycorax and Caliban) who stand for uncontrolled natural energies in alliance with a dark underworld deity, Setebos. The masque is an attempt to rewrite the Persephone myth, so that Persephone escapes the attentions of dusky Dis, need not acknowledge the darkness, and it is perpetual summer. It is also an attempt to filter out all those impurities which might lead to tragedy. Passion is eliminated by strict rules, as in a game of chess. Standing behind the masque (and behind the whole play) is, as Hughes has demonstrated, the story of Dido and Aeneas:

> A central mythic feature of this story, in Virgil's telling, is that Dido's fatal
> passion is dramatized as the goddess Venus' victory over the goddess
> Juno, while her actual death is described as a ritual ministered by Juno,
> Iris and Proserpina.   [*Shakespeare* 419]

Prospero is trying to conjure for his daughter an unfallen world. Ferdinand responds appropriately:

> Let me live here ever;
> So rare a wonder'd father and a wise
> Makes this place Paradise.
>   [IV i 123–5]

But a moment later the vision is rudely shattered ('*to a strange, hollow, and confused noise, they heavily vanish*'). Prospero remembers 'that foul conspiracy Of the beast Caliban' (described by Hughes as 'the emissary of that part of the Goddess which cannot be assimilated . . . what has been excluded from the ego's life' [498]. Prospero can exclude Venus from the nuptials, but only at the cost of ensuring that if she cannot attend as an honoured guest bearing gifts, she will return covertly, from underground, bringing curses. No Art is sufficiently potent or perfect to exclude the goddess totally and permanently.

128

By controlling the moon and tides, Sycorax must also control the menstrual cycle in women. And 'blue-eyed' is a description often applied to Venus. In other words, Sycorax is Venus as she appears to the distorted puritanical vision of Prospero, the Queen of Heaven seen as a witch and a monster. His rejection of her converts her into that, as, in Shakespeare's first poem 'Venus and Adonis', Adonis' rejection of her beauty and bounty had converted her into a ravening boar.

Is Prospero no more than Adonis who, having narrowly escaped the boar, goes into hiding or retreat for decades to perfect his defences against Venus until he is powerful enough to exclude her from his magic circle? Does he succeed in this? Does Shakespeare approve of the attempt? Or is the attempt doomed because, though Sycorax may be dead and Venus distant, the boar survives in Antonio and Caliban even on the island, and presumably marauds everywhere in the world beyond, where Prospero will be without his book and staff?

*   *   *

The scene which above all others justifies Ninagawa's interpretation is Act V, Sc.i, 17–30:

Ariel	Your charm so strongly works 'em
	That if you now beheld them your affections
	Would become tender.
Prospero	Dost thou think so, spirit?
Ariel	Mine would, sir, were I human.
Prospero	And mine shall.

Hast thou, which art but air, a touch, a feeling
Of their afflictions, and shall not myself,
One of their kind, that relish all as sharply
Passion as they, be kindlier mov'd than thou art?
Though with their high wrongs I am struck to th'quick,
Yet with my nobler reason 'gainst my fury
Do I take part: the rarer action is
In virtue than in vengeance: they being penitent,
The sole drift of my purpose doth extend
Not a frown further.

The passage seems unambiguously to confirm that for the first four acts Prospero has been motivated solely by fury at the 'high wrongs' his enemies have done him and a passion for vengeance. If a mere spirit of air is moved to compassion for human suffering when Prospero, a fellow human, is not, then Prospero is less than human. Hitherto he has identified virtue (his sense of righteous injustice) with vengeance. Now it takes Ariel to show him that not only in terms of kindness, but also of 'nobler reason', they are incompatible. It is at this point that Prospero recognizes that his power hitherto has been but 'rough magic' which he now resolves to abjure in favour of the 'rarer action' which is in virtue, conceived now as self-conquest and forgiveness of sins.

Later in the same scene he acknowledges the mistake he has made in keeping Miranda in ignorance of the world. She blithely numbers Sebastian and Antonio among the 'goodly creatures' of her brave new world. Prospero's ''Tis new to thee' implies his recognition that it is really the same old world of incorrigible wickedness and folly, into which his daughter is shortly to be thrust without his protection. She is just as likely as Caliban to be deceived and exploited.

Robert Graves claims that poets can well be judged by the accuracy of their portrayal of the White Goddess, who is the moon, the Queen of Heaven, and the female principle in Nature, creative and destructive both:

> Shakespeare knew and feared her. . . . Her last appearance in the plays is as the 'damn'd witch Sycorax' in *The Tempest*. Shakespeare in the person of Prospero claims to have dominated her by his magic books, broken her power and enslaved her monstrous son Caliban – though not before extracting his secrets from him under colour of kindness. Yet he cannot disguise Caliban's title to the island, nor the original blueness of Sycorax's eyes, though 'blue-eyed' in Elizabethan slang also meant 'blue-rimmed with debauch'. . . . But he is poetically just to Caliban, putting the truest poetry of the play into his mouth:
>
> > Be not afeared; the isle is full of noises,
> > Sounds and sweet airs that give delight and hurt not,
> > Sometimes a thousand twangling instruments
> > Will hum about mine ears; and sometimes voices,
> > That if I then had wak'd after long sleep
> > Will make me sleep again: and then in dreaming
> > The clouds methought would open and show riches
> > Ready to drop upon me; that, when I wak'd
> > I cried to dream again.
> > [*The White Goddess* 426–7]

Wilson Knight agrees that this is 'the truest poetry of the play', and makes even greater claims for it. Caliban, he says,

> makes no distinction between man and spirit, the natural and the supernatural, and sees and hears what to us is wonderful; his every accent is there to prove it. We forget the occasion. We are, for the moment, outside *The Tempest*, but inside the universe; a spiritualistic universe. The universe of the Red Men. [*Dimensions* 123]

In Caliban's poetry, he claims, 'Shakespeare forecasts what may be the future of world literature, concerned less with the fictional than the factual, but with a factuality that encompasses the supernatural' [126].

130

Is it, then, possible to reconcile the apparently opposite interpretations of Kermode and the many critics he speaks for on the one hand, and Graves and Wilson Knight on the other? Perhaps a partial reconciliation is to be found in the final humanizing of Prospero. Prospero, in renouncing his Art, drops all his pretensions to be superhuman. The tempest in Prospero's mind has been a conflict between the light and dark elements warring there. He has attempted to disown the darker areas of the self, what Jung calls the 'shadow-self', as symbolized in Caliban and Sycorax, whose threat and ugliness is in part a product of his own lopsidedness, his puritanical obsessions, his hubristic tendency to behave as though man were capable of becoming god and restoring Paradise.

Only by casting off his magic garments can Prospero find himself. His final acknowledgement of Caliban – 'This thing of darkness I acknowledge mine' – transforms the shadow-self from an unredeemable monster into a creature capable of seeking wisdom and Grace. Prospero returns where he belongs, and leaves Caliban where he belongs, in possession of the island. Is there here a recognition that Prospero has something to learn even from Caliban, that Caliban acknowledged ceases to threaten the overthrow of the state and the psyche, that any healthy and balanced development of the life of the spirit is a corollary of an ability to live fully in the body in harmony with the natural environment?

9 THE GULLING OF GULLIVER

The history of our era is the nauseating and repulsive history of the
crucifixion of the procreative body for the glorification of the spirit, the
mental consciousness. Plato was an arch-priest of this crucifixion. Art,
that handmaid, humbly and honestly served the vile deed, through three
thousand years at least. The Renaissance put the spear through the side
of the already crucified body, and syphilis put poison into the wound
made by the imaginative spear. It took still three hundred years for the
body to finish: but in the eighteenth century it became a corpse, a corpse
with an abnormally active mind: and today it stinketh.   [D.H. Lawrence]

For anyone unfamiliar with *Gulliver's Travels* (or having the usual
hazy memories of it from childhood), the 1997 television adaptation must
have come as a very pleasant surprise. In order to give Swift's rambling and
discursive story a dramatic shape and drive, the adapters very cleverly
invented a new main story-line and set of characters. The whole story takes
place after Gulliver's return from the final voyage. A wicked doctor who lusts
after Gulliver's wife has almost persuaded her that Gulliver must be dead,
when he returns. Under the pretence of helping Gulliver, whose memories of
his extraordinary and extreme experiences are so strong that his hold on the
present is tenuous, he succeeds in getting Gulliver committed to an asylum
for the insane. Most of the first two voyages are given in the flashbacks of
Gulliver's memories. The last he relates at his public hearing before the asylum
doctors to determine whether he shall be allowed to return home. Neither his
own evident rationality (apart from his claim to have had these adventures at
all) nor his wife's loyal plea cut any ice. But Gulliver's son produces a live
Lilluputian sheep, the wicked doctor flees, and Gulliver and his family (once
they have weaned him of his temporary preference for horses) live happily
ever after.

In its own terms the adaptation worked very well. Gulliver's sanity
made him as outlandish and alien in his own society as in any of the strange
lands he had visited. Here the Yahoos rule. The format of the public hearing
sharpened some of Swift's general satire. Why didn't Swift think of it? Perhaps
he did, but had his own reasons for rejecting it, and for not turning his
'prostitute flatterer' into a romantic hero. Of course, to make room for all the
new material, much of the original text had to go. Much bathwater was disposed of, but unfortunately the baby went with it. The baby, the gist of the
matter, in my reading of *Gulliver's Travels,* is precisely the ambiguity of
Gulliver's position. He is certainly not the merely put-upon hero of the adaptation. The issue of his sanity is crucial. In the adaptation this was reduced to
the simple question of whether he was telling the truth (the viewer knowing
all along that he was). The possibility that Gulliver might have had the experiences he claims to have had, but responded to them insanely, or been driven to

132

insanity by them, is never once considered. The main drive of the adaptation is to vindicate Gulliver's sanity (and thereby everything about him). The main drive of the novel is to demonstrate his insanity.

* * *

The first two voyages of *Gulliver's Travels* are splendid satire. But pure satire is, by its very nature, disqualified from the highest ranks of imaginative literature as I have been defining it. It is largely a product of the critical intellect. It is not concerned to explore the depths and recesses of the writer's own psyche. It is judgmental, and that judgement is directed outwards, against fools and rogues, or, in Swift's case, almost the whole human race. There is always the assumption that the writer stands in a privileged position above those he castigates. The charges Swift brings against civilized man, and enforces so mercilessly, are so broad that every reader is intended to come under the lash. Yet satire always gives the reader an easy escape-route – to identify not with the defendant, but with the judge; in this case to identify with Swift against Gulliver. We would never be so gullible or naive as Gulliver.

But the fourth voyage is another matter. Here, it is often claimed, Swift is writing something different, something more like a Utopian romance than a satire. We are, we are told, intended to share Gulliver's horror of the Yahoos and admiration for the Houyhnhnms. Now, suddenly, the satirical gap between the author and his protagonist-victim has gone. Swift and Gulliver are one. The main justification for these assumptions does not derive from the text, but from our knowledge, from other sources, of Swift's opinions, which are frequently interchangeable with those of Gulliver's Houyhnhnm master.

Even if Swift's conscious intention in the last voyage *had* been simply to depict a Houyhnhnm Utopia and to use the Houyhnhnms as a stick to beat Yahoo-like man, that intention was radically subverted in the event. There is perhaps some truth, where the relatively straightforward satire of the first two books is concerned, in Dr. Johnson's claim that once one had thought of little men and big men, the rest was easy. But when Swift thought of Houyhnhnms and Yahoos he found that he had created a potent myth which demanded his engagement at an altogether deeper imaginative level, which demanded the honesty and courage of the greatest imaginative art. The mythic possibilities become Shakespearean. Ferdinand, cast upon an alien shore, finds already living there not just one Caliban and one Prospero, but a whole race of Calibans subjugated and despised by a whole race of Prosperos, who happen to look like horses . . .

Swift was certainly familiar with the controversy on the nature of man which had raged some thirty years earlier between Edward Stillingfleet and John Locke. An attempt was being made to classify each species in accordance with some characteristic unique to it. Thus the horse, as the only whinnying animal, became *animal hinnibile*. Locke had raised philosophical objections to the classification of man as *animal rationale* on the grounds that not all men reason and some other species do in some degree:

> Body, life, and the power of reasoning, being not the real essence of a man, as I believe your lordship will agree; will your lordship say, that they are not enough to make the thing, wherein they are found, of the kind called man, and not of the kind called baboon, because the difference of these kinds is real? If this be not real enough to make the thing of one kind and not of another, I do not see how *animal rationale* can be enough really to distinguish a man from a horse.
>
> [quoted by Ehrenpreis, 135]

Locke also raised the case of a man who took a knock twenty years ago, since when there has been 'not so much appearance of reason in him, as in his horse or monkey'. He argued that both a man without reason and 'the shape of an ass with reason' would have to be classified as distinct species between man and beast.

These ideas threw up rich possibilities for satire, and for more than satire. Swift was interested in the moral rather than purely logical implications. Ehrenpreis sums up the use Swift made of this material:

> The problem seems to be to induce from the assemblage of specimens of mankind a definition which will not only comprehend them but will distinguish them from Yahoos without granting them the properties of Houyhnhnms. At the same time the effect of the varied exhibit is to disprove the validity of current definitions. Perhaps Swift is obliging his readers to acknowledge the paradox that most of them cling to a concept of their species which would exclude their respective selves. . . . Against this background the Yahoos would embody an ironical reflection upon the fact that the bulk of unthinking men do in practice treat external shape as a sounder guide to humanity than reasonable conduct. Further yet, and as the bitterest irony of all, the Yahoos seem Swift's way of showing that for practical purposes one could more easily distinguish man by his vices than by his virtues; for it is certain vices, says Gulliver, that are 'rooted in the very souls of all my species'.
>
> [137–8]

So far, so good. But if this were all, the fourth voyage would be adding little to what had already been done, especially in the second voyage. Ehrenpreis has difficulty in substantiating his sense of the superior and more complex art of the last voyage because he is trapped within the assumption that we must accept that the Houyhnhnms are 'ideals patterns' embodying 'the highest natural virtues', that they are 'beyond criticism', and that 'Gulliver was right to adopt what appears to be their view of humanity'. These assumptions derive not from the text, but from the belief that 'the principles embodied in the Houyhnhnms were normative for everyone'. It is exactly the argument used by Bernard Knox about *Antigone*: that the ideals propounded by Creon and the chorus were at that time universal and therefore must have been shared by Sophocles. In consequence Ehrenpreis is able to do little to defend Swift against his detractors:

> If, says Swift, we were more like the Houyhnhnms in character, we should be better off than we are now: that is his premise. And though his contemporaries, whether Protestant, Roman, or deist, spoke in unison with him, his readers today almost as single-mindedly shout *No*.

But rejection of the Houyhnhnms is not new. In 1818 Coleridge wrote:

> They are not progressive; they have servants without any reason for their natural inferiority or any explanation how the difference acted; and, above all, they, that is Swift himself, have a perpetual affectation of being wiser than their Maker, and of eradicating what God gave to be subordinated and used: the maternal and paternal affection. There is likewise a true Yahooism in the constant denial of the existence of love, as not identical with friendship, and yet always distinct and very often divided from lust.   [reprinted in Donaghue 103–4]

This is all true, except for the totally unjustified conflating of Swift and the Houyhnhnms – 'they, that is Swift himself'. Swift the imaginative artist knew, whatever Swift the abstract thinker might have said, what was lacking in the Houyhnhnms.

Thackeray was another to shout *No*: 'As for the moral, I think it horrible, shameful, unmanly, blasphemous: and giant and great as this Dean is, I say we should hoot him'. Aldous Huxley, Orwell, Leavis, Murry and many others have taken Thackeray at his word. Leavis can be allowed to speak for all these detractors when he says:

> Swift did his best for the Houyhnhnms, and they may have all the reason, but the Yahoos have all the life. Gulliver's master 'thought Nature and reason were sufficient guides for a reasonable animal', but nature and reason as Gulliver exhibits them are curiously negative, and the reasonable animals appear to have nothing in them to guide. . . . The clean skin of the Houyhnhnms, in short, is stretched over a void; instincts, emotion and life, which complicate the problem of cleanliness and decency, are left for the Yahoos with the dirt and the indecorum.
>   [*Common Pursuit* 84–5]

That nature and reason are here exhibited so negatively would not be curious without the assumption, totally unsupported by the text, that Swift was doing his best for the Houyhnhnms. Leavis shifts his ground from Swift to Gulliver's master to Gulliver as if they were interchangeable. It is Gulliver who is doing

135

his best for the Houyhnhnms, and that is exhibited as nowhere near good enough. How can Leavis or any other reader think that we are expected to identify with Gulliver in his praise of Houyhnhnm culture with its total absence of love and reduction of marriage to breeding, when, in the middle of it, Gulliver solemnly recommends as highly deserving our imitation the Houyhnhnm method of educating their young: 'These are not suffered to taste a Grain of *Oats*, except upon certain Days, till Eighteen Years old; nor *Milk*, but very rarely; and in Summer they graze two Hours in the Morning . . .' and so on. These are clearly the ramblings of a madman who, in his blinkered pursuit of 'nature and reason', has lost his own defining humanity.

For Leavis the ultimate sanity about the life of the body was expressed in Lawrence's essay *A Propos of 'Lady Chatterley's Lover'* (1929), and he may have been influenced by Lawrence's outburst against Swift in that essay:

> The mind's terror of the body has probably driven more men mad than ever could be counted. The insanity of a great mind like Swift's is at least partly traceable to this cause. In the poem to his mistress Celia, which has the maddened refrain 'But – Celia, Celia, Celia s***s,' (the word rhymes with spits), we see what can happen to a great mind when it falls into panic. A great wit like Swift could not see how ridiculous he made himself. Of course Celia s***s! Who doesn't? And how much worse if she didn't. It is hopeless. And then think of poor Celia, made to feel iniquitous about her proper natural function, by her 'lover'. It is monstrous.
>
> [*Phoenix II*, 491]

As recently as 1926 Lawrence had written that it was 'honourable, and necessary, to hate society, as Swift did, or to hate mankind altogether, as often Voltaire did' [*Phoenix* 239]. What happened to turn Lawrence so violently against Swift? I surmise that Aldous Huxley, whose essay on Swift appeared in *Do What You Will* in 1929, quoted the offending line to Lawrence out of context. Clearly he had no first-hand knowledge of the poem ('The Lady's Dressing Room'), since Celia is not the poet's mistress, but Strephon's, and the purpose of the poem is to ridicule Strephon for falling into just such a panic:

> His foul imagination links
> Each dame he sees with all her stinks.

In the Introduction to *Pansies* Lawrence had discussed the line at even greater length, making what he took to be the opposite point, that 'the fairest thing in nature, a flower, still has its roots in earth and manure' [*Poems* 417–18]. But this was exactly Swift's point also. If Strephon were not deranged and ridiculous,

> He soon would learn to think like me,
> And bless his ravisht sight to see

Such order from confusion sprung,
And gaudy tulips rais'd from dung.

Strephon's horror at Celia's bodily functions is entirely his iniquity, not hers. Similarly the sublime, sublimated Houynhnhnms in their rejection of the life of the body convert that life (which they cannot banish or do without any more than Prospero can do without Caliban) into filthy Yahoos.

Leavis also underestimates the importance of religious issues in *Gulliver's Travels*, accusing Swift, on the strength of his essays, of 'a complete incapacity even to guess what religious feeling might be' [85]. The Houyhnhnms believe all Yahoos in their country to be degenerate descendants of 'two Originals' from elsewhere. The Houyhnhnms have, however, no myths of their own origins and no interest in metaphysics or the imaginative arts. They have always been and always will be exactly the same. Ernest Tuveson draws our attention to a theological problem which had been raised by Henry More in his *Divine Dialogues* of 1668:

> What about the salvation of rational beings who may well exist in distant planets – as well as in remote places of our own earth? It is suggested that they may be creatures, endowed with reason, who have never experienced the fall. Such beings would have no need of 'that Religion that the sons of *Adam* are saved by.' They would live a perfectly orderly but monotonous existence, and 'no Properties but those either of the *Animal* or *middle* life' would be needed. 'In virtue whereof they may be good *Naturalists*, good *Politicians*, good *Geometricians* and Analysts, good *Architects*, build Cities and frame Commonwealths, and rule over their *brother*-Brutes in those Planets, and make as good use of them as we doe . . .' But this is nothing but a 'middle' life, for all its placid excellence. The heights of human existence, the glory of knowing God, as well as (by implication) the depths, are outside their ken.   [Tuveson 102]

If, as I have argued, many great works of literature are the imagination's indictment of the ego, or the writer's detached intelligence, *Gulliver's Travels* is a particularly clear example of Lawrence's dictum 'Never trust the artist, trust the tale'. To Swift's intelligence the culture of the Houyhnhnms indeed presented itself as wholly rational and therefore wholly desirable. If man were ever to justify the name of *animal rationale*, he would have to behave like the Houyhnhnms and evolve a culture very similar to theirs. Nothing could be clearer, for example, than Swift's statement in a letter to Pope (29 September 1725):

> I have got materials towards a treatise proving the falsity of that definition *animal rationale*; and to show it should be only *rationis capax*. Upon this great foundation of misanthropy (though not Timon's manner) the whole building of my *Travels* is erected.

137

In fact, it seems to me, in the fourth voyage Swift goes rather further than this, possibly further than he knew, calling in question both man's capacity for reason and the desirability of reasoning as a definitive characteristic of a species.

Swift was more than a detached intelligence. To assume that his values in the novel must correspond to those outside it is to subvert the autonomy of the imagination. It gives to a man's opinions, such as he might express in correspondence, a status equal to that of his imaginative work. It denies a writer the right to put himself in the dock rather than the seat of judgement, and to call in evidence against himself (as Coleridge does) just such documents as he might have written when writing from his critical intellect and not from his imagination. If we allow the voyage to the Houyhnhnms to speak for itself we will find that in it Swift accuses both Gulliver and himself of the crime against Nature.

✻   ✻   ✻

It does not at first occur to Gulliver that he has any more in common with a Yahoo than with a baboon. When the suggestion is first made to him that he might be a kind of Yahoo, he bitterly resents it, and attempts, despite the gross physical dissimilarity to get himself accepted as an honorary Houyhnhnm. The Houyhnhnms see Gulliver, despite his ridiculous plumage, as a Yahoo, (and so does the Yahoo female who, coming upon him naked, fancies him as a mate). 'Furred gowns hide all'. Lear might have thought himself of a different species from the naked beggars of his realm until, in his 'madness', he strips himself to a 'poor, bare, forked creature'. Gulliver wraps his nakedness in pretensions to reason; but the Houyhnhnm master is disturbed by what seems to him a difference in kind between Gulliver and the Yahoos to *their* advantage.

> Though he hated the Yahoos of this Country, yet he no more blamed
> them for their odious Qualities, than he did a *Gnnayh* (a Bird of Prey) for
> its Cruelty, or a sharp stone for cutting his Hoof. But when a Creature
> pretending to Reason, could be capable of such Enormities, he dreaded
> lest the Corruption of that Faculty might be worse than Brutality itself. He
> seemed therefore confident, that instead of Reason, we were only
> possessed of some Quality fitted to increase our natural Vices. [ch.v]

This passage exactly corresponds to a letter from Swift to Pope (26 Nov. 1725):

> I tell you after all that I do not hate mankind; it is *vous autres* who hate
> them, because you would have them reasonable animals, and are angry
> for being disappointed. I have always rejected that definition and made
> another of my own. I am no more angry with [Walpole] than I was with
> the kite that last week flew away with one of my chickens, and yet I was
> pleased when one of my servants shot him two days after. [Donoghue 48]

The Houyhnhnm master is more angry and disappointed than Swift because his judgement of mankind depends entirely on information supplied by Gulliver, who has just given him a graphic and enthusiastic description of the Art of War. Gulliver is here at his most obtuse, as he had been at the equivalent point in his relationship with the King of Brobdingnag, where Gulliver's 'admirable Panegyrick' upon his Country had amply justified the king's conclusion that the Natives of that Country were 'the most pernicious Race of little odious Vermin that Nature ever suffered to crawl upon the Surface of the Earth' [ch.vi]. This is the Gulliver described by Swift as 'a prostitute flatterer ... whose chief study is to extenuate the vices and magnify the virtues of mankind' [Donoghue 53].

In both the first two voyages Gulliver had gradually become conditioned to both the values and perspectives of the alien worlds. This produces some of the most ludicrous situations, as where Gulliver solemnly martials evidence in defence of the reputation of the Lilliputian noblewoman accused of sexual indiscretions with him. This pattern is repeated in the last voyage, where Gulliver gradually comes to see the world through Houyhnhnm eyes. But now the process is taken still further. Gulliver and the Houyhnhnms not only converge, but ultimately cross over. The Houyhnhnms (or some of them) come to concede that Gulliver is not a Yahoo, but somewhere midway between the Yahoos and the Houyhnhnms:

> He observed in me all the Qualities of a *Yahoo*, only a little more civilized
> by some Tincture of Reason; which however was in a Degree as far
> inferior to the *Houyhnhnm* Race, as the *Yahoos* of their Country were
> to me.   [ch. ix]

whereas Gulliver himself gradually loses the distinction between himself and the Yahoos:

> At first, indeed, I did not feel that natural Awe which the *Yahoos* and all
> other Animals bear towards them; but it grew upon me by Degrees, much
> sooner than I imagined, and was mingled with a respectful Love and
> Gratitude, that they would condescend to distinguish me from the rest of
> my Species.   [ch. x]

The pompous tone of such passages exactly corresponds to the tone of passages in the earlier voyages where Gulliver is most clearly being set up by Swift as a figure of fun. Why should we take such passages in the fourth voyage to be any less satirical than those in the earlier voyages where Gulliver swallows whole the values of his hosts? In Lilliput he stands on his Lilliputian dignities: 'I had the honour to be a *Nardac*, which the treasurer himself is not; for all the World knows he is only a *Clumglum*, a Title inferior by one Degree' [ch. vi]. In Luggnagg, he expresses the desire to pass his life 'here in the Conversation of those superiour Beings the *Struldbruggs*' [ch. x]. He is fortunately disabused about the Struldbruggs, and his 'keen Appetite for Perpetuity of Life' is much abated. There is no-one to disabuse him about 'the Virtues and Ideas of those exalted *Houyhnhnms*' (since these were, theoretically, the virtues and ideas of everyone in that age); but that is not to say that the reader, suddenly immune to the play of irony in the last voyage, is expected to identify with Gulliver when he writes: 'as I was going to prostrate myself to kiss his Hoof, he did me the Honour to raise it gently to my Mouth', or when he takes those ideas to their logical conclusion: 'And when I began to consider, that by copulating with one of the *Yahoo*-Species, I had become a Parent of more; it struck me with the utmost Shame, Confusion and Horror' [ch. xi].

Though the incongruity of lodging pure reason in the bodies of horses affords occasions for some broad comedy at Gulliver's expense and undermines his efforts to convince both the Houyhnhnms and himself that he is one of them, it is perhaps slightly at odds (horses being such *physical* creatures) with the insistence that, as pure intelligences, they must be above, detached from, their own bodies. Their bodies do not generate physical needs, instincts, emotions, which in any way threaten the absolute rule of reason. With so little bodily life, the shape of their bodies is neither here nor there. Like Shaw's abominable Ancients in *Back to Methuselah*, they would dispense with bodies if they could.

In the Yahoos, on the other hand, we see the flesh at its most rank and gross, soiling everything it touches. We are back to Hamlet's problem. As Gulliver was exactly half way, in size and sense, between the Lilliputians and the Brobdingnagians, so, here, he is half way in all things between Yahoo and Houyhnhnm. So, in the Great Chain of Being, man had been seen as exactly half way between the angels and the beasts, with a body and passions scarcely to be distinguished from the higher beasts, combined with angelic action and godlike reason. In these terms the challenge of being human could be interpreted in two mutually exclusive ways. The puritanical idealist would strive to repudiate everything he shared with the beasts and develop, in isolation, his god-like faculties. This is the ideal to which Gulliver commits himself 'by endeavouring, as far as my inferior Nature was capable, to imitate the *Houyhnhnms*' [ch. x]. It is Gulliver, not Swift, who is willing to eradicate the affections. Swift, on the other hand, sees this as spiritual pride, rejecting the god-given creation and man's ordained place in it.

Gulliver's Travels is not without its positives. Gulliver is judged against a standard of wholeness, humanity and common sense embodied in the King of Brobdingnag and Pedro de Mendez. Gulliver thinks of himself as a truth-seeker, motivated by a desire to grow in virtue and wisdom. He ends up talking only to his horses. For such a quest is doomed without self-knowledge, humanity and humility, and a man is unlikely to have those qualities without the aid of Christ, who is conspicuous by his absence from Gulliver's thinking. Gulliver declares himself to be a Christian, but the only occasion on which this has the slightest effect on his thinking or behaviour is when he refuses to trample on a crucifix. John B. Radner has demonstrated the blindness of

Gulliver to the paramount wisdom all his experiences should teach him, man's need of redemption. (Radner shows that although Swift did not want the *Travels* to be overtly religious, he did build in for those alert to such things a number of significant details. For example, the dates framing the third voyage were in those years Good Friday and Easter Monday; and the date of the concluding letter to Sympson was Easter Sunday.)

We have only Gulliver's word that his chief motivation is the pursuit of virtue and wisdom. In fact his motivation is closer than might at first appear to that other inveterate traveller, Odysseus. He cannot resist the lure of new experience. He has no compunction about deserting his wife and children. He is solipsistic, cruel and proud. He is always on the lookout for opportunities to increase his wealth and prestige. He is much more interested in talking than listening. He wants others to have a high opinion both of himself and of his nation. Another Odysseus-like quality in Gulliver, seldom noted by critics, is his cruelty and ruthlessness. He had earlier shown himself unmoved by the horrors of war. But his attempt to imitate the utilitarian rationalism of the Houyhnhnms leads into much greater inhumanity. Even after he has conceded that men and Yahoos are the same species, this 'gentle Yahoo', as the sorrel nag calls him, kills and skins several Yahoos, including some children, then forces other Yahoos to draw the boat made from and sealed with tallow from these bodies, down to the sea. The whole scene reminds us of the obscenities of the concentration camps.

The responses of the open-minded reader are carefully controlled by Swift, in, for example, the parallels and progression in the structure of each voyage. Just as the reasons for Gulliver's arrival on strange shores get progressively more culpable in his fellow men (first accident, then excusable desertion, then violence from pirates, and finally the treachery of his own men), so his return to his familiar world progresses from joy through contempt to horror. When he returns from Brobdingnag, the first men he sees seem to him 'the most little contemptible Creatures I had ever beheld'. The fault is clearly entirely in Gulliver's eyes:

> As I was on the Road; observing the Littleness of the Houses, the Trees, the Cattle and the People, I began to think myself in *Lilliput*. I was afraid of trampling on every Traveller I met; and often called aloud to have them stand out of the Way; so that I was like to have gotten one or two broken Heads for my Impertinence.
>
> [ch. viii]

The result of his capitulation to the perspectives of the Houyhnhnms is even more distorting and ludicrous, the indiscriminate contempt even more impertinent. He is rescued by some honest Portuguese, who treat him with 'great Humanity', especially their captain, the courteous and generous Pedro de Mendez. Gulliver's response reveals the extent to which his own humanity has deserted him: 'I wondered to find such Civilities from a *Yahoo*. . . . I was ready to faint at the very Smell of him and his Men' [ch. xi]. He cannot endure the presence of his wife and children but retires to his stable to converse with his horses. In refusing to eat bread or drink wine with his family he is rejecting both holy and human communion, stealing from his own nature all the natural man. Is this the man whose admiration for the Houyhnhnms we are expected to share? Gulliver, at the end, has lost the sense that we are all one life. In his own imaginative mode, Swift spells out just as powerfully as Lawrence, that the worship of reason, detached from both the sacred and the human, is unnatural, sterile, and insane.

10 WORDSWORTH – NATURE'S PRIEST OR NATURE'S PRISONER?

In 1798, at the age of 28, Wordsworth claimed that he had long been a 'worshipper of Nature'. For many readers he became, and for some is still, its high priest. There was nothing new at that time in writing poems about nature; but, as Jonathan Bate has shown, there was something very new in the way Wordsworth wrote about it. He rejected the appropriation of nature into the realm of the aesthetic, the reduction of it to the merely picturesque. He transformed our experience of Nature into a religious experience. Moreover, he communicated that experience in terms which are strikingly in accord with our current language of deep ecology, of holistic thinking and biocentric consciousness.

Given his priority and centrality in this, and the body of fine poetry it generated, it is perhaps not surprising that so many readers have not questioned Wordsworth's description of himself, despite the fact that he did not long remain a worshipper of nature after 1798, and by 1802 was committed to the attempt to repudiate it, which lasted the rest of his long life. He continued, of course, to write about nature, but without the inwardness of the early work. His attitude to it become more and more ambivalent and selective, culminating in his reluctant recognition of it as a prison preventing the soul's access to higher things. I shall argue in later chapters that Wordsworth's influence on later English nature poets was not beneficial, and that a great deal of the effort of such poets as Lawrence and R.S.Thomas and Ted Hughes was part of the struggle to escape from its distortions and limitations.

*   *   *

The history of our civilization can be written as the history of our idea of and attitude towards nature; that is, nature considered not just as landscape, flora and fauna, but as all the phenomena, substances, energies, processes, of the universe, including, therefore, all the sciences, human nature, life and death. It is a short step to say that nature is everything. But the fact that we have uses for the word 'unnatural' acknowledges the possibility of repudiating nature in favour of something else, or violating it, or becoming alienated from it. Much religion has involved a rejection of the physical in favour of the metaphysical, of the finite in favour of the infinite, of the temporal in favour of the eternal. Much philosophy has involved a rejection of the real in favour of the ideal. Much scientific and rationalistic thinking has denied spirit, replacing the sacred with the mechanistic. Dualism has become not just one very strange way of looking at the world, but, in the West, the only way. Not only cultural tradition but language itself forces us to think in dualistic and atomistic terms.

Christianity has taught that nature exists for man's exploitation and profit. It has therefore gone hand in glove with materialism and industrialism. The whole drive of our civilization has been based on the assumption that civilization itself is an alternative to nature and superior to it, that mind and technology offer us an alternative method of shaping the world, as though humanity were autonomous. The self-contained consciousness looks out as through windows on a wholly external world full of separate and competing things. It takes a huge effort now to apprehend interrelationships, continuities and wholes, to see the whole of nature as a tree on which humanity is a leaf.

Things got much worse in the eighteenth century with the rise of rationalism and mechanistic science, the start of the industrial revolution and the consequent crowding of people, servants of the machines, factory-fodder, in cities. Blake made his eloquent protest, but not on behalf of nature. His vision was as anthropocentric as it is possible to be: 'All deities reside in the human breast'. According to Crabb Robinson:

> His delight in W[ordsworth]'s poetry was intense. Nor did it seem less notwithstanding by the reproaches he continually cast on W. for his imputed worship of nature, wh. in the mind of Blake constituted Atheism.
>
> [Wilson 333]

Wordsworth's protest was on other grounds. He tried to make men aware of their whole environment, of their dependence on it for health, sanity and ultimate sanctions. And this, as Alfred North Whitehead saw, was the most important and enduring aspect of Romanticism. Here is an extract from Edmund Wilson's summary of Whitehead's argument in *Science and the Modern World*:

> What had really taken place, says Whitehead, is a philosophical revolution. The scientists of the seventeenth century who presented the universe as a mechanism had caused people to draw the conclusion that man was something apart from nature, something introduced into the universe from the outside and remaining alien to all that he found. But a romantic poet like Wordsworth has come to feel the falsity of this assumption: he has perceived that the world is an organism, that nature includes planets, mountains, vegetation and people alike, that what we are and what we see, what we hear, what we feel and what we smell, are inextricably related, that all are involved in the same great entity. Those who make fun of the Romantics are mistaken in supposing that there is no intimate connection between the landscape and the poet's emotions. There is no real dualism, says Whitehead, between external lakes and hills, on the one hand, and personal feelings, on the other: human feelings and inanimate objects are interdependent and developing together in some fashion of which our traditional notions of laws of cause and effect, of dualities of mind and matter or of body and soul, can give us no true idea. The Romantic poet, then, with his turbid or opalescent language, his sympathies and passions which cause him to seem to merge with his surroundings, is the prophet of a new insight into nature: he is describing

144

things as they really are; and a revolution in the imagery of poetry is in reality a revolution in metaphysics.   [5–6]

If Wordsworth's sympathies were not atheistic, they were certainly pagan:

> The world is too much with us; late and soon,
> Getting and spending, we lay waste our powers:
> Little we see in nature that is ours;
> We have given our hearts away, a sordid boon!
> This Sea that bares her bosom to the moon;
> The Winds that will be howling at all hours
> And are up-gathered now like sleeping flowers;
> For this, for everything, we are out of tune;
> It moves us not – Great God! I'd rather be
> A Pagan suckled in a creed outworn;
> So might I, standing on this pleasant lea,
> Have glimpses that would make me less forlorn;
> Have sight of Proteus coming from the sea;
> Or hear old Triton blow his wreathed horn.

This is no mere nostalgia for an Arcadian past, an imaginary golden age when man, nature and the gods were at one; it is a heartfelt plea for a recovery of man's birthright, the squandered blessing of a sacred natural environment in tune with which man can exercise his powers creatively:

> Paradise, and groves
> Elysian, Fortunate Fields – like those of old
> Sought in the Atlantic Main, why should they be
> A history only of departed things,
> Or a mere fiction of what never was?
> For the discerning intellect of Man,
> When wedded to this goodly universe
> In love and holy passion, shall find these
> A simple produce of the common day.

Here, in the early Preface to 'The Excursion', Wordsworth chants 'the spousal verse / Of this great consummation':

> How exquisitely the individual Mind
> (And the progressive powers perhaps no less
> Of the whole species) to the external World
> Is fitted: – and how exquisitely, too,
> Theme this but little heard of among Men,
> The external World is fitted to the Mind;

145

And the creation (by no lower name
Can it be called) which they with blended might
Accomplish: this is our high argument.

There has been general critical agreement that Wordsworth's finest poetry is not 'argument', however high and rhetorically stirring, but those poems or passages which record faithfully, without intrusive interpretation, vivid instances of his relationship with nature before that relationship had been processed into a metaphysic. And at that time Wordsworth had been as guilty as any other boy of crimes against nature, for example his rape of the virgin hazel copse:

The silent trees and Then up I rose
And dragg'd to earth both branch and bough, with crash
And merciless ravage; and the shady nook
Of hazels, and the green and mossy bower
Deform'd and sullied, patiently gave up
Their quiet being: and unless I now
Confound my present feelings with the past,
Even then, when from the bower I turn'd away,
Exulting, rich beyond the wealth of kings,
I felt a sense of pain when I beheld the intruding sky.

['Nutting']

Such unforced testimony to the sacredness of nature and the sacrilege of our dealings with it seems to me Wordsworth's greatest gift.

But Wordsworth's effort failed. Darwinism triumphed – not the Darwinism of Darwin himself, whose work was always motivated by admiration that (as he says in the closing words of *The Origin of Species*) 'from so simple a beginning endless forms most beautiful and most wonderful have been, and are being evolved', but the Darwinism of T.H. Huxley, who saw man as 'compelled to be perpetually on guard against the cosmic forces, whose ends are not his ends, without and within himself', but nevertheless 'susceptible of a vast amount of improvement, by education, by instruction, and by the application of his intelligence to the adaptation of the conditions of life to his higher needs':

That which lies before the human race is a constant struggle to maintain and improve, in opposition to the State of Nature, the State of Art of an organized polity; in which, and by which, man may develop a worthy civilization, capable of maintaining and constantly improving itself, until the evolution of our globe shall have entered so far upon its downward course that the cosmic process resumes its sway; and, once more, the State of Nature prevails over the surface of our planet.   [44–5]

146

After a century of that struggle, it seems now highly unlikely and highly desirable that a state of nature should once again prevail over the surface of our planet.

✳   ✳   ✳

Our strong received sense of Wordsworth as worshipper of and champion of nature derives largely from a few very early poems, especially 'Tintern Abbey'. Here he spells out clearly what he means by 'the external World', declaring himself to be

> A lover of the meadows and the woods,
> And mountains; and of all that we behold
> From this green earth; of all the mighty world
> Of eye and ear, both what they half create,
> And what perceive; well pleased to recognize
> In nature and the language of the sense,
> The anchor of my purest thoughts, the nurse,
> The guide, the guardian of my heart, and soul
> Of all my moral being.

It is precisely this attachment to and high valuation of 'nature and the language of the sense' which both Blake and Coleridge found most objectionable in Wordsworth. In his annotations to Wordsworth, Blake wrote: 'W. must know that what he writes valuable is not to be found in Nature'. Blake's favourite Wordsworth poem was 'Intimations of Immortality', Wordsworth's valediction to nature. Imagination, for Blake, was degraded by any attachment to nature: 'Imagination is the divine vision not of the World, or of Man, nor from Man as he is a natural man, but only as he is a spiritual Man'. It is precisely Blake's refusal to ground his imagination in nature, in this world, which makes the bulk of the later prophetic books the worst poetry written by any major English poet. Blake's career proved that myths and symbols which are not grounded 'in nature and the language of the sense' are dead and become poetic lumber.

But Blake's note was right. It soon became clear that what Wordsworth was worshipping was not nature. Though he continued to use the word, its meaning drifting further and further from the green earth and the world perceived by the senses until it reached a private meaning which specifically excluded these. Reluctant to write off something in which he had invested so much, Wordsworth unconsciously extended and extended the meaning of the word nature to make it cover whatever he now wished to 'write valuable'.

There are several famous passages in book I of *The Prelude* which are usually praised, deservedly, for the immediate, concrete and sensuous manner in which Wordsworth renders his childhood experiences in the natural world. I suggest, however, that it is always the same few passages which critics select because they are, in fact, untypical of Wordsworth, who only 'realizes' experience in this way in order to have its apparent reality displaced by the numinous Powers and Presences he detects behind it. If one reads on, the effect of each of these wonderful passages is immediately dissipated into grandiose misty rhetoric and banal moralizing. Wordsworth is, for the most part, the most insubstantial and unsensuous of poets. Touch, taste and smell are virtually absent from his work. His preferred sights are (and were already in childhood) distant, misty, atmospheric, quickly dissolving into moods:

> Oft in these moments such a holy calm
> Did overspread my soul, that I forgot
> That I had bodily eyes, and what I saw
> Appear'd like something in myself, a dream,
> A prospect in my mind.   [II, 367–71]

The ear is even more important than the eye because sounds are already divorced from substance (or, to use his own perfect word, 'ghostly'); but he could hear the universal song of joy best when his 'fleshly ear . . . slept undisturb'd [432–4].

The tendency for Wordsworth's attention to drift spontaneously from the material world towards the numinous and subjective seems to have been a matter of temperament rather than adult choice:

> I was often unable to think of external things as having external
> existence, and I communed with all that I saw as something not apart
> from, but inherent in, my own immaterial nature. Many times while going
> to school have I grasped at a wall or a tree to recall myself from this abyss
> of idealism to reality.   [Moorman, vol.I 41–2]

A concomitant of this idealism is a tendency to lapse from his early sense of nature as something deeply interfused and unified into Platonic or Cartesian dualism, assuming the old artificial division between internal and external, mind and senses, spirit and substance.

The relationship with nature which in 'Tintern Abbey' and some of the other *Lyrical Ballads* Wordsworth claims he still has, figures in *The Prelude* as something specific to childhood. The past tense is conspicuous in such lines as 'That spirit of religious love in which / I walked with Nature' [II, 376–7]. This is later to be replaced by a quite different spirit no longer 'Subservient strictly to the external things / With which it commun'd [II, 386–7].

*   *   *

The 'Ode: Intimations of Immortality from recollections of early Childhood' spans the crucial years 1802–1804 and contains the whole crisis in little. It is Wordsworth's valediction to Nature. Not that Wordsworth himself saw it in those terms. It's greatness stems in part from the dramatic tension which arises between what he is trying to say, and what insists, despite the counter-insistence of the exclamation marks, on being said. It is very untypical of Wordsworth in its emotionalism, its wild swings of mood, its lack of tranquility. It is the poem in which Wordsworth most gives himself away.

Wordsworth began the Ode in 1802 as a consolation to Coleridge, an answer to 'The Mad Monk' (1800), where Coleridge had written:

> There was a time when earth, and sea, and skies,
> The bright green vale, and forest's dark recess,
> With all things, lay before mine eyes
> In steady loveliness:
> But now I feel, on earth's uneasy scene,
> Such sorrows as will never cease; –
> I only ask for peace;
> If I must live to know that such a time has been!

Wordsworth felt that his own sense of loss was even stronger than Coleridge's, yet that he had found a way to turn the fact that 'such a time had been' to good account, and had found a source of strength in 'what remained behind'. But, perhaps needing all his time and energy for 'The Prelude', he completed at that time only the first four stanzas, evoking the sense of loss but stopping short of the 'abundant recompense'. Before Wordsworth completed the Ode in 1804, Coleridge had plunged even further into dejection and written his own Ode to it:

> There was a time when, though my path was rough,
>   This joy within me dallied with distress,
> And all misfortunes were but as the stuff
>   Whence Fancy made me dreams of happiness:
> For hope grew round me, like the twining vine,
> And fruits, and foliage, not my own, seemed mine.
> But now afflictions bow me down to earth:
> Nor care I that they rob me of my mirth;
>   But oh! each visitation
> Suspends what nature gave me at my birth,
>   My shaping spirit of Imagination.

Wordsworth was stimulated to finish the 'Immortality Ode' as an antidote to this.

The Ode is badly named. Nowhere, not even in this poem, does Wordsworth show the slightest interest in the idea of survival after death. The Ode is not about immortality, but about the Platonic notion of pre-existence. Yet Wordsworth never really committed himself to a belief in pre-existence either. He wrote to Miss Fenwick:

> I took hold of the notion of pre-existence as having sufficient foundation
> in humanity for authorizing me to make for my purpose the best use of it
> I could as a poet.

By this he means, I take it, that everyone can bear testimony to 'that dream-like vividness and splendour which invest objects of sight in childhood'. But he invests this seeming with such transcendental permanent reality that life itself becomes, in comparison, the dream, the unreality.

The opening of the poem might seem at first glance to be simple praise of nature:

> There was a time when meadow, grove and stream,
>   The earth, and every common sight,
>   To me did seem
>   Apparell'd in celestial light,
> The glory and the freshness of a dream.

But 'apparell'd in celestial light' suggests that the light is not a property of things, but borrowed from heaven. The second stanza confirms that Wordsworth is *not* talking about nature's own beauty, but what he calls in *The Prelude* 'a superadded soul / A virtue not its own', an 'auxiliar light' from the mind, which seemed to transfigure common sights, as in a dream. In the 'Elegiac Stanzas' he calls it 'The light that never was, on sea or land, / The consecration, and the Poet's dream'. When the dreamer wakes, the 'visionary gleam' fades 'into the light of common day', and that light, whatever concessions are made to nature's beauties and pleasures, is not enough to live by. Once the 'vision splendid' has been lost, the ordinary sight which remains is no better than blindness. Hence to be 'Nature's Priest' is possible only to 'the Youth' still attended by the 'vision splendid'. The whole poem is about the source and status of that vision, and what can be done about its apparently inevitable loss.

Why should the moon look round her with particular delight when the heavens are bare? The point is that the moon does not depend on objects for her delight, is not subservient to external things. She delights in her capacity to illuminate the heavens with her own radiance; that radiance *is* her delight. The Child of Joy does the same in his world. He can transfigure every 'common sight' with the radiance of his own joy: 'To unorganic natures I transferr'd / My own enjoyments' [*Prelude* II 410–11]. The radiant world delights him: it is irradiated by his delight. The process is circular, unless we postulate a source of that joy beyond both child and nature (as the moon must borrow her light from the sun). This applied to almost all Wordsworth's poetry. But in the early years he gave nature at least half the credit for what she merely reflected from his own mind. Coleridge saw that much more clearly than Wordsworth himself:

> thy soul received
> The light reflected, as a light bestowed.
> ['To William Wordsworth']

The poem is organized primarily around images of light and darkness, sight and blindness. It opens with a real sunrise. The sun is associated with spring, flowers, birdsong, warmth, love, vitality; nevertheless, it cannot draw the narrator into its festival because he is no longer capable of spontaneous joy. He strains towards a second-hand joy through the shouts of the shepherd boy. But all the songs of joy being sung around him merely serve to remind him of what is lost. He tries to listen to them, but what he hears is cataracts, and mountain echoes, and night winds. He has become much more receptive to sounds than sights, particularly those 'sounds that are / The ghostly language of the ancient earth / Or make their dim abode in distant winds'. Such sounds are closely related to pre-natal experience, not in heaven, but in the womb. Wordsworth's heaven is always described as a tranquillity at the centre of a fostering, nurturing universe whose heartbeat is indistinguishable from his own. Psychologists call this the 'oceanic' experience. It follows naturally enough that when he returns to his heaven at the end of the Ode it is no longer rendered in terms of light, but as a sea. Children, having not yet begun their long trek inland towards alienation in a harsh world, still playing on the shore, can 'hear the mighty waters rolling evermore'.

In the first four stanzas there had been no mention of pre-existence. When he continued the poem in 1804 he plunged straight into the subject with a startling paradox:

> Our birth is but a sleep and a forgetting:
> The Soul that rises with us, our life's Star,
> Hath had elsewhere its setting,
>   And cometh from afar:
>   Not in entire forgetfulness,
> But trailing clouds of glory do we come
>   From God, who is our home.

This is stated as a categorical fact – no metaphor. Given this datum, the child's vision is the only reality. Life is a dream. In the early books of *The Prelude* birth was a release of creativity and access of vision consequent upon the marriage of the soul with nature. Now it is an exile into blindness and sterility. In the second book of *The Prelude* the 'Presence' which irradiated and exalted for the infant Babe 'all objects through all intercourse of sense' was the earthly Mother:

> No outcast he, bewilder'd and depress'd;
> Along his infant veins are interfus'd

151

> The gravitation and the filial bond
> Of nature, that connect him with the world.
>   [260–3]

By 1804 the early metaphors of marriage and motherhood have been replaced
by those of alienation and adoption:

> Earth fills her lap with pleasures of her own;
> Yearnings she hath in her own natural kind,
> And, even with something of a Mother's mind,
> And no unworthy aim,
>   The homely Nurse doth all she can
> To make her Foster-child, her Inmate Man,
>   Forget the glories he hath known,
> And that imperial palace whence he came.

Nature is thus relegated to a side-show, a box of toys.

In 'The Prelude', to call the infant 'an inmate of this *active* universe'
meant simply that he, like Lucy, dwelt with Nature. Now the word 'Inmate',
following the 'shades of the prison-house' in the previous stanza, suggests
rather that Earth is no more than an orphanage. Even parental love is now
part of the conspiracy to lull the child into a 'dream of human life', the world
of false appearances, noise, mad endeavour and role-playing. The child, of
course, has no means of knowing that he is Philosopher, Prophet and Seer.
He blindly strives to become as blind as adults, imitating the behaviour of all
the other actors in the human comedy until custom lies upon him 'with a
weight / Heavy as frost, and deep almost as life!' The shades of the prison-house
now modulate into the darkness of the grave. Life is no longer even a dream;
it is a death.

Having sunk to this nadir of dejection, Wordsworth now attempts to
pull himself up by his own bootstraps. The saving grace is memory. The adult
can still remember and interpret his childhood experiences, not for the sake
of recapturing the lost joys, rather

>   those obstinate questionings
> Of sense and outward things,
> Fallings from us, vanishings;
> Blank misgivings of a Creature
> Moving about in worlds not realiz'd . . .

This tentative, exploratory 'creature' sounds like Ted Hughes' wodwo, except
that Wordsworth arbitrarily attributes these questionings not to a natural
curiosity about the world and openness to experience but to supernatural
'recollections' of 'that immortal sea / Which brought us hither'. Wordsworth
can no longer possess the deepest truths as his birthright, or augment the

sunrise with his own joy, but he can, as his own sun sets, send out from his eye the sober colouring of 'soothing thoughts that spring / Out of human suffering'.

The Ode contains some of the most memorable lines in English poetry. They are all lines about what is lost. There is no point in claiming that

> Though nothing can bring back the hour
> Of splendour in the grass, of glory in the flower;
> We will grieve not, rather find
> Strength in what remains behind

if all the vitality of the poem, all the *poetic* power, is in the grief, and none in the supposedly surviving strength. The attempt in the last stanza to claim that only one delight has been relinquished, is desperate, and the compensation, that the years will bring 'the philosophic mind', hollow.

Coleridge did not like the poem. He felt that the idea of pre-existence was merely fanciful, and yet the whole argument of the poem rested on it; otherwise the vast claims made for the child would be absurd.

It is a pity that Yeats' notion of the world soul, or Jung's of the collective unconscious, was not available to Wordsworth. Some such notion would have enabled him to account for the lost vision without dualism, without the assumption that the vision must derive from somewhere elsewhere, somewhere outside and superior to nature. According to Jung, the collective unconscious could be described as

> a collective human being combining the characteristics of both sexes, transcending youth and age, birth and death, and, from having at its command a human experience of one or two million years, practically immortal. If such a being existed, it would be exalted above all temporal change; the present would mean neither more nor less to it than any year in the hundredth millenium before Christ; it would be a dreamer of age-old dreams and, owing to its limitless experience, an incomparable prognosticator. It would have lived countless times over again the life of the individual, the family, the tribe, and the nation, and it would possess a living sense of the rhythm of growth, flowering and decay.
>
> [quoted in Baring 42]

Baring and Cashford argue that in Neolithic times 'this vision was still a living reality and had not yet become a memory and a dream':

> Jung, striving to restore to the psyche this forgotten knowledge of the unity and sacrality of all life, knew that the Neolithic experience is not dead and gone, but still lives on in us as the archaic ground of the twentieth-century psyche. It is found, for instance, in the spontaneous

world of the child, which is lost with the adaptation to a desacralized
society.   [105]

                ❊   ❊   ❊

Wordsworth tried to have it both ways. Both the Ode and *The Prelude* oscillate
between two poles, a belief that this world – 'the very world which is the
world / Of all of us' is 'the place in which, in the end, / We find our happiness,
or not at all' [Book X 726–8], and the equally strong belief that

> Our destiny, our nature, and our home
> Is with infinitude, and only there.
> [Book VI 538–9]

It is when the tension between these two is lost, when all is subsumed in the
one 'great thought / By which we live, Infinity and God', that the great years
end and the long decline begins.

By the time we get to book XI the 'glorying' in Nature celebrated in
'Tintern Abbey' has been replaced by a devastating sense of loss, a dejection
almost as guilt-ridden as Coleridge's, and for much the same reasons. This
book records a war within, as the new Wordsworth in the name of Reason
repudiates history, passion and poetry:

> Thus strangely did I war against myself;
> A Bigot to a new Idolatry
> Did like a Monk who hath forsworn the world
> Zealously labour to cut off my heart
> From all the sources of her former strength.
> [74–8]

Reason ('logic and minute analysis') came between Wordsworth and the 'soul
of Nature':

> 'Tis true that earth with all her appanage
> Of elements and organs, storm and sunshine,
> With its pure forms and colours, pomp of clouds
> Rivers and mountains, objects among which
> It might be thought that no dislike or blame,
> No sense of weakness or infirmity
> Or ought amiss could possibly have come,
> Yea, even the visible Universe, was scanned
> With something of a kindred spirit, fell
> Beneath the domination of a taste
> Less elevated, which did in my mind
> With its more noble influence interfere,
> Its animation and its deeper sway.   [108–120]

He can find no justification or extenuation for his presumption in 'sitting thus in judgement' over nature, for these 'barren intermeddling subtleties', unless it be 'inherent in the Creature ... A twofold Frame of body and of mind' [168–70]. Wordsworth was subsequently able to shake off this habit. But he could no longer tap the sources of his former strength: 'the hiding-places of my power / Seem open; I approach, and then they close' [336–7]. He comes very close to Coleridge when he speaks of 'this later time, when storm and rain / Beat on my roof at midnight', and of himself as 'thus restored / Or otherwise'. The ending of book XI is very subdued and chastened, his vision of nature purged of all joy, glamour and rhetoric:

> And afterwards, the wind and sleety rain
> And all the business of the elements,
> The single sheep, and the one blasted tree,
> And the bleak music of that old stone wall,
> The noise of wood and water, and the mist
> Which on the line of each of those two Roads
> Advanced in such indisputable shapes,
> All these were spectacles and sounds to which
> I often would repair and thence would drink,
> As at a fountain.   [376–85]

Though Wordsworth claimed to have been able to shake off the habit of analytical and judgemental reasoning, he continued to define Nature (and, for that matter, God) as more and more to be identified with 'the mind of man'.

The final book of *The Prelude* expands on the ending of the Ode. There much larger claims are made for these 'philosophic minds':

> By sensible impressions not enthrall'd,
> But quicken'd, rouz'd, and made thereby more apt
> To hold communion with the invisible world.
> Such minds are truly from the Deity,
> For they are Powers; and hence the highest bliss
> That can be known is theirs, the consciousness
> Of whom they are habitually infused
> Through every image, and through every thought,
> And all impressions; hence religion, faith,
> And endless occupation for the soul
> Whether discursive or intuitive;
> Hence sovereignty within and peace at will.
>   [103–14]

Hence the growing preference for those impressions which most lend themselves to conversion into images of the ideal and infinite. The wonderfully rendered vision of the 'huge sea of mist' seen from the top of Snowdon by moonlight has to be reduced to 'the perfect image of a mighty mind, / Of one that feeds upon infinity' [69–70], and further reduced in the 1850 version to a mere reflection, 'emblem' or 'type / Of a majestic intellect' [66–7]

> a mind sustained
> By recognitions of transcendent power,
> In sense conducting to ideal form,
> In soul of more than mortal privilege.
> [74–7]

The closing lines of *The Prelude* are addressed to 'Prophets of Nature'. Wordsworth offers to

> Instruct them how the mind of man becomes
> A thousand times more beautiful than the earth
> On which he dwells, above this Frame of things
> . . .
> In beauty exalted, as it is itself
> Of substance and of fabric more divine.

'The earth', 'this Frame of things', what we normally mean by nature, may be beautiful, but it can lull the senses into a sleep of death unless 'sanctified / By reason and by truth', products exclusively of 'the mind of man'.

About the time he finished *The Prelude* Wordsworth translated three sonnets by Michaelangelo which he found full of 'excellent' meaning. One of them contains the lines:

> Heav'n born, the Soul a heav'n-ward course must hold;
> Beyond the visible world She soars to seek,
> For what delights the sense is false and weak,
> Ideal Form, the universal mould.

It seems that by 1805 Wordsworth could have found excellent meaning in St. Augustine:

> And men go forth and admire lofty mountains and broad seas, and roaring torrents, and the ocean, and the course of the stars, and turn away from themselves while doing so.

In 1806 Wordsworth wrote 'The White Doe of Rylstone'. Nature is now of interest to him only in so far as it can be purified and spiritualized out of all recognition. He later claimed that the poem was the 'highest' he had ever produced, culminating in 'nothing less than the Apotheosis of the Animal':

Throughout, objects derive their influence not from properties inherent in themselves . . . but from such as are *bestowed* upon them by the minds of those who are conversant with or affected by those objects. . . . The mere physical action was all unsuccessful; but the true action of the poem was spiritual – the subduing of the will and all inferior passions, to the perfect purifying and spiritualizing of the intellectual nature; while the Doe, by connection with Emily is raised, as it were, from its mere animal nature into something mysterious and saintlike.

[Moorman, II, 113]

❋   ❋   ❋

In the Preface to the *Lyrical Ballads* Wordsworth had described the human mind as the 'mirror of the fairest and most interesting properties of nature'. Now the relationship is reversed, nature being of interest only when it mirrors the fairest properties of the human mind, the highest aspects of his own nature – grandeur, permanence, tranquillity. He admitted, in 'Ruth' that an 'irregular' nature could equally well find in the natural world images of kindred irregularity – images of tumult, impetuosity and voluptuousness. The values, therefore, come first, from a source other than nature. Whence?

> I had been taught to reverence a Power
> That is the very quality and shape
> And image of right reason . . .

The argument is circular, since by 'right reason' Wordsworth means what he has been 'taught to reverence', conditioned to believe at his mother's knee. Leavis speaks of his 'upbringing in a congenial social environment, with its wholesome simple pieties and the traditional sanity of its moral culture, which to him were nature' [*Revaluation*, 171]. They were, indeed, second nature. But in the poems they become Nature, a source of unquestionable moral absolutes with a vaguely supernatural sanction. Terrific encounters with Nature are reduced to messages he could have got from any commonplace book. One of the fearful 'visitations' ('low breathings coming after me') is not to chastise the young Wordsworth for being a 'fell destroyer' of woodcocks, but for stealing 'the bird / Which was the captive of another's toils'. Nature deploys its fearful powers to enforce the law of property. This unquestioning assurance of certain certainties for no better reason than that he learned them as a blessed Babe is surely disabling in a major poet, especially when they are supported by an unscrupulous manipulation of 'the external world'.

Wilson Knight had less admiration than Leavis for 'simple pieties' and 'traditional sanity':

Ethically, Wordsworth never breaks new ground. The established values remain intact, whereas poetry's more normal business is to *reclaim* territory from evil possession, to redeem rather than reject, seizing on essential good: of which the great prophet is Nietzsche.

[*The Starlit Dome*, 82]

In *The Will to Power* Nietzsche wrote:

The insipid and cowardly concept 'nature' devised by nature enthusiasts (– without any instinct for what is fearful, implacable and cynical in even the 'most beautiful' aspects), a kind of attempt to read moral Christian 'humanity' into nature – Rousseau's concept of nature, as if 'nature' were freedom, goodness, innocence, fairness, justice, an idyll – still a cult of Christian morality fundamentally. – Collect together passages to see what the poets really admired in, e.g., high mountains, etc. Complete ignorance the presupposition for this cult –

Wordsworth wanted Nature to confirm for him that love, joy, beauty and goodness were not just fragile human values but cosmic absolutes:

> For the man
> Who, in this spirit, communes with the Forms
> Of Nature, who with understanding heart
> Both knows and loves such objects as excite
> No morbid passions, no disquietude,
> No vengeance and no hatred – needs must feel
> The joy of that pure principle of love
> So deeply, that, unsatisfied with ought
> Less pure and exquisite, he cannot choose
> But seek for objects of a kindred love
> In fellow creatures and a kindred joy.
> . . . he looks round
> And seeks for good; and finds the good he seeks.

Of course, if you resolutely turns a blind eye to everything potentially morbid or disquieting, and seek out that which confirms your pre-existing optimistic metaphysic, that is what you find. What value can we attach to an optimism which refuses to acknowledge anything which does not support it? Wordsworth casts Nature in the role of cosmic parent, priest and Sunday School teacher, and what is being taught is perilously close to 'all's right with the world'. It is not surprising that the book Wordsworth most hated was Voltaire's *Candide*, which had already demolished that position.

In 1879 Leslie Stephen wrote:

He seems at times to have overlooked that dark side of nature which is recognized in theological doctrines of corruption, or in the scientific theories about the fierce struggle for existence. . . . Is there not a teaching

158

of nature very apt to suggest horror and despair rather than a complacent brooding over soothing thoughts? ['Wordsworth's Ethics']

Stephen's phraseology betrays the influence of Darwin, but of course it had not needed Darwin or 'scientific theories' to reveal the 'fierce struggle for existence' in Nature. Nine years before the appearance of *The Origin of Species* (1859) Tennyson published *In Memoriam*:

> Are God and Nature then at strife,
> That Nature lends such evil dreams?
> So careful of the type she seems,
>   So careless of the single life.
>
>   . . . . . .
>
> 'So careful of the type?' but no.
> From scarpèd cliff and quarried stone
> She cries, 'A thousand types are gone:
>   I care for nothing, all shall go.
>
> 'Thou makest thine appeal to me:
> I bring to life, I bring to death:
> The spirit does but mean the breath:
>   I know no more.' And he, shall he,
>
> Man, her last work, who seemed so fair,
> Such splendid purpose in his eyes,
> Who rolled the psalm to wintry skies,
>   Who built him fanes of fruitless prayer,
>
> Who trusted God was love indeed
> And love Creation's final law –
> Though Nature, red in tooth and claw
>   With ravine, shrieked against his creed –
>
> Who loved, who suffered countless ills,
> Who battled for the True, the Just,
> Be blown about the desert dust,
>   Or sealed within the iron hills?

In the very year in which Keats and Wordsworth met, Keats wrote:

> I was at home
> And should have been most happy, – but I saw
> Too far into the sea, where every maw

> The greater on the less feeds evermore. –
> But I saw too distinct into the core
> Of an eternal fierce destruction, . . .
> The Shark at savage prey, – the Hawk at pounce, –
> The gentle Robin, like a Pard or Ounce,
> Ravening a worm.
> ['Epistle to John Hamilton Reynolds']

Blake was well aware of 'the image of Eternal Death' in nature:

> The Spider sits in his labour'd Web, eager watching for the Fly.
> Presently comes a famish'd Bird & takes away the Spider.
> [*Vala*, Night the First]

Exactly a century before Stephen's book, David Hume's *Dialogues Concerning Natural Religion* had been published. There Hume's spokesman, looking at the 'immense Profusion of Beings' in the Universe, concludes:

> How hostile and destructive to each other! How insufficient all of them for their own Happiness! How contemptible or odious to the Spectator! The whole presents nothing but the Idea of a blind Nature, impregnated by a great vivifying Principle, and pouring forth from her Lap, without discernment or parental Care, her maim'd and abortive Children.

Shakespeare acknowledged the 'dark side of nature', those 'monsters of the deep' that prey on each other. In *The Book of Job* the young eagles 'suck up blood'. Wordsworth seems blankly unaware of the case made so irresistibly there that the mind of man is totally unfitted to comprehend those monstrous powers of the natural world, Behemoth and Leviathan. Hesiod, eight centuries B.C., was well aware that

> Fish, fowl, and savage beasts, (whose law is power)
> Jove lets each other mutually devour.

The purpose of Aldous Huxley's rather heavy-handed essay 'Wordsworth in the Tropics' was to suggest that there it might have been more difficult for him to avoid the seamy side of Nature:

> A few months in the jungle would have convinced him that the diversity and utter strangeness of Nature are at least as real and significant as its intellectually discovered unity. Nor would he have felt certain, in the damp and stifling darkness, among the leeches and the malevolently tangled rattans, of the divinely Anglican character of that fundamental unity.

160

But Wordsworth did not need to go to the tropics to see savage nature. He saw hawks every day, and turned a blind eye, as Hopkins was to do, to their natures, to that Nature of which the hawk is symbol, and to the God of hawks.

Yet despite frequent attacks of this kind Wordsworth's influence in this respect has been so pernicious and long-lasting that it was still possible even after the second world war for a poet (R.S. Thomas in poems like 'The Welsh Hill Country' or Ted Hughes in poems like 'Thrushes', 'Pike' and 'Hawk Roosting', for example) to shock English readers simply by refusing to look at nature in a Wordsworthian way.

*   *   *

Wordsworth eventually came to realize that his earlier confidence 'that Nature never did betray the heart that loved her' was no more than 'the Poet's dream'. He 'could have fancied that the mighty Deep / Was even the gentlest of all gentle Things' ['Elegiac Stanzas'] until it took his brother in 1805. That 'deep distress', he claimed, humanized his soul. Though no longer a worshipper of Nature, he continued to write about it, and when the deep religious feeling is removed, what is left is often mawkish sentimentality.

It would obviously be absurd to suggest that Wordsworth was ignorant of nature, especially of high mountains. But extraordinarily little of the knowledge he had about nature gets into the poems. There are very few animals in Wordsworth, and hardly any of those are predators. In 'The Fountain', for example, is the amazing assertion that all birds die of old age, and a 'beautiful and free' old age at that. Wordsworth is interested, for poetic purposes, in flowers and butterflies, because they are conventionally beautiful, and in songbirds for the sake of their pretty songs. Because of its pleasant nostalgic, romantic or literary associations, the murderous cuckoo is a 'blessed Bird'. No major poet has written sillier poems than Wordsworth, for example 'The Redbreast and the Butterfly':

> What ail'd thee Robin that thou could'st pursue
>   A beautiful Creature,
> That is gentle by nature?
> Beneath the summer sky
> From flower to flower let him fly;
> 'Tis all that he wishes to do.
> The Chearer Thou of our in-door sadness,
> He is the Friend of our summer gladness:
> What hinders, then, that ye should be
> Playmates in the sunny weather,
> And fly about in the air together?
> Like the hues of thy breast
> His beautiful wings in crimson are drest,
> A brother he seems of thine own:
> If thou wouldst be happy in thy nest,

> O pious Bird! whom Man loves best,
> Love him, or leave him alone!

Wordsworth would have had less objection, presumably, had the butterfly been still a caterpillar. This is surely what Nietzsche means by ignorance. Wordsworth seems not to realize that there are forces dictating behaviour in the natural world other than sentimental human notions of beauty and love. There is a lack of respect for the animal world implied by the relentless anthropomorphism.

An almost permanent slumber sealed Wordsworth's spirit to prevent him giving due recognition to the fact that other creatures, including other people, have life-modes of their own which have nothing to do with human morality or aesthetics or the growth of his own mind. He cannot allow anything to have a life of its own. If we think of poets as conjurors able to pull rabbits (lumps of energy alive and kicking) out of their hats, Wordsworth's unusual trick is to make them disappear into his. We think of him as a man of wide and deep sympathies until we realize how many of his experiences are valued only as visitations from Nature in the process of framing 'a favor'd Being', how many of his characters are of interest to him only in so far as they have something to teach him. Their raison-d'être is precisely to enlarge his own sympathies. The leech-gatherer, for example, is described, with astonishing solipsism, as 'Like a man from some far region sent / To give me human strength, by apt admonishment'. If Wordsworth had not happened along at that moment, the leech-gatherer's whole life would have been wasted. It is this aspect of the poem that Lewis Carroll seized on in his brilliant parody 'Upon the Lonely Moor'.

Shelley also wrote a parody of Wordsworth which constitutes (as all the best parodies do) perceptive criticism:

> He had a mind which was somehow
>   At once circumference and centre
> Of all he might feel or know;
> Nothing ever went out, although
>   Something did ever enter.
>
> He had as much imagination
>   As a pint pot; – he never could
> Fancy another situation
> From which to dart his contemplation
>   Than that wherein he stood.
>   ['Peter Bell the Third']

It is very shocking to hear Wordsworth, of all poets, accused of lacking imagination. But if imagination is indeed, as Shelley implies, the means whereby the mind escapes from the tyranny of the ego, enters situations not its own, encounters and admits the not-self, then Wordsworth is indeed lacking in it. His 'spots of time' are all moments of increased awareness of self.

Lawrence also wrote a parody of 'Peter Bell'. The lines which had particularly provoked him were those in which Wordsworth mocks Peter's soullessness:

> A primrose by a river's brim
> A yellow primrose was to him,
> And it was nothing more.

Here is Lawrence's parody, which is little known:

> A primrose by the river's brim
> A yellow primrose was to him
>   And a great deal more –
>
> A primrose by the river's brim
> Lit up its pallid yellow glim
>   Upon the floor –
>
> And watched old Father William trim
> His course beside the river's brim
>   And trembled sore –
>
> The yokel, going for a swim
> Had very nearly trod on him
>   An hour before.
>
> And now the poet's fingers slim
> Were reaching out to pluck at him
>   And hurt him more.
>
> Oh gentlemen, hark to my hymn!
> To be a primrose is my whim
>   Upon the floor,
>   And nothing more.
>
> The sky is with me, and the dim
> Earth clasps my roots. Your shadows skim
>   My face once more . . .
>   Leave me therefore
>   Upon the floor;
>   Say *au revoir* . . .

Ah William! The 'something more' that the primrose was to you, was yourself in the mirror. And if the yokel actually got as far as beholding a 'yellow primrose', he got far enough. You see it is not so easy even for a poet to equilibrate himself even with a mere primrose. He didn't leave it with a soul of its own. It had to have his soul. And nature had to be sweet and pure, Williamish. Sweet-Williamish at that!   [*Phoenix II*, 448–9]

What Lawrence means by 'equilibrate himself' he explains in another essay:

How marvellous is the living relationship between man and his object! be it man or woman, bird, beast, flower or rock or rain: the exquisite frail moment of pure conjunction, which, in the fourth dimension, is timeless. If it is to be life, then it is fifty per cent. me, fifty per cent. thee: and the third thing, the spark, which springs from out of the balance, is timeless.
     [*Phoenix II*, 434–5]

A splendid example of such a living relationship would be that between Lawrence and the pine tree outside his New Mexico ranch:

I think no man could live near a pine tree and remain quite suave and supple and compliant. Something fierce and bristling is communicated. The piny sweetness is rousing and defiant, like turpentine, the noise of the needles is keen with aeons of sharpness. In the volleys of wind from the western desert, the tree hisses and resists. It does not lean eastward at all. It resists with a vast force of resistance, from within itself, and its column is a ribbed, magnificent assertion. . . . I am conscious that it helps to change me, vitally. I am even conscious that shivers of energy cross my living plasm, from the tree, and I become a degree more like unto the tree, more bristling and turpentiney, in Pan.   [*Phoenix* 25]

This is a far cry from

> One impulse from a vernal wood
> May teach you more of man,
> Of moral evil and of good,
> Than all the sages can.
> ['The Tables Turned']

Lawrence's pine tree has nothing to teach, least of all of moral good and evil. Wordsworth cannot see the trees for the moralized wood. Even in the finest poems and passages about his encounters with nature, the impulses Wordsworth receives are all too often rendered as moral teachings rather than strange emanations not reducible to human terms. Even in 'Nutting', with its lovely sense of the 'quiet being' of the unravaged copse, there is no attempt to relate to the hazels other than morally, or to render their unique nature, and we are fobbed off with the hackneyed poetic diction of 'shady nook' and 'mossy bower'.

Wordsworth, too, had begun by defining the Lawrencean balance as 'the first / Poetic spirit of our human life'. The mind of the child, like that of the true poet

> Creates, creator and receiver both,
> Working but in alliance with the works
> Which it beholds.
>
> [*Prelude* II 273–5]

It was a balance which, as we have seen, he could not sustain against the internal pressure to make the creating mind 'lord and master', both centre and circumference of the external universe:

> I had a world about me; 'twas my own,
> I made it; for it only liv'd to me,
> And to the God who look'd into my mind.
>
> [III 142–4]

Since this God seems to have little else to do but look into Wordsworth's mind, he becomes no more than an attribute and apotheosis of that mind. What Wordsworth more and more 'writes Valuable' and seems to be worshipping is the capacity of his own mind to experience a sense of sublimity and transcendence (what Keats called 'the Wordsworthian or egotistical sublime').

11 THE CURSE OF THE ALBATROSS

There is no shortage of minute descriptions of nature in Coleridge's early journals and notebooks. He attempted, with a graphic precision similar to Hopkins', to record something of 'the marvellous distinctiveness & unconfounded personality of each of the million millions of forms, & yet the undivided Unity in which they subsisted' [*Notebooks* II 2344]. Yet, unlike Hopkins, he was rarely able to turn this abundant material ('the lovely shapes and sounds intelligible / Of that eternal language' ['Frost at Midnight'] to poetic account. The reasons for this failure are many and complex. One of the most overt, present from the beginning of his poetic career, is theological. In the early years he was happy to attach a high value to nature in aesthetic terms (the picturesque), and these terms shade off into the moral as he uses nature as a repository of symbols to help him organize and objectify his otherwise elusive and intangible thoughts. It was a world accessible to the mind, yielding patterns of order and unity, and therefore a source of stability and health on which he could depend at times of inner turmoil. Nature, he tried for a while to believe, was given by God for this very purpose. The personal God in whom he believed was a reasonable being who gave men god-like reason in order to apprehend Truth. This is not far removed from the teachings of Aquinas on which Hopkins based his evaluation of nature. But for Coleridge there was no Duns Scotus to mediate between the spiritual austerity of Aquinas and the sensuality of the nature-loving poet. Coleridge's Christianity was not a religion of blessings and creation and incarnation, but of sin, redemption and transcendence. He spoke of his 'natural inheritance of Sin and Condemnation' [*Notebooks* III 4005]. He was in constant fear that to attach any spiritual or theological value to the world of objects perceived by the senses would be to lay himself open to the heresy of pantheism. The attraction of a pantheistic vision is evident in Coleridge's work even before he met the persuasive expression of it in such early Wordsworth poems as 'Tintern Abbey'. In 1795 he wrote:

> And what if all of animated nature
> Be but organic Harps diversely fram'd,
> That tremble into thought, as o'er them sweeps
> Plastic and vast, one intellectual breeze,
> At once the Soul of each, and God of all?

But such thoughts are quickly dismissed as 'unhallow'd', 'shapings of the unregenerate mind' ['The Eolian Harp']. He agreed with Blake that 'whosoever believes in Nature disbelieves in God', and considered it a 'fearful error' even to regard the universe as an attribute of God's deity. He strove, therefore, to keep his God out of the world. It was the opposite tendency in Wordsworth which deeply worried him:

This inferred dependency of the human soul on accident of birth-place
and abode, together with the vague, misty, rather than mystic, confusion
of God with the world, and the accompanying nature-worship, of which
the asserted dependence forms a part, is the trait in Wordsworth's poetic
works that I most dislike as unhealthful, and denounce as contagious.

[*Collected Letters* V, 59]

Coleridge saw himself as obliged to make a choice between his attraction to
nature and his determination 'to fight the bloodless fight / Of Science, Freedom, and the Truth in Christ'. There are other, perhaps deeper reasons for
Coleridge's inability to become a worshipper of nature, to which we shall
return later.

But for one year, the *annus mirabilis* of 1797–8, the combination of
Coleridge's strong emotional response to nature and the irresistible influence
of Wordsworth was able to overcome both his intellectual predilections and
his theological convictions to the extent that he could describe himself as 'all
adoration of the God in Nature'. There is a letter to Thelwall (16 October
1797) written partly in verse and partly in prose. The verse contains the lines:

Struck with the deepest calm of joy, I stand
Silent with swimming sense; and gazing round
On the wide Landscape, gaze till all doth seem
Less gross than bodily, a living Thing
Which acts upon the mind and with such Hues
As cloath th'Almighty Spirit when he makes
Spirits perceive his presence!

This passage begins like Wordsworth, but in the last two lines drifts towards
Coleridge's characteristically more spiritual vision. The prose part of the same
letter makes Coleridge's position much clearer (and much further from
Wordsworth's):

Frequently all *things* appear *little*, all the knowledge that can be acquired
child's play; the universe itself! what but an immense heap of *little*
things? . . . My mind feels as if it ached to behold and know something
great, something *one* and *indivisible*. And it is only in the faith of that
that rocks or waterfalls, mountains or caverns, give me the sense of
sublimity or majesty. But in this faith *all things* counterfeit infinity.

That ambiguous word 'counterfeit' is a long way from the neutral word 'cloath'
in the verse passage. The first six of the nine meanings listed in the O.E.D.
involve the intention to deceive. Is there already, in Coleridge's choice of this
word (when functioning as thinker, not poet) a hint of his later rejection of
pantheism as 'a handsome Mask that does not alter a single feature of the
ugly Face it hides'. Nature is here equated with the devil, or rather with the

167

serpentine Pagan goddess whom Coleridge's deepest imagination found so inescapable and so terrifying:

> Alas! Alas! that Nature is a wary wily long-breathed old witch, tough-lived as a turtle, & divisible as the polyp repullulative in a thousand snips and cuttings, integra et in toto. She is sure to get the better of Lady Mind in the long run & to take her revenge too . . .   [*Notebooks*]

She was also, unfortunately for him, his muse, and her revenge for his defection was to withdraw the gift and the consolations of creativity.

*   *   *

The main difference as poets between Wordsworth and Coleridge at this time was, it seems to me, that Wordsworth was disturbed by the unconscious and disliked as unhealthful Coleridge's dependence on it. Wordsworth valued nature partly because it gave him something solid and external to hold on to and to help him resist the pull of the unconscious. For the same reason, he wrote always in the past tense, long after the event, recollecting emotion in tranquillity. Coleridge plunged into the dark or lurid turbulence of his own emotions at that moment. Wordsworth worked largely in images, Coleridge in symbols. Wordsworth always knew, or thought he knew, exactly what he was doing. Coleridge liked his own poetry best when he didn't understand it. Of some lines in 'The Destiny of Nations' which were later to provide him with much of the symbolic framework of 'The Ancient Mariner':

> . . . When Love rose glittering, and his gorgeous wings
> Over the abyss fluttered with such glad noise,
> As what time after long and pestful calms,
> With slimy shapes and miscreated life
> Poisoning the vast Pacific, the fresh breeze
> Wakens the merchant-sail uprising.

he wrote:

> These are very fine Lines, tho' I say it that should not: but, hang me, if I know or ever did know the meaning of them, tho' my own composition.
>   [*Poetical Works*, 140]

Wordsworth could never have said that. Wordsworth's conception of poetry was almost pedagogic, Coleridge's shamanic. Dorothy Wordsworth's first wondering response to him was that he had more of the 'poet's eye in a fine frenzy rolling' than she had ever witnessed. Opium, though taken as a pain-killer, no doubt helped to propel Coleridge on his shamanic voyages on the sacred rivers and strange seas of his own unconscious.

Thus, fortunately for us, Coleridge's creative imagination habitually bypasses the censorship of his theology.

✢   ✢   ✢

'Kubla Khan' dates from 1797 or 1798. Coleridge's famous account of it as an opium dream interrupted by a person from Porlock was not written until the occasion of its publication in 1816, and may have been invented to forestall accusations of incoherence. The poem would not otherwise seem incomplete. His dismissive description of it as no more than 'a psychological curiosity' would serve the same purpose. Six years earlier, in a notebook, he had described it simply as 'composed in a sort of reverie'. By this he meant a state of day-dreaming in which the intellect and ego are in abeyance, but the imagination is released, allowing symbols to well up from the depths of the unconscious and combine to form a pattern pregnant with deeper and more universal meanings than any the poet could arrive at in his normal state of consciousness. Whitman spoke of this reverie as 'a trance, yet with all the senses alert – only a state of high, exalted musing – the tangible and material with all its shows, the objective world suspended or surmounted for a while, and the powers in exaltation, freedom, vision – yet the senses not lost or counteracted'; and Hughes speaks of 'the necessary trance'.

All great romantic poems are composed in some such state, though in 'Kubla Khan' Coleridge seems to have entered a particularly deep reverie, to have released particularly potent symbols, and to have had the courage to let them work without subsequent interference or interpretation. They are metaphors for his own nature conceived at such a depth that they are also metaphors for ours. The whole poem is to communicate its meanings entirely through such symbols. Coleridge himself has no definitive access to their meaning. We must make of them what we can, allowing them to play upon each other, upon whatever else we happen to know of Coleridge or of other literature, and upon our own imaginations.

> In Xanadu did Kubla Khan
> A stately pleasure-dome decree:
> Where Alph, the sacred river, ran
> Through caverns measureless to man
> Down to a sunless sea.
> So twice five miles of fertile ground
> With walls and towers were girdled round:
> And there were gardens bright with sinuous rills,
> Where blossomed many an incense-bearing tree;
> And here were forests ancient as the hills,
> Enfolding sunny spots of greenery.

Within these few lines Coleridge has established the basic polarities of the poem by juxtaposing the pleasure-dome and the sacred river, that which is designed and built by and for man, and that which is natural and 'measureless to man'. The polarities are sacred and profane, artificial and natural, human and non-human, fertile and sterile, life and death. Within the walls these polarities are to be reconciled. The odd word 'so' beginning the second sentence may simply mean that everything was built because Kubla Khan had decreed it, or that the walls were built to create a self-enclosed world where life could be dedicated to pleasure, a pagan paradise of atonement, where walls do not exclude mother earth but girdle her, and she responds to this nurture by blossoming and enfolding. The attempt is vast, not to reject life or any part of it, but to bring everything into accord with man and his pleasure. The walls must therefore enclose the whole above-ground stretch of the river of life, from source to sink.

What had no doubt impressed itself deeply on Coleridge in the passage from Purchas which had inspired 'Kubla Khan' was the inclusiveness of Kubla's enclosure, and his determination to ensure the benison of nature by pouring forth, 'with his own hands', the milk of thousands of white mares 'in the aire, and on the earth, to give drink to the spirits and Idols which they worship, that they may preserve the men, women, beasts, birds, corne, and other things growing on the earth'. If nature accepts the sacrifice, she responds with milk and honey-dew of her own, and man and nature are at one.

In the second stanza the female suggestions become more intense and finally explicitly sexual. The opening phrase 'But oh!' indicates that something dreadful is about to be described. That 'deep romantic chasm which slanted / Down the green hill athwart a cedarn cover!' is no less than the groin of Mother Earth, a place simultaneously savage, holy, enchanted and demonic, the fount and origin of all life. The earth, like a woman in labour, breathes in 'fast thick pants', then suddenly gives birth to a mighty fountain tossing huge dancing fragments of rock (of which, perhaps, the palace is built). And this giving birth, this eruption of creative energy, is perpetual, a 'ceaseless turmoil'. Then the river settles down to meander gently for five miles, watering the woods and gardens, until it reaches the caverns through which it sinks into 'a lifeless ocean'. The sacred river is a symbol of life itself, that undifferentiated life which the Greeks called *zoë*, nature's fertilizing energy available for a time to man to channel into his creative purposes; energies born in the turmoil of sex and blood, and doomed, after a term, to be dissipated in the destructive tumult of death.

Midway between the fountain and the caverns, between birth and death, Kubla Khan builds his pleasure-dome, from which can be heard both the turmoil of the rising waters and the tumult of the falling waters in a 'mingled measure' which is the music and the dance of a life in harmony with both. Whereas a spire or Gothic arch is a symbol of the aspiration to detach the spirit from the earth, the dome-shape, like Lawrence's rainbow (and, behind him, the rainbow of Genesis) is a symbol of the reconciliation of heaven and earth, body and spirit. It is a symbol of fulfilment, rounded and complete, like a breast. Its wholeness constitutes its holiness. It is thus the opposite of Shelley's 'dome of many-coloured glass', which is life staining 'the white radiance of Eternity' ['Adonais'], of Tennyson's Palace of Art, a 'lordly pleasure-house' specifically designed to exclude the world and its cycles and tumult, and of Yeats' Byzantium, which also repudiates nature in favour of art, and neglects 'sensual music' in favour of 'monuments of unageing intellect'. Moreover, this 'miracle of rare device' (art) seems to have been constructed to be as sunny as possible, reaching upwards, but also to extend down into the earth where there are caves of ice. Kubla's domain reaches horizontally through time from long before birth ('ancestral voices') to the distant future (prophesies of its own inevitable destruction), and also vertically through space from the sun to the under-earth, from the highest to the lowest, the hottest to the coldest extremes available to man's senses. Had it sought pleasure by attempting to exclude the ancestral voices and the tumult it would have been merely escapist and self-indulgent. Had it allowed them to prevail, dejection would have supervened and condemned the whole enterprise to remain unfinished.

Kubla Khan might more easily have enclosed only that section of the river which meandered gently for five miles, and all within his walls would have been gardens and pleasure-dome. The palace of art was often thought of as dedicated to beauty, shutting out the world where ignorant armies clash by night. That, for Coleridge, would have been mere fancy, not imagination which must pay all its debts to reality. T.H. Huxley was to speak of the highest human activity as building, in opposition to the state of nature, the state of art. What Kubla builds in his palace and Coleridge in his poem is in defiance of that opposition. Here art admits its total dependence on nature. All fertility and creativity ultimately depend on the sacred river. 'Great creating Nature' creates the gardener and the artist too. The 'miracle of rare device' may be the product of a human brain, but that in turn is a product of nature and subservient to its laws. Coleridge regarded the ability to achieve such reconciliation of opposites as the highest power of the poet:

> The poet, described in ideal perfection, brings the whole soul of man into activity.... He diffuses a tone and spirit of unity, that blends, and (as it were) *fuses*, each into each, by that synthetic and magical power, to which we have exclusively appropriated the name of imagination. This power ... reveals itself in the balance or reconciliation of opposite or discordant qualities.   [*Biographia Literaria*, ch.XIV]

In the closing section the poet claims that in order to create the poetic equivalent of 'that dome in air' he would have to recapture a 'deep delight' he had once experienced in a vision of a 'damsel with a dulcimer'. The fount of inspiration is associated, again, with woman, or female muse, who acts as intermediary between poet and nature. Her song is always a symphony because she sings, spontaneously, in harmony with nature (which men, for reasons which will emerge in 'Dejection', are no longer capable of). Coleridge always associated his loss of inspiration with his failure to establish a satisfactory relationship with a woman. Given that inspiration, from woman or any other source, the poet is transformed into the prophet or shaman, who makes the dangerous journey, on behalf of us all, into the depths of the psyche, the spirit world, to return half-crazed, but with healing truths. This truth-teller is always feared by rationalists, materialists, and by those who simply want to be left alone to go to the wedding feast, to make money, to read the newspaper, or to write yet another book of post-modern critical theory. As Ted Hughes says:

> How can a poet become a medicine man and fly to the source and come back and heal or pronounce oracles? Everything among us is against it.

He has also been feared and persecuted by the devotees of revealed religion, and was therefore feared, and ultimately proscribed by Coleridge's Christian self. The struggle between Coleridge's Unleavened self and his Christian self is brilliantly described in Hughes' essay 'The Snake in the Oak' (*Winter Pollen*, 1994).

✢   ✢   ✢

Wordsworth's ponderous and patronizing list of the 'great defects' of 'The Ancient Mariner' which he included in his preface to the second edition of the *Lyrical Ballads* reveals that he was unable to read the poem Coleridge had actually written, unable to recognize the symbolic meaning of the plot, the characters or the imagery:

> First that the principal person has no distinct character, either in his profession of Mariner, or as a human being who having been long under the control of supernatural impressions might be supposed himself to partake of something supernatural: secondly, that he does not act, but is continually acted upon: thirdly, that the events having no necessary connection do not produce each other; and lastly, that the imagery is somewhat too laboriously accumulated.

It is significant that Coleridge was an outstanding interpreter of Shakespeare. Coleridge too, whether he knew it or not, was perpetually generating metaphors for his own nature. He described himself as 'seeking, as it were *asking* for, a symbolical language for something within me that already and forever exists'. He is searching, in other words, for archetypes. Speaking of 'The Ancient Mariner' he claimed that what gives these 'shadows of imagination' their credibility is the 'semblance of truth' they receive from his 'inward nature'.

There is every bit as much of Coleridge's 'inward nature' in 'The Ancient Mariner' as in 'Dejection', but translated into some of the most striking, memorable and universal objective correlatives in literature. The strongest, most deeply felt stanza in the poem is not one of the macabre highlights, but the painful reiteration of

> Alone, alone, all, all alone,
> Alone on a wide wide sea!
> And never a saint took pity on
> My soul in agony.

The strongest element throughout the poem is this agony compounded of loneliness, desolation and remorse. In the notebooks we can see this agony searching for its symbols:

> in that eternal and delerious misery –
> wrathfires –
>   inward desolations –
>   an horror of great darkness
> great things that on the ocean
>   counterfeit infinity –

The theme is exactly the same as that of the abortive long poem 'The Wanderings of Cain' which Coleridge abandoned in order to write 'The Ancient Mariner'. It was to be about 'guilt, suffering, expiation and wandering . . . The scene was desolate; as far as the eye could reach it was desolate'. And Cain was to be punished by God not only for a senseless killing, but 'because he neglected to make a proper use of his senses'.

If Coleridge is himself the mariner, what had he killed to give him such remorse? Clearly it was no bird or external creature, but a part of himself. In 1808 he was to write: 'O had I health and youth, and were what I once was – but I played the fool, and cut the throat of my Happiness, of my genius, of my utility'. Self-murder is not too strong an image for several ways in which Coleridge already felt that he had senselessly killed the best part of himself, his capacity for loving.

At the time of writing 'The Ancient Mariner' Coleridge had never been to sea. Some years later he was at sea and saw men shooting at a hawk from the ship, and wrote – 'Poor Hawk! O Strange Lust of Murder in Man! – It is not cruelty. It is mere non-feeling from non-thinking'. The shooting of the albatross is motiveless because in the unawakened consciousness of the mariner it is too trivial an act to need a motive; it is no different from shooting at a bottle. A mariner is one who cuts himself off from the living body of mankind and sails to silent seas where 'no living thing was to be seen'. In this he is a perfect symbol of the reclusive thinker whose abstruse researches take him further and further from nature and common human experience. The imagination cannot deal in abstract things. To reject nature and the life of the senses is necessarily to exile the Muse and starve imagination. The poet's tongue 'through utter drought' is 'withered at the root'. But the poet who is honest and humble and courageous enough (as Coleridge, for one glorious year was) to admit that this has happened, to accept responsibility for it, to allow the suffering imagination to exact its terrible revenges, opens the way through ego-death to a rebirth of imagination and glorious reconciliation with the transfigured Muse.

This account by no means exhausts the significance of the killing of the albatross. There are also more deeply personal and more universal dimensions. Several critics have noted the heavily sexual imagery of the poem. The poem includes its own representative auditor in the form of the wedding-guest, disgusted by and afraid of the mariner yet held by his glittering eye. He is equally pulled by the merry din of the wedding, the feast, the rose-red bride, and the dreadful tale of the withered mariner, whose cross-bow is later to suggest (like the dead albatross hanging from his neck) both an inverted crucifix and a perverse alternative (like Adonis' spear) for normal, generative, perhaps even sacramental, phallic activity. The mariner later projects onto the surface of the Sargasso Sea the obscene contents of his own disordered psyche. As Wilson Knight describes it:

It is a lurid, colourful, yet ghastly death-impregnated scene, drawn to express aversion from physical life in dissolution or any reptilian manifestation; and, by suggestion, the sexual as seen from the mentalized consciousness as an alien, salty, reptilian force. It is a deathly paralysis corresponding, it may be, to a sense of sexually starved existence in the modern world; certainly 'water, water everywhere, nor any drop to drink' fits such a reading. [*The Starlit Dome*, 85–6]

That the water-snakes symbolize the passions, especially sexual passions, cannot be doubted. In 'Pantisocracy' Coleridge had written:

> And dancing to the moonlight roundelay,
> The wizard Passions weave an holy spell.

The curse is merely the extension to the external world of what has already happened inside the mariner. Wind symbolizes both inspiration and creative energy. It was the albatross (love) that had 'made the breeze to blow'. Now the sea itself, source of all life, is stagnant. Rain cannot fall, for the mariner has dammed up the spring of love in his own heart. Hughes writes:

Considering the situation as a game, one could say the Christian Crossbow Self has won the first round, and in winning has forced onto the bird and the sea of the Female . . . a state like death, and onto itself a life of horror, dumbly staring at the world of its own death-dealing rejection, a world that seems to putrefy. [*WP* 455]

Lawrence's 'Snake' is a poem clearly inspired, in part, by 'The Ancient Mariner'. Here the phallic snake excites horror by entering a symbolically female 'fissure', miming the sex act. The narrator, in his attempt to kill the snake (come to drink from a common source of water), combines in one act the mariner's killing of the albatross and his horror at the writhing of the water-snakes. Immediately, the narrator regrets it:

> I despised myself and the voices of my accursed human education.
> And I thought of the albatross,
> And I wished he would come back, my snake.
>
> For he seemed to me again like a king,
> Like a king in exile, uncrowned in the underworld,
> Now due to be crowned again.
>
> And so, I missed my chance with one of the lords
> Of life.
> And I have something to expiate:
> A pettiness.

The mariner, too, comes to see 'God's creatures of the calm' as lordly, having their appointed place in the scheme of things. Coleridge's gloss compares them with the stars:

> The blue sky belongs to them, and is their appointed rest, and their native country and their own natural homes, which they enter unannounced, as lords that are certainly expected and yet there is silent joy at their arrival.

Lawrence's earlier explication of serpent symbolism applies equally to his own later poem and to 'The Ancient Mariner':

> If there is a serpent of secret and shameful desire in my soul, let me not beat it out of my consciousness with sticks. It will lie beyond, in the march of the so-called subconsciousness, where I cannot follow it with my sticks. Let me bring it to the fire to see what it is. For a serpent is a thing created. It has its own *raison d'être*. In its own being it has beauty and reality. . . . For the Lord is the lord of all things, not of some only. And everything shall in its proportion drink its own draught of life.
>
> [*Phoenix*, 677–9]

[It is interesting to note that the spirit of Sicily during Coleridge's visit in 1804 released him from the voice of his education and his deep-seated horror of the reptilian: 'O this savage and unforgettable scene! Huge Stones and huge Trees, & small & large Trees and stones . . . & the savage women in the

Torrent, hairy menlike legs – Oleander! Ivy! Myrtle / and all the pot herbs – lovely Lizards The Paradise.']

The albatross is the opposite of the mariner. Despite its prodigious wings, it chooses to descend to share the lot of men, in sheer fellowship. When its body is later hung about the neck of the mariner instead of the cross, the parallel with Christ is made specific. It represents also the last tenuous link between the mariners and the rest of life. The mariner's act is therefore an unconscious claim to be able to do without this link with man, nature and God-in-nature. It is an act of pure hubris.

But the powers symbolized by the albatross cannot really be killed. They can be repudiated and violated. This treatment only serves to drive the energies underground ('nine fathom deep') where they work destructively, and are inaccessible to human understanding or control, glimpsed only in dreams and nightmares. Everything is reversed. Instead of the glorious sun of dawn we have 'the bloody sun at noon' (a god of wrath). Instead of the moon as protective virgin ('Mary Queen') we have the White Goddess in her other aspect as witch and whore:

> Her skin was as white as leprosy,
> Her lips were red, her looks were free,
> Her locks were yellow as gold:
> The Night-mare LIFE-IN-DEATH was she,
> Who thicks man's blood with cold.

The triple goddess can save and inspire, but she can, provoked, turn men mad. The mariner's glittering eye signifies that he is moonstruck, lunatic.

Coleridge's Nature here manifests itself as Christian and Pagan powers simultaneously. While the Polar spirit works from below, concerned, like the Eumenides, only to avenge the sacrilege of the spilt blood of the guest, the Angels working above are concerned to transform the curse into redemptive suffering leading to at least partial expiation and redemption. The outcome is something of a compromise.

The Hermit makes godly hymns in the wood, celebrating both Nature and God. His altar is a moss-covered oak-stump. He does not cut himself off from other men but 'loves to talk with mariners'. The Nature he knows and worships, however, is far from Wordsworth's 'vernal wood'. It contains Love and processes of redemption and rebirth, but also, indivisibly, decay, fear, pain and death:

> Brown skeletons of leaves that lag
> My forest-brook along;
> When ivy-tod is heavy with snow,
> And the owlet whoops to the wolf below,
> That eats the she-wolf's young.

The mariner/shaman/poet has made his psychic journey into the spirit world and returned to the human world, come full circle to his point of departure, but transformed by his experiences, half-crazed, but bearing healing truths for mankind. R.D. Laing describes the voyage in these terms:

> This journey is experienced as going further 'in', as going back through one's personal life, in and back and through and beyond into the experience of all mankind, of the primal man, of Adam and perhaps even further into the being of animals, vegetables and minerals. In this journey there are many occasions to lose one's way, for confusion, partial failure, even final shipwreck: many terrors, spirits, demons to be encountered, that may or may not be overcome. . . . We are so out of touch with this realm that many people can now argue seriously that it does not exist. It is very small wonder that it is perilous indeed to explore such a lost realm.
> [*The Politics of Experience*, 104–5]

The imaginative, prophetic, healing power is as much a curse as a blessing. The gift of prophecy was from the first often accompanied by the curse of never being believed. Few wish to listen to such truths, or can accept them having listened. The mariner's impact is disastrous – the Pilot falls into a fit; the Pilot's boy goes permanently insane; the Hermit can scarcely stand and cannot shrieve him; the wedding guest turns away from the wedding 'like one that hath been stunned / And is of sense forlorn'.

It is as though Coleridge had had the experience, but his Christian self refused to allow him to hold on to its meaning. As Hughes puts it:

> Coleridge experiences his Pagan 'regression' as a breakthrough to a vision of greater spiritual meaning: his vision of the beauty of the sea-snakes, which renews his (the Mariner's) spiritual being, and redeems all the horrors of his Christian adventure. Nevertheless, when Coleridge's habitually dominant Christian attitude reasserts itself, after this brief, mystical reversal, the returned Mariner's experience is recounted, and heard, not as a vision of greater spiritual meaning, a revelation of the divine glory of the total creation, but as something unspeakably dreadful, incomprehensibly ominous and disheartening, a tale too terrible to be told or heard, like a curse.
> [*WP* 451]

  ✱ ✱ ✱

Wordsworth did all he could to discourage Coleridge from going on writing in the manner of the great poems, where Coleridge had sought symbols for inner realities, even when those realities were disturbing or disgusting. But even without Wordsworth's influence, he would probably have sought increasingly symbols only for the pure and perfect, and these he found in other people rather than in the natural world or in himself. His use of symbols becomes increasingly self-conscious; they degenerate from being the forgotten or

hidden truths of his own nature to being fully conscious emblems and ana-
logues for intellectual ideas and ideals. His refusal of unconscious symbols
bars him from the sources of his finest poetry. By 1802 the only remaining
subject for distinguished poetry is his lament for what is lost. In March of that
year Coleridge wrote 'the Poet is dead in me'.

    The date Coleridge gave his 'Dejection' ode (4 April 1802), though we
know the ode was not composed on any single day, is significant. Early April
is a time when one might hope for a resumption of creativity. At the beginning
of the *Canterbury Tales* Chaucer takes for granted that as the sweet showers
of April engender the flowers, and the sunshine and gentle breezes prick the
hearts of birds into song, so these same impulses will stimulate the hearts of
men into both physical and spiritual activity. When the natural world ceases
to give a man's soul this 'wonted impulse', or his soul ceases to be able to
receive it, he experiences a particularly acute and modern form of dejection
we call alienation – a sense of being cut off from the sources of life and from
its potential fruitfulness:

> Sometimes when I earnestly look at a beautiful Object or Landscape, it
> seems as if I were on the *brink* of a Fruition still denied.
>
> [*Notebooks* III 3767]

When T.S. Eliot wanted to create a sense of the loss of harmony between
human feelings and the seasonal rhythms of the natural world, he began *The
Waste Land* with an inversion of the beginning of the *Canterbury Tales*:

> April is the cruellest month, breeding
> Lilacs out of the dead land, mixing
> Memory and desire, stirring
> Dull roots with spring rain.

Wordsworth's creativity was similarly cruel to Coleridge – 'Life's joy rekindling
roused a throng of pains' ['To William Wordsworth']. The flowers of spring are
welcomed, though Coleridge could now find no other use for them than to
strew them upon his own grave.

    The word 'dull' is prominent also at the beginning of Coleridge's ode.
His inspiration now is not worth calling a wind, merely a 'dull sobbing draft,
that moans and rakes / Upon the strings of this Aeolian lute, / Which better
far were mute'. The first stanza is a prayer for wind and rain, not the gentle
breezes and showers of Chaucer, but a 'squally blast' with slant driving rain.
So dull are his feelings that he cannot imagine that anything less than a
full-blown storm 'might startle this dull pain, and make it move and live!' He
is not praying for the pain to go away, but for it to blossom into expression,
which would itself be some relief. As it is, his depression is locked within
him:

> A grief without a pang, void, dark and drear,
> A stifled, drowsy, unimpassioned grief,
> Which finds no natural outlet, no relief,
> In word, or sigh, or tear –

It is a self-absorbed stifling grief which prevents him responding or relating to anything outside himself. Yet a poet is, by his own definition, one who can send his soul, his imagination, abroad to commune with the other, the not-self.

The danger is that this poem too will turn in upon itself, licking its own sores, like a Hamlet soliloquy. His only hope is an external beacon or guiding star. He addresses the poem to his beloved Sara, his muse, and an embodiment of that Joy which is the mortal enemy of Dejection.

It had been a balmy and serene evening, full of birdsong, lovely cloud formations, followed by sparkling stars and a crescent moon – a scene which at one time would have filled Coleridge with joyful emotions. Now, though his eyes register the beauty, he feels nothing, as if the connection between his outward senses and his inner feelings had been severed. From this he concludes:

> I may not hope from outward forms to win
> The passion and the life, whose fountains are within.

The image of the fountain, together with the description of his dejection as a 'smothering weight' on his breast, reminds us of 'The Ancient Mariner', whose lack of feeling had caused him to shoot the albatross, whose heavy body was then hung about his neck. This weight fell from him and the natural intercourse of nature – wind and rain – resumed only when his spontaneous feelings were released like a fountain. But if Coleridge himself understood 'The Ancient Mariner' he was unable to act on or live by what it said to him. By repudiating nature and 'the natural man', the life of the body, he severed himself from the tree of life: he shot the albatross. And the spring of love which gushed from his heart, for Sara Hutchinson, was no blessing, but itself a curse.

Intercourse, either with outward forms through the senses or with the archetypes of his own unconscious, always stimulated Coleridge to desire sexual intercourse with women. Not only was such intercourse banned by religious law as adulterous, but any overt sexuality, even with his wife, had come to seem to Coleridge to be a capitulation to the lowest in himself. His ultimate requirement from Sara was that she should be a living embodiment of absolute purity and a symbol of perfection. He must therefore protect her from his own degrading sexual desires, and from any touch of nature. He thus violated both Sara herself, and the 'natural man' in his own nature. His determination that his sexual drives should be repressed drove him to reject the whole natural world, which became a source of temptation rather than strength.

Coleridge has by now committed himself to the belief that man's intellectual and spiritual faculties are higher than nature, and that the forms of nature must be subjugated to the intellect. Like Blake he believed that without man nature would be barren, or, in his own words, 'an inanimate cold world'. Yet no sooner has he claimed that 'in our life alone does Nature live: Ours is her wedding garment, ours her shroud', than he is driven to define the Joy which issues from the soul as 'Life, and Life's effluence, cloud at once and shower':

> Joy, Lady! is the spirit and the power,
> Which wedding Nature to us gives in dower.

What we give to Nature, it seems, we have received from her.

The claim that the loss of his 'shaping spirit of Imagination' can be laid at the door of too much 'abstruse research' seems but a rationalization or evasion of the real 'viper thoughts' which are not allowed into this poem, but emerge under cover of nightmares in 'The Pains of Sleep' ('desire with loathing strangely mixed', 'life-stifling fear, soul-stifling shame'), and more explicitly, despite the use of ciphers, in the notebooks.

As the poem begins once more to coil around itself, Coleridge seeks to project his soul outwards again by paying attention to the wind which has now got up. He first interprets the sound of it as a 'scream of agony' or the groans of a routed army. But suddenly the noise ceases, and in the profound silence which follows, he imagines a less frightening tale:

> 'Tis of a little child
> Upon a lonesome wild,
> Not far from home, but she hath lost her way:
> And now moans low in bitter grief and fear,
> And now screams loud, and hopes to make her mother hear.

This tale is 'tempered with delight' because of its implication that there are such things as home and mother waiting to be found. The child seeks its home. The mother seeks her child. They are not far apart. The child has lost her way only for a while. Coleridge is obviously that lost child. Home is where he belongs. The mother is the loving female, whether an actual loving woman, or Nature, or his own anima. In the final stanza the storm becomes a 'mountain-birth' which can only mean that Sara, with the stars hanging bright over her dwelling, is to be the virgin mother out of whom the whole of creation is to be reborn, purified and unified in her:

> To her may all things live, from pole to pole,
> Their life the eddying of her living soul!

The prayer is desperate, and could not be answered. Neither Sara nor anyone else could redeem Coleridge from the damage he continued to inflict upon himself.

Not least in the causes of his dejection was the knowledge that he had so desperately mismanaged his own sensibilities, that there had been

> a long and blessed interval, during which my natural faculties were allowed to expand, and my original tendencies to develop themselves: my fancy, and the love of nature, and the sense of beauty in forms and sounds.
>
> [*Biographia* I, 10]

That he had once 'traced the fount whence streams of nectar flow', had fed on honey-dew, and drunk the milk of Paradise.

Coleridge was never able to recover Joy from without or within:

> In vain we supplicate the Powers above;
> There is no resurrection for the Love
> That, nursed in tenderest care, yet fades away
> In the chilled heart by gradual self-decay.
> ['Love's Apparition and Evanishment']

What remained was work without hope:

> Work without Hope draws nectar in a sieve,
> And Hope without an object cannot live.
> ['Work without Hope']

Nor can poetry live without access to nature, either in its outward forms or its inward symbols.

Norman Fruman sums up Coleridge's later life:

> The later Coleridge presents a poignant image of severely diminished emotional range and response. Suppressing the 'natural man' in himself, he willingly embraced the role of sedentary semi-invalid over the last eighteen years of his life. He left his wife when he was just thirty-four years old – never having been an ardent husband – and for the next twenty-eight years he was celibate, and struggled mightily to banish sexual images from his mind. He spent the long Highgate years more or less in the garb and stance of a priest, clad from head to toe in black, and declaiming against the evils of the age and the animal in us all. He was still a young man when he ceased to be a husband, father, brother, or lover to anyone.
>
> [Gravil, 75]

His alienation was complete, most notably, perhaps, in his alienation from the life of the body. In the *Biographia* Coleridge speaks of

the seeming identity of body and mind in infants, and thence the
loveliness of the former; the commencing separation in boyhood, and the
struggle of equilibrium in youth: thence inward the body is first simply
indifferent; then demanding the translucency of the mind not to be worse
than indifferent; and finally all that presents the body as body becoming
almost of an excremental nature.   [II 263]

(Here is Blake's 'Vile Body'.) But the buried life of the body is still, as late as
1825, capable of crying out its distress in the poetry:

> All Nature seems at work. Slugs leave their lair –
> The bees are stirring – birds are on the wing –
> And Winter slumbering in the open air,
> Wears on his smiling face a dream of Spring!
> And I the while, the sole unbusy thing,
> Nor honey make, nor pair, nor build, nor sing.
>   ['Work without Hope']

Like Hopkins he felt himself to be 'time's eunuch' (a word which occurs,
encoded, in the *Notebooks*). And the result, as always, was not the hoped for
soaring of the life of the spirit, but spiritual paralysis. In his own epitaph he
described himself as 'he who many a year with toil of breath / Found death in
life'.

12 THE CRIME AGAINST HEATHCLIFF

In the context of the nineteenth-century English novel, the most striking feature of *Wuthering Heights* is its originality. Other novelists, including her sisters, dealt with relationships, manners and morals in a highly civilized society. Emily Brontë had no social life, few relationships outside the household, and neither knew nor cared about the world beyond Haworth. Her inner life was turbulent and passionate. She found on the moors around her living manifestations of those same forces which warred within her. There is little place for nature in the English novel before Hardy; none for wild nature, even in the rural novels. Dorothy van Ghent writes:

> In George Eliot's *Adam Bede*, where there is relatively a great deal of 'outdoors', nature is man's plowfield, the acre in which he finds social and ethical expression through work; this is only a different variety of the conception of nature as significant by virtue of what man's intelligential and social character makes of it for his ends. [251]

Emily Brontë's own nature led her to wild nature as its mirror, subsuming Heaven and Hell. She exulted in the freedom, wildness and purity of the moor, its summer profusion and blossom and birdsong, its space for the spirit to soar in. She knew also the wuthering wind on the heights, the desolation, the inhuman cruelty of its storms and winters. Still, she chose the heath as her heaven, even if that meant choosing exposure and death. So the landscape of the novel is also her own psychic and spiritual landscape, which she explores with single-minded unfaltering honesty.

In comparison with Emily Brontë's, Coleridge's was a 'coward soul'. Emily Brontë's relationship with Nature was not complicated by any Christian affiliation. Her imagination was not cowed by guilt. Like Blake she was well aware of the dehumanizing influence of Christianity, as preached and practised in England at that time. So confident was she in her inner lights that there is no sense of the breaking of taboos in her attack on religion. Her Blake-like confidence in the abnormality and unnaturalness of it enables her to treat it largely in a comic mode, which takes for granted that the reader will share the writer's norms. It was very disconcerting for her first readers to find their sympathies being drawn into an alliance through comedy against the most sacrosanct beliefs of the time. Joseph is almost the only spokesman in the novel for religion, which in his mouth becomes gibberish. His vocation, we are told, was to be where there was plenty of wickedness to reprove. Emily Brontë must have known Wesley's description of Yorkshire: 'that place suits me best where so many are groaning for redemption'. The effect is to make it impossible to take seriously, to puncture and empty of all moral or spiritual content, such words as 'wickedness' and 'redemption'. The poetry of the novel transfers that charge to another set of words and images altogether.

Unlike Blake, she found in Nature the only heaven she needed. Unlike Wordsworth, she yearned for no imperial palace elsewhere. Catherine's dreams of such a place are nightmares of alienation and exile. Emily Brontë must, from an early age, have rejected the 'lumber' thrust upon her in the form of Methodist tracts, and rebelled against the patriarchal God in all his forms in favour of the God within her breast, the 'Almighty ever-present Deity / Life':

> Vain are the thousand creeds
> That move men's hearts, unutterably vain,
> Worthless as withered weeds
> Or idlest froth amid the boundless main
> ['No coward soul is mine']

How she would have loved Whitman:

> Divine am I inside and out, and I make holy whatever I touch or am
>   touch'd from,
> The scent of these arm-pits aroma finer than prayer,
> This head more than churches, bibles, and all the creeds.
> ['Song of Myself' 24]

Like him she believed that Life was Undying and infinite, and was not offended by its 'perpetual transfers and promotions' [49]:

> With wide-embracing love
> Thy spirit animates eternal years
> Pervades and broods above,
> Changes, sustains, dissolves, creates and rears

>   . . .

>   There is not room for Death
> Nor atom that his might could render void
> Since thou art Being and Breath
> And what thou art may never be destroyed.

This is amazingly close to Whitman's

> The smallest sprout shows there is really no death,
> And if ever there was it led forward life, and does not wait at the end
>   to arrest it,
> And ceas'd the moment life appear'd.
> All goes onward and outward, nothing collapses,
> And to die is different from what anyone supposed, and luckier. [6]

184

With Whitman she could have written: 'I bequeath myself to the dirt to grow from the grass I love' [52]. Catherine, in her grave, achieves this atonement: 'It was dug on a green slope, in a corner of the kirkyard, where the wall is so low that heath and bilberry plants have climbed over it from the moor; and peat mould almost buries it.' [205]

Unlike Hopkins, no fear of 'death's worst, winding sheets, tombs and worms and tumbling to decay' could frighten her, no promise of heaven seduce her, from her attachment to mother earth:

> Indeed, no dazzling land above
> Can cheat thee of thy children's love . . .
> We would not leave our native home
> For *any* world beyond the Tomb.
>   ['I see around me tombstones grey']

Life includes pain and death. If Life cannot be sustained on earth, it continues under it. There is nothing aesthetic or anthropomorphic or in any way selective about Emily Brontë's Nature. It is as harsh as any depiction of nature in our literature. While Wordsworth's birds die of happy old age, Emily Brontë's are lucky if they manage to leave the nest.

The most potent single metaphor of her own nature is wind. Her choice of title for *Wuthering Heights* indicates her own awareness of its centrality. Wind represents all the 'wandering elementals' which, if let into our consciousness, would make impossible the continuance of our complacent round of reading, thinking and human relationships. Wind at its most beneficent is the breath of life. At its most destructive it is the wind which twists and stunts and kills. At the Heights, the 'atmospheric tumult' is such that 'the narrow windows are deeply set in the wall, and the corners defended with large jutting stones' [46]. Etymologically, 'window' means 'wind's eye'; and the eye is the window of the soul. A window is like a delicate membrane keeping out ghosts, demons, all the dark, anarchic forces which inhabit what we would prefer to think of as the safely locked cellar of the unconscious. Heathcliff's eyes are described as 'the clouded windows of hell'.

In *Wuthering Heights*, the window does come in. Its breaking is associated with violent emotions, bloodshed, violation and the supernatural. What has there been shut out is not only the stormy elements, but a child from her rightful spiritual home and inheritance. You cannot shut out death and danger without shutting out nature, and therefore life and love.

In every other chapter in this book the criminal is male and the victim female (or the female component in the male psyche). In many women writers this would also be the case; but in Emily Brontë these roles are conflated – she refuses all sexual discriminations. Nature presents itself to her as the universal mother insofar as it is the womb and tomb of life; but between those extremes it is rather that which is other than her own vulnerable femaleness, the not-self beyond the ego (or the ego extending without limit), wild, free, energetic, challenging, harsh. Not Nature the loving or devouring mother, but Nature the exhilarating elemental exposure of heath and cliff, 'where the wild wind blows on the mountain side'.

Deprived from early childhood of a mother, Emily Brontë might have been expected to be particularly exposed to the pressures of a patriarchal society. But because of her own extreme independence of spirit (or bloody-mindedness), she seems to have been totally immune to whatever pressures were put upon her from the outside to modify her ideas or behaviour in any way. The relatively high degree of conventionality in her sisters indicates that the pressures were there. The combination of Emily Brontë's character and circumstances gave her the terrible choice between death-in-life and life-in-death. Like her sisters, she could have tried to make what she could of society and human relationships, even perhaps marriage, and have repressed as childish her immortal longings. But she was wiser than Cathy and knew what would have to be given up. Rather she chose not to reject her inner life, but to nurse it and live through it and defend it against the world. But because, despite the rare tolerance of Patrick Brontë, her spirit was under continual siege, it drove her further into isolation, harshness, and a degree of brutality against both herself and others. It was a cold wind which bit her breast. She chose what seemed to her the lesser of two evils. The good which was not available to her in life, she sought in her art.

*　　*　　*

Charlotte Brontë claimed that Heathcliff

> exemplified the effects which a life of continued injustice and hard usage
> may produce on a naturally perverse, vindictive, and inexorable
> disposition. Carefully trained and kindly treated, the black gypsy-cub
> might possibly have been reared into a human being, but tyranny and
> ignorance made of him a mere demon. The worst of it is, some of his
> spirit seems breathed through the whole narrative in which he figures: it
> haunts every moor and glen, and beckons in every fir-tree of the Heights.
>
> [Petit 33–4]

Her prejudices against him are exactly those of Mrs. Earnshaw, who was 'ready to fling it out of doors: she did fly up – asking how he could fashion to bring that gypsy brat into the house' [77]. The child's obscure origins and dark colouring do not make him a gypsy, and gypsies, in any case, are human beings. No-one heeds Earnshaw's warning: 'you must e'en take it as a gift of God; though it's as dark almost as if it came from the devil'. The injustice and hard usage begin at once. Spontaneous rejection is the child's first experience at the Heights, before he can have done anything to deserve it. We know nothing of his natural disposition or his origins. Having been found in Liverpool, he could be, as Nelly later tells him, the son of the Emperor of China for all they know, or even a bastard of Earnshaw's. It is the very obscurity of his origins, geographically, racially and morally, which determines that he shall be persecuted. That Heathcliff should be given the name of a son who had died feeds their suspicion that he is a fairy changeling.

The name itself suggests something inhuman. Again and again his face is described as clouding, brightening, overcast, like a landscape. He is not, at first, physically ugly. He can look handsome or repulsive according to his mood, as a landscape changes with the weather. It is deprivation which later affects both his disposition and his appearance. We need not assume that cruelty and spite come naturally to him. Hatred is his anodyne, the only means by which he can relieve the pain of his constant frustration and humiliation. Hindley's treatment of him is, as Nelly says, 'enough to make a fiend of a saint'. Heathcliff becomes a fiend only when his life becomes a hell.

Wuthering Heights demands to be read in such a way that Heathcliff functions simultaneously on three levels. On the surface he is an autonomous character in a drama which is comprehensible in ethical and social terms. Here he exemplifies the effects of cruelty and deprivation upon the young, acts as a critic of the artificial social and moral refinement of the Lintons, and dies broken by the sterile and destructive passions of hate and revenge. The second level is that we have already discussed in relation to his name, a permanent, indestructible reality against which all social values are seen to be flimsy and ephemeral, all moral values relative or impertinent:

My love for Linton is like the foliage in the woods. Time will change it, I'm well aware, as winter changes the trees. My love for Heathcliff resembles the eternal rocks beneath – a source of little visible delight, but necessary.

[122]

It is not really a matter of 'love'. It is not because the two halves love each other that an oak resists splitting (the metaphor is Catherine's). In passages like these we must be aware also of the third level, the psycho-spiritual. When Cathy says that Heathcliff is necessary to her, and that she *is* Heathcliff, she is speaking quite literally; for at this level Heathcliff is a projection of an essential part of Cathy's own being, the very ground of it. Stevie Davies describes Heathcliff as 'Catherine before she fell into her adult female biology and status. . . . He is the illicit access forged (at the price of life itself) from the subconscious to the conscious world . . . the electrifying and spellbinding hoardings of the imagination' [80].

The unforgivable sin committed in the novel is the separation of Catherine and Heathcliff, which corresponds to the attempted violation of Emily Brontë's integrity by the imposition on it of a narrowly feminine role. Heathcliff is thus, among other things, Cathy's *animus. Animus* is everything women are taught and expected (in those days were virtually obliged) to suppress. It is the unacknowledged content of the unconscious clamouring for expression and acceptance, and turning violent in its desperation. Emma Jung writes of the *animus*:

In the dreams and fantasies of even happily married women, a mysteriously fascinating masculine figure often appears, a demonic or divine dream or shadow lover . . . a kind of inherent primal phenomenon.

Shuttle and Redgrove refer to the 'dangerous *negative animus*, the destructive masculine spirit in women'. If a deep instinctual process in a woman is ignored or rejected, they say:

then its spirit will return with all the evolutionary power of those instinctual processes that grew us and continue to energize our physical being. You could say in this way, that the Christian Devil was a representation of the animus of the menstruating woman, in so far as the Christian ethic has Satanised woman and her natural powers. [126]

The novel itself is Emily Brontë's way of releasing and conversing with this body of repressed, exiled energy and information. The purpose of the first generation story is simply to let it speak, to let it find its own way to whatever reintegration it can; of the second to subject it to criticism in full consciousness and to attempt to initiate a process of healing there to avoid a repetition of those agonies.

Wuthering Heights is no mere *cri de coeur*. The elder Cathy is deprived of father as well as mother, and no-one at the Heights is able to control her. Nelly is little older than Cathy, and Joseph simply provokes out-and-out defiance. Thus Emily Brontë goes out of her way to avoid blaming anyone or anything other than Cathy herself for her fate. Deprivation seems to be the common lot of childhood, and leads invariably to distortion. Yet, though other characters in the first generation seem helpless, Cathy is given total existential freedom. She behaves as though nothing need ever be paid for. She thinks she can have all the advantages of a conventional marriage, of wealth, leisure and social status, even of love, as it is normally understood, without any surrender of freedom or even of Heathcliff. She colludes with, almost initiates, the parting from Heathcliff. He certainly blames no-one else: 'Because misery, and degradation, and death, and nothing that God or Satan could inflict would have parted us, *you*, of your own will, did it' [197]. Thus Emily Brontë defends herself by demonstrating in Cathy's defection to the Lintons and Thrushcross Grange how fatal it would have been to her own integrity to make any such concessions.

The total identification with Heathcliff, the total possession by the animus, left Cathy with no means of satisfying her social needs and softer affections but to reject Heathcliff (as it seemed to him) and the Heights in favour of Edgar Linton and Thrushcross Grange. At the low lying Grange, with its high garden wall, there is no wind at all. There, in the absence of Heathcliff (the three years of which occupy a mere two pages) her life is in abeyance; she virtually ceases to live. On his return she becomes 'an angel' and radiates sunshine through the house for several days. But her absolute need for Heathcliff is again thwarted.

The parallel has often been observed between this passage from *Wuthering Heights* (Catherine speaking of Heathcliff):

> If all else perished, and *he* remained, I should still continue to be; and if all else remained, and he were annihilated, the Universe would turn to a mighty stranger. I should not seem a part of it. [122]

and this stanza from 'No coward soul':

> Though Earth and moon were gone
> And suns and universes ceased to be
> And thou wert left alone
> Every Existence would exist in thee.

More often than not, the comparison has been used to misinterpret the poem. The passage from the novel is assumed to be romantic hyperbole, and that assumption is carried over into the poem, as though a Gondal heroine were here speaking to her lover. In fact the whole poem after the first stanza is addressed to Life, 'almighty ever-present Deity', the God within her breast. The poem has nothing to do with romantic love, and the novel, despite the plays and films ('the greatest love-story ever told'), precious little. In its proper context, the stanza can only mean that Life is not only in worlds and creatures and atoms, but in 'Being and Breath', which in turn must mean the animating spirit of love which 'pervades and broods over' the cycles of creation and dissolution alike. The word 'love' comes clear when we take the full value of the associated terms, 'holding fast', 'anchored', 'wide-embracing'; and still clearer when we remember how the equivalent passage in the novel is introduced:

> I cannot express it; but surely you and everybody have a notion that there is, or should be, an existence of yours beyond you. What were the use of my creation if I were entirely contained here? [122]

Love is what prevents any living creature from being an island. It is the albatross, the water-snake, the interdependence of all living things, their common sacredness. Catherine is not saying that she cannot live without Heathcliff the man. She is saying that she cannot live without her soul, her soul being the opposite of her ego. The self-centred ego can live on, a sort of death-in-life, without awareness of the rest of life; but the soul dies when its links are severed with Nature, that is, with everything beyond itself, with Life.

For all the loving care lavished on her Cathy begins to die simply for lack of the Breath of Life. Her spirit cries to return to the Heights to hear 'that wind sounding in the firs by the lattice'. The novel makes no distinction between her need for Heathcliff and her desire to be 'among the heather on those hills' where she can be 'herself', 'half savage and hardy and free'. Before

189

she can recognize her visitors she must wean 'her eyes from contemplating the outer darkness' [165]. That outer darkness is now her only reality. In her last illness Cathy cries out: 'I'm sure I should be myself were I once among the heather on those hills. Open the window again wide: fasten it open!' [163]. Yet the body cannot bear total exposure. Heathcliff and Cathy reject book, thought, and (insofar as they never regard each other as separate people) relationships. They throw open the windows of their souls to the wind, and achieve that total reunion with each other and with nature which they have yearned for; but the price is death. Cathy challenges Heathcliff to find a way to her 'not through that Kirkyard', but can herself conceive of no other adequate reunion, and Heathcliff accepts that way with relish: 'by the time Linton gets to us, he'll not know which is which!' [319].

*　　*　　*

In life, Emily Brontë felt she must choose, like the elder Cathy, between the window fastened open and the window soldered closed. She chose the former, life-in-death, rather than what would have been, for her, death-in-life. In her art she could imagine other possibilities, windows which shut out the wuthering wind, but can be opened to admit the breeze of life and love. The whole structure of the second half of the novel implies that she was well aware that life is not always a matter of such stark choices; that it does offer possibilities of harmony and fruition if a middle ground can be created between the pampered airlessness of the Grange and the wuthering exposure of the Heights. Here she moves from a tragic mode of fated beings to the mode of Shakespearean comedy, where problems are soluble, where distortion is not allowed to progress beyond the point of no return, where people who are naturally decent and loving can, with a little help from the author, modify the conditions of their lives to allow for a reconciliation of opposites, and move, accompanied by images of sunshine and fertility, towards maturity and happy marriage.

The first half of the novel is singularly non-judgemental; but the second half acknowledges that Cathy/Heathcliff had asked for too much in the name of selfhood and freedom. No human being can merge herself wholly with the life-force. There was ultimately something infantile in their outrageous demands. There must be constraints and modifications, out of respect for the conditions life itself imposes on human beings, out of respect for other people with their different natures, out of respect for one's own body's limitations.

Emily Brontë was fascinated by the effects of both heredity and environment. Linton Heathcliff, inheriting the worst qualities of both parents, seems to lack the capacity to become a viable human being. But even a good seed will produce a healthy plant only if it has space, soil and nourishment. The human equivalents of these are freedom (within reason), home and love. Hareton and the younger Cathy, though motherless and vulnerable are born of love and not lacking in vitality. Hareton's birth is accompanied by auspicious imagery of sunshine:

On the morning of a fine June day, my first bonny little nursling, and the last of the ancient Earnshaw stock, was born. We were busy with the hay in a far-away field, when the girl that usually brought our breakfasts came running, an hour too soon, across the meadow and up the lane, calling me as she ran. 'Oh, such a grand bairn!' she panted out. 'The finest lad that ever breathed!'.   [104]

Here is ripening sun, fertility, nourishment, and a clear indication in the phrase 'bonny little nursling' that, despite the death of the mother, the child will not entirely lack maternal care. Ten chapters later, the same imagery reappears:

Still I thought I could detect in his physiognomy a mind owning better qualities than his father ever possessed. Good things lost amid a wilderness of weeds, to be sure, whose rankness far over-topped their neglected growth; yet, notwithstanding, evidence of a wealthy soil that might yield luxuriant crops, under other and favourable circumstances.
                                                                    [231]

Cathy is not quite 'a second edition of the mother', but very near it. She combines the best features of either side:

She was the most winning thing that ever brought sunshine into a desolate house – a real beauty in face, with Earnshaws' handsome dark eyes, but the Lintons' fair skin, and small features, and yellow curling hair. Her spirit was high, though not rough, and qualified by a heart sensitive and lively to excess in its affections. That capacity for intense attachments reminded me of her mother; still she did not resemble her; for she could be soft and as a dove, and she had a gentle voice, and pensive expression. her anger was never furious, her love never fierce; it was deep and tender   [224]

Cathy 'grew like a larch', while Hareton suffered under Heathcliff's attempt to 'see if one tree won't grow as crooked as another, with the same wind to twist it'. It is not only the same wind, the same deprivation which had deformed Heathcliff's life; it is also virtually the same tree. Hareton is as much a second edition of Heathcliff as Cathy is of Catherine, though completely unrelated to him. Inheritance, therefore, cannot be the determining factor.

Emily Brontë clearly wishes to recapitulate the childhood of Heathcliff and Catherine with a few small but decisive adjustments. These adjustments are partly genetic, but mainly environmental. Heathcliff probably could have made Hareton as crooked as himself had he been able to keep up the pressure. What Heathcliff is denying Hareton is, in its largest sense, education. Without that, Hareton's natural intelligence becomes ineffective, so that Cathy asks 'Is he all he should be?... or is he simple – not right?' [254] Nelly rebukes her for despising him so unjustly: 'Had *you* been brought up in his circumstances, would you be less rude? He was as quick and intelligent a child as ever you were' [282].

Heathcliff is not the only source of the deprivation. The Heights are still exposed and wuthering. When Cathy as a child looked out from her nursery window to Penistone Crags, Nelly 'explained that they were bare masses of stone, with hardly enough earth in their clefts to nourish a stunted tree'. Joseph is still the malign human embodiment of the spirit of the Heights. Zillah has replaced Nelly. She acquiesces in the worst excesses of Heathcliff's regime.

Though education means for Emily Brontë anything which fosters the healthy growth of the whole personality, she does not despise formal learning. Hareton's illiteracy is presented as perhaps the most shameful manifestation of his degradation. His reclamation is effected by a combination of love and books. Books have made several earlier appearances in the novel. The first separation of Heathcliff and Catherine resulted from an incident involving the burning of books – the lumber thrust upon the children by Joseph which made Catherine resolve that she hated a good book. But primarily we have associated books with Thrushcross Grange with its well-stocked library in which Edgar had read, unaware, during Catherine's fatal illness. It is something to be spurned or destroyed or over-written if it cannot be seen to contribute directly to the life of wilful passion. At the Grange it offers a refuge and a retreat, an alternative, neatly-processed version of human life and nature which prepares Cathy very badly for her exposure to the reality at the Heights.

We picture Catherine as an outcast gazing through an open lattice towards the Heights while a bitter wind rustles the pages of an unread book Edgar has left on the sill for her. The younger Cathy's position at the Heights is exactly the contrary, exiled against her will from the Grange with its library of well-read, well-loved books, the books she has smuggled in burned or con-fiscated, escaping at last through the very lattice at which her mother's ghost is to beg admittance of Lockwood. Her home is the Grange, but it is not her heaven:

> Mine was rocking in a rustling green tree, with a west wind blowing, and
> bright, white clouds flitting rapidly above; and not only larks, but
> throstles, and blackbirds, and linnets, and cuckoos pouring out music on
> every side, and the moors seen art a distance, broken into cool dusky
> dells, but close by, great swells of long grass undulating in waves to the
> breeze; and woods and sounding water, and the whole world awake and
> wild with joy. [280]

Home for Cathy is not a retreat, an artificially cultivated park surrounded by a high wall. It is a place to move out from to confront life in all its fullness. She is not attracted by the hot dreamy stillness and unbroken blue of Linton's heaven. In hers there is wind and cloud, but not storm. Her mother's moors are there, but 'at a distance'. Cathy's heaven is filled with birdsong. Her list of songbirds cannot fail to remind us of the birds which filled her mother's imagination shortly before her death – wild duck, pigeon, moorcock and lapwing, all birds commonly shot. The lapwing in particular dominates her thoughts, a bird with a plaintive cry, feigning a broken wing to protect the young, helpless and exposed in their ground nest. Heathcliff once set a trap over such a nest so that the parents dare not come, and they found the nest 'full of little skeletons' the following winter. This image of the deserted nest, the vulnerability of the young, wanton cruelty, suffering and death, contains within it the central theme of the novel.

When books, towards the end of the novel, come to play a more positive role, it is not so much their content that matters as the fact that they symbolize a human faith in communication and social intercourse. The importance of the books is established long before Hareton is able actually to read them. The first sympathetic act of co-operation towards Cathy he makes, or is allowed to make, is when he reaches down some books in the dresser which are too high for her. From her cruel mockery of Hareton's efforts to teach himself to read (stealing from her and profaning books 'consecrated by other associations') she progresses gradually to the point of neatly wrapping a handsome book and tying it with riband as a peace offering, grudgingly accepted, together with the promise 'if he take it, I'll come and teach him to read it right' [345].

Love effects a remarkable transformation:

> His honest, warm, and intelligent nature shook off rapidly the clouds of ignorance and degradation in which it had been bred; and Catherine's sincere commendations acted as a spur to his industry. His brightening mind brightened his features, and added spirit and nobility to their aspect.
>
> [351–2]

The human transformation is only the first of a series of transformations it generates. The process of the first generation where the house helped to distort its occupants is now reversed. Joseph's currant bushes are displaced to make room for an importation of plants from the Grange. Lockwood, on his next visit, is greeted with 'a fragrance of stocks and wall-flowers' and is amazed to find the gate unlocked and doors and lattices open. Nelly has also been 'transplanted' from the Grange, and fills the house with 'Fairy Annie's Wedding'.

Of course this transformation is made possible only by the collapse of Heathcliff. Cathy expresses her compassion for Linton in the words: 'He'll never let his friends be at ease, and he'll never be at ease himself!' [286] The idea of being at ease, like the idea of being at home, is central, and particularly relevant to Heathcliff. The opposite of ease is torment. It is torment Heathcliff expects to suffer for the rest of his life after the death of Catherine. The best he can hope for is the distraction of his revenge. And it is torment with which he curses Catherine's ghost. It is the need for ease which, after eighteen years of torment, drives Heathcliff to Catherine's grave, to make preparation for their reunion in death. Heathcliff's heaven is six feet under ground.

In the final chapter each generation simultaneously reaches its heaven. Hareton and Cathy stand at the threshold of a life of rewarding fruitfulness. They are at ease with themselves, each other and the world. Their children will lack for nothing. But they feel it necessary to end the three-hundred-year Earnshaw occupation of Wuthering Heights. They must put a distance between themselves and unaccommodated nature; they commit themselves, like Shakespeare's late heroines, to a civilized living which neither capitulates to nature, nor cuts itself off from nature's sustaining sources of vitality.

13 HAWTHORNE AND THE CRIME AGAINST WOMAN

In 'The Custom House', Hawthorne's semi-autobiographical introduction to *The Scarlet Letter,* the narrator claims to have found an old document outlining the story of a beautiful young woman, Hester Prynne, who married a scholarly man much older than herself and slightly deformed, Roger Chillingworth, who then sent her ahead to prepare a home in the young Puritan colony of Boston. But her husband did not follow, and all her enquiries drew a blank, until both she and the entire community had to assume him to be dead. After some years of quasi-widowhood, Hester and a charismatic young divine, Arthur Dimmesdale, fall passionately in love. Dimmesdale recoils in horror at his sin, and fails to come forward when Hester, visibly pregnant, is condemned as an adulteress. She bears her child in prison, and is then condemned to wear for the rest of her life a scarlet letter A for adulteress on her breast. The narrator's imagination is aroused by this story, and he resolves to elaborate it in the form of a novel.

The Scarlet Letter has been much misread, for reasons similar to the misreading of *Gulliver's Travels* we have already discussed, that is, a failure to respond adequately to imagery and tone (particularly irony) and to distinguish between the author and the narrator – a problem also, as we shall see, at the root of most misreadings of Conrad's *Heart of Darkness.*

Taking his lead from Melville's comments on Hawthorne, Leslie Fiedler argues that the great artist should be a truth-teller, and that to be a truth-teller is to be a nay-sayer:

> There is some evidence that the Hard No is being spoken when the writer seems a traitor to those whom he loves and who have conditioned his very way of responding to the world. When the writer says of precisely the cause that is dearest to him what is always and everywhere the truth about all causes – that it has been imperfectly conceived and inadequately represented, and that it is bound to be betrayed, consciously or unconsciously, by its leading spokeman – we know that he is approaching an art of real seriousnes if not of actual greatness. The thrill we all sense but hesitate to define for ourselves – the thrill of confronting a commitment to truth which transcends all partial allegiances – comes when Dante turns on Florence, Molière on the moderate man, de Sade on reason, Shaw on the socialists, Tolstoy on the reformers, Joyce on Ireland, Faulkner on the South, Graham Greene on the Catholics, Pasternak on the Russians and Abraham Cahan or Nathaniel West on the Jews. [Fiedler 7]

To this list could be added many more examples including Sophocles, Euripides and Aristophanes on Greece, the Gawain poet on Christian chivalry, Swift on reason, Hawthorne on Puritanism . . .

What Fiedler means by a Hard No, is a blanket no, on the assumption, in Melville's words, that 'all men who say *yes,*lie'. All partial, selective, or relative nos Fiedler dismisses as sentimental and righteous. *No! in Thunder* was first published in 1960, and it is perhaps no coincidence that in 1960 the theatre of the absurd was at its most popular, for the blanket no is close to the rather facile no of absurdism, based as it was on the assumption that since the universe itself is meaningless and valueless, so must be everything within it. A Hard No to satisfy Fiedler would presumably be Hamlet's starting point':

> How weary, stale, flat, and unprofitable
> Seem to me all the uses of this world!
> Fie on't, ah fie, 'tis an unweeded garden
> That grows to seed; things rank and gross in nature
> Possess it merely.

It follows from this that Ophelia, far from being a rose of May, is as fat a weed as Claudius. Such a starting point precludes action, since what would be the point in operating upon a patient diseased in every organ, every cell. The logical conclusion is Lear's great No! in thunder: 'Crack Nature's moulds, all germens spill at once'. Yet Lear's madness repudiates everything Cordelia lives and dies for, the possibility of redemption. Had he remained in it he would have killed the physician, and the fee bestowed upon the foul disease.

But most of the nay-saying in literature has not been of this kind. The no of satire, for example, invariably implies fundamental truths, positives or norms against which these particular people, this behaviour or belief, can be measured and found woefully inadequate, so the louder the no, the stronger the implied yes. The greatest artists are not content to diagnose the symptoms of the world's diseases. They are in the business of seeking cures, and the hard cure is a hard yes, which is far harder than the hardest no. To opt out is an easy option. In that search the writer must run the risk of both sentimentality and righteousness.

I am also doubtful about Melville's 'thunder'. Surely thundering is more the mode of the preacher than the artist, who is often obliged by the distance between his own way of seeing the world and that of his readers to adopt a more subtle and covert strategy such as that of Swift, Emily Brontë or Conrad, forcing the more receptive readers at least to respond at a deeper, more fully human, level than the narrator, and also, therefore, at a deeper level than their own usual, socially, culturally and morally conditioned, selves. Melville himself elsewhere made exactly this point:

> For in this world of lies, Truth is forced to fly like a sacred white doe in
> the woodlands; and only by cunning glimpses will she reveal herself, as in
> Shakespeare and other great masters of the great Art of Telling the Truth
> – even though it be covertly, and by snatches.

> ('Hawthorne and His Mosses')

Those novelists who have chosen to dispense with such strategies and confront their readers with an open challenge have often regretted it. Hardy, writing half a century after Hawthorne, and in a less puritanical culture, subtitled *Tess of the d'Urbervilles* 'A Pure Woman', but the obloquy this earned him marked the beginning of the end of his novel writing; and Lawrence's decision to write honestly and openly about adulterous sex in *Lady Chatterley's Lover* earned him only a lasting reputation as a pornographer

*   *   *

Lawrence's heroine Ursula Brangwen devotes herself to discovering how the life that is in her wants to be lived. She is fortunate in belonging to the first generation in which this is, though still with many difficulties, possible. Her predecessors were all tragic figures.

Women have not, of course, been the only victims, since men have been equally pressurized to eradicate or sublimate all those qualities which lie towards the female end of the spectrum of their own natures. Lawrence's snake symbolizes the 'phallic consciousness', which is the bridge or atonement between male and female natures. But the voice of his education says to the protagonist in 'Snake':

> If you were a man
> You would take a stick and break him now, and finish him off.

It was that same voice which drove Oedipus and Creon and Pentheus and Adonis and Angelo and the Ancient Mariner to their self-destruction, the voice which insists on defining manhood and womanhood from the outside, in terms of a spoken or unspoken creed.

Existentialism, though half-baked as a philosophy, provided many terms and concepts which were fertile for the writing and reading of literature. The challenge to every man or woman is to live authentically, in good faith, that is, in terms of how the life that is in us needs to be lived. This is the opposite of selfishness, since the most fundamental needs will be found to involve the interdependence of all individuals not only with each other but also with the whole non-human world for a full and balanced sexual and communal, physical and spiritual life. To live in bad faith is to give up the struggle, to capitulate to the dead forms, collusions and mutilations which any society ('other people') attempts to impose in its pursuit of power at the expense of life.

The greatest novel produced by Existentialism is Sartre's *Nausea*, where there is a wonderful chapter on the Municipal Art Gallery, where generations of worthies, the moral guardians and exemplars of the community, are enshrined. They 'raised fine children, taught them their rights and duties, religion, and respect for the traditions which had gone to the making of France. Bright colours had been banished, out of a sense of decency'. They appear to be sitting in harsh judgement on their successors: 'his judgement pierced me like a sword and called in question my very right to exist'.

I looked at them in vain for some link with trees and animals, with the thoughts of earth or water. . . . They had enslaved the whole of Nature: outside themselves and in themselves.

Hawthorne has a very similar passage:

On the wall hung a row of portraits, representing the forefathers of the Bellingham lineage. . . . All were characterized by the sternness and severity which old portraits so invariably put on; as if they were the ghosts, rather than the pictures, of departed worthies, and were gazing with harsh and intolerant criticism at the pursuits and enjoyments of living men.

The necessary allegiance of the creative writer to imagination, since imagination is bound to be in opposition to the pseudo-rational structures of society and its enforced orthodoxies at any time, predisposes him to some form of existential revolt. The writer *must* favour Antigone against Creon, Dionysos against Pentheus, the Green Knight against the Christian/chivalric code, Venus against Adonis, Cleopatra against Octavius Caesar, even Caliban against Prospero and the Yahoos against the Houyhnhnms.

Every age and culture has had its equivalent of Existentialism. In Puritan New England in the seventeenth century it was Antinomianism, a belief that the law which came from within should overrule both civil and religious law. Another explicit connection which Hawthorne also makes twice, once at the beginning and once, as a reminder, well into the story, is with the most famous figure in the history of Antinomianism, Ann Hutchinson. All his original readers would have known that Ann Hutchinson was banished from Massachusetts in 1638 for advocating the intuitive revelation of God in preference to scriptures and laws. Though there was no evidence of any sexual relationship, she seduced intellectually one of the most prominent divines of the time, John Cotton, who later repudiated her.

Hawthorne is at pains to conflate in the reader's mind Ann Hutchinson and his heroine Hester Prynne. He recognizes that the Puritans were right to fear all who claimed such freedom, defying the law, whether in theory, as in the case of Ann Hutchinson, or in practise, as in Hester's case (though the two overlap), since they were in effect proposing an alternative definition of the sacred, an alternative divinity, the same divinity which Hawthorne as imaginative artist, is bound to worship. As priestesses of this divinity, Ann Hutchinson and Hester are both 'sainted'.

Once fully in his imaginative mode what overrides all else is Hawthorne's conviction of the evil, the spiritual corruption and pollution (his own terms) of Puritanism. According to Melville Hawthorne never said yes to anything. On the contrary, so virulent is his hatred of the Puritans that it seems that anyone persecuted by them must be in the right – Quakers, Antinomians, Indians, even adulterers. The Puritan writers frequently described heretical thought as the spawning of bastards. Given the nature of Puritan legitimacy, every form of illegitimacy, including the sexual, becomes, for Hawthorne, a virtue.

*   *   *

My references to Swift and satire may seem to have little possible relevance to *The Scarlet Letter*. Yet Hawthorne himself makes this very connection quite explicitly in the first paragraph of 'The Custom House', his autobiographical introduction to the novel. There Hawthorne tells us that 'the example of the famous 'P.P., Clerk of this Parish', was never more faithfully followed' than it is to be in 'The Custom House'. Hawthorne must have assumed that *The Memoirs of P.P., Clerk of this Parish* was sufficiently famous for most of his readers at least to know that it was a satirical production of the Scriblerus Club, which consisted of Swift, Pope, John Gay, Thomas Parnell, Dr. Arbuthnot, and Robert Harley, Earl of Oxford, and was an anonymous parody of such tedious autobiographies as Bishop Gilbert Burnet's *A History of His Own Times*. An even more famous joint production of the club was *The Memoirs of Martinus Scriblerus*, which contained passages by Swift which he later developed in *Gulliver's Travels*. The concluding part of 'The Custom House' (where Hawthorne reminds us that he is using the 'tone' of *The Memoirs of P.P.*) purports to establish the authenticity of the documents on which *The Scarlet Letter* is based in terms almost identical with those used by Swift in his fictitious publisher's preface to *Gulliver's Travels,* where the publisher promises that 'if any Traveller hath a Curiosity to see the whole Work at large, as it came from the Hand of the Author, I will be ready to gratify him'. Hawthorne writes:

> The original papers, together with the scarlet letter itself, . . . are still in my possession, and shall be freely exhibited to whomsoever, induced by the great interest of the narrative, may desire a sight of them.

Why should Hawthorne be at such pains to tell us that he is faithfully following the example of a fake and satirical autobiography (drawing particular attention to his tone), unless to alert the reader of the novel to the distance between himself and the narrator, and to the fact that we are to take the narrator's judgement to be no more reliable than Gulliver's? The narrator tells us, for example, that the illegitimate Pearl is 'an imp of evil, emblem and product of sin' who had 'no right among christened infants'. In the authentic voice of Gulliver he then describes those infants as 'playing at going to church, perchance; or at scourging Quakers; or taking scalps in a sham-fight with the Indians; or scaring one-another with freaks of imitative witchcraft'. In this ironic context the word 'christened' is drained of all positive meaning, and once such terms are subverted, there is no longer any meaning in the words 'evil' and 'sin'. In 'The Gentle Boy', a story about the scourging of Quakers, Hawthorne uses the same Swiftian technique:

For her voice had been already heard in many lands of Christendom; and she had pined in the cells of a Catholic Inquisition, before she felt the lash, and lay in the dungeons of the Puritans. Her mission had extended also to the followers of the Prophet, and from them she had received the courtesy and kindness, which all the contending sects of our purer religion united to deny her.

The word 'pure' is irredeemably tainted in such a context, and a non-Christian religion actually gains in moral and spiritual stature by virtue of being rejected by all Christian 'sects'. Even towards the end of the novel, the narrator is obtuse enough to tell us that Hester has learned 'much amiss' in losing her reverence for 'the clerical band, the judicial robe, the pillory, the gallows, the fireside, or the church'. The actual effect is to devalue both fireside and church by relegating them behind the mere trappings of authority ('gowns and furred robes hide all'), and the instruments of institutionalized cruelty.

Hawthorne's control of tone and narrative voice in *The Scarlet Letter* is not as consistent as Swift's or Emily Brontë's. When the narrator speaks of flowers as 'the floral tribe' he sounds like Lockwood, but he is by no means, like Gulliver or Lockwood, merely absurd. He is more like Nelly Dean in that he incorporates the judgement of society at its best, its most humane and balanced. The reader is temporarily seduced, for example, into accepting the narrator as expressing an adequate degree of criticism and rejection of the early Puritan settlers, Hawthorne's ancestors, founders of the whole culture he had inherited. The narrator expresses the orientation to what he narrates of that part of Hawthorne himself which functions as objective historian, surveyor, custom-house official, would-be member of a community.

The strong emotions which the story aroused in Hawthorne as he wrote it are communicated to the reader in spite of, not because of, the attitude of the narrator. The reader is gradually lured into the position of finding the narrator inadequate to the human situation. He compromises with the moral evil of Puritanism and shows himself to be a true descendent of his witch-burning ancestors in the very act of disowning them. He prides himself on a degree of enlightened tolerance and humanity which distinguishes him from his forbears, but the reader soon becomes impatient with his equivocations, feeling that a more courageous and passionate partisanship, a more thoroughgoing rejection of them, is called for.

Hawthorne deliberately widens the gap between himself and the customs officer by claiming that the latter had lost all interest in literature and in nature; that the faculty of imagination had become 'suspended and inanimate' within him. The customs officer is precisely Hawthorne minus imagination. The figure presented to us in 'The Custom House' and ever-present as narrator in the story which follows would be totally incapable of writing *The Scarlet Letter*. There is another Hawthorne at work, whose allegiances are elsewhere, Hawthorne the Artist, for whom that calling, with its inevitable Alienation, is an imperative demanding quite the opposite of the narrator's attempt at objectivity, at being fair to all concerned, demanding that the story be told not in a careful historical, social, moral and religious context (or only superficially, deceptively so), but in a manner which subverts all that, subverts Hawthorne himself as ordinary person, in terms of the permanent realities of the human spirit, of human needs at the level of the individual psyche depending as it does on an unmediated relationship with the non-human world. Art is as subversive of law and conventional morality as Adultery, and this is the A which burns on the breast of the customs officer as he instinctively feels a kinship with Esther.

❋ ❋ ❋

Any reader who doubts that, despite the apparent identification of Hawthorne with the narrator in 'The Custom-House', they are in fact worlds apart, need only compare the narrator of *The Scarlet Letter* with the narrator of *The Blithedale Romance*, published only two years later. Though Miles Coverdale in *The Blithedale Romance* is not exactly Hawthorne, we can hardly doubt that he is a great deal closer to Hawthorne than the narrator of *The Scarlet Letter*. The *Romance* has a contemporary setting, and is partly autobiographical; and the narrator is presented as a poet with liberal and progressive sympathies. The admiration which Hawthorne clearly feels for Hester he dare not, within the context of *The Scarlet Letter*, express overtly; but his admiration for Zenobia can be expressed through Coverdale, in an explicitly progressive context, quite outspokenly. The other essential difference is that Zenobia does not have the stigma of the scarlet letter to contend with. She keeps her sexual history to herself, and Coverdale is unable to discover it. His interest in it, however, is sympathetic, not judgemental. It seems that she has lived a passionate, somewhat reckless life, and there may well have been adultery involved at some point in it. But one feels that, should Coverdale have discovered this, it would not have made much difference to his estimate of her.

The terms in which he expresses that estimate are, in relation to *The Scarlet Letter* (of two years earlier), very revealing. Before Coverdale even arrives at Blithedale he sets up a dichotomy between the constricting and joyless pressure of traditional forms and the beauty and freshness of what nature perpetually offers. By the time the snow has passed through city smoke and immediately been trodden by countless boots, its freshness has been quite extinguished: 'Thus the track of an old conventionalism was visible on what was freshest from the sky'. Once into the countryside, he fills his lungs with 'air that had not been spoken into words of falsehood, formality and error, like all the air of the dusky city'. Poetry is by definition the opposite of such words: 'true, strong, natural, and sweet – something that shall have the notes of wild birds twittering through it, or a strain like the wind-anthems in the woods'.

Zenobia's only ornament, which she hardly needs, but which perfectly expresses her character, is a fresh exotic flower (no-one knows where they come from) which she wears in her hair every day. What arouses in Coverdale an attitude almost of worship is simply Zenobia's unconstrained and shameless womanliness. She carries her sex with a nobility which suggests that she is and knows herself to be an avatar of the goddess. The womanliness she embodies is a far cry from the pattern of domesticated and repressed womanliness the puritans had imposed on their women. She scorns the 'petty restraints which take the life and colour out of other women's conversation'. In most other women 'their sex fades away, and goes for nothing':

> Not so with Zenobia. One felt an influence breathing out of her such as we might suppose to come from Eve, when she was just made, and her Creator brought her to Adam, saying, 'Behold! Here is a woman!' Not that I would convey the idea of gentleness, grace, modesty and shyness, but of a certain warm and rich characteristic , which seems, for the most part, to have been refined away out of the feminine system.

'Warm' and 'rich' are precisely the terms we associate with Hester. These are women whose sexuality is luxuriant. Coverdale speaks of Zenobia's 'flesh-warmth' and 'full bust'. She is not at all 'maiden-like', but mellow, blooming, and generous. Hawthorne presents Zenobia as a prototype for all women, as 'womanliness incarnated': 'The image of her form and face should have been multiplied all over the earth'.

These are the very characteristics which would have forced the Puritan community to take action against Hester whether she had been guilty of adultery or not. The adultery is a pretext. Zenobia is in Coverdale's eyes admirably 'free'. In the eyes of the Puritans such freedom in a woman threatens their whole precarious structure. 'Free' is seen as 'wild', and 'wild' is close to 'demonic'. Both women bring the full power of their womanliness to bear in attempting to reclaim men who have sacrificed their manhood for the life of the spirit or of an abstract ideal. They are united in the image of the 'perfectly-developed rose', which puts to shame the mean and dismal world of men.

❄   ❄   ❄

The narrator in *The Scarlet Letter* is interested in the document he finds as a historical record of events unique to their time and place, and the fates of the individuals caught up in them. So, of course, is Hawthorne. But his imagination seized upon seventeenth century New England not only because of the continuity with his own world and the need he felt to repudiate the cruelty of his Puritan forebears, but because that world offered in a dramatic, extreme, yet realistic form, an image of the persecution of the female, of the passional self, of the individual spirit, which he saw as characteristic of all patriarchal societies. That historical moment presented him with a very clear and extreme image of the sickness of our Western culture almost since its inception. The founders of monotheistic religions and their heirs, the founding fathers of Christianity, had, looming large among their many problems, the problem of the female. In the not-too-distant past the female had reigned supreme as the great Goddess, 'great creating Nature' as Shakespeare called her, by virtue of her magical ability to create life. Many societies had been matriarchal. The male rebellion against the dominance of the female had necessarily involved the degradation not only of actual women, but of Nature herself, and of those qualities in the male psyche which came to be seen as unmanly – the qualities Jung called the anima. Great creating Nature herself becomes that which must be put behind the bars of a prison-house or fenced out in the darkness of the surrounding forest with all its abominations. Nature was handed over to the devil. The great goddess Anath became Anathema, a witch and a whore, a scarlet woman, and that was the primal 'A'.

Peter Redgrove and Penelope Shuttle write:

> As Savramis points out in his splendidly titled *The Satanizing of Women*, the Christian Western world identified woman with sin. She was 'an advance guard of hell', she was 'a frightening worm in the heart of man'. She was 'the devil's gate'. The witch-hunters saw themselves 'As representatives of a theology that satanizes sexuality as such, equates women with sexuality, and seeks to destroy the female sex in order to eliminate "wicked" sexuality in favour of a man-ruled Christian world'. The infamous manual for inquisitors that was written for use at witch-trials, *The Hammer of Witches* or *Malleus Maleficarum*, is distinguished from other works on heresy in that it is 'solely and exclusively devoted to the persecution and destruction of the female sex'.
>
> [*The Wise Wound*, 214]

Women were condemned to death for curing 'without having studied', by which was meant for studying nature rather than the scriptures.

*   *   *

Like Nellie Dean the narrator of *The Scarlet Letter* is set up as representative of the best the social, exclusively human and rational world has to offer, only to be exposed as radically inadequate. That inadequacy is conveyed in two ways. First there is the play of irony directed against him in his very tone of voice, which is distinctly more formal, conventional, pious and pompous than the voice of Hawthorne in his other fictions, particularly in the *Romance*. Second there is the imaginative power generated by the prose especially in its imagery (again as in *Wuthering Heights*) on those many occasions where it by-passes the narrator and plays directly (though often subliminally) upon the sensibilities of the reader.

Once we have realized that we cannot take our bearings from the narrator, we are obliged to take them partly from common humanity, but also largely, whether we realize it or not, from the powerful and persistent imagery. Since the imagery of *The Scarlet Letter* derives almost entirely from the natural world, presented to us in terms of wildness, profusion, variety, fructifying warmth and beauty, the bearings which derive from it are at the polar extreme from the values of the Puritans, expressed, as they are, in terms of order, uniformity, rigidity, coldness, deformity and disease. *The Scarlet Letter* is a dramatic poem, as dependent on patterns and accumulations and clashes of imagery as any Shakespeare play.

Even before Hester makes her appearance, the imagery begins to do its work. The pious and commonplace narrative voice is completely subverted by the far stronger and deeper meaning of the imagery. The prison is presented to us as 'that black flower of civilized society', but the obvious meaning of the wild rose bush at the prison door is evaded. We are told that it 'may serve to symbolize some sweet moral blossom that may be found along the track, or relieve the darkening close of a tale of human frailty and sorrow'. Already a gap is created between the natural meaning of a symbol, that is the meaning any reader would give to it if it were left uninterpreted by the narrator, and the interpretation the narrator in fact gives it. The word 'sweet' is sentimental and the word 'moral' sententious, and Hawthorne knows it. Far from illustrating some sweet moral in a Puritan chapbook, the rose speaks 'from the deep heart of Nature'. It is inherently and traditionally a symbol of sexual love, and the word 'wild' means sexual love not regimented or coerced by Puritanical restrictions. The tale's interpretation of itself is as far removed from the contemporary idea of morality as Ann Hutchinson was from the 17th century Puritan idea of a saint. What the rose at the door of the prison clearly symbolizes is the Puritans' inability to expel Nature entirely from their community, and the inability of their cruellest laws and punishments to expunge the flowering of the human heart, especially in women and in sexual love.

The tale's image patterns and therefore moral bearings are exactly those of Blake in the *Songs of Experience*, for example in 'The Garden of Love':

> I went to the Garden of Love,
> And saw what I never had seen:
> A Chapel was built in the midst,
> Where I used to play on the green.
>
> And the gates of this Chapel were shut,
> And 'Thou shalt not' writ over the door;
> So I turn'd to the Garden of Love
> That so many sweet flowers bore;
>
> And I saw it was filled with graves,
> And tomb-stones where flowers should be;
> And Priests in black gowns were walking their rounds,
> And binding with briars my joys & desires.

So, in *The Scarlet Letter*, the preoccupation with sin demands that the most necessary structures are the prison and the scaffold. Though the scaffold is situated beneath the eaves of Boston's earliest church, it is the scaffold and not the church which is the centre of communal and spiritual life. The church is never described, and no scene takes place within it.

The rose is the true symbol for what the Puritans attempt, with their scarlet letter, to transform into its opposite, shame, the invisible worm in the bud. In this context the word 'moral' takes on a Blake-like irony. Hester is a wild rose flowering even within the prison or Chapel, at the very heart of the Puritan enterprize, the essential life they cannot destroy. The true home for such a rose is a 'bed of crimson joy' [Blake, 'The Sick Rose'].

The second time in the novel that our attention is drawn to actual roses takes place in a garden with 'closely shaven grass', thought otherwise overgrown, where there are both rose-bushes and apple-trees –

> probably the descendents of those planted by the Reverend Mr.
> Blackstone, the first settler of the peninsula; that half-mythological
> personage who rides through our early annals, seated on the back of a
> bull.

Blackstone had so disliked the Puritans that he had ridden off to join the Indians. Snow's *History of Boston* (1825) describes him seated on a bull. Hawthorne extended his mythology by placing him (in 'The Maypole of Merry Mount'), without any evidence, in the pagan community at Merry Mount. He sounds very like the renegade Catholic priest in Brian Freil's *Dancing at Lughnasa*. In this garden Pearl cries for a red rose. When asked by the Reverend Mr. Wilson who made her, she 'announced that she had not been made at all, but had been plucked by her mother off the bush of wild roses, that grew by the prison-door'.

The attachment of shame not only to sin but to sex and to the human body was still characteristic of Hawthorne's society. Within five years of the publication of *The Scarlet Letter*, Whitman published the first edition of *Leaves of Grass,* and openly confronted the criminality of Puritanism in terms Hawthorne must have applauded. Later Whitman wrote, having given several examples of crippling fear of sex and the body in his own time:

> A civilization in which such things as I have mentioned can be thought or
> done is guilty to the core. It is not purity, it is impurity, which calls
> clothes more decent than the naked body . . . It is not innocent but guilty
> thought which attaches shame, secrecy, baseness and horror to great and
> august parts and functions of humanity.

          *   *   *

The opening scene of the novel is a scene of moral outrage directed by an entire community against one woman. The narrator shares the outrage:

> Here, there was the taint of deepest sin in the most sacred quality of
> human life, working such effect, that the world was only the darker for
> this woman's beauty, and the more lost for the infant that she had borne.

The narrative voice uses all the standard epithets for Hester's 'crime' and 'sin', but we are encouraged to let the novel make quite another valuation. Hester behaves 'with natural dignity'. The very badge of her shame she has transformed with 'so much fertility and gorgeous luxuriance of fancy' that it becomes a fitting ornament for her beauty, charcterized by abundant hair and richness of complexion. She has thus transformed her punishment into a further act of rebellion, since it is 'greatly beyond what was allowed by the sumptuary regulations of the colony'. All in all she presents her persecutors with a rival divinity, an image of 'Divine Maternity', since 'her beauty shone out, and made a halo of the misfortune and ignominy in which she was enveloped'. Like Ann Hutchinson, she is 'sainted' despite all the community's efforts to demonize her.

The scene cannot but bring to mind the woman taken in adultery in *St. John* viii. There is no reluctance among Hester's accusers to cast the first stone, which implies that they all believe themselves to be without sin. Hawthorne's view of that claim is clear, especially in 'Young Goodman Brown'. The narrator describes the loss of faith in the goodness of others as 'one of the saddest results of sin', but to endorse that, the reader would have to doubt that 'the outward guise of purity' is often a lie, and, even where it is not, would have to prefer the 'unsunned snow' in a 'pure' matron's bosom to the scarlet letter emblazoned on Hester's.

What Hawthorne conspicuously refuses to do in the value judgements of the narrator, that is overtly endorse Hester, he does not only in the telling of her tale and depiction of her character, but also through copious powerful symbolism. It is impossible to imagine Hawthorne himself, as opposed to his narrator, to be capable of such moralistic mindless clichés as 'a woman stained with sin'. Even the narrator cannot deny that the scarlet letter itself is transformed by Hester into something startlingly beautiful, scarlet and gold, the colours of rich life, which are also colours associated with the Indians and the seamen, occasional visitors grudgingly tolerated by the community. On the first page the tale establishes a clear polarity between the negative characteristics of the Puritans, uniformity, dreariness, rigidity, inhumanity, and the positives associated with all those they persecute or exclude.

The modern reader feels simply outrage against everyone in that community other than Hester. We feel that it is evil to participate in such sadism or to allow it to proceed without protest or intervention. In so responding, we are not allowing ourselves to respond in terms of modern sophisticated, emancipated, secular values, but in terms enforced by the tale itself. The scene is presented by Hawthorne in such a way as to force the reader, even his contemporary readers conditioned to stand with the crowd against Hester, to stand rather with her on the scaffold, wishing we had the power to hurl the whole crowd into the pit. The values Hawthorne enforces are not those he declares. His failure to declare them shifts the onus to do so onto the reader.

With great courage and integrity Hawthorne keeps from us all information about Hester's adultery. We learn nothing of her relationship with Dimmesdale, the circumstances, the occasion, who took the initiative. Hawthorne will not pry into any of this. It is all, morally, beside the point. The point is that Hester's judges are as ignorant as we are of these matters, that the law takes no congnisance of them, that the idea of sin has become dissociated from actual human living and needs. The life of the body and all human feelings have been subjugated to a rigid legalistic grid of moral prescriptions and proscriptions. Hawthorne rejects, above all, labels. He knows that a marriage can be evil and an adulterous relationship good, and that one law for the lion and the ox is oppression.

Hester has harmed no-one other than the husband she expects never to see again and believes to be dead. Chillingworth himself admits that, as a man misshapen and in decay, 'having given my best years to feed the hungry dream of knowledge' (like George Eliot's Casaubon), he should have had nothing to do with budding youth and beauty such as Hester's. Their marriage he describes as 'false and unnatural'. But she had challenged a sacrosanct patriarchal system. As in Mosaic law, her sin is codified, and, once made public, provides the community with the opportunity to cast almost literal stones in perfect self-righteousness. Sadistic self-righteousness is not codified as a sin. On the contrary it is exalted as the community's primary weapon against the codified sins. This is the point, misunderstood by his entire congregation again and again, of Dimmesdale's sermons. He is misunderstood because he insists on making the point either in general terms or in relation (absurdly in their eyes) to himself. He gets through to some of them at last only by the silent exposing of his breast. Though Hawthorne makes the point early in the novel that some of the ruthless matrons complaining that Hester has been let off so lightly have also committed adultery, or worse, the main point is that even those who are as upright, pure, moral, as they seem, are participants in a conspiracy of evil.

Hester is herself a wild rose bush from which grows Pearl, that 'lovely and immortal flower'. The narrator's gloss about 'rank luxuriance' can do little to offset the superiority of 'rank' to 'rigid' established by the imagery. The passion the narrator describes as 'rank', Hester describes as 'consecrated'. Since it is consecrated to nature and the human heart, that is, to the Puritan, evil. Hawthorne leaves the reader to decide, on the strength of the tale and its imagery, which is the more appropriate term.

Hester has no wish 'forever to do battle with the world', only to 'be a woman in it'. Certain attributes are 'essential to keep her a woman'; these are the absolutes she must live by, and they are defined as 'Love', 'Passion' and 'Affection'. These, even if they cannot escape it, will always transcend 'the iron framework of reasoning'. Hawthorne is not proposing any such simplistic distinction as that men live by the mind, women by the emotions. Ann

Hutchinson was far more intelligent than her persecutors. Hester 'imbibed this spirit':

> She assumed a freedom of speculation, then common enough on the
> other side of the Atlantic, but which our forefathers, had they known of it,
> would have held to be a deadlier crime than that stigmatized by the
> scarlet letter.

(In fact, long after Hawthorne's day, it was still unacceptable, even across the Atlantic, for women to speculate freely on such matters, as Ibsen's Mrs Alving, who also offered herself to her pastor, was to learn in *Ghosts*.) Had it not been for her responsibilities to Pearl, Hester

> might have come down to us in history, hand in hand with Ann
> Hutchinson, as the foundress of a religious sect. She might, in one of her
> phases, have been a prophetess. She might, and not improbably would,
> have suffered death from the stern tribunals of the period, for attempting
> to undermine the foundations of the Puritan establishment.

On the contrary, what Hawthorne believed was that a rigid rationality, cut off from all other human attributes, would always be perverse, sterile and inhuman – what Blake called single vision. What Hawthorne sought, what all imaginative artists by definition seek, was wholeness, in man and woman.

The scarlet letter does not do its work on Hester. Her suffering brings wisdom, but not the wisdom of repentance. She comes to see that her husband's guilt is far deeper than her own:

> She deemed it her crime most to be repented of, that she had ever
> endured, and reciprocated, the lukewarm grasp of his hand. . . . And it
> seemed a fouler offence committed by Roger Chillingworth, than any
> which had since been done him, that, in the time when her heart knew
> no better, he had persuaded her to fancy herself happy by his side.

Did George Eliot have this in mind when she created the relationship between Dorothea Brooke and Casaubon in *Middlemarch*?

Though the simple request to be a woman in the world is denied to Hester, it is to be realized in her daughter, who represents not simply the next generation, but that inevitable future when the long succession of reincarnations of the victimized goddess will win back that freedom with their suffering. Pearl's name may evoke the painful origins of the actual pearl, a perpetual irritation in the bosom of its mother – beauty growing out of suffering. Since Pearl is the offspring of an adulterous relationship, has not been subjected to the discipline of a formal education which would have extinguished the joy of life in her, and is conspicuously wild and unpredictable in her behaviour, the Puritans have no option but to see her as an 'imp of evil'. In that culture there were no words available even to Hester to describe Pearl's wildness other than those associated with the demonic. This is no excuse for the many critics who have seen her in the same light.

But the stronger association of the name is surely the 'pearl without price' which is an image of the kingdom of heaven in *Matthew* 13. In spite of himself, the narrator has to confess that physically Pearl was immaculate, 'worthy to have been brought forth in Eden'. Moreover, she has a 'native grace', combining the 'wild-flower prettiness of a peasant baby' with the 'pomp of an infant princess'. Indeed the only characteristic he can point to in support of the accusation of perversity is her wildness: her nature 'lacked reference and adaptation to the world into which she was born':

> It was as if she had been made afresh, out of new elements, and must perforce be permitted to live her own life, and be a law unto herself, without her eccentricities being reckoned to her for a crime.

She spontaneously claims an existential or Antinomian freedom, and because her mother is exiled to the forest-fringe of the community, escapes its 'wholesome regimen for the growth and promotion of all childish virtues', not least that 'frequent application of the rod, enjoined by Scriptural authority'. That she should be so 'full of merriment and music' in itself cries out for the repression meted out to the rival community at Merrymount.

Again there are close parallels in Blake. At the centre of Blake's rebellion was the conviction that the main purpose of life was not to enchain what he called the energies, which only provokes them to destructive manifestations, but to release them into creative activity. Hester observes in Pearl 'so fierce a training of the energies that were to make good her cause, in the contest that must ensue'. Blake's 'A Little Girl Lost' begins with this epigraph:

> *Children of the future Age*
> *Reading this indignant page,*
> *Know that in a former time*
> *Love! Sweet Love! was thought a crime.*

Blake's little girl is somewhat older than Pearl, and has her first experience of sexual love in an unsupervised and therefore unfallen world:

> Once a youthful pair,
> Fill'd with softest care,
> Met in garden bright
> Where the holy light
> Had just remov'd the curtains of the night.
>
> There, in rising day,
> On the grass they play;

> Parents were afar,
> Strangers came not near,
> And the maiden soon forgot her fear.

But her later meeting with her father desecrates her joys and desires, smearing them with the serpent-slime of sin, vomiting poison on the bread and the wine.

> To her father white
> Came the maiden bright;
> But his loving look,
> Like the holy book,
> All her tender limbs with terror shook.

Pearl several times invites her father to join hands with Hester and herself. But it never seems to occur to Dimmesdale that he might have any obligations in the eyes of God towards Hester and Pearl. The only thing he feels he ought to share with them is their public humiliation. He denies Pearl a family and therefore drives her into greater wildness. She is like the child Anna Brangwen in Lawrence's *The Rainbow,* lacking the security which the rainbow arch of an achieved marriage symbolizes. His desertion leaves Hester, as Lawrence says of Tom Brangwen, 'like a broken arch thrust sickeningly out from support', and that unsupported weight presses on Pearl.

While Dimmesdale moves in perpetual gloom, Pearl generates or attracts her own private pool of sunshine. She has a deep fund of vital energy, the lack of which, as well as guilt, is what Dimmesdale is dying of, a life-giving energy which is denied its circuit in a family, except for one remarkable moment. Dimmesdale takes her hand:

> The moment that he did so, there came what seemed a tumultuous rush of new life, other life than his own, pouring like a torrent into his heart, and hurrying through all his veins, as if the mother and the child were communicating their vital warmth to his half-torpid system. The three formed an electric chain.

But Dimmesdale, as Pearl sees, is neither bold nor true. He is too self-centred to accept the gift of love and life. He 'had extended his egotism over the whole expanse of nature'.

The same discrepancy we noted in the interpretation of the wild rose bush exists on a larger scale in relation to the forest. All the passing references to the forest assume the standard Puritan associations of darkness and evil. The forest is precisely what the colonists have come to eradicate, and Dimmesdale in particular had come from a great English university 'bringing all the learning of the age into our wild forest-land'. But when we actually enter and experience the forest, its meaning is exactly the opposite. Its beauties are not presented as the product of mere rankness. It would be absurd, given his lifelong, minutely recorded love of Nature, to assume that Hawthorne is speaking in his own person when he condemns Hester for 'breathing the wild, free atmosphere of an unredeemed, unchristianized, lawless region' and for being in sympathy with 'that wild, heathen Nature of the forest, never subjugated by human law, nor illuminated by higher truth'. Hawthorne had spent a large part of his life shunning that subjugated humanized world. Not only are such sentiments completely out of keeping with his attitude to Nature as expressed in his Notebooks (was he not a close friend of Thoreau?) but also with the forest as we experience it in this novel.

Dimmesdale behaves as though he had only two alternatives, to keep silent as he does until the end, or to publicly confess and join Hester and Pearl on the scaffold. There is a third alternative, which his role as the spiritual leader of a Christian community in fact enforces on him, that is to do what Christ would have done, what Christ did in a similar situation with the woman taken in adultery. He should have opposed the communal cruelty in the name of compassion and common humanity. As Hester says to him in the forest: 'What hast thou to do with these iron men, and their opinions? They have kept thy better part in bondage too long already'. It seems for a moment that his better part might yet be redeemable. He feels joy for the first time since his 'sin':

> It was the exhilarating effect – upon a prisoner just escaped from the dungeon of his own heart – of breathing the wild, free atmosphere of an unredeemed, unchritianized, lawless, region. His spirit rose, as it were, with a bound, and attained a nearer prospect of the sky, than throughout the misery which had kept him grovelling on the earth.

With great daring Hawthorne has Dimmesdale attribute his momentary redemption and resurrection to the forest leaves and his decision to seek the 'better life' in adultery:

> O Hester, thou art my better angel! I seem to have flung myself– sick, sin-stained, and sorrow-blackened – down upon these forest-leaves, and to have risen up all made anew, and with new powers to glorify Him that hath been merciful?

In the forest 'never subjugated by human law, nor illumined by higher truth', Hester achieves her apotheosis. She frees her abundant hair, 'dark and rich'. Her smile 'seemed gushing from the very heart of womanhood':

> Her sex, her youth, and the whole richness of her beauty, came back from what men call the irrevocable past, and clustered themselves, with her maiden hope, and a happiness before unknown, within the magic circle of this hour. . . . All at once, as with a sudden smile of heaven, forth burst

the sunshine, pouring a very flood into the obscure forest, gladdening each green leaf, transmuting the yellow fallen ones to gold.

For Pearl, especially, it is a moment of atonement with all the flora and fauna of the forest : 'The truth seems to be that the mother-forest, and these wild things which it nourished, all recognized a kindred wildness in the human child'. She decks herself with flowers like Perdita at the sheep-shearing: 'See with what natural skill she has made those simple flowers adorn her! Had she gathered pearls, and diamonds, and rubies, in the wood, they could not have become her better'.

What would have happened if Dimmesdale had allowed himself to be persuaded to run away with Hester, and they had escaped the attentions of Chillingworth? Surely we never believe for a moment that this could happen. Chillingworth would necessarily be on the ship with them, since he is a part of Dimmesdale, his chilling worth, his disabling, dehumanizing self-subjection to the quest for spiritual purity. Once out of the forest and the company of Hester and Pearl, his new found freedom can express itself only in the blanket negation of blasphemy. Remove his 'dynasty and moral code' and there is nothing for him to fall back on but his 'buckramed habit of clerical decorum'. His final act, far from being an act of 'honesty and courage' as some critics have called it, is his total, fatal capitulation to a set of evil values which have eaten their way into his breast, cauterized his heart. The difference between Hester and Dimmesdale is that her scarlet letter is external; it can be thrown off or worn with ostentatious scorn. His is internal. It defines him. It is his life. The aspiration towards purity and perfection itself emerges as evil.

The forest, for all its positive associations, is not a place where people can live and start a family. They could have tried to found an alternative community, but, apart from physical hardship and the dangers from the Indians, the Puritans would soon have stamped out such an attempt, as they stamped out the attempt at Merry Mount. As for going back to Europe, there would always be the crippling fear of discovery, since even two centuries later the adulterous or 'impure' woman is invariably destroyed. Emma Bovary, Anna Karenina, Tess, show that no patriarchal society will (can by definition) tolerate adultery.

Hawthorne is, like Flaubert, Tolstoy, Hardy, strongly aware of marriage as a social institution, of the unlikelihood of fulfilment on the run or in exile. If you are locked into a society which forbids your personal fulfilment, the situation is tragic. There was a powerful convention in fiction that however sympathetic the writer might be to an adulterous heroine, the moral code must be respected to the extent that she must end the novel dead. *Madame Bovary* (1856) and *Anna Karenina* (1873) both end with the death of the heroine; and despite his claim that she is a 'pure woman' and the fact that her supposed sin was not in any case adulterous, Hardy's Tess (1893) ends on the gallows. The mere fact that Hester is still alive and relatively happy at the end is therefore highly subversive. It was not until Lawrence and Joyce in the nineteen-twenties that novelists dared to openly celebrate adultery.

Hawthorne's heroine is a scarlet woman who glories in her 'sin'; the villain the betrayed husband; the most sinful member of the community its spiritual leader. By the end of the novel, the scarlet letter itself is transformed, even in the eyes of the citizens, until they begin to read it as standing for Able. The reader recognizes, in the pun with Abel, Hawthorne's affirmation of Hester's innocence. But what he has planted in the minds of his readers is that the true interpretation is Angel. Red begins as the colour of evil and shame, but becomes, through Hawthorne's alchemy, the colour of inextinguishable life.

The last we hear of Hester, she is giving comfort and counsel to wounded, wasted and wronged women, assuring them that

at some brighter period, when the world should have grown ripe for it, in Heaven's own time, a new truth would be revealed, in order to establish the whole relation between man and woman on a surer ground of mutual happiness.

The Scarlet Letter is Hawthorne's contribution to that ripening and revelation.

14 WHITMAN AND THE VOICE OF NATURE

In 1844, when Whitman was a twenty-five-year-old journalist, Emerson published his essay on 'The Poet'. There he claimed for the poet that

> beyond the energy of his possessed and conscious intellect, he is capable of a new energy (as of intellect doubled on itself), by abandonment to the nature of things; that, beside his privacy of power as an individual man, there is a great public power, on which he can draw, by unlocking, at all risks, his human doors, and suffering ethereal tides to roll and circulate through him: then he is caught up into the life of the Universe, his speech is thunder, his thought is law, and his words are universally intelligible as the plants and animals.

He spoke of the man with such power as 'the conductor of the whole river of electricity':

> Nothing walks, or creeps, or grows, or exists, which must not in turn arise and walk before him as exponent of his meaning. Comes he to that power, his genius is no longer exhaustible. All the creatures, by pairs and by tribes, pour into his mind as into a Noah's ark, to come forth again to people a new world.

Such a man, he claimed, would be under the protection of Pan:

> Thou true land-lord! sea-lord! air-lord! Wherever snow falls, or water flows, or birds fly, wherever day and night meet in twilight, wherever the blue heaven is hung by clouds, or sown with stars, wherever are forms with transparent boundaries, wherever are outlets into celestial space, wherever is danger, and awe, and love, there is Beauty, plenteous as rain, shed for thee, and though thou shouldest walk the world over, thou shalt not be able to find a condition inopportune or ignoble.

Whitman felt these words were written to him; they gave him his vocation. His own definition of that vocation was henceforth to be in very similar terms. The Preface to the first (1855) edition of *Leaves of Grass* is full of echoes of Emerson's essay:

> The greatest poet hardly knows pettiness or triviality. If he breathes into anything that was before thought small, it dilates with the grandeur and life of the universe. . . . The land and sea, the animals, fishes and birds, the sky of heaven and the orbs, the forests, mountains and rivers, are not small themes – but folks expect of the poet to indicate more than the beauty and dignity which always attach to dumb real objects – they

214

expect him to indicate the path between reality and their souls. . . . What do you think is the grandeur of storms and dismemberments, and the deadliest battles and wrecks, and the wildest fury of the elements, and the power of the sea, and the motion of nature, and the throes of human desires, and dignity and hate and love? It is that something in the soul which says, Rage on, whirl on, I tread master here and everywhere – Master of the spasms of the sky and of the shatter of the sea, Master of nature and passion and death, and of all terror and all pain.

Yet even when he is closest to Emerson, there are significant distinctions. It is clear that Whitman's scope is much greater than Emerson's, with his crippling reduction of all meaning to Beauty. Emerson's Nature is altogether more placid and benevolent than Whitman's, and is accorded no value whatsoever in and for itself. Whitman's credo in the 1855 Preface begins 'Love the earth and sun and the animals', and he does not mean what Emerson would have meant by that: value them as 'commodities', that is, for the many ways in which they are useful to man.

Emerson's response to the first *Leaves of Grass* was as warm as if Whitman had written it himself. But Emerson soon cooled as he became aware of the radical differences between his own position, particularly in relation to nature, and that of Whitman. He wrote of Thoreau in a journal entry in 1862: 'Perhaps his fancy for Walt Whitman grew out of his taste for wild nature, for an otter, a woodchuck, or a loon'. And in 1873 Emerson omitted Whitman altogether from his anthology *Parnassus*.

In 'The Poet', Emerson frequently used the word 'nature', but did not define it or explain his apparently high valuation of it, since he had already done that at great length in *Nature* (1836). It is almost inconceivable that Whitman, having read *Nature*, could subsequently address Emerson as 'Master' and attach so much importance to his approval; for Emerson's 'Nature' is a far cry from Whitman's. It is as though Emerson here gathers together, simplifies and systematizes the elements most hostile to nature in the thought of Socrates, Plato, Aquinas, Blake, Wordsworth and Coleridge.

Whitman's vision is biocentric or geocentric. Emerson's is blatantly anthropocentric. Nature, he claims, is provision made for the support, delight and profit of man. As in Hopkins, the attempt to demonstrate that all things exist for the benefit of man becomes at times ludicrous: 'Therefore is Space, and therefore Time, that man may know that things are not huddled and lumped, but sundered and individual'. Man is the one perfect being: 'All other organizations appear to be degradations of the human form'. Godlike man 'is himself the creator in the finite'. Emerson echoes Sophocles' Ode to Man: 'Who can set bounds to the possibilities of man?' Nature 'offers all its kingdoms to man as the raw material which he may mould into what is useful. Man is never weary of working it up. . . . More and more, with every thought, does his kingdom stretch over things, until the world becomes, at last, only a realized will, – the double of the man'. He even refers specifically to the

Antigone in terms which suggest a very strange interpretation of that play, linking it with nineteenth-century science: 'a spiritual life has been imparted to nature', 'the solid seeming block of matter has been pervaded and dissolved by a thought':

> Thus even in physics, the material is ever degraded before the spiritual. The astronomer, the geometer, rely on their irrefragable analysis, and disdain the results of observation. The sublime remark of Euler on his law of arches, 'This will be found contrary to all experience, yet is true;' had already transferred nature into the mind, and left matter like an outcast corpse.

These attitudes lead to an equally distorted reading of *The Tempest*. Shakespeare, he claims, shares with Prospero 'the power of subordinating nature', of making free with 'the most imposing forms and phenomena of the world', thus asserting 'the predominance of the soul'. The claim that nature is 'a metaphor of the human mind' is rich for poetry and no detriment to nature; but for Emerson it was only that. The male intellect, hungry for knowledge and power, is the ultimate sanction.

Emerson's universe is strictly dualistic, 'composed of Nature and the Soul', and idealistic, every material form pre-existing in the mind of God. He even finds it perfectly conceivable that nature does not exist, and does not see that its non-existence would have any bearing on the existence of man. Only the tyranny of the senses binds us to nature 'as if we were a part of it'. In Emerson's terms, Whitman's is an 'unrenewed understanding': 'To the senses and the unrenewed understanding, belongs a sort of instinctive belief in the absolute existence of nature. In their view, man and nature are indissolubly joined'.

No poet has ever been less dualistic and idealistic than Whitman ('materialism first and last imbuing'):

> Most writers have disclaimed the physical world and they have not over-estimated the other, or soul, but have underestimated the corporeal. How shall my eye separate the beauty of the blossoming buckwheat field from the stalks and heads of tangible matter? How shall I know what life is except as I see it in the flesh? I will not praise one without the other or any more than the other.

By 1881 Whitman went much further, affirming, at the end of his eulogy of all the parts and functions of the human body added to 'I Sing the Body Electric':

> O I say these are not the parts and poems of the body only, but of the soul,
> O I say now these are the soul!

216

It was precisely this element in Whitman which made him, for Lawrence, 'a great moralist' and 'a great changer of the blood in the veins of men':

> Whitman was the first heroic seer to seize the soul by the scruff of her neck and plant her down among the potsherds. . . . Stay in the flesh. Stay in the limbs and lips and in the belly. Stay in the breast and womb. Stay there, Oh, Soul, where you belong. . . . The great home of the Soul is the open road. Not heaven, not paradise. . . . The soul is neither 'above' nor 'within'. It is a wayfarer down the open road.   [*Studies* 180–1]

The result is 'a morality of actual living, not of salvation'.

Emerson held the Socratic view that to every man who pursues truth and virtue, every form will eventually become 'an open book' revealing its 'inner life and final cause'. Nature is a great schoolroom for the human understanding. Animals, for example, exist to give us lessons. And nature never did betray the heart that loved her. This leads to morally base conclusions, such as that grinding debt is 'a preceptor whose lessons cannot be foregone, and is needed most by those who suffer from it most'. Whitman said that Wordsworth 'lacks sympathy with men and women', and might have said the same of Emerson.

Whitman later came to wonder 'that years ago I began like most youngsters to have a touch (though it came late, and was only on the surface) of Emerson-on-the-brain – that I read his writings reverently, and address'd him as "Master", and for a month or so thought of him as such' ['Emerson's Books (The Shadows of Them)']. By this date, 1880, what struck Whitman most about Emerson was his 'cold and bloodless intellectuality' and his egotism or anthropocentrism: 'His final influence is to make his students cease to worship anything – almost cease to believe in anything, outside of themselves'.

Then there was the distance Emerson had deliberately put between himself and Nature, the cultivated artificiality of his perceptions and his style, the narrowness of his vision. Thoreau said of the first *Leaves of Grass* 'it is as if the beasts spoke'. Nothing could have been further from the voice of Nature than that of Ralph Waldo Emerson:

> Though the author has much to say of freedom and wildness and simplicity and spontaneity, no performance was ever more based on artificial scholarships and decorums at third of fourth removes, (he calls it culture,) and built up from them. It is always a *make*, never an unconscious *growth*. It is the porcelain figure or statuette of lion, or stag, or Indian hunter – and a very choice statuette too – appropriate for the rosewood or marble bracket of parlor or library; never the animal itself, or the hunter himself. Indeed, who wants the real animal or hunter? What would that do amid astral and bric-a-brac and tapestry, and ladies and gentlemen talking in subdued tones of Browning and Longfellow and art?

217

The least suspicion of such actual bull, or Indian, or of Nature carrying
out itself, would put all those good people to instant terror and flight.

Had Whitman shared the ideas and attitudes of Emerson, his poetry
would necessarily have been as bad as Emerson's.

*   *   *

No critic, as far as I am aware, has ever denied that Whitman has many and
major faults. The later editions of *Leaves of Grass* are overblown and run to
seed. Whitman's poetry must, like Blake's, Wordsworth's or Lawrence's, be
read selectively. But there remains a substantial quantity of wonderful poetry
which Whitman could not have produced had he written in a more crafts-
manlike and self-critical way. There are poems, some of them very long poems,
which do not suffer from any of his faults, or in which the faults themselves
are transfigured and become virtues. Let us look, for example, at the problem
of Whiman's egotism.

Whitman was a notorious egotist in his life; in his art a professional
egotist. He made no bones about it, writing, in one of his many anonymous
reviews of *Leaves of Grass*: 'There can be no two thoughts about Walt
Whitman's egotism. That is avowedly what he steps out of the crowd and turns
and faces them for' [Quoted by Zweig, 274]. Perhaps all artists are in this
sense egotists. But Whitman is so much more blatant than any other. The first
line of the first poem in the first *Leaves of Grass* was 'I CELEBRATE MYSELF',
('Song of Myself' did not yet have a title). And we need go no further than that
poem to harvest:

I resist anything better than my own diversity

I have pried through the strata and analyzed to a hair,
And counselled with doctors and calculated close and found no sweeter
fat than sticks to my own bones.

Walt Whitman . . . a kosmos

Divine I am inside and out, and I make holy whatever I touch or am
  touched from;
The scent of these arm-pits is aroma finer than prayer,
This head is more than churches or bibles or creeds.

I dote on myself . . . there is that lot of me, and all so luscious

I am an acme of things accomplished, and I an encloser of things to be.

All forces have been steadily employed to complete and delight me

I sound my barbaric yawp over the roofs of the world.

Many readers can see no reason why they should listen. If Wordsworth is the egotistical sublime, surely Whitman is the egotistical ridiculous. How can anyone take him seriously? Such readers have missed the whole point, and missed it threefold. First, they have missed the humour. Whitman is joyously clowning and teasing. 'Song of Myself' is (among many other things) a great comic poem. To his over-earnest followers who wanted him to be a prophet or philosopher, Whitman would say: 'Why, I pride myself on being a real humorist underneath everything else' [quoted by Reynolds, 507]. But this is not the crude humour of gross exaggeration and gigantism only. It is Whitman's tricksy technique for subverting the normal standards of his readers, luring us, under cover of comedy, beyond the limitations of our usual, narrowly reasonable and realistic secularism and anthropocentrism. It echoes some of the high-spirited conceits of Donne or Marvell, and was rightly recognized by Emerson as wit. Whitman's provocative strategy is similar to Blake's in *The Marriage of Heaven and Hell*, and for ultimately similar purposes. The jester unyokes the imagination of his audience. Underneath the egotist and blusterer is the humorist; but underneath the humorist is the healer and the seer.

Whitman's 'egotism' is the opposite of the hubristic egotism of the Greek heroes. Whitman saw himself as a hero, in accordance with Emerson's lofty prescription for the ideal poet, but not at all the aggressively male and selfish hero of the ancient epics. He tells the Muse to 'cross out please those immensely overpaid accounts, / That matter of . . . Odysseus' wanderings' ['Song of the Exposition']. Nothing could be further from the self-honing spirit of Odysseus than the open spirit in which Whitman sets out on his imaginative exploration of the sea of life:

> O we can wait no longer,
> We too take ship O soul,
> Joyous we too launch out on trackless seas,
> Fearless for unknown shores on waves of ecstasy to sail,
> Amid the wafting winds, (thou pressing me to thee, I thee to me,
>   O soul,)
> Caroling free, singing our song of God,
> Chanting our chant of pleasant exploration.
>
> ['Passage to India']

Odysseus' self was forged in opposition and contradistinction to everything else in heaven and earth: he does not have the imagination to know or care, still less to feel what others feel. Whitman's self grows by assimilating experience, relationships, not by assimilating others. Such assimilation requires an opening of the self to imaginative identification: 'I am the man . . . I suffered . . . I was there'. His pride is exactly balanced by his sympathy, so that it sets him apart, distinct, without setting him above or beyond. His pride is absolute, not relative, a recognition that every part of him is a miracle, and therefore representative of the vast miracle of creation, the wheeled universe. 'Song of Myself' may begin 'I CELEBRATE MYSELF', but it continues: 'And what I assume you shall assume, / For every atom belonging to me as good belongs to you'. Whitman wanted to compel 'every reader to transpose himself or herself into the central position, and become a living fountain' [Matthiessen 1941, 650]. When a man tells us he is wonderful, we recoil. When he tells us we are equally wonderful, we warm to him. When he tells us a pismire or a blade of grass is equally wonderful, we must forget both our egotism and his and listen to a wisdom beyond both:

> Come I should like to hear you tell me what there is in yourself that is
>   not just as wonderful,
> And I should like to hear the name of anything between Sunday morning
>   and Saturday night that is not just as wonderful.
>
>   ['Who Learns My Lesson Complete']

Thus the second usual mistake shades into the third, which is to fail to register that the voice speaking to us is frequently, especially in 'Song of Myself', not only the voice of Walt Whitman, a 'single, separate person', or even the all-suffering voice of humanity, but also, as far as he can translate it, the voice of Nature herself, of the earth ('His analogy the earth complete in itself enfolding in itself all processes of growth effusing life and power for hidden purposes'), of the 'kosmos'. In an attempt to make this unmistakable, Whitman added to the 1860 *Leaves of Grass* a poem explaining exactly what he meant by 'Walt Whitman, a kosmos':

> Who includes diversity and is Nature,
> Who is the amplitude of the earth, and the coarseness and sexuality of
>   the earth, and the great charity of the earth, and the equilibrium also,
> Who has not look'd forth from the windows the eyes for nothing, or
>   whose brain held audience with messengers for nothing,
> Who contains believers and disbelievers, who is the most majestic
>   lover,
> Who holds duly his or her triune proportion of realism, spiritualism,
>   and of the aesthetic or intellectual,
> Who having consider'd the body find all its organs and parts good,
> Who, out of the theory of the earth and of his or her body understands
>   by subtle analogies all other theories,
> The theory of a city, a poem, and of the large politics of these States;
> Who believes no only in our globe with its sun and moon, but in other
>   globes with their suns and moons,
> Who, constructing the house for himself or herself, not for a day but
>   for all time, sees races, eras, dates, generations,
> The past, the future, dwelling there, like space, inseparable together.
>
>   ['Kosmos']

He also later added to the first section of 'Song of Myself' a new passage concluding: 'I permit to speak at every hazard, / Nature without check with original energy'.

These efforts to spell it out would not have been necessary if Whitman had been able to rely on anything better than wilful incomprehension in the majority of his few readers. For example, between two of the most notorious examples of 'egotism' in my list – 'The scent of these arm-pits . . .' and 'I dote on myself . . .' – is a passage of sixteen lines purporting to describe 'the spread of my own body', which includes 'shaded ledges and rests', 'tilth', 'root of washed sweet-flag, timorous pond-snipe, nest of guarded duplicate eggs', 'hay', 'trickling sap of maple, fibre of manly wheat', 'sun', 'vapors', 'brooks and dews', 'winds', 'fields, branches of live-oak'. This is far too much to be merely metaphor. It is an example of Whitman's consistent refusal to distinguish what he called the 'microcosmic' Walt Whitman from the macrocosm of which his own body was a part containing the whole (since 'all truths wait in all things'). He is always faithful to his sense of his own body as continuous with the earth both in space and time. Under a broadly farcical line such as

[I] am stucco'd with quadrupeds and birds all over

lies a fully developed holistic philosophy such as that of Merleau-Ponty:

> Immersed in the visible by his body, itself visible, the see-er does not appropriate what he sees; he merely approaches it by looking, he opens himself to the world. . . . Visible and mobile, my body is a thing among things; it is caught in the fabric of the world, and its cohesion is that of a thing. But because it moves itself and sees, it holds things in a circle around itself. Things are an annex or prolongation of itself; they are incrusted into its flesh, they are parts of its full definition; the world is made of the same stuff as the body. [55]

Whitman had no fear of contradicting himself, since nature is full of contradictions. He would have agreed with Blake that 'without contraries is no progression'. 'Song of Myself' is a unique fusion of extreme megalomaniac egotism and extreme self-sacrificial humility, of metaphysical wit and romantic afflatus, of clowning and high seriousness, of contrivance and inspired prophetic vision.

The attempt to speak with the voice of Nature was described by Whitman as a 'great language experiment'. Of course it has to be much more than that; it has to be also what Zweig calls 'an adventure of personal change' [231], for 'poems of depth' must be, Whitman claimed, 'actual emanations from the personality and life of the writers'. It may be that the change came suddenly, as a visitation, if section 5 of 'Song of Myself' is autobiographical. Whitman is here addressing his own soul:

I mind how we lay in June, such a transparent summer morning;
You settled your head athwart my hips and gently turned over upon
    me,
And parted the shirt from my bosom-bone, and plunged your tongue
    to my barestript heart,
And reached till you felt my beard, and reached till you held my feet.

Swiftly arose and spread around me the peace and joy and knowledge
    that pass all the art and argument of the earth;
And I know that the hand of God is the elderhand of my own,
And I know that the spirit of God is the eldest brother of my own,
And that all the men ever born are also my brothers . . . and the
    women my sisters and lovers,
And that a kelson of the creation is love;
And limitless are leaves stiff or drooping in the fields,
And brown ants in the little wells beneath them,
And mossy scabs of the wormfence, and heaped stones, and elder and
    mullen and pokeweed.

A kelson is a bar bolted to the keel holding it and the timbers together. His own oceanic experience initiated him into a world where everything holds together by the power of love, that is sympathy, interaction, mutual dependence, a world therefore of atonement between body and soul, man and God. And the word for that newly perceived indivisible whole is Nature, where love declares itself as limitless leaves of grass. Every weed, ant or worm becomes henceforth a token of that love, a letter from God:

I find letters from God dropped in the street, and every one is signed
    by God's name,
And I leave them where they are, for I know that others will
    punctually come forever and ever.

This is Whitman at his closest to Hopkins, who also found God where 'weeds, in wheels, shoot long and lovely and lush'.

Or it may be that the change took place gradually over the period 1850–1855. (Either way Whitman acquired the 'vision splendid' at about the age at which Wordsworth lost it.) In that case, the first steps would have been necessarily negative, a clearing of the ground, a recognition of and rejection of single vision, a shedding of all the layers of falsity and insulation and complacency and conformity which seal the spirit and prevent us, in Lawrence's words, from coming at 'the real naked essence of our vision'. It is the Romantic tradition of the Aeolean harp or wind-bells. Whitman anticipates Nietzsche's call: 'Not I! Not I! but a *God* through my instrumentality' (which Lawrence rephrased as 'Not I, not I, but the wind that blows through me!'). But Whitman uses the trope with a disarming comic literalness: 'The sound of

the belched words of my voice . . . words loosed to the eddies of the wind'
['Song of Myself']. And Whitman was so uniquely successful in achieving this
freedom and openness and nakedness, this escape from the tyranny of the
ego, that he was even able to by-pass, much of the time, that argument with
himself which generates the creative energy of Shakespeare and Swift, Conrad
and Yeats. He silenced the argumentative self, tense with self-doubt, irritably
reaching after facts and reasons. He achieved precisely that 'negative capability' which Keats mistakenly attributed to Shakespeare: 'I have no mockings
or arguments . . . I witness and wait'. In order to relax and listen and watch,
he found that he had to 'stop thinking' in the ordinary sense.

> What is marvellous? what is unlikely? what is impossible or baseless, or
> vague? after you have once just opened the space of a peachpit and given
> audience to far and near and to the sunset and had all things enter with
> electric swiftness softly and duly without confusion or jostling or jam.
>
> [Preface to 1855 *Leaves of Grass*]

In such a man 'his thoughts are the hymns of the praise of things' [1855
Preface]. It is the 'intuitive reason' which Coleridge hoped would some day
accompany the resolving of miracles into laws:

> what we now consider as miracles in opposition to ordinary experience,
> we should then reverence with a yet higher devotion as harmonious parts
> of one great complex miracle, when the antithesis between experience
> and belief would itself be taken up into the unity of intuitive reason.
>
> [*The Friend* vol.i, 519]

Whitman became, in Zweig's words, 'a voice various and broad enough
to say "everything"' [249]. It was a voice so different from any heard before
that it seemed to Thoreau 'a little more than human'. It may be rather that, if
the poet is indeed 'the equable man' – 'Not in him but off from him things are
grotesque or eccentric or fail in their sanity' – then it is the other voices which
are less than fully human. In *St. Mawr* Lawrence claims that a man in whom
Pan is not dead would be 'all the animals in turn, instead of one, fixed,
automatic thing, which he is now, grinding on the nerves'. Whitman shares
with Lawrence and Hughes this ability to 'be all the animals in turn', to identify
with the non-human creation:

> The soul or spirit transmits itself into all matter – into rocks, and can live
> the life of a rock – into the sea, and can feel itself the sea – into the oak,
> or other tree – into an animal, and feel itself a horse, a fish, or bird – into
> the earth – into the motions of the suns and stars – A man is only
> interested in anything when he identifies himself with it – he must
> himself be whirling and speeding through space like the planet Mercury –
> he must be driving like a cloud – he must shine like the sun – he must be

orbic and balanced in the air, like this earth – he must crawl like the pismire – he must – he would be growing fragrantly in the air, like the locust blossoms – he would rumble and crash like the thunder in the sky – he would spring like a cat on his prey – he would splash like a whale.

[quoted by Zweig, 174]

'Song of Myself' was to be 'a poem in which all things and qualities and processes express themselves – the nebula – the fixed stars – the earth – the grass, waters, vegetable, sauroid, and all processes – man – animals' [ibid 211].

Whitman was particularly interested in the voices of animals. When he said that he had been searching for twenty-five years for the right word to express what the twilight note of the robin meant to him, he was not speaking of some Flaubertian mot juste, nor of some super-descriptive or onomatopoeic word. Lawrence felt that certain voices, particularly animal voices, were not merely audible, but could 'sound on the plasm direct'. In 'Tortoise Shout' he lists many such sounds, including the song of the nightingale: 'I remember the first time, out of a bush in the darkness, a nightingale's piercing cries and gurgles startled the depths of my soul'. The spirits dictating to Yeats stopped when an owl hooted outside, saying 'We like that sort of sound'. Hughes comments:

And that is it: 'that sort of sound' makes the spirits listen. It opens our deepest and innermost ghost to sudden attention. It is a spirit, and it speaks to spirit.   [WP 125]

Many natural sounds, but especially the voices of birds, opened up depths of Whitman's soul, spoke to him nakedly of the fundamentals of life and death.

> I think I will do nothing for a long time but listen,
> And accrue what I hear into myself . . . and let sounds contribute
>   toward me.
>
> I hear the bravuras of birds . . .   ['Song of Myself' 26]

He would summon such voices, like a shaman, to help him enter unfamiliar or forbidding regions of the spirit:

> Having studied the mocking-bird's tones and the flight of the
>   mountain-hawk,
> And heard at dawn the unrivall'd one, the hermit thrush from the
>   swamp-cedars,
> Solitary, singing in the West, I strike up for a New World.
>   ['Starting from Paumanok']

These birds are not chosen at random. Preparing himself to 'translate' a story of loss and death, he sings

> Out of the cradle endlessly rocking,
> Out of the mocking-bird's throat, the musical shuttle.

Preparing himself spiritually for his great threnody on Lincoln, he invokes the voice of the hermit thrush:

> Song of the bleeding throat,
> Death's outlet song of life ..

*   *   *

So to the 'great language experiment', as Whitman called it, for such ideas and attitudes have profound implications for style:

> But to speak in literature with the perfect rectitude and insouciance of the movements of animals and the unimpeachableness of the sentiment of trees in the woods and grass by the roadside is the flawless triumph of art. . . . The greatest poet has less a marked style and is more the channel of thoughts and things without increase or diminution, and is the free channel of himself. He swears to his art, I will not be meddlesome, I will not have in my writings any elegance or effect or originality to hang in the way between me and the rest like curtains. I will have nothing hang in the way, not the richest curtains. What I tell I tell for precisely what it is. Let who may exalt or startle or fascinate or soothe I will have purposes as health or heat or snow has and be as regardless of observation.
>
> [1855 Preface]

The first of the Rules for Composition Whitman laid down for himself in his notebooks was 'A perfectly transparent, plate-glassy style, artless, with no ornaments'. He defined the 'Divine style' as 'perfect transparent clearness, sanity and health'.

So the first stage, stylistically, is also negative, a going naked: to tear down the curtains of received poetic style, the style of Longfellow and Tennyson, even, it seemed to Whitman, of much of Shakespeare. He had to get out from under what Hughes has called the 'suffocating maternal octopus' of the English poetic tradition. Of Tennyson's 'De Profundis' Whitman wrote: 'It has several exquisite little verses, not simple like rosebuds, but gem-like like garnets or sapphires, cut by a lapidary artist'. Had Lawrence come across this when he contrasted the 'treasured gem-like lyrics of Shelley and Keats' with the 'perfect rose' of Whitman's verse, 'only a running flame, emerging and flowing off, and never in any sense at rest, static, finished'? There are many passages in Lawrence's preface to the American edition of his *New Poems* which might easily come from Whitman's 1855 preface:

> There must be the rapid momentaneous association of things which meet and pass on the for ever incalculable journey of creation: everything left

in its own rapid, fluid relationship with the rest of things. . . . Whitman pruned away his clichés – perhaps his clichés of rhythm as well as of phrase. And this is about all we can do, deliberately, with free verse. We can get rid of the stereotyped movements and the old hackneyed associations of sound or sense. We can break down those artificial conduits and canals through which we do so love to force our utterance. We can break the stiff neck of habit. We can be in ourselves spontaneous and flexible as flame, we can see that utterance rushes out without artificial form or artificial smoothness. But we cannot positively prescribe any motion, any rhythm.

If nothing is being done deliberately, what determines that the utterance shall be verse at all? In the earliest surviving version of his essay on Whitman, Lawrence attempted his own answer to this question:

It takes the greatest soul of all to be quite straightforward and direct. In the long run rhetoric and circuitous elaboration and gorgeous language must take second place. . . . If we look at Whitman's verse form, again we see a dual intention. At its best it springs purely spontaneous from the well-heads of consciousness. The primal soul utters itself in strange pulsations, gushes and strokes of sound. At his best Whitman gives these throbs naked and vibrating as they emerge from the quick. They follow, pulse after pulse, line after line, each one new and unforeseeable. They are lambent, they are life itself. Such are the lines. But in the whole, moreover, the whole soul speaks at once: sensual impulse instant with spiritual impulse, and the mind serving, giving pure attention. The lovely blood-lapping sounds of consonants slipping with fruit of vowels is unsurpassed and unsurpassable, in a thousand lines. Take any opening line, almost. – 'Out of the cradle endlessly rocking –' or again 'By the bivouac's fitful flame' or 'When lilacs last in the dooryard bloom'd' – it goes straight to the soul, nothing intervenes. There is the sheer creative gesture, moving the material world in wonderful swirls. The whole soul follows its own free, spontaneous, inexplicable course, its contractions and pulsations dictated from nowhere save from the creative quick itself. And each separate line is a pulsation and a contraction. There is nothing measured or mechanical. This is the greatest poetry. But sometimes, again, Whitman dumps us down cartloads of material, cartload upon cartload. All is shovelled out uninspired. How weary one grows of 'A Song for Occupations', for example!   (*Studies* 368–9)

The course of Whitman's inspiration is not entirely inexplicable; it's shapes and rhythms do not come from nowhere. F.O. Matthiessen suggests that for Whitman 'poetic rhythm was an organic response to the centers of experience – to the internal pulsations of the body, to its external movements in work and in making love, to such sounds as the wind and the sea' [1941, 564]. He was well aware of the effect of the ebb and flow of the Long Island breakers, 'rolling in without intermission, and fitfully rising and falling', upon his style:

> Its analogy is *the Ocean*. Its verses are the liquid, billowy waves, ever rising and falling, perhaps sunny and smooth, perhaps wild with storm, always moving, always alike in their nature as rolling waves, but hardly any two exactly alike in size or measure (metre), never having the sense of something finished and fixed, always suggesting something beyond.
>
> [quoted in Matthiessen 1941, 566–7]

It was not until 1879 that Whitman, after travelling through the prairies and the Rockies, suddenly felt that he had discovered the 'law' of his own poems in the spirit of place – 'this grim yet joyous elemental abandon – this plenitude of material, entire absence of art, untrammel'd play of primitive Nature – the chasm, the gorge, the crystal mountain stream, repeated scores, hundreds of miles – the broad handling and absolute uncrampedness' ['An Egotistical "Find"']. The 'untrammel'd play of primitive Nature' he also found in many other forms, but especially in vegetation, which provides him with this commonest analogy for his own lines: 'Drawing language into line by rigid grammatical rules, is the theory of the martinet applied to the processes of the spirit, and to the luxuriant growth of all that makes art' [quoted by Zweig 208–9]. Whitman refuses to train or lop the tendrils of his verse to fit the rectilinear trellis of the printed page. They sprawl, luxuriate, turn back upon themselves. Yet the result is far from a shapeless tangle, and very far from prose:

> Whitman's verse – with the exception that it is not metered – is farther removed from prose than is traditional verse itself, for the reason that traditional verse, is, like prose, composed in sentences, whereas Whitman's verse is composed in lines.
> [Ross 363]

Whitman's verse line obliterates the distinction between form and content. The comma at the end of the line is not to mark a grammatical division, but to indicate that the living organism which is the line takes its life and meaning from its place in the larger pattern (Whitman called it the 'ensemble'), which does in the real world and could theoretically in the poem extend to infinity: 'such joined unended links' – 'I will thread a thread through my poems that time and events are compact'. The commas are his stitches. The poem or verse paragraph breaks into the endless chain at some more or less random point, and drops out when enough examples have been accumulated to suggest the whole. Each poem is an excerpt from 'the only complete, actual poem' which is Nature.

Another characteristic anti-grammatical feature is the absence or deferment of verbs, particularly of transitive verbs:

There is a peculiar force in the true descriptive style, which takes over when one surrenders self in favour of the object; it is the force of unbroken continuity. Verb forms, instead of coming to an end, as transitive action, directed from the agent at the world . . . participate instead in a continuum in which every action is reflexive, intermediate between passive and active. [Massey 54]

Zweig suggests that as Wordsworth's steady tread over the Lakeland fells or round his garden paths determined his basically iambic rhythm, so Whitman, also an ambulatory poet, took his poetic rhythms from his walking rhythms, strolling, loitering, with frequent lingering to register and soak in some feature of the scene. There was the powerful influence of music, particularly the operatic aria and recitative. There were the rhythms of Hebrew parallelism mediated by the King James bible.

There seem to be no specifically literary influences. The only earlier free verse I know which is anything like Whitman's is Christopher Smart's in 'Jubilate Agno', which Whitman could not have known. On his cat Jeoffry Smart writes:

For by stroking him I have found out electricity.
For I perceived God's light about him both wax and fire.
For the Electrical fire is the spiritual substance, which God sends from heaven to sustain the bodies both of man and beast.
For God has blessed him in the variety of his movements.
For, though he cannot fly, he is an excellent clamberer.
For his motions upon the face of the earth are more than any other quadrupede.
For he can tread to all the measures upon the music.
For he can swim for life.
For he can creep.

It cannot be coincidence that Smart, like Whitman, was driven to such verse by an overwhelming need to praise and celebrate the created world, to fuse the physical and the spiritual, treating every creature as a sacred microcosm of the whole. Either could have written, as Whitman did in 'Starting from Paumanok' 'all the things of the universe are perfect miracles, each as profound as any'.

Blake's unfettered verse in the prophetic books should theoretically have been similar to Whitman's, but is so only on the rare occasions when Blake celebrates the colours, sounds and movements of the natural world:

Thou seest the gorgeous clothed Flies that dance & sport in summer
Upon the sunny brooks & meadows; every one the dance

Knows in its intricate mazes of delight artful to weave,
Each one to sound his instruments of music in the dance,
To touch each other & recede, to cross & change & return. [*Milton*]

Whitman did not discover Blake in his formative years, and when he did so, was as struck by the differences as by the resemblances:

Of William Blake & Walt Whitman Both are mystics, extatics but the difference between them is this – and a vast difference it is: Blake's visions grow to be the rule, displace the normal condition, fill the field, spurn this visible objective life, & seat the subjective spirit on an absolute throne, wilful and uncontrolled.

[Gohdes 53]

When Blake removed the fetters of metrical verse, he had, unlike Whitman and Smart, no other shaping force available to him, no analogies with what Whitman called the 'organic body' and believed to be the necessary shaper of the poetic imagination.

It is unlikely that Whitman was imitating translations of primitive poetry; yet his own has the authentic ring of the genuine primitive. How easily, for example, these lines (or any others) of the Australian Aborigine 'Moon-Bone Cycle' would transpose into a Whitman poem:

A duck comes swooping down to the Moonlight Clay Pan, there at the
  place of the Dugong . . .
From far away. I saw her flying over, in here at the clay pan ...
'I carried these eggs from a long way off, from inland to Arnhem
  Bay . . .
Because I have eggs, I give to my young the sound of the water.'
Splashing and preening herself, she ripples the water, among the
  lotus . . .
Backwards and forwards, swimming along, rippling the water,
Floating along on the clay pan, at the place of the Dugong.

Whitman's, like Caliban's, is the poetry of facts: 'A fact truly and absolutely stated . . . acquires a mythological or universal significance'. Hopkins agreed: 'But indeed I have often felt when I have been in this mood and felt the depth of an instress or how fast the inscape holds a thing, that nothing is so pregnant, so straightforward to the truth as simple 'yes' and 'is'.' It is an attempt to reclaim what our ordinary language and habitual responses have almost killed off, the ability to pay attention to Being, to what is actually and continually offered by life; not the search for deeply hidden underlying meanings, but the simple reception of what is at hand and manifest. The discipline of reducing one's style to that ('the Divine style') is as great as the disciplines of formal artifice and elaboration Hopkins nevertheless more frequently pursued.

What would a poetry of simple 'yes' and 'is' be like? The nearest Hopkins himself got to it was probably in 'Pied Beauty':

> Glory be to God for dappled things –
>> For skies of couple-colour as a brinded cow;
>>> For rose-moles all in stipple upon trout that swim;
> Fresh-firecoal chestnut-falls; finches' wings;
>> Landscape plotted and pieced – fold, fallow and plough;
>> And all trades, their gear and tackle and trim.

Even here there are the usual Hopkins adjectival pyrotechnics (which would surely pass Whitman's test of imperiously proving themselves); but basically it is a list, and for some items in the list – 'finches' wings' – mere naming is enough.

Whitman shared with Hopkins a faith in language as capable of supplying the poet with far more than he needs. Where Whitman fails in expression he does not blame his tools. The English language is 'brawny enough, and limber and full enough' (1855 Preface):

> Never will I allude to the English Language or tongue without exultation. This is the tongue that spurns laws, as the greatest tongue must. It is the most capacious vital tongue of all, – full of ease, definiteness, and power, – full of sustenance.   ['An American Primer']

The right words exist. 'Words strain, / Crack and sometimes break, under the burden' [T.S. Eliot, 'Burnt Norton'] only when they are severed from substance and turned into concepts. Any such slipping of language was a clear sign to Whitman that he was misusing it, not keeping faith with the denotative roots and human history of language. Words without referends in the world of common human experience are mere marks on the page:

> Were you thinking that those were the words, those upright lines?
>> those curves, angles, dots?
> No, those are not the words, the substantial words are in the ground
>> and sea,
> They are in the air, they are in you.   ['Song of the Rolling Earth']

Words transcribe experience, and a poet's vocabulary must be the very index of his being:

> Latent, in a great user of words, must actually be all passions, crimes, trades, animals, stars, God, sex, the past, might, space, metals, and the like – because these are the words, and he who is not these plays with a foreign tongue, turning helplessly to dictionaries and authorities.
>
> ['An American Primer']

To describe with vivid adjectives may help the reader to see more clearly and may fire the reader's own imagination, but it also puts the poet as word-smith between us and the object. The charge of the poet's own feelings is real and valuable, but it jams the original charge of the unadorned name, which is what Whitman was after. He believed that the poet could, by pristine naming, mime and renew the creation itself.

Many readers shudder at Whitman's catalogues. Even Lawrence called them 'all those lists of things boiled in one pudding-cloth!' [*Studies* 174]; but the proof of the pudding is in the eating. 'They call the catalogue names', said Whitman, 'but suppose they do? It *is* names: but what could be more poetic than names?' [Traubel 324]. In the *Primer* he claimed that '*names* are magic. – One word can pour such a flood through the soul'. Names are magic, the list Divine. Some of Whitman's lists are undeniably tiresome, examples of what Hopkins called Parnassian, attempts to repeat a proven formula without new inspiration. Others are wonderful, charged, exuding freshness. What distinguishes them?

Clearly any old random list of names will not constitute a poem. There must be something to impart that sense of wonder, a boldness and urgency in the diction, the rhythms, the interrelationships, or all of these, a coherence. The inner logic of the list is at its clearest in 'There Was a Child Went Forth', where it follows the cycles of the seasons, the physical movements of the child as it moves outwards from the cradle and familiar farmstead to the noisy streets of the city and the 'huge crossing at the ferries', and the emotional and spiritual growth of the child through schooldays, adolescence with its doubts and yearnings, independent manhood in the world of crowds and commerce, to the spiritual maturity of the man now capable of imaginative self-projection and self-abnegation, of relating to and taking its spiritual orientation from Nature, of writing this poem and the first *Leaves of Grass*, of justifying in the telling, the tallying and witnessing, in the ultimate visionary fullness and calm, the claim made at the poem's beginning and end:

> The village on the highland seen from afar at sunset . . . the river between,
> Shadows . . . aureola and mist . . . light falling on roofs and gables of white or brown, three miles off,
> The schooner nearby sleepily dropping down the tide .. the little boat slacktowed astern,
> The hurrying tumbling waves and quickbroken crests and slapping;
> The strata of colored clouds . . . the long bar of maroontint away solitary by itself . . . the spread of purity it lies motionless in,
> The horizon's edge, the flying seacrow, the fragrance of saltmarsh and shoremud;
> These became part of that child who went forth every day, and who now goes and will always go forth every day,
> And these become of him or her that peruses them now.   [139]

A more complex example would be 'Spontaneous Me'. We need look only at the opening to see what Whitman is up to.

> Spontaneous me, Nature,
> The loving day, the mounting sun, the friend I am happy with,
> The arm of my friend hanging idly over my shoulder,
> The hillside whiten'd with blossoms of the mountain ash,
> The same in autumn, the hues of red, yellow, drab, purple, and light
> and dark green
> The rich coverlet of the grass, animals and birds, the private
> untrimm'd bank, the primitive apples, the pebble-stones,
> Beautiful dripping fragments, the negligent list of one after another as
> I happen to call them to me or think of them,
> The real poems.

Certainly this is a list, entirely lacking in main verbs, but it is by no means as negligent or accidental as Whitman would have us suppose. We cannot say how conscious Whitman was of the shaping imagination at work, but at work it certainly is, in accordance with his claim that 'imagination and actuality must be united'.

The grouping of the items into lines is, as always, highly significant. To distribute the first five other than two and three would wreck the delicate web of meanings. In the first line, 'spontaneous me' and 'Nature' are not just items one and two in a random list. The usual dualistic distinction between self and not-self is fudged by the possibility that 'Nature' is not item two at all, but in apposition to 'spontaneous me', another way of saying the same thing. Whitman has the knack of expressing distinction and identity simultaneously ('always a knit of identity, always distinction'). 'Spontaneous me' is me at my most natural, and, (this poem coming shortly after 'Song of Myself') we are already familiar with the idea of self as a microcosm of Nature. The second line has a similar rich ambiguity. Are the three items also one? Is the sun also the friend? That the day is 'loving' suggests that it is; and 'mounting' has a sexual connotation.

We are not allowed to know (perhaps Whitman does not know) to what extent the language is metaphorical, or which items in the list are metaphors for which others. There is a striking example of this in 'I Sing the Body Electric':

> Bridegroom night of love working surely and softly into the prostrate
> dawn,
> Undulating into the willing and yielding day,
> Lost in the cleave of the clasping and sweet-flesh'd day.

It is impossible to tell whether this is love-making as a metaphor for dawn, or dawn for lovemaking. The distinction is eliminated between the creative acts of man and those of Nature.

Once we are tuned to this sort of language, we realize that the arm of the friend is also a blossom-heavy branch of mountain ash hanging over the hill's shoulder. The flora and fauna can be a 'coverlet' only if we abandon the distinction between the earth itself and a recumbent human body. The list of autumn colours begins predictably enough, but the word 'drab', used as a colour, alerts our attention to the less common observation that, even in late autumn, shades of green still predominate. Four adjectives, 'private', 'untrimm'd', 'primitive' and 'dripping', condition our response to the subsequent images. When we remember that the title of the section of *Leaves of Grass* to which 'Spontaneous Me' belongs is 'Children of Adam', and that the first line of that section is 'To the garden the world anew ascending', everything falls into place. The apples are the apples of Eden, here cleansed of all association with sin, and restored to an unfallen world heavy with 'real poems', created things in rich 'clusters' (the original title of the poem), dripping with dew, renewed every day with the sun. The feeling is identical with Hopkins' response to spring:

> What is all this juice and all this joy?
> A strain of the earth's sweet being in the beginning
> In Eden garden. ['Spring']

The poem seems to answer less to its own title than to Whitman's uncharacteristic reference to 'the curious chess-game of a poem'.

Most of Whitman's lists are less carefully shaped than this. Even some of the more blatant of them seem to me to succeed, partly by the provocation of their very blatancy, which becomes at last a kind of heroic simplicity and candour, and partly by the astute placing, here and there, of equally simple but unexpected words, partly because of Whitman's ability to juxtapose and relate the items in such a way that the whole is greater than the sum of its parts, not an inert linear catalogue, but a living organism.

Malcolm Cowley claims that 'I Sing the Body Electric' suffers from 'the addition of a final section that is not in the least electric, being merely a long anatomical catalogue' [xxxvi]. I do not find it so. Nearly every line has its unexpected word or perspective – 'drop and tympan of the ears', 'the waking or sleeping of the lids', 'neck-slue', 'hind-shoulders, and the ample side-round of the chest', 'man-root', 'knee-pan'. The list moves downwards starting at the top of the head. The words for the parts of the body are particularly strong, and Whitman lets them do their work, sometimes the delicate words, iris, lids, nostrils, the hard words, jaws, knuckles, ribs, the shapely words, shoulders, scapula, sinews, the flexible words, wrist, joints, sockets. Having reached the heel, he moves to the internal organs, and it is here that we meet the typical Whitman refusal to discriminate between one organ and another, between organs and their functions, between those functions and the emotions associated with them, between the basic emotions and the life that is in us, between that life and the soul:

> Sympathies, heart-valves, palate-valves, sexuality, maternity,
> Womanhood and all that is a woman, and the man that comes from
>   woman,
> The womb, the teats, nipples, breast-milk, tears, laughter, weeping,
>   love-looks,
> love-perturbations and risings ...

Thirty-six long lines without a stop and without a verb between the third line and the penultimate. The flat list – 'Head, neck, hair, ears . . .' gradually modulating to include 'all attitudes, all the shapeliness, all the belongings of my or your body or of anyone's body, male or female', to include features common to all yet expressing unique character: 'The continual changes of the flex of the mouth, and around the eyes', all culminating in 'the exquisite realization of health' in a living human-being not anatomized or vivisected but assembled before our eyes:

> O I say these are not the parts and poems of the body only, but of the
>   soul,
> O I say these are the soul!

✻   ✻   ✻

'Song of Myself' was a poem addressed to America at a particular moment in its history, a poem with large political and cultural pretensions. These have been fully discussed by others. In any case, Whitman's own priorities are clear enough:

> After you have exhausted what there is in business, politics, conviviality,
> love, and so on – have found that none of these finally satisfy, or
> permanently wear – what remains? Nature remains; to bring out from
> their torpid recesses, the affinities of a man or woman with the open air,
> the trees, fields, the changes of seasons – the sun by day and the stars of
> heaven by night.   ['New Themes Entered Upon']

Democracy itself he sees as dependent on 'a living and enthusiastic sympathy with Nature':

> I conceive of no flourishing and heroic elements of Democracy in the
> United States, or of Democracy maintaining itself at all, without the
> Nature-element forming a main part – to be its health-element and
> beauty-element – to really underlie the whole politics, sanity, religion and
> art of the New World.   ['Nature and Democracy – Morality']

Carlyle's *Sartor Resartus* (1833) was Whitman's holy book:

Carlyle's 'Natural Supernaturalism,' by means of an unassisted transaction between the ordinary object and the dishabituated eye, effects authentic miracles. 'Custom blinds us to the miraculousness of daily-recurring miracles.' 'The true use' of his book, he reveals at its end, has been 'to exhibit the Wonder of daily life and common things.' His hero, when his 'mind's eyes were . . . unsealed, and its hands ungyved,' had awakened 'to a new Heaven and a new Earth.' Now if the reader would only 'sweep away the Illusion of Time,' 'how were thy eyesight unsealed, and thy heart set flaming in the Light-sea of celestial wonder!' Then all would be brought to the enduring vision of the glory in the grass – the recognition that 'through every grass-blade . . . the glory of a present God still beams.'

[Abrams, 384]

'I know of nothing else but miracles', wrote Whitman. And the breaking of the customary human limits of space and time is perhaps the most striking feature of 'Song of Myself':

> My ties and ballasts leave me . . . I travel . . . I sail . . . my elbows rest
>   in the sea-gaps,
> I skirt the sierras . . . my palms cover continents,
> I am afoot with my vision.

In the first pages of his first notebook Whitman wrote: 'Bring all the art and science of the world, and baffle and humble it with one spear of grass'. The first poem in the first *Leaves of Grass* opens with the self 'observing a spear of summer grass'. Grass is a recurring motif throughout 'Song of Myself' and has the sixth section to itself.

Whitman does not presume to explain the grass. He knows what it is no more than a child. But it suggests many analogies, metaphors and hints. One of these is much the strongest, and anticipates the ending of the poem – the hint of death. Behind the whole of *Leaves of Grass* stands the biblical text:

> All flesh is grass, and all the glory of man as the flower of grass.
> The grass withereth, and the flower thereof falleth away.
>   [*The First Epistle General of Peter* i. 24]

'Song of Myself' is an attempt to define and substantiate a material Divinity which is 'more than churches or bibles or creeds'. It is a running dialogue with the Bible, challenging Judeo-Christian attitudes. Often Whitman starts from an unspoken biblical text, such as 'all flesh is grass', and then gives his own anti-biblical commentary or development:

What do you think has become of the young and old men?
And what do you think has become of the women and children?

They are alive and well somewhere;
The smallest sprout shows there is really no death,

And if ever there was it led forward life, and does not wait at the end
    to arrest it,
And ceased the moment life appeared.

All goes onward and outward ... and nothing collapses,
And to die is different from what any one supposed, and luckier.

'What is the grass?' could be said to be the question to which the Eleusinian
Mysteries were the answer, and Whitman's answer is much the same.

    Whitman admits from the outset the losses, leakage and wastage of
time, 'time the destroyer' as Eliot calls it, time 'like the river with its cargo of
dead negroes, cows and chicken coops'. But he does not conclude that death
owns everything. That vision has been traditional from the Greeks to Eliot
and Beckett. Behind it is the assumption that nothing which does not last for
ever is of real value, that the achievements of man are mocked by time and
cancelled by death. It has never been more forcefully expressed than by
Hopkins:

>   Million-fueled, nature's bonfire burns on.
> But quench her bonniest, dearest to her, her clearest-selved spark
> Man; how fast his firedint, his mark on mind, is gone!
> Both are in an unfathomable, all is in an enormous dark
> Drowned. O pity and indignation! Manshape, that shone
> Sheer off, disseveral, a star, death blots black out; nor mark
> Is any of him at all so stark
> But vastness blurs and time beats level.
>   ['That Nature is a Heraclitean Fire
>   and of the comfort of the Resurrection']

Nature is an everlasting bonefire. It can be redeemed only in terms of a
reality elsewhere, outside space and time, for Hopkins the Resurrection, which
transforms the matchwood of this world into the 'immortal diamond' of eternity; for Eliot 'the timeless' which intersects our mundane 'reality', transfigures
it, and redeems the time. 'East Coker' gives us a vision of time without any
such redeeming intercession:

> Two and two, necessary coniunction,
> Holding each other by the hand or the arm

Which betokeneth concorde. Round and round the fire
Leaping through the flames, or joined in circles,
Rustically solemn or in rustic laughter
Lifting heavy feet in clumsy shoes,
Earth feet, loam feet, lifted in country mirth
Mirth of those long since under earth
Nourishing the corn. Keeping time,
Keeping the rhythm in their dancing
As in their living in the living seasons
The time of the seasons and the constellations
The time of milking and the time of harvest
The time of the coupling of man and woman
And that of beasts. Feet rising and falling.
Eating and drinking. Dung and death.

The imagery circles and sinks from the dance around the bonfire which celebrates the 'dignified and commodious sacrament of marriage', through bestial
coupling to the grave. The language sinks from the humane Elizabethan prose
of Thomas Elyot to the ultimate reduction of 'dung and death'. But such a
passage entirely loses its charge in the context of Whitman, for whom such
words as 'loam', 'earth', 'coupling', 'beasts', 'dung' and 'death' have none of the
pejorative weight, the suggestion of despiritualization, which Eliot takes for
granted.

For the writer like Beckett without belief in any such alternative
reality, Nature becomes absurd and disgusting. Beckett's Watt launches into
a comic parody of Whitman:

The crocuses and the larch turning green every year a week before the
others and the pastures red with uneaten sheep's placentas and the long
summer days and the new-mown hay and the wood-pigeon in the
morning and the cuckoo in the afternoon and the corncrake in the
evening and the wasps in the jam and the smell of the gorse and the look
of the gorse and the apples falling and the children walking in the dead
leaves and the larch turning brown a week before the others and the
chestnuts falling and the howling winds and the sea breaking over the pier
and the first fires and the hooves on the road and the consumptive
postman whistling *The Roses Are Blooming in Picardy* and the standard
oil-lamp and of course the snow and to be sure the sleet and bless your
heart the slush and every fourth year the February débâcle and the
endless April showers and the crocuses and then the whole bloody
business starting all over again. A turd.

Beckett specifically rejects the grass, as a symbol of Nature at its most
seductive and dangerous:

'I am the cow, which, at the gates of the slaughterhouse, realises all the absurdity of pastures. A pity she didn't think of it sooner, back there in the long lush grass. Ah well. She still has the yard to cross. No one can take that away from her.'   [*Eleuthéria*]

That moment of total lucidity, awakening from the sleep of life, is for Beckett the only meaning and dignity and justification of it all.

But the implied rebuttal of Whitman misfires, since the negative elements Watt introduces with such Irish venom are all there in Whitman, even in 'Song of Myself' – the dead leaves, the howling storms, the consumptive postman, the circularity ('faithfulness') of Nature. Late in his life Whitman attended a sermon in which the preacher used the Whitmanesque phrase 'the rounded catalogue divine complete'. Whitman strongly objected to the sermon because the catalogue 'entirely ignored . . . the following':

> The devilish and the dark, the dying and diseas'd,
> The countless (nineteen-twentieths) low and evil, crude and savage,
> The crazed, prisoners in jail, the horrible, rank, malignant,
> Venom and filth, serpents, the ravenous sharks, liars, the dissolute;
> (What is the part the wicked and the loathsome bear within earth's
>   orbic scheme?)
> Newts, crawling things in slime and mud, poisons,
> The barren soil, the evil men, the slag and hideous rot.
>   ['The Rounded Catalogue Divine Complete']

Whitman's catalogue is complete because it by no means leaves out these things. Even in 'Song of Myself', his most buoyant and optimistic poem, they have their place, not only in whole sections such as the story of the murder of the four hundred and twelve young men, but in every catalogue with any pretension to completeness. The very long section 15 offers a fair sample of human activities in America. It does not depict nineteen-twentieths 'low and evil, crude and savage' (that is partly a debating point against the preacher, partly a measure of Whitman's darker vision in later life). Nineteen-twentieths are morally neutral or unevaluated. The President is juxtaposed to the prostitute, with no discriminating judgement implied. The list is long enough and inclusive enough and carefully balanced enough to ensure that whatever moral evaluations individual readers might supply, they will span the whole gamut from the universally pleasing ('The regatta is spread on the bay . . . how the white sails sparkle!') to the universally abhorrent:

> The malformed limbs are tied to the anatomist's table,
> What is removed drops horribly in a pail.   [37]

This completeness of Whitman's catalogues makes it difficult for him to put his thumb in the balance either against the tragic vision (Lawrence) or in favour of it (Hardy, Beckett, early Hughes). The dark side is acknowledged, brought into sharp focus, given its full emotional and moral weight, yet never allowed to fill the frame, to supplant one's awareness of all that is not dark. The sea, for example, is not simply the destroyer, perfecting its killers, polishing its bones, casting ashore its wreckage and wastage, as in Eliot's 'Dry Salvages' or Hughes' 'Relic'. This is only one of its faces:

> Sea of stretched ground-swells!
> Sea breathing broad and convulsive breaths!
> Sea of the brine of life! Sea of unshovelled and always-ready graves!
> Howler and scooper of storms! Capricious and dainty sea!
> I am integral with you . . . I too am of one phase and of all phases.
>
> [46]

Whitman will not, however high or low his own feelings, detach any list from its context in Nature: 'Shall I make my list of things in the house and skip the house that supports them?' The house is the house of life, in which death has its honoured and essential place, but no more honoured or essential than, for example, sex. We have seen that Whitman cannot speak for long about the earth without mention, directly or indirectly, of sex. In the third section of 'Song of Myself' he expresses this in the lines:

> Urge and urge and urge,
> Always the procreant urge of the world.
>
> Out of the dimness opposite equals advance . . . Always substance and
>   increase,
> Always a knit of identity . . . always distinction . . . always a breed of
>   life.

For a man whose very thinking was now a matter of the marriage of opposites, the knitting of identity out of distinction by means of analogies and correspondences ('the subtle knot that makes us man'), the most striking and close correspondences between human experiences and the larger processes of the natural world were exactly those experiences which seemed to Eliot to reduce human life to animality and spiritual barrenness, 'birth and copulation and death' ['Sweeney Agonistes']. These are the great themes of 'Song of Myself', the chief means of sharing in those larger processes, and therefore the chief sources of spirituality. Like Lawrence Whitman felt that copulation was participation in the divine 'sexuality of the earth' ['Kosmos']. Writing a poem was the imaginative equivalent of making love, which was in turn the human equivalent of the sunrise or of creation itself:

> Something I cannot see puts upwards libidinous prongs,
> Seas of bright juice suffuse heaven.

Such lines gain part of their force by their daring inversion of some of the greatest lines of religious poetry. I am reminded here, for example, of Vaughan's lines:

> But felt through all this fleshly dress
> Bright shoots of everlastingness.
> ['The Retreat']

In the religious tradition it is always the dull earth which is suffused by bright shafts of spirit from above.

Whitman felt with Blake that puritanical religion had an appalling burden of guilt. Whitman claimed that it had 'led to states of ignorance, repressal, and covered over disease and depletion, forming certainly a main factor in the world's woe'. The subject of sexuality 'should be redeemed from the pens and tongues of blackguards and boldly brought into the demesne of poetry – as something not gross and impure, but entirely consistent with highest manhood and womanhood and indispensable to both'.

The woman who watches in hiding the twenty-eight young men bathing naked does so in a spirit which is the opposite of that in which the insane Pentheus watches the Bacchantes. She is like the Lady of Shallott as she 'hides handsome and richly drest aft the blinds of the window'; but her looking is not fatal to her. On the contrary, her imaginative participation renews her sanity, initiating her belatedly into her own womanhood, in an inversion of baptismal rites. What Reynolds calls the 'purifying fusion of sex and nature' in the diction and imagery and rhythms works so well that this remarkable passage retains its innocence even if we read it as suggesting that the woman is masturbating.

The same cleansing rhetoric operates also on a much larger scale throughout Whitman.

'Nothing can jar him', Whitman said of the poet in his 1855 Preface, '– suffering and darkness cannot – death and fear cannot'. Though Whitman's sympathy is genuine, and amply demonstrated in the passages about suffering, darkness, death and fear in 'Song of Myself', the suffering and fear of the hounded slave and the mashed fireman is not his own, and he is able to remain unshaken by it only within the conceit which controls the whole poem, that agonies are one of his changes of garments: 'My hurt turns livid upon me as I lean on a cane and observe'. But there is a moment in 'Song of Myself' when Whitman's god's-eye vision makes him desperate. He has just described the terrible sea-fight:

> Formless stacks of bodies and bodies by themselves . . . dabs of flesh
> upon the masts and spars,
> The cut of cordage and dangle of rigging . . . the slight shock of the
> soothe of waves,

Black and impressive guns, and litter of powder-parcels, and the
    strong scent,
Delicate sniffs of the seabreeze . . . smells of sedgy grass and fields by
    the shore . . . death-messages given in charge to survivors,
The hiss of the surgeon's knife and the gnawing teeth of his saw,
The wheeze, the cluck, the swash of falling blood . . . the short wild
    scream, the long dull tapering groan,
These so . . . these irretrievable.

In spite of his efforts to extend the scene to take in the soothe of the waves
and the assurance of the grass, he is for the moment mastered by a fit of
nausea, stunned by 'the dull unintermitted pain'. He feels the full force of
Eliot's recognition that 'time is no healer: the patient is no longer here'. But
he recovers, discovering himself to be 'on a verge of the usual mistake', that
is, the mistake of lapsing into partial vision, separating the crucifixion from
the resurrection:

That I could look with a separate look on my own crucifixion and
    bloody crowning!
I remember . . . I resume the overstaid fraction,
The grave of rock multiplies what has been confided to it . . . or to any
    graves,
The corpses rise . . . the gashes heal . . . the fastenings roll away. [38]

Like Hopkins, Whitman finds comfort in the resurrection, but his
resurrection is not to another world redeemed from time and with a body of
immortal diamond.

The fear of death in Eliot and Beckett is part of a larger fear of everything which might threaten self-possession. It is essentially fear of the not-
self, rationalized as disgust. It extends to cover sex and love, the whole life
of the body, which, unlike the mind, cannot maintain itself aloof from the
rest of the physical world. Thus the hatred of copulation and procreation in
Eliot and Beckett is not only on account of its cyclic nature ('We give birth
astride of a grave'), but also on account of its sheer physicality. To such
temperaments matter itself is corrupt and insupportable. For Eliot Nature is
reducible to 'dung and death', for Beckett to 'a turd'. But in Whitman's poetic
vocabulary even these terms are transfigured; dung and death are part of
the miracle and holy. He accepts the 'perpetual transfers and promotions' of
mortality:

And as to you corpse I think you are good manure, but that does not
    offend me,
I smell the white roses sweetscented and growing,
I reach to the leafy lips . . . I reach to the polished breasts of melons,

And as to you life, I reckon you are the leavings of many deaths,
No doubt I have died myself ten thousand times before.   [49]

Hence he finds 'dung and dirt more admirable than was dreamed, / The super-natural of no account'. In 'This Compost' he again inverts the traditional terror of the grave, fearing not what the earth will do to his body, but what his body might do to the earth. He wonders that 'the resurrection of the wheat' appears out of the graves of men, and fears that what men put back into the earth, including their 'distemper'd corpses', must at last poison the earth and halt its procession of miracles:

> Now I am terrified at the Earth, it is that calm and patient,
> It grows such sweet things out of such corruptions,
> It turns harmless and stainless on its axis, with such endless
>   successions of diseas'd corpses,
> It distills such exquisite winds out of such infused fetor,
> It renews with such unwitting looks its prodigal, annual, sumptuous
>   crops,
> It gives such divine materials to men, and accepts such leavings from
>   them at last.

His highest ambition is the fullest possible atonement with the earth:

> I bequeath myself to the dirt to grow from the grass I love,
> If you want me again look for me under your bootsoles.
>   [52]

This is Whitman's serio-comic version of Christ's words: 'Lift up the stone and there thou shalt find me'. It is also, perhaps, an expression of the same spirit Baring and Cashford detect in one of the famous Lascaux cave paintings, where, while a bison dies, a rhinoceros drops his dung:

> The dung of the rhinoceros . . . is given such prominence as to suggest
> that, even in the act of apparently passing out of the life cycle, the dung
> still contains the seeds of fruit or grain that will begin a new cycle.   [37]

        ✤   ✤   ✤

It would be misleading to suggest that 'Song of Myself', written at the outset of his long career, could be taken, alone, to speak for Whitman. In later life Whitman experienced plenty of suffering and fear in his own person, and could no longer maintain the omnivorous optimism of his thirties. In 1860 it seemed that no-one wanted his work, no-one would employ him, no-one return his love. Whitman has his equivalent of the 'Immortality' and 'Dejection' odes, and of Hopkins' terrible sonnets: it is 'As I Ebb'd with the Ocean of Life'. Here Whitman is 'baffled, balked, bent'. All the effort and high expectations of

Leaves of Grass has come to nothing, 'a few . . . dead leaves'. As Hopkins came to feel himself reduced to 'chaff', 'mortal trash', 'matchwood', so Whitman feels that his life, like the beach at low tide, is strewn with husks, lines of débris underfoot, 'chaff, straw, splinters . . . scum'. It needed a great imaginative effort to hold together the Walter Whitman who was as capable as other men of crimes and complacencies and despiriting failures, and the 'microcosmic' Walt Whitman afoot with his vision and blessed with universal atonement. At those times when he could not lift his vision above the beach detritus he doubted whether he had ever really achieved any of it. Perhaps the earlier ecstasies had been merely, in Hopkins' words 'self-yeast of spirit', or in his own 'all that blab whose echoes recoil upon me':

> But that before all my arrogant poems the real Me stands yet
>   untouch'd, untold, altogether unreach'd,
> Withdrawn far, mocking me with mock-congratulatory signs and bows,
> With peals of distant ironical laughter at every word I have written,
> Pointing in silence to these songs, and then to the sand beneath.
> I perceive I have not really understood any thing, not a single object,
>   and that no man ever can,
> Nature here in sight of the sea taking advantage of me to dart upon me
>   and sting me,
> Because I have dared to open my mouth to sing at all.

Of these lines R.W.B. Lewis has written:

> It is an image of immeasurable effect. And it is, so to speak, a triumph
> over its own content. Anyone who could construct an image of the higher
> power – the one he aspires toward – standing far off and mocking him
> with little satiric bows and gestures, comparing and consigning his verses
> to the sandy debris under his feet: such a person has already conquered
> his sense of sterility, mastered his fear of spiritual and artistic death,
> rediscovered his genius, and returned to the fullest poetic authority.
> Within the poem, Whitman identifies the land as his father and the fierce
> old sea as his mother; he sees himself as alienated no less from them than
> from the real Me, and he prays to both symbolic parents for a
> rejuvenation of his poetic force, a resumption of 'the secret of the
> murmuring I envy'. But the prayer is already answered in the very
> language in which it is uttered; Whitman never murmured more
> beautifully; and this is why, at the depth of his ebbing, Whitman can say,
> parenthetically, that the flow will return. [28]

There is frustration, loss, humiliation, dereliction, but never despair, never repudiation or a desire to become immortal diamond. The sea-drift has its own beauty, and even in the ooze exuding from his dead lips he sees 'the prismatic colors glistening and rolling'. The effect is comparable with 'those are pearls that were his eyes', or the sea-change which transfigures the broken body of Simon in *Lord of the Flies*.

And Whitman does continue to sing, no longer with 'barbaric yawp' but softly and poignantly. Like the 'noiseless patient spider' he sends out filament after filament into 'the vacant vast surrounding'. The later years yielded not only the great elegies, but such lovely sparkles from the wheel as 'To the Man-of-War Bird' and 'The Dalliance of Eagles', poems such as 'Passage to India' which fearlessly explore the deeps, the incomparable prose of *Specimen Days*, through all the suffering of premature old-age and paralyzing illness to that serene valediction 'Good-Bye My Fancy!':

> Long indeed have we lived, slept, filter'd, become really blended into
> one;
> Then if we die we die together, (yes, we'll remain one,)
> If we go anywhere we'll go together to meet what happens,
> May-be we'll be better off and blither, and learn something,
> May-be it is yourself now really ushering me to the true songs, (who
> knows?)
> May-be it is you the mortal knob really undoing, turning – so now
> finally,
> Good-bye – and hail! my Fancy.

15 HOPKINS AND THE RELIGION OF THE DIAMOND BODY

Isn't 'fall' and 'redemption' quite a late and new departure in religion and in myth: about Homer's time? Aren't the great heavens of the true pagans – I call these orphicising 'redemption' mysteries half-christian – aren't they clean of the 'Salvation' idea, though they have the re-birth idea? and aren't they clean of the 'fall', though they have the descent of the soul? The two things are quite different. In my opinion the great pagan religions of the Aegean, and Egypt and Babylon, must have conceived the 'descent' as a great triumph, and each Easter of the clothing in flesh as a supreme glory, and the Mother Moon who gives us our body as the supreme giver of the great gift, hence the very ancient Magna Mater in the East. This 'fall' into Matter . . . this 'entombment' in the 'envelope of flesh' is a new and pernicious idea arising about 500 B.C. into distinct cult-consciousness – and destined to kill the grandeur of the heavens altogether at last.

[D.H. Lawrence]

I entreat you, my brothers, *remain true to the earth,* and do not believe those who speak to you of superterrestrial hopes! They are poisoners, whether they know it or not. They are despisers of life, atrophying and self-poisoned men, of whom the earth is weary: so let them be gone! Once blasphemy against God was the greatest blasphemy, but God died, and thereupon these blasphemers died too. To blaspheme the earth is now the most dreadful offence, and to esteem the bowels of the Inscrutable more highly than the meaning of the earth.

[Nietzsche]

Hopkins' fascination with what he began in 1868 to call the 'inscapes' of the natural world is evident from the earliest diaries and journals, but in the eighteen-sixties it seems to have been a combination of aesthetics, draughts-manship and natural history, having no connection with his religious con-cerns. Suddenly, in 1870, his inscapes acquire a new dimension and meaning: 'I do not think I have ever seen anything more beautiful than the bluebell I have been looking at. I know the beauty of our Lord by it' [*Journals* 199]. Later that year there follows a description of the Northern Lights, which ends:

This busy working of nature wholly independent of the earth and seeming to go on in a strain of time not reckoned by our reckoning of days and years but simpler and as if correcting the preoccupation of the world by being preoccupied with and appealing to and dated by the day of judgement was like a new witness to God and filled me with delightful fear.

[200]

This fusing of aesthetic and religious experience, both grounded in natural inscapes, has been attributed to the influence of Duns Scotus; but Hopkins did not read Duns Scotus until 1872. If it is attributable to an outside influence at all, then that influence is St. Ignatius. Hopkins' commentaries on the *Spiritual Exercises* date from the same period (1877–81) as his most joyful and spontaneous poems and are very close to them in spirit:

CREATION THE MAKING OUT OF NOTHING, bringing from nothing into being: once there was nothing, then lo, this huge world was there. How great a work of power! . . .
It is a book he has written, of the riches of his knowledge, teaching endless truths, full lessons of wisdom, a poem of beauty ...
'The heavens declare the glory of God!' The birds sing to him, the thunder speaks of his terror, the lion is like his strength, the honey like his sweetness; they are something like him, they make him known, they tell of him, they give him glory. [*Sermons* 238–9]

God dwells in creatures . . . God works and labours for me in all created things on the face of the earth . . . All things therefore are charged with love, are charged with God and if we know how to touch them give off sparks and take fire, yield drops and flow, ring and tell of him. [193–5]

But there was within Catholic teaching another tradition entirely, a tradition in the ascendant in Victorian England and much more in accord with the general morality and spirituality of the time, a tradition which regarded nature with fear and hostility, which defined nature and grace as mutually exclusive opposites, and aligned the natural world, the flesh and the devil (and woman) against God:

Hence the soul cannot be possessed of the divine union, until it has divested itself of the love of created beings. [St. John of the Cross]

Though for several years Hopkins managed to avoid this dualism, it became at last the cross on which he was crucified. Nature, which was for him in 1877 the divine creative fire of God playing through the physical, temporal world, 'the dearest freshness deep down things', 'a strain of the earth's sweet being in the beginning / In Eden garden', a standard of purity against which the corruption of the human world was to be judged, became by 1888 'nature's bonfire', 'world's wildfire', a heap of trash and matchwood reducing itself to ashes, a joke, and good riddance, since it was a dangerous distraction from what really matters, the only thing of true value, the immortal diamond of the redeemed soul, redeemed from world, flesh and devil. I want to try to understand the apparently unavoidable process (for a great poet who was also a Jesuit priest at that time) by which this total inversion of values took place.

✻ ✻ ✻

When Hopkins entered the Jesuit order he welcomed the discipline he felt he needed to restrain his independent spirit and restrict his manifold interests. This meant burning most of his poems, curbing his passion for music, and giving up learning Welsh (since he could hardly pretend that his sole motive had been the conversion of Wales). It did not mean giving up his interest in the natural world and its inscapes, since it was but a short step to reinterpret these as precisely those phenomena which testified most strongly to the presence of God or Christ in creation, and therefore the most likely to help him to praise God. His moments of aesthetic insight could now be glorified as epiphanies, perceptions of the sacred, encounters with Christ. Scotus confirmed him in this, and extended his range by pointing out that it was in their characteristic action even more than in appearance and design that created things revealed their innermost being and divine purpose.

It was not long before Hopkins took the next short step, to the realization that the value of such experiences need not be private, but carried an obligation to bear witness, and that the only adequate way of testifying, for him, would be the writing of poems, for only the language of poetry could match the pattern of inscape and the charge of instress. And for this purpose it would have to be a very special and original kind of poetry which Hopkins knew he had in him, but which he knew to be beyond any of his contemporaries (with the possible and grudging exception of Whitman).

Out of this perfect matching of his religious vocation with his poetic gifts and love of nature came the great celebratory poems of the years 1877 to 1881. His effort now was not just to register physical and temporal externals, phenomena, but to interpret them as expression of the innermost, as laws of being. If this can be achieved, the object, formerly a mere eye-chaos, or, if perceived as beautiful, mere 'brute beauty' or geometry, is transfigured, becomes radiant with a meaning which is far from merely metaphorical because a tangible example of the spirit of God, the body of Christ, in this world, affording, for those of us who are not saints, our only direct experience of him in this life.

There are several Hopkins poems which seem to embody a sacramental Christianity perfectly in accord with deep ecology – 'God's Grandeur', 'Spring', 'The Sea and the Skylark', 'Pied Beauty', 'Binsey Poplars', 'Inversnaid', 'Ribblesdale'.

Let us look closely at 'God's Grandeur'.

> The world is charged with the grandeur of God.
> It will flame out, like shining from shook foil;
> It gathers to a greatness, like the ooze of oil
> Crushed.

The fourth word is charged with meanings, and plunges us deep into Hopkins' distinctive poetic and religious world. The primary meaning is, of course, electrical. It suggests that God flows through the world as an energizing current, that everything in creation is therefore connected to everything else, part of the same circuit, and also to God, the source. It also suggests that the world is a huge battery in which creative energy lies latent, in which is stored an infinite potential for renewal. All processes, natural and human, are dependent on this energy, which can be manifested in very different ways. At one extreme as light, like the sudden lightning which flashes from a sheet of multifaceted silver-foil when it is shaken; at the other as steady pressure which, with such slowness that it is barely detectable, crushes the seed to release its innermost oil. It need not surprise us that Hopkins should choose examples from the world of human industry rather than the natural world, since his main theme in this poem is man's misuse of what God provided specifically for his use, such as 'coal and rockoil for artificial light and heat' [*Sermons* 90].

> Why do men then now not reck his rod?
> Generations have trod, have trod, have trod;
> And all is seared with trade; bleared, smeared with toil;
> And wears man's smudge and shares man's smell: the soil
> Is bare now, nor can foot feel, being shod.

This strange juxtaposition of 'then' and 'now', closely followed by the word 'generations', reminds us of the first time men disobeyed God. No sooner had God charged the world with life than he put men in charge of it, and charged them not to eat of the tree of knowledge. The subsequent history of the race has been a compounding of that first recklessness. Only man has the freedom to disconnect himself from the divine circuit, and this he has systematically done, especially since the industrial revolution. The sacred flame was entrusted to man, and he has seared the world with it. Oil has been extracted not only from plants, but from the earth itself, and smeared over everything. The shod foot treading earth bare is a potent image of alienation, of man in self-imposed exile from his home 'in Eden garden' ['Spring']. Hughes expresses Adam Kadmon's glad acceptance of the earth as his proper home in the image of 'the sole of a foot/ Pressed to world-rock', to which he says 'I was made/ For you'.

The sestet testifies to that in nature which seemed to Hopkins inextinguishable:

> And for all this, nature is never spent;
> There lives the dearest freshness deep down things
> And though the last lights off the black West went
> Oh, morning, at the brown brink eastward springs –
> Because the Holy Ghost over the bent
> World broods with warm breast and with ah! bright wings.

At the very moment when nature seems utterly spent, the first token of renewal appears. The world bent with toil, or under the burden of man's works and sins, is transformed into the image of an egg the hatching of which, under the warm breast of the dove, will release the 'dearest freshness' of innocence, joy, love, creativity, which still lives under the hard shell of greed, complacency and materialism. The Holy Ghost as dove broods over the world in both senses, pondering the crime, but also renewing victimized nature. In the 'May Magnificat' Hopkins calls Mary the 'mighty mother' and compares her to a throstle on its eggs, which 'Forms and warms the life within; / And bird and blossom swell / In sod or sheath or shell'.

'Spring' wonderfully evokes the rush and richness of new life, the intercourse of heaven and earth, as shooting weeds, birdsong and peartree leaves all 'brush the descending blue'. The vision of 'Pied Beauty' is even more ecstatically holistic, triumphantly unifying all the dualistic opposites of high and low, large and small, swift and slow, light and dark, human and non-human, change and permanence. The vision of 'Hurrahing in Harvest' is the same, until the last two lines, where aspiration towards God expresses itself as a hurling off of earth. It is not clear whether the heart only half hurls earth off because it has not quite achieved the boldness which would be needed to kick the cumbering earth off completely, or whether the poet wishes to have the best of both worlds, like Lawrence's St. Matthew:

> I have mounted up on the wings of the morning, and I have dredged
> down to the zenith's reversal.
> Which is my way, being man.
> Gods may stay in mid-heaven, the Son of Man has climbed to the
> Whitsun zenith,
> But I, Matthew, being a man
> Am a traveller back and forth.
> So be it.

The ambiguity is, as we shall see, a more serious matter in 'The Windhover'.

In 'God's Grandeur' Hopkins seems to doubt man's capacity, try as he may, to do any permanent damage to the earth. In 'Binsey Poplars' and 'Ribblesdale' he becomes progressively less confident. As joy and confidence tend to produce in Hopkins verbal exuberance, sadness produces a moving simplicity. His dear aspens are 'All felled, felled, are all felled . . . Not spared, not one'. 'Ten or twelve, only ten or twelve / Strokes of havoc' have unselved the scene. Hopkins stresses the vulnerability of the natural world, how easily we can threaten its complex and delicate functions:

> Since country is so tender
> To touch, her being so slender,
> That, like this sleek and seeing ball
> But a prick will make no eye at all.

We must beware, however, of imputing too much ecological consciousness to Hopkins. What we do when we 'delve or hew – Hack and rack the
growing green!' may be to wreck an ecosystem and alter the world's climate,
but this is of course not what Hopkins means. He means simply that the
beauty of that 'sweet especial scene' is now lost for ever, so that 'After-comers
cannot guess the beauty been'.

In 'Ribblesdale', 'selfbent' man, 'so tied to his turn', so thriftless, reaves
'our rich round world bare / And none reck of world after'. There is no doubting
Hopkins' 'care and dear concern'. But Hopkins does not show much awareness
of connections between one part of nature and another, of interdependence,
only of the independent connection of each creature to God and to the individual who knows how to touch it. Perhaps we read into 'God's Grandeur' the
idea of a circuit. The created world does not present itself to Hopkins as a
system, rather an aggregation of single and separate miracles, each conceived
and charged by God for a specific and very precise purpose (could we but see
it). And this purpose is not in relation to the rest of creation, but only in
relation to the augmenting of God's glory by praise and the saving of souls.

This will become clearer if we look at two more of Hopkins' most
famous poems, 'The Windhover' and 'As Kingfishers Catch Fire'.

> I caught this morning morning's minion, king-
> dom of daylight's dauphin, dapple-dawn-drawn Falcon, in his riding
> Of the rolling level underneath him steady air, and striding
> High there, how he rung upon a wimpling wing
> In his ecstasy! then off, off forth on swing,
> As a skate's heel sweeps smooth on a bow-bend: the hurl and gliding
> Rebuffed the big wind. My heart in hiding
> Stirred for a bird, – the achieve of, the mastery of the thing!

'Caught' does not mean simply 'caught sight of'. The diction, rhythm, imagery,
will not allow for so mundane a meaning. It means that Hopkins caught,
perhaps for the first time, the spiritual significance of the falcon, brought it
home to his heart, thereby transforming it to Falcon, the type of Christ our
Lord, prince of heaven. The wonderful mimetic recreation of the characteristic
hovering of the kestrel (also known as a standgale), which rides the wind with
the steadiness of a skilled horseman who moves with his mount, always level
in relation to it, however it may roll and threaten to hurl him, or of a skater
whose skill performing figures of eight enables him to triumph over those
forces which seek to bring him down, is not there merely in order to give us
a vivid description of a kestrel, as in a nature poem. It is there, along with all
the medieval chivalric splendour, to fuse Falcon and Christ in one composite
image of mastery, mastery of all dangers, temptations, everything which con-
spires to overthrow the heroic spirit, everything, that is, the poet's heart is in
hiding from. We hear in the apparently throw-away phrase 'my heart in hiding'
an echo of 'The swoon of a heart that the sweep and the hurl of thee trod /

Hard down with a horror of height' ['The Wreck of the Deutschland'], and a hint of the heart to which he will later say 'Here! creep, / Wretch, under a comfort serves in a whirlwind'. At the time of writing 'The Windhover' Hopkins both feared the height and the danger of exposure to the big wind and longed for the whirl of wings, the fling of the heart and the towering grace. The danger is that the higher the aspiration the greater the temptation to pride, and therefore the deeper the hurtle of hell. The heart hides in true humility before the spiritual achievements of Christ and his saints, but also, perhaps, in envy of the outward trappings of valorous action, its pride and plume, which might precede a fall, as it did for Arthur's chevaliers. He does not know whether his life of obscurity and renunciation, in clerical black, is a manifestation of courage or cowardice. His heart stirs for the very thing it is in hiding from (as Eliot's heart stirred for and cowered from 'the awful daring of a moment's surrender').

At the beginning of the sestet this stirring articulates itself as a prayer for the resplendent qualities of the bird. Since the Falcon is also the Prince summoned by the King of daylight to perform his chivalric deeds in high heaven, Hopkins is praying to become something much more than a cavorting kestrel, he is praying for God to buckle on him the shining armour which will transform the drab priest into the most favoured hero and man-of-action whose exploits are emblazoned upon him and flash upon the world: 'Brute beauty and valour and act, oh, air, pride, plume, here / Buckle!'. That the strong verb 'Buckle!' should be carried over and given the extra stress of beginning a line, that it should seem, therefore, to have the exclamation mark to itself, and that it should be followed by the uniquely capitalized 'AND', makes it the crux of the poem. It seems that in the very process of carrying the word over it has acquired a second and rapidly overriding meaning. As the last word of the first line of the sestet, its primary meaning seems to be 'fasten'; as the first word of the second line – 'Buckle! AND the fire that breaks from thee then' – it has become 'cave in'. The breaking of fire from something which has broken open is a favourite Hopkins image. It reappears in the very next poem as 'Fresh-firecoal chestnut-falls', freshly fallen chestnuts, that is, as bright as the fire which breaks from a fallen firecoal, which before it fell might have seemed as dead as a chestnut's husk. More important, it is taken up in the closing lines of this poem, in the 'blue-bleak embers' which 'Fall, gall themselves, and gash gold-vermilion'. To 'buckle' means then, primarily, to crumple, to cave in and break open. Christ does combine within himself all the admirable attributes of the falcon, but adds to them a quite different attribute which infinitely outshines them, his spiritual beauty, which shone brightest not in chivalric performance or any acts in which pride might plume itself, but in self-sacrifice, in the galling and gashes of the crucifixion. The fire that breaks from Christ then is the vermilion of blood which is simultaneously the gold of Grace.

Hopkins defines instress as 'a moulding force which succeeds in asserting itself over the resistance of cumbersome and restraining matter'.

Thus the instress of the falcon is that which gives it the name of windhover or standgale, the force which gives it mastery over the big wind. The instress of Christ (self-sacrificial Love) is his triumph over the evil inherent in unredeemed matter ('mortal trash'). What instress did Hopkins desire for himself? Poetic inspiration ('the roll, the rise, the carol, the creation'), or the conquest of all such aspirations? The ostentatious skill of the windhover is also perhaps an image of Hopkins' pride in his own flamboyant poetic mastery, his triumph over the resistance of cumbersome language. Was his pride in that entirely for the greater glory of God?

The phrase 'O my chevalier!' implies a choice of the second meaning of 'buckle' and reverses the prayer of two lines earlier. The poet now prays not to ride in public and in pride, but to be ridden in humble obscurity. Christ is now Hopkins' chevalier because the poet's overweening heart is now the horse, that which must be broken ('rung upon the rein') and mastered ('Thou mastering me God'). What must be subdued is precisely that in him which rebelled against the humiliation of a life spent in obscurity ('in hiding') and 'stirred for a bird'. ('I am no wing/ To tread emptiness' says Hughes' Adam.) He can console himself that as 'sheer plod' burnishes the plough-share, so the self-renunciation of his own plodding life might burnish his soul. Not for him that honour which is 'flashed off exploit' ['St. Alphonsus Rodriguez']; rather the 'mastery in the mind' of 'Morning, Midday and Evening Sacrifice'. There are the resplendent crusading knights; there are the saints and martyrs whose wounds testify to their struggles; and there are those who have, outwardly, nothing to show for a life of dedication and renunciation and inner strife. St. Alphonsus Rodriguez was 'a laybrother of our Order, who for 40 years acted as hall porter to the College of Palma in Majorca; he was, it is believed, much favoured by God with heavenly light and much persecuted by evil spirits' [Poems 252]. It was Hopkins' hope that his own inconspicuous 'war within' during years and years 'of world without event' might be similarly favoured.

The word 'buckle' is thus perhaps the turning point in Hopkins' work at which breaks into the celebratory mood a recognition of the need to renounce the very things he found most attractive in nature, the mortal beauty which made his blood dance. Whatever is not so sacrificed becomes hostage to 'surly the mere mould'.

'The Windhover' could only have been written by someone who had closely watched and admired the behaviour of kestrels. But that is not the main subject of the poem. As the subtitle 'To Christ our Lord' warns us, it is about Christian martyrdom. There is, of course, no reason why Hopkins should not draw upon the natural world in this way. But when we look at the use he habitually makes of nature, we may become aware of some strain between, on the one hand, the claims he makes for nature as being charged with God, and the expectation this gives rise to (which is satisfied in Whitman) that what he is doing when he looks at nature is attempting to 'see into the life of things' that he might thereby know God, and on the other the extent to which what he sees in nature is determined by relatively external correspondences to preconceptions about God, Christ and Creation which have been arrived at without reference to the natural world as anyone would see it without such preconceptions.

'As kingfishers catch fire' is perhaps the poem in which Hopkins most triumphantly marries his own vision to that of St. Ignatius and Duns Scotus. The poem speaks and spells itself very clearly, and in high spirits, racing from one half-line inscape to the next. It moves effortlessly from nature to music to man to Christ to God.

We can make allowances, in 'The Windhover' for the fact that it is not primarily a poem about a kestrel, that other aspects of the behaviour of the kestrel might have been relevant for other purposes, and that Hopkins has every right to select whatever aspect of the bird he likes for this particular poem. But the more poems we read, the more we become aware that the principle of selection is always the same, and 'As kingfishers catch fire' makes clear that it is not really a matter of selection at all:

> Each mortal thing does one thing and the same:
> Deals out that being indoors each one dwells;
> Selves – goes itself; *myself* it speaks and spells;
> Crying *What I do is me: for that I came.*

In ringing and telling of itself, the creature rings and tells of God, who, according to St. Ignatius, made the creature for the purpose of helping men to praise him. Knowing how to touch things means, therefore, identifying and taking into one's heart whatever distinctive quality of the creature most matches a quality of Christ or God. Only this could explain Hopkins' inordinate enthusiasm for 'St. Patrick's Breastplate', a translation of a fifth-century poem ascribed to St. Patrick, which Hopkins described in May 1870 as 'one of the most remarkable compositions of man':

> I bind unto myself to-day
> The virtues of the star-lit heaven,
> The glorious sun's life-giving ray,
> The whiteness of the moon at even,
> The flashing of the lightning free,
> The whirling wind's tempestuous shocks,
> The stable earth, the deep salt sea,
> Around the old eternal rocks.

What Hopkins touches and seeks to bind unto himself is usually a distinctive form of beauty, (with a particular preference for effects of light, as in the first half of the St. Patrick quotation), or of power (as in the second). He is not, it seems to me, saying that everything a kingfisher characteristically does gives God glory, or even that everything it does is a revelation of its innermost being, and therefore of God's purpose in creating kingfishers. Rather, he is attempting to isolate one characteristic, and that a visual effect upon an implied watcher, as the sole purpose of the existence of kingfishers (or dragonflies, or kestrels, or any other creatures). 'And the world is full of things and events, phenomena of all sorts, that go unwitnessed [*Correspondence* 7]'. Hopkins regrets this 'want of witness'. Nothing has meaning for him without it. Just as it needs the human participant to tumble a stone over the rim of a roundy well or tuck a string, so it needs him to register the kingfisher catching fire or the dragonfly drawing flame. Kingfishers and dragonflies are particularly appropriate because their distinctive colouring is not pigment but structural colour, depending on the reflection of light (from the sun symbolizing God) striking the creature at a certain angle, into the eyes of the beholder. As it is the sole purpose of a man to keep grace, so it is the sole purpose of the kingfisher to help him to do so by flashing through beams of sunlight when he happens to be watching, or of a kestrel to hover on a big wind when he happens to be watching. This, to the non-Catholic at least, is somewhat absurd – absurdly anthropocentric. Kingfishers do not flash through sunbeams in case someone might be watching, but as part of the process of catching fish. Hawks and kingfishers speak and spell themselves in their efficiency as killers. This need not, as Hughes has shown, compromise their sacredness. Hughes' kingfisher catches both fish and fire:

> Through him, God
> Marries a pit
> Of fishy mire.
>   And look! He's
> – gone again.
>   Spark, sapphire, refracted
> From beyond water
> Shivering the spine of the river.
>   ['The Kingfisher']

Hopkins discounts the whole of the rest of the life of the kingfisher, including that characteristic action after which it is named, and of which the flashing between trees is an incidental part, and even the catching fire goes for nothing if the beholder is wanting. He discounts all the creatures which are never seen at all, because they live too remote from human beings, or are too small to be noticed. Descartes had clearly stated the problem:

> It is not at all probable that all things have been created for us in such a manner that God has no other end in creating them. . . . We cannot doubt that an infinitude of things exist, or did exist, though they may have ceased to do so, which have never been beheld or comprehended by man, and have never been of any use to him.   [quoted by Lovejoy, 188]

Gray had made the point in the famous lines:

Full many a gem of purest ray serene,
  The dark unfathom'd caves of ocean bear;
Full many a flower is born to blush unseen,
  And waste its sweetness on the desert air.

But what was for Gray merely an unquestioning anthropocentrism was for Hopkins a theological tenet, that all non-human creatures had been created solely as revelations to man of aspects of the beauty and glory of God. Yet Hopkins seems to have been oblivious of the wastefulness of creation, if indeed it had been created purely for men to witness. In the year Hopkins entered the Jesuit order, Alfred Russell Wallace was writing his account of the birds of paradise he had seen in the Malay Archipelago:

I thought of the long ages of the past, during which the successive generations of this little creature had run their course – year by year being born, and living and dying amid these dark and gloomy woods, with no intelligent eye to gaze upon their loveliness; to all appearance such a wanton waste of beauty. It seems sad, that on the one hand such exquisite creatures should live out their lives and exhibit their charms only in these wild inhospitable regions; while on the other hand, should civilized man ever reach these distant lands, and bring moral, intellectual and physical light into the recesses of these virgin forests, we may be sure that he will so disturb the nicely-balanced relations of organic nature as to cause the disappearance, and finally the extinction, of these very beings whose wonderful structure and beauty he alone is fitted to appreciate and enjoy. This consideration must surely tell us that all living things were *not* made for man. Many of them have no relation to him. The cycle of their existence has gone on independently of his, and is disturbed or broken by every advance in man's intellectual development; and their happiness and enjoyments, their loves and hates, their struggles for existence, their vigorous life and early death, would seem to be immediately related to their own well-being and perpetuation alone.
  [*The Malay Archipelago and the Birds of Paradise*, 223–4]

  Hopkins also discounts everything which is not counted beautiful or in some other way impressive to human sensibility (or current fashions of sensibility). But if the world is charged with God's grandeur, how can one creature be counted more beautiful than another? Sir Thomas Browne wrote:

I hold there is a general beauty in the works of God, and there is no deformity in any kind or species of creature whatsoever. I know not by what logic we call a Toad or a Bear or an Elephant ugly; they being created in those outward shapes and figures which best express the action of their inward forms.
  [*Religio Medici*]

One might have expected this position to appeal strongly to Hopkins, but he is locked into an aestheticism which deduces, rather, the inward beauty (or otherwise) from the outward.

The principle that 'outward beauty is the proof of inward beauty' seems to Hopkins to sanction his obsession with youthful good-looks, his loathing of the poor on account of their ugliness, and his admiration for soldiers on account of their scarlet uniforms, as if the *raison d'être* of soldiers were to look 'manly' on parade, rather than to kill and be killed. In glorifying 'the spirit of war' he sets up Christ as example:

> Mark Christ our King. He knows war, served this soldiering through;
> He of all can reeve a rope best. ['The Soldier]

Why not 'thrust a bayonet best'? Hopkins has to admit that in assuming that all redcoats are manly 'the heart ... makes believe ... feigns', for even 'our redcoats, our tars' are 'but foul clay' ['The Soldier']. A bugler boy 'breathing bloom of a chastity in mansex fine' kneels 'in regimental red' for his First Communion. Hopkins prays for his safety with pleas which 'Would brandle adamantine heaven with ride and jar, did / Prayer go disregarded' ['The Bugler's First Communion']. But Hopkins calls his own sincerity in question when he writes to Bridges: 'I am half inclined to hope the Hero of it may be killed in Afghanistan' [92].

But when Hopkins turns his attention to the unfallen world of non-human creatures, such feigning is no longer necessary. He can proclaim with absolute conviction that the apparel proclaims the beast.

In his commentary on the *Spiritual Exercises* Hopkins claims that although other creatures are able to give God less glory than man, since they do it unknowingly, 'nevertheless what they can *they always do*' [*Sermons* 239]. It follows that the kestrel gives God glory in all its actions. Can we allow Hopkins, in retrospect, to divorce the hovering of the kestrel so totally from the predatory purpose of that hovering? In 1872 Hopkins had recorded that 'a big hawk flew down chasing a little shrieking bird close beside us' [*Journals* 221]. What did that tell him about God? What God made the tiger? What of the God who demands of Job

> Doth the hawk fly by thy wisdom, and stretch her wings toward the
> south?
> Doth the eagle mount up at thy command, and make her nest on high?
> She dwelleth and abideth on the rock, and the strong place.
> From thence she seeketh the prey, and her eyes behold afar off.
> Her young ones also suck up blood: and where the slain are, there is
> she. [39:26–30]

The God who answers Job out of the whirlwind ridicules his hubristic claim to understanding, and his anthropocentric view of the natural world. God's purposes stretch far beyond the human world 'to cause it to rain on the earth, where no man is; on the wilderness, wherein there is no man'. He asks Job, and through him mankind:

> Wilt thou hunt the prey for the lion? or fill the appetite of the young lions.
> When they couch in their dens, and abide in the covert to lie in wait?
> Who provideth for the raven his food? when his young ones cry unto God, they wander for lack of meat. [38:39–41]

Hopkins cannot cope with such a God, the chief of whose works is Behemoth. He faces the problem of mortality and the problem of suffering, but he turns away from the problem of predation. Even Tennyson, (Alfred Lawn Tennyson as Whitman called him), a frippery poet for the most part, his 'thoughts commonplace and wanting in nobility', had in that 'divine work' *In Memoriam* registered with compelling power and honesty that Nature 'red in tooth and claw' shrieks against a creed such as Hopkins', a creed of love, beauty, and purposes centred exclusively on individual human beings.

The nearest Hopkins comes to the problem is in a curiously and uncharacteristically evasive passage in one of his Liverpool sermons [25 October 1880]. Here his attempt to demonstrate his anthropocentric view of creation collapses with a whimper:

Therefore all the things we see are made and provided for us, the sun, moon, and other heavenly bodies to light us, warm us, and be measures to us of time; coal and rockoil for artificial light and heat; animals and vegetables for our food and clothing; rain, wind, and snow again to make these bear and yield their tribute to us; water and the juices of plants for our drink; air for our breathing; stone and timber for our lodging; metals for our tools and traffic; the songs of birds, flowers and their smells and colours, fruits and their taste for our enjoyment. And so on: search the whole world and you will find it a million-million fold contrivance of providence planned for our use and patterned for our admiration.

But yet this providence is imperfect, plainly imperfect. The sun shines too long and withers the harvest, the rain is too heavy and rots it or in floods spreading washes it away; the air and water carry in their currents the poison of disease; there are poison plants, venomous snakes and scorpions; the beasts our subjects rebel, not only the bloodthirsty tiger that slaughters yearly its thousands, but even the bull will gore and the stallion bite or strike; at night the moon sometimes has no light to give, at others the clouds darken her; she measures time most strangely and gives us reckonings most difficult to make and never exact enough; the coalpits and oilwells are full of explosions, fires, and outbreaks of sudden death, the sea of storms and wrecks, the snow has avalanches, the earth landslips; we contend with cold, want, weakness, hunger, disease, death, and often we fight a losing battle, never a triumphant one; everything is full of fault, flaw, imperfection, shortcoming; as many marks as there are of God's wisdom in providing for us so many marks there may be set against them of more being needed still, of something having made of this very providence a shattered frame and a broken web.

Let us not now enquire, brethren, why this should be; we most sadly feel and know that so it is. [*Sermons* 90]

Hopkins had no answer to the passage in David Hume's *Dialogues of Natural Religion* (1779), where Hume demonstrates that the existence of God cannot be proved by the argument that design in Nature implies a designer:

One would imagine, that this grand production had not received the last hand of the maker; so little finished is every part, and so coarse are the strokes, with which it is executed. Thus, the winds are requisite to convey the vapours along the surface of the globe, and to assist men in navigation: But how oft, rising up to tempests and hurricanes, do they become pernicious? Rains are necessary to nourish all the plants and animals of the earth: But how often are they defective? how often excessive? Heat is requisite to all life and vegetation; but is not always found in the due proportion. On the mixture and secretion of the humours and juices of the body depend the health and prosperity of the animal: But the parts perform not regularly their proper function. What more useful than all the passions of the mind, ambition, vanity, love, anger? But how oft do they break their bounds, and cause the greatest convulsions in society? There is nothing so advantageous in the universe, but what frequently becomes pernicious, by its excess or defect; nor has nature guarded, with the requisite accuracy, against all disorder or confusion. The irregularity is never, perhaps, so great as to destroy any species; but is often sufficient to involve the individuals in ruin and misery.

Hopkins badly needs a Trickster figure to account for what went wrong without having to blame God. But the rigid dualism of good and evil prevents Satan from playing this role in Christianity. Hopkins has to choose between a totally good creation by God or a totally evil one by Satan. At the outset he chooses the former, but remains deeply troubled by inescapable discrepancies until, in his final despair, he swings perilously close to the latter, a belief that Nature is a Heraclitean fire deserving no better than to be reduced to ashes, and redeemable, somewhere elsewhere, only by the Resurrection.

* * *

Hopkins is a master of rhythm. I do not mean of the theory of rhythm, but the instinctive matching of rhythm and sense which could not be fabricated in terms of any theory. So expressive is his rhythm that there are places where one feels one could get the essential meaning from the rhythm alone. A particularly striking example is the ending of 'Felix Randall'. In 'child, Felix, poor Felix Randall' the rhythm loses all impetus, is drowned in grief. Then comes the steady accumulation of rhythmic power to the triumphant and inevitable conclusion:

> How far from then forethought of, all thy more boisterous years,
> When thou at the random grim forge, powerful amidst peers,
> Didst fettle for the great grey drayhorse his bright and battering
>   sandal!

But perhaps his most expressive rhythms are to be found in the poem in which he departed furthest from any kind of rhythmic regularity and the stringencies of the sonnet form – 'The Leaden Echo and the Golden Echo', of which he said 'I never did anything more musical'. Under the text he wrote: 'I have marked the stronger stresses, but with the degree of the stress so perpetually varying no marking is satisfactory. Do you think all had best be left to the reader?'

It was this poem which prompted Bridges to comment on the similarity between Hopkins and Whitman, which provoked Hopkins' 'De-Whitmanizer':

> I always knew in my heart Walt Whitman's mind to be more like my own than any other man's living. As he is a very great scoundrel this is not a pleasant confession. And this also makes me the more desirous to read him and the more determined that I will not.   [*Letters to Bridges*, 155]

It is no coincidence that most of Hopkins' favourite poets were 'scoundrels'. Tennyson, he claims, 'has not that sort of ascendancy Goethe had or even Burns, scoundrel as the first was, not to say the second; but then they spoke out the real human rakishness of their hearts and everybody recognised the really beating, though rascal vein' [*The Correspondence of G.M. Hopkins and R.W. Dixon*, 25]. But how could this ascetic dedicated priest, this lonely, disciplined writer of highly-wrought poems, recognize such kinship with a pagan sensualist, a loafer on the open road sending his barbaric yawp over the roofs of the world? The very qualities Whitman accepted in himself, fostered, inflated, Hopkins tried to sacrifice. Yet Hopkins knew that these differences were but superficial, that in their response to nature, in the seriousness of their commitment to writing from the heart, in religious sensibility even, they were akin.

There are plenty of parallels in the poetry, but it is in their informal prose, when stylistic differences are at a minimum, that Hopkins and Whitman come closest. Hopkins did not know Whitman's diaries which record inscapes almost interchangeable with his own:

> July 14, 1878. My two kingfishers still haunt the pond. For nearly an hour I indolently look and join them while they dart and turn and take their

airy gambols, sometimes far up the creek disappearing for a few moments, and then surely returning again, and performing most of their flight within sight of me, as if they knew I appreciated and absorb'd their vitality, spirituality, faithfulness, and the rapid, vanishing, delicate lines of moving yet quiet electricity they draw for me across the spread of the grass, the trees, and the blue sky. [*Whitman* 743]

July 22 1878. Now, indeed, if never before, the heavens declared the glory of God. It was to the full sky of the Bible, of Arabia, of the prophets, and of the oldest poems. There, in abstraction and stillness, (I had gone off by myself to absorb the scene, to have the spell unbroken,) the copiousness, the removedness, vitality, loose-clear-crowdedness, of that stellar concave spreading overhead, softly absorb'd into me, rising so free, interminably high, stretching east, west, north, south – and I, though but a point in the centre below, embodying all. As if for the first time, indeed, creation noiselessly sank into and through me its placid and untellable lesson, beyond – O, so infinitely beyond! – anything from art, books, sermons, or from science, old or new. The spirit's hour, religion's hour – the visible suggestion of God in space and time – now once definitely indicated, if never again. The untold pointed at – the heavens all paved with it. The Milky Way, as if some superhuman symphony, some ode of universal vagueness, disdaining syllable and sound – a flashing glance of Deity, address'd to the soul. [748–9]

Hopkins' diary entry for 23 January 1866 reads like missing lines from 'Spontaneous Me' or 'I Sing the Body Electric':

Lobes of the trees. Cups of the eyes. Gathering back the lightly hinged eyelids. Bows of the eyelids. Pencil of eyelashes. Juices of the eyeball. . . . Juices of the sunrise. Joins and veins of the same. [*Journals* 72]

Hopkins did not know 'Song of Myself', where he would have found: 'Seas of bright juice suffuse heaven' and

To me the converging objects of the universe perpetually flow, All are written to me, and I must get what the writing means.

I see something of God each hour of the twenty-four, and each moment then, In the faces of men and women I see God, and in my own face in the glass.

There are equally surprising echoes of style. Whitman, too, loved alliteration. In 'The Sleepers' alone, Hopkins might have found 'sparkles of starshine', 'a show of the summer softness', and even 'a gay gang of blackguards with mirthshouting music'.

Knowing nothing of these, it seems that Hopkins' extraordinary identification with Whitman, and also his disapproval, is based solely on 'a strong impression of his marked and original manner and way of thought and in particular of his rhythm'. Of course Hopkins knew that Whitman's 'way of thought' tended towards the pantheistic and pagan, and this cannot be separated from the 'savagery' of his art. For Whitman strove to make his verse a free channel for the voice of the spirit who formed all scenes, who, in scenes such as the American south-west, could only be seen (as Lawrence also was to see him there) as savage:

> Spirit that form'd this scene,
> These tumbled rock-piles grim and red,
> These gorges, turbulent-clear streams, this naked freshness,
> These formless wild arrays, for reasons of their own;
> I know thee, savage spirit – we have communed together,
> Mine too such wild arrays, for reasons of their own
> ['Spirit that Form'd this Scene']

Hopkins knew this poem. Such formless wild creations of a formless wild god are not at all what Hopkins wanted to see in God's works nor to recreate in his own. The phrase 'for reasons of their own' indicates the most crucial difference between Hopkins and Whitman. Hopkins' theology did not allow for such autonomy in the non-human world. Mary Midgley gives Kant (as well as common sense) the credit for breaking out of 'the Egoist squirrel cage':

> The world in which the kestrel moves, the world that it sees, is, and will always be, entirely beyond us. That there are such worlds all around us is an essential feature of our world. . . . It is not a device for any human end. It does not need that external point. It is in some sense . . . an end in itself.
>
> [359]

The question of rhythm is also crucial:

> Extremes meet, and (I must for truth's sake say what sounds pride) this savagery of his art, this rhythm in its last ruggedness and decomposition into common prose, comes near the last elaboration of mine.
>
> [*Letters to Bridges*, 157]

There is nothing in any of the passages Hopkins knew which comes particularly near to the elaboration (if such it is) of 'The Leaden Echo and the Golden Echo'. But if Bridges was more familiar with Whitman, there are certainly echoes he might have heard:

> Come then, your ways and airs and looks, locks, maiden gear,
>   gallantry and gaiety and grace,
> Winning ways, airs innocent, maiden manners, sweet looks, loose
>   locks, long locks, lovelocks, gaygear, going gallant, girlgrace –

Such lines might well have reminded Bridges of lines of Whitman, for example:

> Love-thoughts, love-juice, love-odor, love-yielding, love-climbers, and
>   the climbing sap,
> Arms and hands of love, lips of love, phallic thumb of love, breasts of
>   love, bellies press'd and glued together with love,
> Earth of chaste love, life that is only life after love . . .
>
> ['Spontaneous Me']

Usually the similarity of minds between Hopkins and Whitman is masked by their opposite ideologies, as their similarity in metre is masked by their opposite and extreme theories of metre, each of which was something of a pose. Whitman's style was no more a 'barbaric yawp' than Hopkins' was calculated artifice. But Hopkins' inspiration was not always 'buckled within the belt of rule', crammed and cramped into sonnets. It was twice allowed to find its own free form. The other example, 'Epithalamium', brings us even closer to Whitman.

The poem is little known. Hopkins imagines himself

>   where a candycoloured, where a gluegold-brown
> Marbled river, boisterously beautiful, between
> Roots and rocks is danced and dandled, all in froth and
>   water-blowballs, down.

He hears a shout

> And the riot of a rout
> Of, it must be, boys from the town
> Bathing: it is summer's sovereign good.

> By there comes a listless stranger: beckoned by the noise
> He drops towards the river, unseen
> Sees the bevy of them, how the boys
> With dare and with downdolphinry and bellbright bodies huddling out,
> Are earthworld, airworld, waterworld thorough hurled, all by turn and
>   turn about.

He hies to a neighbouring secluded pool ('the best there'), throws off his clothes, 'offwrings' his boots 'Till walk the world he can with bare his feet', and enters the water:

> Here he will then, here he will the fleet
> Flinty kindcold element let break across his limbs
> Long. Where we leave him, froliclavish, while he looks about him,
>   laughs, swims.

This comes very close to section 11 of 'Song of Myself', where a listless woman in hiding observes twenty-eight young men bathing, and in imagination joins them:

> Dancing and laughing along the beach came the twenty-ninth bather,
> The rest did not see her, but she saw them and loved them . . .
> The young men float on their backs, their white bellies bulge to the
>   sun, they do not ask who seizes fast to them,
> They do not know who puffs and declines with pendant and bending
>   arch,
> They do not think whom they souse with spray.

'Epithalamium' (1888) is by far the most relaxed and high-spirited of the late poems. The 'listless stranger' is clearly Hopkins himself ('to seem the stranger lies my lot'). Though he cannot join the 'dare' and 'downdolphinry' of the boys, he can at least cast off his cares with his clothes:

> No more: off with – down he dings
> His bleachèd both and woolwoven wear:
> Careless these in coloured wisp
> All lie tumbled-to

It is a frolicsome poem, clearly releasing Hopkins' repressed desire to enter the world of joy-in-life, to acknowledge the healing power of nature in itself, the earth and its elements as man's natural home. But of course 'our Law' does not allow it, overrules imagination. He takes it all back, retreats into hiding, with the disingenuous excuse that it is all an allegory:

> Enough now; since the sacred matter that I mean
> I should be wronging longer leaving it to float
> Upon this only gambolling and echoing-of-earth note –
> What is . . . the delightful dene?
> Wedlock. What is water? Spousal love.

It is not. Nothing Hopkins can say now can denature the delightful dene, or turn the 'fleet, flinty kindcold element' into anything but water. Both are far too real, too 'there', too concrete and sensory, too specific, to be reducible to allegory. This is Hopkins painfully renouncing what the poet in him found sacred but the priest could not. This is the crime against nature and his own

263

nature he was virtually to accuse himself of a few months later in 'Thou art indeed just, Lord'.

✳   ✳   ✳

Not only was the teaching of St. Ignatius and Duns Scotus wholly anthropocentric; it also encouraged in Hopkins a heightened sense of unique selfhood. If it is possible to touch God in other creatures, how much more so can we know him in other men:

> Our law says: Love what are love's worthiest, were all known;
> World's loveliest – men's selves. Self flashes off frame and face.
> ['To what serves Mortal Beauty']

and how much more fully and directly in ourselves. Hopkins' intense sense of self borders at times on the narcissistic and solipsistic:

> When I consider my selfbeing, my consciousness and feeling of myself, that taste of myself, of *I* and *me* above and in all things, which is more distinctive than the taste of ale or alum, more distinctive than the smell of walnutleaf or camphor. . . . Nothing else in nature comes near this unspeakable stress of pitch, distinctiveness, and selving, this selfbeing of my own . . . Searching nature I taste *self* but at one tankard, that of my own being. [*Sermons* 123]

Again the closeness to Whitman, Whitman taking the self to be the world in little, is astonishing:

> I dote on myself, there is that lot of me and all so luscious
> ['Song of Myself' 24]

But Whitman's exaltation of self is always qualified by his comedy –

> The scent of these arm-pits aroma finer than prayer

– and balanced by an equally exaggerated humility:

> I project my hat, sit shame-faced, and beg.   [37]

The conclusion of Hopkins' commentary is 'that I am due to an extrinsic power' [128]; but once the conviction of the identity of self and Christ is lost, the strands of selfhood are untwisted, and the way is opened for the terrible recriminations of the years in Ireland:

> I am gall, I am heartburn. God's most deep decree
> Bitter would have me taste: my taste was me;

264

Bones built in me, flesh filled, blood brimmed the curse.
Selfyeast of spirit a dull dough sours. I see
The lost are like this, and their scourge to be
As I am mine, their sweating selves; but worse.
                    ['I wake and feel the fell of dark']

Hopkins accuses himself of the sin of Adam, 'rebelling against God his lawgiver and judge' [*Sermons* 67]. What form could this 'selfyeast of spirit' have taken but that, believing himself to be praising God in his creation, he had in fact been praising himself:

Cheer whom though? the hero whose heaven-handling flung me, foot trod
Me? or me that fought him? O which one?   ['Carrion Comfort']

In the last poems, the conviction that to be oneself is to be Christ can no longer be sustained. The 'unspeakable stress of pitch' becomes 'pitched past pitch of grief', where to the musical meaning is added the sense of shipwreck and of being thrown away as of no worth – a 'Jack, joke, poor potsherd'. The temptation is to 'choose not to be'.

In 'That Nature is a Heraclitean Fire and of the Comfort of the Resurrection', the charge which had sanctified the world in 'God's Grandeur' becomes 'world's wildfire' reducing it to ash. Man, nature's 'clearest-selvèd spark', goes into the bonfire with the rest. The poor Jackself is now mere matchwood. Yet none of this really matters, within this poem, for Hopkins has the master card, the last trump, up his sleeve – the resurrection which will transform his 'mortal trash' into 'immortal diamond'. It is no longer good enough as it was in 'The Leaden Echo and the Golden Echo' that the body should be recovered in its youthful beauty ('not the least lash lost') at the resurrection. The desperate need to defeat time, decay and death results, as it always does in poetry ('Ode to a Grecian Urn', 'Sailing to Byzantium') in an exchange of the living body for something cold, hard, and as incapable of living as dying. Freud described this wish for a self-contained and immortal body as both infantile and narcissistic.

'That Nature is a Heraclitean Fire' is the last poem with Hopkins' characteristic bravura – inventive diction, sweeping rhythms, clinching rhymes, triumphant coda. The result is a fine but, in comparison with the poems around it, a closed poem. It ends with not the hope but the certainty of the resurrection, leaving no room for other possibilities or for creative interpretation by the reader in terms of his or her nature and experience. It is clear from the surrounding poems that it is not true to Hopkins' real state, in which the only comfort which served was that 'all Life death does end, and each day dies with sleep' ['No worst, there is none']. The well-wrought poem, in its closed circularity, is itself a life-belt for the drowning self, as the externally-validated doctrine of the resurrection is its beacon. The whole human being, whose last strands are being untwisted, is excluded from the conclusion of the poem in favour of the confident believer.

What Hopkins is undergoing in these last years is the experience Simone Weil calls 'affliction':

> Affliction is essentially a destruction of personality, a lapse into anonymity . . . it is a pulverisation of the soul by the mechanical brutality of circumstances. . . . Unless constrained by experience, it is impossible to believe that everything in the soul – all its thoughts and feelings, its every attitude towards ideas, people and the universe, and, above all, the most intimate attitude of the being towards itself – that all this is entirely at the mercy of circumstances. . . . When thought finds itself, through force of circumstance, brought face to face with affliction, it takes immediate refuge in lies, like an animal dashing for cover.
>
> ['On Science, Necessity and the Love of God']

It can also take refuge in the comforts of faith, which, whether true or false in the absolute, is always poetically false unless poetically substantiated. Poetry has nothing to do with 'truths' handed down from above, only with those less comforting truths the imagination dredges up from below. In this poem Hopkins commits one of the original sins of Hughes' Adam:

> Wrapped in peach-skin and bruise
> He dreamed the religion of the diamond body.
>
> ['Adam']

The loss of the sense of self as something unique, eternal, and of infinite worth, was devastating to Hopkins, who needed a personal and special providence not to be shared with mere sparrows. Again there is a strong contrast with Whitman who would happily grant everything he claimed for himself to a blade of grass, and who viewed his inevitable dissolution with equanimity.

✤   ✤   ✤

I am, I suppose, moving towards the suggestion that Whitman's open style is morally superior to Hopkins' style of the middle period in that Hopkins', like most highly wrought styles, is an attempt to impose an aesthetic or rhetorical order on material which might otherwise threaten the control and security of the ego. Hopkins' Ignatian theology, his anthropocentrism, narcissism, aestheticism, his inscapes, his elaborate over-complex style, are all symptoms of the same syndrome, of the kind of hubristic or ego-defensive imagination which, according to Janos Pilinszky 'places the stylistic certainty of appearances before the self-forgetful incarnation of the world' ['Creative Imagination in Our Time'].

The unique Hopkins style is 'counter, original, spare, strange'. It enables us to share the thoughts and feelings of a refined sensibility. No-one would wish to be without the famous poems which exemplify it. But they are not Hopkins' finest. The greatest poetry in the language is the simplest. Not the simplicity of innocence, but a strong, naked, irreducible simplicity on the far side of experience, usually of breakdown, which dispenses with verbal richness or complexities ('the poetry does not matter'). No longer, at this level, do words strain and slide away from meanings. The language is capable, we know, of perfect expression, 'a condition of complete simplicity' ['Little Gidding']:

> I am a very foolish fond old man,
> Fourscore and upward, not an hour more or less;
> And, to deal plainly,
> I fear I am not in my perfect mind.
> Methinks I should know you and know this man;
> Yet I am doubtful: for I am mainly ignorant
> What place this is, and all the skill I have
> Remembers not these garments; nor I know not
> Where I did lodge last night. Do not laugh at me;
> For, as I am a man, I think this lady
> To be my child Cordelia. [*King Lear* IV vii 60–9]

The greatest lines are utterly purged of style:

> To-morrow, and to-morrow, and to-morrow.

> Never, never, never, never, never.

Only the greatest poets have touched this level of self-abnegation. It is touched again and again in the last sonnets, where Hopkins speaks directly, unselfconsciously, out of the spiritual nakedness and sterility of his 'winter world'. They came, he says, 'like inspirations unbidden and against my will'. Ostensibly, he is praying and pleading that his work might become more rewarding and his poetic inspiration return, but the insistent imagery of fertility in both the human and the natural worlds tells another story. His last cries are addressed not to the God of 'yonder', but of here and now, to the 'lord of life', who has cut him off from all that sustains life, from the common life-need of water, and from the communion of natural life to which even the birds and plants belong.

Hopkins' inability to find 'Thirst's all-in-all in all a world of wet' reveals, consciously or unconsciously, in its echo of 'Water, water, every where, / Nor any drop to drink', his sense of spiritual kinship with the Ancient Mariner. Hopkins knew the spectre of Life-in-Death, the loneliness of a soul in agony, the curse of spiritual drought. Does he also share the mariner's guilt, the deep knowledge of a crime against nature and his own nature, like a dead bird hanging about his neck? It was a full acceptance and spontaneous blessing of all the creatures he had formerly despised, of their lordly autonomy, which released the Ancient Mariner from his curse, and allowed nature to resume her fertile processes:

> To Mary Queen the praise be given!
> She sent the gentle sleep from Heaven,
> That slid into my soul.
>
> . . .
>
> And when I awoke, it rained.

Mary Queen provides for Coleridge here a continuity with the great pagan Queen of Heaven, who was, according to Hughes 'the goddess of Catholicism, who was the goddess of Medieval and Pre-Christian England, who was the divinity of the throne, who was the goddess of natural law and of love, who was the goddess of all sensation and organic life' [WP 110]. This is very much the goddess Hopkins had celebrated in 'The May Magnificat', where he comes close to saying that May is Mary's month because she is no other than the great Mother Goddess of earth's renewal. When he asks the 'mighty mother' why May is her month she answers with her own question: 'What is Spring?', to which she answers 'Growth in every thing –'

> Flesh and fleece, fur and feather,
> Grass and greenworld all together;
>> Star-eyed strawberry-breasted
>> Throstle above her nested
>
> Cluster of bugle blue eggs thin
> Forms and warms the life within;
>> And bird and blossom swell
>> In sod or sheath or shell.
>
> All things rising, all things sizing
> Mary sees, sympathizing
>> With that world of good,
>> Nature's motherhood.

Hopkins continues to celebrate 'Spring's universal bliss' until, almost as an afterthought, he awkwardly drags himself back from the pagan world:

> This ecstasy all through mothering earth
> Tells Mary her mirth till Christ's birth
>> To remember and exultation
>> In God who was her salvation.

The atonement of body and spirit, nature and God, pagan and Christian, which Hopkins had almost achieved at that time is finally abandoned in 'Spelt from Sibyl's Leaves'. Here everything his sacramental vision had unified is unwound, dismembered, back to a stark dualism which is death to poetry, except the terrible poetry of the death of poetry:

> Let life, waned, ah let life wind
> Off her once skeined stained veined variety upon, all upon two spools;
>   part, pen, pack
> Now her all in two flocks, two folds – black, white; right, wrong;
>   reckon but, reck but, mind
> But these two; ware of a world where but these two tell, each off the
>   other; of a rack
> Where, selfwrung, sheathe-and-shelterless, thoughts against thoughts
>   in groans grind.

The great mother has now turned dragonish:

> In her death-throes, nature has defensively manifested herself to him her
> unacceptable, demonic aspect, embodying the primeval fear of the
> monstrous, devouring female. Hopkins can no longer integrate and
> reconcile the energies of his inner dragon, his unfallen self, and is
> consigning her to the darkness, separating the female from the male,
> 'black' from 'white', 'wrong' from 'right'.
>
> [from an unpublished essay by Ann Mackay]

Hopkins, like Wordsworth, now finds himself excluded from Nature's festival, but does not for that reason end in repudiation of her. His faith in her proves at the last more resilient than his faith in a God outside nature. At the same time that he is crying out for a diamond body, he is pleading for impregnation and conception, for the creative life of the living body. These are, of course, metaphors for grace and for poetic inspiration. But it is surely highly significant that in searching for appropriate metaphors for those things which constituted for him the very meaning and justification of life, he should turn so often, so insistently and powerfully, to sexual metaphors and the closely related metaphors drawn from nature's capacity for self-renewal, nature's never-lost in-built grace.

Hopkins would have agreed with Wordsworth that the making of metaphors is 'the great spring of the activity of our minds, and their chief feeder' ['Preface' to the *Lyrical Ballads*]. Wordsworth adds, astonishingly: 'From this principle the direction of the sexual appetite and all the passions connected with it, take their origin'. It is ironic that the poet of all poets whose metaphors most vindicate this claim should have been a celibate priest whose sexual appetite was doomed to lead only to secret and sterile sin.

The last two sonnets are driven by sexual imagery. 'To R.B.' is a cry from Hopkins' widowed anima, his muse, his soul, a cry for impregnation ('live and lancing like the blowpipe flame'), for sunshine and spring rain. But in 'Thou art indeed just, Lord' he is himself the lacking father, castrated and impotent:

> See, banks and brakes
> Now, leaved how thick! laced they are again
> With fretty chervil, look, and fresh wind shakes
> Them; birds build – but not I build; no, but strain,
> Time's eunuch, and not breed one work that wakes.
> Mine, O thou lord of life, send my roots rain.
> ['Thou are indeed just, Lord']

These by no means lagging lines, stripped of all consolations from above, and of all the ego-protection of an imposed style, speak out of the real desolation of the heart. They echo hollowly the joyful shout at Eleusis: 'The people, looking up to heaven, cry "Rain!", and, looking down to earth, cry "Conceive!": *hye, kye'* [Baring 381], and the opening of the Prologue to *The Canterbury Tales*, which testifies to a spiritual life in men which is not cut off from the fertile processes of the natural world, but continuous with them:

> Whan that Aprill with his shoures soote
> The droghte of March hath perced to the roote,
> And bathed every veyne in swich licour
> Of which vertu engendred is the flour;
> Whan Zephirus eek with his sweete breeth
> Inspired hath in every holt and heeth
> The tendre croppes, and the yonge sonne
> Hath in the Ram his halve cours yronne,
> And smale foweles maken melodye,
> That slepen al the nyght with open ye
> (So priketh hem nature in hir corages);
> Thanne longen folk to goon on pilgrimages . . .

Nature pricked Hopkins' heart that spring, but in so doing only taunted him and brought home to him the horror of the chasm which had now opened up for him between nature and God.

16 THE CASE OF THE MISSING ELEPHANTS – CONRAD'S *HEART OF DARKNESS*

'Heart of Darkness' is, obviously, a savage indictment of colonialism. As Conrad wrote in a letter, what was going on in the Congo was 'the vilest scramble for loot that ever disfigured the history of human conscience and geographical exploration'. But it needs no imaginative novelist to tell us this. It was not the realization of this alone which made the Congo experience so transforming: 'Before the Congo, I was just a mere animal', he told his friend Edward Garnett. Months after his return he wrote: 'I am still plunged in deepest night, and my dreams are only nightmares'. That 'deepest night', the heart of darkness, was not merely the folly and greed of certain Belgian traders. It was clearly something within Conrad which the experience had forced him to confront.

On the surface of the story, the darkness is the jungle, the African wilderness, but it is not a story which allows us long to remain on the surface. At an early stage in his tale Marlow reveals that the journey into the dark heart of Africa has for him the character of a quest into his own inner darkness:

> It was the farthest point of navigation and the culminating point of my experience. It seemed somehow to throw a kind of light on everything about me – and into my thoughts. [11]

As the company doctor had told him, 'the changes take place inside, you know' [65].

*　　*　　*

In Jane Austen's *Mansfield Park* Sir Thomas Bertram is the guardian of most of the novel's positives, a man of kindness, conscience and justice, a man of sound English decency. The plot needs him to be absent for some months, so Jane Austen sends him off to Antigua on 'business'. His 'Estate' there has been 'making poor returns'. No character in the novel has any curiosity about the nature of this 'business' which is the source of their wealth and on which their life of luxury and idleness depends; nor does Jane Austen expect any reader to be interested in it. It is highly likely that to obtain cheap labour for his estate, Sir Thomas would have been involved, like all the other absentee landlords, in the slave trade. The issue of slavery is raised only to be immediately dropped as beyond the concerns of a novel whose world ends at Portsmouth. Antigua is but a name. Jane Austen defined her art as 'the little bit (two inches wide) of Ivory on which I work with so fine a brush'. 'Ivory' here is a dead image, completely cut off from any awareness of what ivory is, where it comes from, and what must be paid for even two inches of it in terms of suffering and death. Perhaps at that time only Blake and Coleridge were capable of making such connections – connections made by few at any time. Ivory is still intermittently a legal trade.

Even the socially and economically conscious novelists of the later nineteenth century were concerned exclusively with abuses within England. Yet this was the age of Empire, and England a trading even more than a manufacturing nation. The Liverpool dockers and Lancashire cotton workers went on strike rather than handle cotton from the slave-owning estates of the West Indies. Conrad picks up the thread where it begins in London or Brussels and follows it, in pursuit of the ultimate truth, into the heart of darkness, which is simultaneously at the other end of the earth and within every human heart.

Like *Wuthering Heights* 'Heart of Darkness' is a box within a box within a box – a meaning within an initially confident but ultimately inadequate narration, within another, still less dependable narration. The first narrator is anonymous, but his attitudes, together with the fact that his friends are a Director of Companies, a Lawyer and an Accountant, place him as a member of the decent, complacent conspiracy of trade. What these companies are and where they operate is a question not to be asked. The 'work' of these men is not 'out there' in the darkness beyond the luminous estuary, but behind them, in London, 'the biggest, and the greatest, town on earth'. They are, in Eliot's words 'assured of certain certainties'. They are much the same certainties Marlow takes to Africa with him. The first white man he meets at the first station there is also an accountant. He 'had verily accomplished something':

> In the great demoralization of the land, he kept up his appearance. That's backbone. His starched collars and got-up shirt-fronts were achievements of character. . . . And he was devoted to his books, which were in apple-pie order. [26]

His achievements include coping with distractions not experienced by his London counterpart:

> The groans of this sick person [a dying agent] distract my attention. And without that it is extremely difficult to guard against clerical errors in this climate. [27]

The first narrator expatiates upon 'the great spirit of the past', on 'all the men of whom the nation is proud', their ships 'like jewels flashing in the night of time'. These conquerors, 'adventurers', 'settlers', traders, 'hunters for gold or pursuers of fame' (he names such pirates and sackers of cities as Sir Francis Drake), are indiscriminately described as 'bearers of a spark from the sacred fire' – heirs of Prometheus.

Marlow's first words – 'And this also has been one of the dark places of the earth' – lead us to anticipate an end to this claptrap. Marlow avoids the worst of the first narrator's verbal clichés, but not his clichés of thought. For him, too, dark means simply uncivilized. To be a man is to get on with your work, to 'face the darkness . . . without thinking much about it'. For the incomprehensible is 'also detestable', and 'what saves us is efficiency'.

> The conquest of the earth, which mostly means the taking it away from those who have a different complexion or slightly flatter noses than ourselves, is not a pretty thing when you look into it too much. What redeems it is the idea only. An idea at the back of it; not a sentimental pretence but an idea; and an unselfish belief in the idea – something you can set up, and bow down before, and offer a sacrifice to . . .   [10]

Marlow has plenty of opportunity in what follows to justify his distinction between 'sentimental pretence' and his own redeeming 'idea'. His superiority is evident in his clear-sighted recognition that it is 'not a pretty thing', but virtually forfeited by his distaste for looking into anything 'too much'.

Again Marlow parades his superiority to his 'excellent aunt' who, having been taken in by 'all that humbug' treats him 'like an emissary of light': 'I ventured to hint that the company was run for profit'. But again Marlow undercuts his own position immediately afterwards by his generalizations on 'how out of touch with truth women are':

> They live in a world of their own, and there had never been anything like it, and never can be. It is too beautiful altogether, and if they were to set it up it would go to pieces before the first sunset. Some confounded fact we men have been living contentedly with ever since the day of creation would start up and knock the whole thing over.   [18]

We are to learn what 'facts' he is prepared to live with. He descends by the end into lies far more sentimental and damning than those of the first narrator or his aunt.

If Marlow's 'redeeming idea' is not that the colonist is 'something like an emissary of light', what is it? He is shortly to be describing colonialism as 'rapacious and pitiless folly'. His sense of taking part in 'a sordid farce' is strengthened by the superior reality, the naturalness, of the natives:

> Now and then a boat from the shore gave one a momentary contact with reality. It was paddled by black fellows. . . . They shouted, sang; their bodies streamed with perspiration; they had faces like grotesque masks – these chaps; but they had bone, muscle, a wild vitality, an intense energy of movement, that was as natural and true as the surf along their coast. They wanted no excuse for being there.   [19–20]

What is Marlow's excuse for being there? The next black men he sees are a chain-gang. They toil past him 'with that complete, deathlike indifference of unhappy savages'. He admits that he is 'a part of the great cause of these high and just proceedings'. A moment later he steps into 'the gloomy circle of some Inferno':

Black shapes crouched, lay, sat between the trees leaning against the trunks, clinging to the earth, half coming out, half effaced within the dim light, in all the attitudes of pain, abandonment, and despair. Another mine on the cliff went off, followed by a slight shudder of the soil under my feet. The work was going on. The work! And this was the place where some of the helpers had withdrawn to die. They were dying slowly – it was very clear. They were not enemies, they were not criminals, they were nothing earthly now, – nothing but black shadows of disease and starvation, lying confusedly in the greenish gloom. Brought from all the recesses of the coast in all the legality of time contracts, lost in uncongenial surroundings, fed on unfamiliar food, they sickened, became inefficient, and were then allowed to crawl away and rest. [24]

Marlow gives one a ship's biscuit, then returns to his own affairs:

I went to work the next day, turning, so to speak, my back on that station. In that way only it seemed to me I could keep my hold on the redeeming facts of life. Still, one must look about sometimes . . . I asked myself sometimes what it all meant. [33]

He answers himself 'unreal' or 'absurd', and turns away again:

I've never seen anything so unreal in my life. And outside, the silent wilderness surrounding this cleared speck on the earth struck me as something great and invincible, like evil or truth, waiting patiently for the passing away of this fantastic invasion.

A wilderness is by definition something the civilized man turns his back on. Marlow will never discover whether it is evil or truth. The 'redeeming facts of life' shrink to a speck, and that speck Marlow identifies with Kurtz.

From the moment he sees the French gunship 'incomprehensible, firing into a continent', Marlow registers mercilessly the 'insanity', the 'lugubrious drollery' of all he sees. A vast hole is being dug to no purpose. There is a hole in the bottom of the pail of the man trying to put out a fire. There is a brickmaker unable to make any bricks because some essential materials cannot be found and will never be sent. It is a sick real-life version of 'The Hunting of the Snark':

He came as a Baker: but owned, when too late –
And it drove the poor Bellman half mad –
He could only bake Bridecake – for which, I may state,
No materials were to be had.

But Marlow's easy recourse to the words 'absurd' and 'unreal' is a way of shrugging off responsibility.

If he has already lost faith in 'the work', Marlow retains to the end his faith in 'work' and efficiency, oblivious of the fact that all his work is part of 'the work'. He deliberately blinkers himself henceforth to the point where all he can see is rivets – 'a certain quantity of rivets – and rivets were what really Mr. Kurtz wanted, if he had only known it' [40–41]. Marlow rationalizes his escapism by claiming that he likes 'what is in the work, – the chance to find yourself. Your own reality – for yourself, not for others – what no other man can ever know. They can only see the mere show, and never can tell what it really means' [41]. In the circumstances this is pathetic. The truth comes out a few pages later:

> When you have to attend to things of that sort, to the mere incidents of
> the surface, the reality – the reality, I tell you – fades. The inner truth is
> hidden – luckily, luckily. But I felt it all the same; I felt often its
> mysterious stillness watching me at my monkey tricks, just as it watches
> you fellows performing on your respective tight-ropes for – what is it?
> half-a-crown a tumble –   [49]

Here Marlow is asked to be civil by one of his listeners. He apologizes. Don't rock the boat. 'And what does the price matter, if the trick be well done?' But he cannot allow himself to go on thinking of his work as no more than monkey-tricks. At the end he is still justifying himself in terms of his 'power of devotion to an obscure back-breaking business', even when this is no more than 'the faith in your ability for the digging of unostentatious holes to bury the stuff in', the 'stuff' being dead hippo. [71]

When Marlow signed his contract in Brussels, he sold his soul to the company. Marlow himself had an inkling of this ('It was just as though I had been let into some conspiracy' [15]). Brussels itself had always made him think of 'a whited sepulchre' [14]. Was he aware of the rest of that quotation from *Matthew* 23:27?

> Woe unto you, scribes and Pharisees, hypocrites! for ye are like unto
> whited sepulchres, which indeed appear beautiful outward, but are within
> full of dead men's bones, and of all uncleanness.

Minutes after landing at the first station, the inkling deepens into an appalling warning:

> I foresaw that in the blinding sunshine of that land I would become
> acquainted with a flabby, pretending, weak-eyed devil of a rapacious and
> pitiless folly. How insidious he could be, too, I was only to find out several
> months later and a thousand miles farther.   [23]

The warning goes unheeded. Blindly he follows in the footsteps of a Faust-like man who, blessed with great gifts and the highest principles, had been betrayed and degraded by that devil into setting himself up as a god, and using the power that gave him to indulge in 'abominable satisfactions' in the devil's name. Is Marlow's very name an echo of that of Christopher Marlowe, who sold himself to the highest bidder, and followed so closely in the steps of his overreaching hero? Kurtz' final cry: 'The horror! The horror!' is a condensation of the last lines of Faustus.

*　　*　　*

The narrator has told us that the Thames is 'a waterway leading to the uttermost ends of the earth', though it is not until the final sentence of the story that the pride of that claim is qualified by his realization that it also 'seemed to lead into the heart of an immense darkness'. Marlow connects the black wool being knitted 'feverishly' by the old woman in the Company offices with the white wool round the neck of the dying Negro. Had he not bid her goodbye with the words *morituri te salutant*? There are many such connecting threads. The *raison d'être* for the whole show is ivory.

At each trading station on the Congo, 'the word ivory', we are told, 'would ring in the air for a while – and on we went again into the silence'. The word rings like a refrain on, it seems, every page of 'Heart of Darkness', once we have reached the Congo; and so it should, since it is the holy grail all these 'pilgrims' are seeking, the 'spell' which holds them captive, the tune to which is danced 'the merry dance of death and trade' [20]. Yet though the word 'ivory' chimes insistently, we hear surprisingly little about this substance for which so many men are dying, about where it comes from before it comes into the hands of the traders, or goes to after it leaves them. Nowhere does Marlow mention what this precious substance is used for back in the civilized world. We must make our own connection with the 'bones' the Accountant is toying with on the first page of the story, the dice on which some young Roman is imagined to have squandered his fortune [9], and the billiard-ball to which Kurtz' bald head is compared. These are the invaluable end-products. For the shareholders back in Europe the ivory is converted into wealth which buys leisure for the cultivation of civilized values, the best of which, like the rectitude of Marlow's listeners or the innocence, beauty and honour of the Intended, is founded on a lie.

The price which has to be paid is not only the sordid deaths of so many 'pilgrims' and negroes. Marlow speaks of ivory-traders as if they were involved in a mining operation: 'To tear treasure out of the bowels of the land was their desire, with no more moral purpose at the back of it than there is in burglars breaking into a safe. Who paid the expenses of the noble enterprise I don't know; but the uncle of our manager was leader of that lot' [44]. In Norman Sherry's *Conrad* [p.58] is an obscene photograph of the man himself, Alexandre Delcommune, standing proudly with his rifle by the side of a pile of thirteen hippopotamus heads. Marlow is, at this stage of the story, secure in his moral superiority to such people. But is there not a certain moral obtuseness in the comparison with burgling, and the refusal to look too closely into who paid and what was paid for such enterprises?

> The word 'ivory' rang in the air, was whispered, was sighed. You would think they were praying to it. A taint of imbecile rapacity blew through it all, like a whiff from some corpse. [33]

What corpse? 'Ivory' is a processed, polished word, an evasion, a 'whited sepulchre'. Only three times, towards the end, does Marlow use the word 'tusks', and only once, in the entire story, the word 'elephant' (which slips out in another context). One gathers from Marlow that the traders get the ivory from the natives, and ivory is just something the natives happen to have plenty of. The final link in the chain is one Marlow shrinks from acknowledging, the slaughter, the agony, the protracted deaths of thousands of elephants. The elephants are conspicuous by their absence from Marlow's consciousness.

This would perhaps be a slender thread on which to hang a charge of moral obliquity against Marlow were it not part of a complex web of such threads woven by Conrad. It is, in fact, characteristic of Marlow, in moral or psychological matters, to come to the brink and then turn away with a failure of nerve. The darkness fascinates him, draws him, but he cannot, as Kurtz had done, look into its heart. He is no fool. He knows his limitations. It is not so much that he lacks imagination as that he fears that his imagination might take him out of his depth, as Kurtz' had taken him for all his 'genius'.

And it is not only elephants. There is no description, or even naming, of any of the flora and fauna of Africa. There are many descriptions of the jungle, but always in vague terms, as an impenetrable barrier or incomprehensible face. Marlow obviously fears it. He prefers to stay on his boat, in the little world where he is master. He is very ambivalent about the jungle, and never even attempts to reconcile his wildly fluctuating responses to it. At one extreme he regards it, as he had done those first natives, as providing a standard of reality and sanity against which the artificial human settlements can be judged: 'the silence of the land went home to one's very heart – its mystery, its greatness, the amazing reality of its concealed life' [90]. But at the other extreme it is 'the lurking death', 'the hidden evil', 'the unseen presence of victorious corruption'. We remember his description of the Romans in Britain having to live in the midst of 'the incomprehensible, which is also detestable'. Since he refuses to enter the jungle, either in the body or in imagination, it can only be for him a mirror, or a screen on which he projects whatever preconceptions are already in his mind, the blank gaze of a sphinx:

> I wondered whether the stillness on the face of the immensity looking at us two were meant as an appeal or as a menace. What were we who had strayed in here? Could we handle that dumb thing, or would it handle us?

I felt how big, how confoundedly big, was that thing that couldn't talk, and perhaps was deaf as well. What was in there? I could see a little ivory coming out from there, and I had heard Mr. Kurtz was in there. I had heard enough about it, too – God knows! Yet somehow it didn't bring any image with it – no more than if I had been told an angel or a fiend was in there. [38]

It is like the surrounding darkness into which, in Lawrence's *The Rainbow*, Ursula gazes from the little clearing lit by man's consciousness, and sees there gleams which might be the swords of angels or the flash of fangs.

Marlow's ambivalence about the jungle explains his failure to understand Kurtz. Before he meets Kurtz, he takes him to be a gifted, good and brave man, whose brightness has been heightened, not extinguished, by the surrounding darkness. After having met him, Marlow regards him as one who has simply gone too far into the darkness, too far from the sanity of rivets, and has succumbed to the horror, the nameless abominations, which lurk there. But as we have seen there is no reason to suppose that the jungle contains anything of the sort. The horror Kurtz finally sees is inside his own skull. It is not, as Marlow thinks, the dying Kurtz who is a 'hollow sham', but 'the original Kurtz' [98]. The journalist who sums Kurtz up as an 'extremist', who would have made a splendid leader of an extreme party – 'any party' [104] – is close to the mark. In his zeal for the cause of 'the Suppression of Savage Customs', Kurtz had claimed 'unbounded' power for good for the white races: 'we approach them [savages] with the might as of a deity' [72]. His extremism manifests itself in 'burning noble words', soaring perorations. To put such a man in a position where everything is permitted ('there was nothing on earth to prevent him killing whom he jolly well pleased' [81]), is to subject him to the same test to which Shakespeare subjects Angelo. And the result is the same: Benevolence suddenly collapses and is supplanted by its opposite: 'Exterminate all the brutes!' [72].

And the vital twist, the mysterious chemical change that converts the resisting high-minded puritan to the being of murder and madness, is that occult crossover of Nature's maddened force – like a demon – into the brain that had rejected her. [Ted Hughes, *WP* 114]

Marlow is no such extremist. Unlike Kurtz he can recognize a 'remote kinship' with the savages and their customs. He admits that there is even an 'appeal' to him in the 'fiendish row' [52]. In this he is like Escalus, who suggests to Angelo that he, in certain circumstances, might have done that for which he now condemns Claudio. Angelo denies his common humanity with fornicators, as Kurtz with savages, and that part of himself he denies then turns upon him and overturns the whited sepulchre of his psyche. It is, apparently, a common psychological phenomenon, this sudden psychic flip from extreme high-mindedness to extreme viciousness, from the tightest discipline to utter licence.

Later Marlow comes to the brink of understanding:

> But the wilderness had found him out early, and had taken on him a
> terrible vengeance for the fantastic invasion. I think it had whispered to
> him things about himself which he did not know, things of which he had
> no conception till he took counsel with this great solitude – and the
> whisper had proved irresistibly fascinating. It echoed loudly within him
> because he was hollow at the core . . .   [83]

The ellipsis is Marlow's. It is his way of saying 'I don't want to go any further
down that path'. A moment later he interrupts his informant, shouting : 'I
don't want to know anything of the ceremonies used when approaching Mr.
Kurtz'. To know more would be too 'withering to one's belief in mankind' [95].
It would be to reveal that the heart of darkness is not only in Kurtz: it is in
Marlow himself: it is in the best of men. It is the heart of man.

                                        *   *   *

Marlow peeps over the edge and is permitted to draw back his hesitating foot.
But he has seen enough to alienate him temporarily from his species:

> I found myself back in the sepulchral city resenting the sight of people
> hurrying through the streets to filch a little money from each other, to
> devour their infamous cookery, to gulp their unwholesome beer, to dream
> their insignificant and silly dreams. . . . Their bearing, which was simply
> the bearing of commonplace individuals going about their business in the
> assurance of perfect safety, was offensive to me like the outrageous
> flauntings of folly in the face of a danger it is unable to comprehend.   [102]

Unlike the Ancient Mariner, he has no desire to enlighten them, stops no
unwilling wedding guest in the street; merely regards himself as not very well,
suffering from a feverish imagination. Though he is subsequently to tell his
tale to equally complacent people, he shows little sign of finding them offen-
sive, and they regard him as no more than a good spinner of yarns.

Marlow has, he tells us, a temperamental aversion to lying:

> You know I hate, detest, and can't bear a lie, not because I am straighter
> than the rest of us, but simply because it appals me. There is a taint of
> death, a flavour of mortality in lies – which is exactly what I hate and
> detest in the world – what I want to forget. It makes me miserable and
> sick, like biting something rotten would do.   [38–9]

Yet he ends the story a liar, a purveyor of the shabbiest humbug, a sentimental-
ist and a moral coward.

Marlow calls the Intended's ignorance a 'great and saving illusion'.
What it saves is not so much the Intended as Marlow himself from the darkness

of the truth. That the Intended should express her grief that she will never see Kurtz again with the words 'never, never, never' is one of Conrad's most savage ironies, reminding us, as it does, of Lear's lament for Cordelia, a young and innocent woman who did not need to be protected from the truth, who not only had an aversion to sentimental lies but saw that even the whitest of them leads to the triumph of evil, for whom truth, not illusion, was redeeming, even if it lead to the overthrow of the state and her own death. A character in Ted Hughes' *Eat Crow* says of Lear's line: 'the king is using this word NEVER like a knife, to carve up his own insides. . . . He's forcing it down into the last, deepest cellars and underground resistance of his life-illusion' [16]. Nothing could be further than the Intended's use of the word to seal her ignorance from any staining truth. And this 'innocence' is what Marlow ultimately sets up, bows down before, and offers a sacrifice to, the sacrifice of his own integrity, his real innocence. He becomes an accomplice in the great lie and the great crime.

Conrad has often been accused of identifying too closely with Marlow, of failing to see how inadequately Marlow interprets his experiences and how suspect is the probity and integrity on which he so prides himself. Conrad is certainly, to a large extent, Marlow. Marlow's values are Conrad's: the belief in the redeeming idea of colonialism (Conrad was still able to speak, after his Congo experience, of 'the civilizing work in Africa'), efficient work as an end in itself, irrespective of its purpose (like the British officer in *Bridge on the River Kwai*). But the Conrad who is Marlow is Conrad the seaman, Conrad the employee, the member of society, perhaps even the author of the worst of his fiction; it is not Conrad the author of 'Heart of Darkness'. Marlow, in spinning his yarn, makes himself the hero of it – again unlike the Ancient Mariner; offers himself with disingenuous modesty as the standard by which others are judged. But his creator accepts the curse of the Ancient Mariner, which is also the curse of the great imaginative writer, the obligation to accuse himself, to tell the deepest truth that is in him, however humiliating that may be. If Conrad, Conrad the man, was a 'mere animal' before the Congo, after it he was, in the judgement of Conrad the writer, a mere criminal. Marlow is his criminal self.

Whether the writer accuses himself of complicity in a larger, almost universal crime, or of some unique aberration (for which it would be best for all concerned if he were put out of his misery), as in the case of Kafka, the truth the imagination unlocks is always general, always representative. I, the hypocrite reader, must recognize such a writer, even a writer as extreme and eccentric as Baudelaire, as 'mon semblable, – mon frère' [Preface to *Fleurs du Mal*]. We are all guilty of Marlow's crime.

What was happening in the Congo in the eighteen-nineties is not just a regrettable page of history. Almost every act we perform (or neglect to perform) has endless repercussions. Every product we buy, investment we make, job we do, is one end of a chain which leads, in many cases, to the ends of the earth. The other end is a burning rainforest, a desecrated waterway, animals dying needlessly in fear and pain, native peoples evicted, exploited or exterminated. Like Marlow we prefer not to follow the chain too far. Like his London friends we prefer not to follow it at all. At one point Marlow turns on them with scathing words we might well apply to ourselves:

> Here you all are, each moored with two good addresses, like a hulk with two anchors, a butcher round one corner, a policeman round another, excellent appetites, and temperature normal – you hear – normal from year's end to year's end. [68]

But Marlow returns to Europe to become part of the great conspiracy of silence. In 1946 Jung wrote:

> But already we are fascinated by the possibilities of atomic fission and promise ourselves a Golden Age – the surest guarantee that the abomination of desolation will grow to limitless dimensions. And who or what is it that causes all this? It is none other than that harmless (!), ingenuous, inventive and sweetly reasonable human spirit who unfortunately is abysmally unconscious of the demonism that still clings to him. Worse, this spirit does everything to avoid looking himself in the face, and we all help him like mad. [*Collected Works*, 9.i.253]

Marlow turned back from the brink. Conrad the man looked over, then turned back. Conrad the artist looked himself (and therefore Western man) in the face long enough to create this one supreme work. So dark, so terrible a vision had to be externalized in a work of art, in order to exorcise it from his thoughts if not from his dreams. Life must go on.

Eliot twice took epigraphs from 'Heart of Darkness'. Two quotations from Eliot seem particularly apt here, the first for Marlow:

> Human kind
> Cannot bear very much reality. ['Burnt Norton']

the second for Conrad

> After such knowledge, what forgiveness?
> ['Gerontion']

17 LAWRENCE AND THE RESURRECTION OF PAN

At the beginning of the Christian era, voices were heard off the coasts of Greece, out to sea, on the Mediterranean, wailing: 'Pan is dead! Great Pan is dead!'
[D.H. Lawrence, 'Pan in America']

The three books which meant most to Lawrence in his formative years were the Authorized Version of the Bible, the Congregational Hymnbook, and Palgrave's *Golden Treasury of Songs and Lyrics*. Palgrave was crammed with Wordsworth, who exerted a more powerful influence on Lawrence than any other writer, an influence which proved to be a very mixed blessing.

Some of the earliest Wordsworth poems memorably gave voice to sentiments of 'natural piety' which would no doubt have been Lawrence's in any case, contrasting 'Nature's holy plan' with 'what man has made of man' ('Written in Early Spring'). But as early as 'The Crown' (1915) Lawrence was ridiculing Wordsworth's anthropomorphism and sentimentality:

Let no one suffer, they have said. No mouse shall be caught by a cat, no mouse. It is a transgression. Every mouse shall become a pet, and every cat shall lap milk in peace, from the saucer of utter benevolence. This is the millennium, the golden age that is to be, when all shall be domesticated, and the lion and the leopard and the hawk shall come to our door to lap milk and to peck the crumbs, and no sound shall be heard but the lowing of fat cows and the baa-ing of fat sheep. . . . The tiger, the hawk, the weasel, are beautiful things to me; and as they strike the dove and the hare, that is the will of God, it is a consummation.
[*Reflections*, 275–6, 297]

Yet he never quite escaped its influence. What sounds would Lawrence rather hear than lowing and baa-ing? He seems deaf to what Hughes calls the 'screeching finales' of the victims of predators. It is possible to praise the perfection of the predator without discounting the prey. When Hughes claims that the tiger 'blesses with a fang' ('Tiger-Psalm'), he has earned the right to make such a claim by paying full attention to suffering:

Creation quaked voices –
It was a cortège
Of mourning and lament
Crow could hear and he looked around fearfully.
['Crow Tyrannosaurus']

Even Crow is not entirely heedless, but has the grace to weep as he walks and stabs.

The Wordsworth poem which remained Lawrence's favourite for most of his life was the 'Intimations' Ode, which no doubt helped to imprint in him the dualism against which he had to struggle for so long. For though Lawrence quickly came to rebel against Wordsworth's rejection of earth in favour of heaven and of body in favour of soul, and to reverse that choice, he accepted for many years that such a choice had to be made.

Another classic dualist text which Lawrence met early was Plato's *Phaedrus*:

> Pure was the light and pure were we from the pollution of the walking sepulchre which we call a body, to which we are bound like an oyster to its shell.
>
> [57]

In Plato's (or Socrates') parable, the mind or ego is the driver of a chariot drawn by two horses, one white (spirit) and one black (body). The parable seeks to justify any amount of cruelty to the body and its needs and desires:

> The driver . . . jerks the bit from between the teeth of the lustful horse, drenches his abusive tongue and jaws with blood, and forcing his legs and haunches against the ground reduces him to torment.
>
> [63]

This image of cruelty to a horse, representing the delicate sensitivity of the body, affected Lawrence so powerfully that he returned to it several times in his works. In *Women in Love* there is Gerald's bullying of the Arab mare at the level crossing, which prefigures his later relationships with women and his final self-destruction. In *St. Mawr*, Rico precipitates the crisis when he treats the stallion exactly as Plato had recommended. In *Women in Love* the horse threatens to fall backwards on top of its rider; in *St. Mawr* it actually does so. It is a part of themselves, their own affective life, their Pan life, that such riders are damaging. Lou sees Pan in St. Mawr. In his 'London Letter' to *The Laughing Horse*, Lawrence equates the death of Pan with the death of 'the horse in us'. In The First Lady Chatterley, Connie and Clifford argue about Plato's parable, which Connie sees as suicidal, a recipe for disaster.

Gradually Lawrence came to see all cruelty, perversion, pollution and sterility as a direct result of such blasphemous conceit as that of Socrates and Plato. Lawrence first responded by flying to the opposite extreme:

> My great religion is a belief in the blood, the flesh, as being wiser than the intellect. We can go wrong in our minds. But what our blood feels and believes and says, is always true. The intellect is only a bit and a bridle.
>
> [L I 503]

Lawrence is here quoting the Psalms: 'Be ye not as the horse, or as the mule, which have no understanding: whose mouth must be held in with bit and bridle' [32:9]. This is the Christianity of St. John of the Cross, Augustine, Aquinas, and the Puritans ('to whom all things are impure') down to

Lawrence's day. In the same year in which Lawrence began *Lady Chatterley's Lover*, Eliot quoted with approval St. John of the Cross: 'Hence the soul cannot be possessed of the divine union, until it has divested itself of the love of created beings'.

Lawrence soon saw the need to modify his position and began to write on this issue in a spirit of reconciliation. In *The Rainbow*, the rainbow itself was a symbol of reconciliation, harmony, between the sexes, between the universe and the innermost, between God and man. The rainbow is also the crown in the essay of that name: 'The iridescence which is darkness at once and light, the two-in-one'. Lawrence here modifies traditional dualism by arguing that the lion (body) and unicorn (spirit) are not fighting for ultimate victory, which would be the death of both, but for equilibrium. Yet even here there is no questioning the basic duality of existence. Whether he took sides or strove for reconciliation, Lawrence perpetuated a dualism he was unable to see beyond until he reached the American South-West.

✳   ✳   ✳

The elements of Lawrence's vision were there from the start – his love of nature and his ability to activate the responses of others to it, his hatred of urban ugliness and mechanization, his respect for the life of the body and its feelings. No great writer had ever been in a better position, growing up in a miner's home in the Nottinghamshire/Derbyshire coalfield, to know first-hand the truth of Wendell Berry's assertion that

> Fossil fuels have always been produced at the expense of local ecosystems and of local human communities. The fossil-fuel economy is the industrial economy par excellence, and it assigns no value to local life, natural or human. [10]

As early as 1909 Lawrence expressed this as powerfully as it has ever been expressed in the opening paragraph of 'Odour of Chrysanthemums':

> The small locomotive engine, Number 4, came clanking, stumbling down from Selston with seven full waggons. It appeared round the corner with loud threats of speed, but the colt that it startled from among th gorse, which still flickered indistinctly in the raw afternoon, outdistanced it at a canter. A woman, walking up the railway-line to Underwood, drew back into the hedge, held her basket aside, and watched the footplate of the engine advancing. The trucks thumped heavily past, one by one, with slow inevitable movement, as she stood insignificantly trapped between the jolting black waggons and the hedge; then they curved away towards the coppice where the withered oak-leaves dropped noiselessly, while the birds, pulling at the scarlet hips beside the track, made off into the dusk that had already crept into the spinney. In the open, the smoke from the engine sank and cleaved to the rough grass. The fields were dreary and

forsaken, and in the marshy strip that led to the whimsey, a reedy
pit-pond, the fowls had already abandoned their run among the alders, to
roost in the tarred fowl-house. The pit-bank loomed up beyond the pond,
flames like red sores licking its ashy sides, in the afternoon's stagnant
light. Just beyond rose the tapering chimneys and the clumsy black
headstocks of Brinsley Colliery. The two wheels were spinning fast up
against the sky, and the winding-engine rapped out its little spasms. The
miners were being turned up. [*Prussian Officer* 181]

The engine has the dignity of a number, but the woman has no name. The
engine is a ludicrously ineffective machine, yet all life which cannot fly away
(including the human beings trapped by the economic system) are subject to
it. Nature here seems to have given up the struggle against pollution, as though
succumbing to some hellish disease spreading from the pit-bank. The locomo-
tive is only an extension of the larger, equally clumsy and spasmodic machine,
the colliery itself. We do not need to be told that the miners are often turned
up maimed or dead. The paragraph is far more than background or scene
painting. The subsequent story renders its meanings in terms of the specific
tragedy of a single family.

And these meanings remain constant throughout Lawrence's life. They
emerge most notably in the Wiggiston chapter of *The Rainbow*, the 'Industrial
Magnate' chapter of *Women in Love*, and in Connie's drive through Tevershall
in *Lady Chatterley's Lover*. There Connie sees

the utter negation of natural beauty, the utter negation of the gladness of
life, the utter absence of the instinct for shapely beauty which every bird
and beast has, the utter death of the human intuitive faculty. [152]

The cinema offers *A Woman's Love* as a degraded substitute for the Eros
which has been exiled to its last fastness in the woods artificially preserved
for Clifford, the presiding Mammon, to look out on, shoot pheasants in, and
drive his motorized wheelchair through. The pit-banks are the visible stinking
excrement of the whole operation.

The beginning of *The Rainbow* harks back to a pre-industrial paradise.
The early Brangwens had lived in cyclic, not in linear or historical time – an
earthbound life with all the advantages and disadvantages of rootedness. The
main disadvantage was the mental and imaginative and spiritual inertia. After
the day's work was over there was nothing for them to do but gaze into the
back of the fire. The industrial revolution, arriving belatedly here, brings not
only the pits, but also improved communications and education, the lure of
travel, knowledge, experience – ever widening circles of consciousness. The
whole organization of the novel is in terms of the dualistic alternatives of the
horizontal (the land, the life of the senses) and the vertical (Lincoln Cathedral,
mental or spiritual aspiration), with the possibility held out of reconciliation
in the arched (the rainbow). Ursula pursues a series of false rainbows

(transcendental religion, romantic love, knowledge). The true rainbow she sees at the end of the novel symbolizes the reconciliation of all the opposites, worker and employer, man and woman, body and spirit, man and God, but it is only a momentary vision. It tells her, very vaguely, how the life that is in her wants to be lived, but not how to live it.

Lawrence's search for the life proper to his species was interrupted by the war. The war put a spear through the side of his hopes for mankind. The news from the front and the moral debacle at home combined with his ill-health, marital problems, and the persecution of himself and his work by the authorities to produce a misanthropy verging on madness. By the time he finished *The Rainbow*, the ordinary human world had come to seem to him a dead shell, like the dead shells of all the individual egos of which it is composed, artificially insulating humanity from nature and its gods. Ursula's rainbow vision becomes possible only when she has broken that shell, suffered an ego-death, and thereby entered another more real world where inner and outer realities are no longer polarized.

Lawrence was later to call this period of his life his 'nightmare', and the novel which came out of it, *Women in Love*, would be well described as 'a nightmare of mental disintegration and spiritual emptiness'. The hero, Birkin, imagines a future world, after some debacle, cleansed of humanity – 'just the long grass waving, and a hare sitting up'. Birkin recapitulates many of Lawrence's own earlier mistakes. His attachment to the shell of a dead world of ideas and values is what has to be violently broken when Hermione smashes a ball of lapis lazuli onto his head. Birkin, barely conscious, walks to a nearby hillside, takes off his clothes, rolls in the vegetation, presses himself against the trees. It is not delirium, any more than the behaviour of the Bacchantes was delirium. It is a return to sanity, a rediscovery of where he belongs and what really matters. The coolness and subtlety of the vegetation comes into his blood and heals him:

> Why should he pretend to have anything to do with human beings at all? Here was his world, he wanted nobody and nothing but the lovely, subtle, responsive vegetation, and himself, his own living self.   [107]

Of course he cannot stay there, and Lawrence is far from advocating a return to nature in that simplistic sense – he was later to satirize the hermit's attempt to be through with the world of men. The point is rather that nature should be there, within and without us, a perpetual source of healing and renewal.

Before 1914 Lawrence's work had been anthropocentric, concerned almost exclusively with human relationships, with nature as a background – a very lively and prominent background, but a background nonetheless. Subsequently it became much more central. What saved Lawrence's sanity in the worst days of the war was his deepening faith in the non-human world as a source of health and wholeness:

What massive creeping hell is let loose nowadays. It isn't my disordered
imagination. There is a wagtail sitting on the gate-post. I see how sweet
and swift heaven is.   [*Letters*, II, 331]

In the years which followed, Lawrence's fiction suffered from his loss
of belief in people. You can't have novels without people. But you can have
poems without people. Lawrence's greatest work of the immediate post-war
period was his finest collection of poems *Birds, Beasts and Flowers*.

*   *   *

In *The First Lady Chatterley* Lawrence was to write of 'a new flux that would
change one away from the old self as a landscape is transfigured by earthquake
and lava floods'. Sicily changed Lawrence in just such a way, and provided
him with rich imagery of such transformation. What emerges through the
fissure in these poems is not angels but streams of red-hot lava, royal snakes,
hounds of hell pursuing Persephone. All the flora and fauna of Sicily are but
manifestations of a deeper more potent life in the underworld, the world under
the world.

Lawrence's creed, which he offers as an alternative to Benjamin
Franklin's narrowly anthropocentric creed, focuses on the opening up of communications between the human and the non-human, the self and the not-self,
the conscious and the unconscious. Lawrence believed:

'That I am I.'

'That my soul is a dark forest.'

'That my known self will never be more than a little clearing in the
  forest.'

'That gods, strange gods, come forth from the forest into the clearing
  of my known self, and then go back.'

'That I must have the courage to let them come and go.'

'That I will never let mankind put anything over me, but that I will try
  always to recognize

and submit to the gods in me and the gods in other men and women.'

[*Studies* 22]

These strange gods are symbolized in the poems by birds, beasts and flowers.
There are several poems, 'Snake', 'Man and Bat' and 'Fish', for example, about
how difficult it is even to simply let them come and go, to shed all the humanistic assumptions which mankind (the voice of one's education) has been putting
over one all one's life. The strong temptation is to anthropomorphize flora and
fauna, which is an attempt to accommodate them to that which is known.

Lawrence's misanthropy was in one sense a sickness, but in another
a healthy purging of his hitherto anthropocentric vision and of what was left
of the anthropomorphic attitude to Nature of his youth. Man now appears on
the scene, if at all, as the intruder, the aberration, who, in the presence of the

sacred, can think of nothing better to do than to try to kill it (or, in psychological terms, refuse to acknowledge it, drive it into the seething darkness of the unconscious).

In 'Snake' Lawrence castigates the mistakes not only of unregenerate men, but also of his own earlier self, concentrating into a few minutes of poetic time an education in consciousness which had taken him decades. For by the end of the poem the narrator, our representative, has learned that he must expiate the pettiness of the whole perverse rigmarole of sin and guilt which Western Man has allowed to be foisted onto his psyche.

The narrator's problem is as much with the fissure into which the snake draws itself as with the phallic snake itself. In the fruit poems he calls it 'the female part'. But of course the fissure is very much more than the vagina. It is, among other things, an image for the creative or mythic imagination, corresponding to Joseph Campbell's description of myth as 'the secret opening through which the inexhaustible energies of the cosmos pour into human cultural manifestation' [*Hero*, 13]. As early as 1915, Lawrence had used the image in connection with the female, with prophetesses and 'some of the great women saints': 'the truth came as through a fissure from the depths and the burning darkness that lies out of the depth of time'. The fate of Cassandra at the hands of the male (including Apollo) Lawrence takes to be

> symbolic of what mankind has done to her since – raped and despoiled and mocked her, to their own ruin. It is not your brain you must trust to, nor your will – but to that fundamental pathetic faculty for receiving the hidden waves that come from the depths of life, and for transferring them to the unreceptive world. It is something which happens below the consciousness, and below the range of the will – it is something which is unrecognised and frustrated and destroyed.   [L II 297–8]

In *Kangaroo* we find:

> Alone like a pythoness on her tripod, like the oracle alone above the fissure into the unknown. The oracle, the fissure down into the unknown, the strange exhalations from the dark, the strange words that the oracle must utter. Strange cruel, pregnant words: the new term of consciousness.
>   [310]

And in a 1926 letter to Rolf Gardiner: 'We'll have to establish some spot on earth, that will be the fissure into the under world, like the oracle at Delphos' [V 591]. We are familiar with the Delphic oracle, through Greek tragedy, as the oracle of Apollo; but Lawrence is clearly thinking of the original Delphic oracle which was the Oracle of Mother Earth. (Cashford and Baring speak of 'her priestesses, sitting in the hot sun beside cracks in the earth' [305].) When Apollo wounded Python with his arrows, the serpent fled to the Oracle at Delphi 'but Apollo dared follow him into the shrine, and there despatched him beside the sacred chasm' [Graves, *Greek Myths* I, 76]. Zeus demanded expiation, but Apollo, having coaxed the secret of prophesy from Pan, 'seized the Delphic Oracle and retained its priestess, called the Pythoness, in his own service'.

For Lawrence Etna was such a 'fissure into the under world'; and the debate within him between the voice of spontaneous reverence for the creatures of that world, and the voice of his education, is a debate between Dionysos and Apollo, with Apollo, the apotheosis of reason, characteristically resorting to violence. Since the narrator in the poem is not Lawrence but a representative of our civilization it is essential that Apollo wins, by fair means or foul, leaving the man 'accursed'. He repents too late, seeing belatedly that the snake is

> Like a king in exile, uncrowned in the underworld,
> Now due to be crowned again.   [CP 351]

We cannot but think of Lucifer, once brightest of angels, and of what Frederick Carter calls 'the mysterious triple communion in the garden between woman and snake and man from which it would seem came the discovery of seed and its purpose' [BM 29]. The assault on the snake is a version of the primal sin, which, for Lawrence, was not the eating of the apple but the bruising of the head of the serpent. Kate Leslie in *The Plumed Serpent* is the new Eve, released, at last, from the compulsion to violate the serpent:

> It was a snake, with a subtle pattern along its soft dark back, lying there over a big stone, with its head sunk down to earth.
> It felt her presence, too, for suddenly, with incredible soft quickness, it contracted itself down the boulder, and she saw it entering a little gap in the bottom of the wet wall.
> The hole was not very big. And as it entered it quickly looked back, poising its little, dark, wicked, pointed head, and flickered a dark tongue. Then it passed on, slowly easing its dark length into the hole.
> When it had all gone in, Kate could see the last fold still, and the flat little head resting on the fold, like the devil with his chin on his arms, looking out of a loop-hole. So the wicked sparks of the eyes looked out at her, from within the recess. Watching out of its own invisibility.
> So she wondered over it, as it lay in its hidden places. At all the unseen things in the hidden places of the earth. And she wondered if it was disappointed at not being able to rise higher in creation: to be able to run on four feet, and not keep its belly on the ground.
> Perhaps not! Perhaps it had its own peace. She felt a certain reconciliation between herself and it.   [425]

The witty, throwaway style of 'Peach' or 'Figs' will not serve when it is a matter of recognizing and submitting to the gods of snakes, bats or fishes.

What is needed is a technique for shutting out the voices of education and 'listening-in to the voices of the honourable beasts that call in the dark paths of the veins of our body, from the God in the heart' [*Phoenix* 759]. Description pulls us towards betraying similes. A pike is not, in the last analysis, 'like a lout on an obscure pavement'. He is not like anything in our world:

> I had made a mistake, I didn't know him,
> This grey, monotonous soul in the water,
> This intense individual in shadow,
> Fish-alive.
>
> I didn't know his God.
> I didn't know his God.   ['Fish']

Lawrence had an almost occult insight into the being of non-human creatures, even into the spirit of landscapes; but in the best poems of *Birds, Beasts and Flowers*, having gone further than any other English poet into the non-human life mode, he has to acknowledge the essential unknowability of it and stand in silent awe, in the presence of gods not his. One of those gods was Lucifer, once brightest of angels, now exiled to the underworld, but 'due to be crowned again'. According to Jung, when God cast Lucifer out of heaven, he cut off a vital part of himself, his link with the world of the flesh; he repudiated nature itself. Lawrence always associated Satan with fallen Pan.

Lawrence also frequently gives to the god of the flora and fauna and of the underworld of the human unconscious the name of Dionysus or Hades (Pluto), who, according to Heraclitus, are one. The courage to admit messengers from that realm is only a stage in the journey. Much greater courage is needed to abandon the world of normal human consciousness altogether and follow those messengers back through the fissure into their world. That shamanic journey, is already adumbrated in one or two of the fruit poems, 'Grapes' for example:

> And if we sip the wine, we find dreams coming upon us
> Out of the imminent night.
> Nay, we find ourselves crossing the fern-scented frontiers
> Of the world before the floods, where man was dark and evasive
> And the tiny vine-flower rose of all roses, perfumed,
> And all in naked communion communicating as now our clothed
>   vision can never communicate.

Even beyond the journey into 'naked communion' is the leave-taking, the 'Orphic farewell' of dissolution described in 'Medlars and Sorb Apples':

> Going down the strange lanes of hell, more and more intensely alone,
> The fibres of the heart parting one after the other

And yet the soul continuing, naked-footed, ever more vividly
   embodied
Like a flame blown whiter and whiter
In a deeper and deeper darkness
Ever more exquisite, distilled in separation.

For the full exploration of that dark region, without benefit of intoxication, we must wait for Lawrence's last poems, when he had to prepare
himself in imagination for the 'imminent night' of death. The only fully open
soul is that of a dying man. 'Bavarian Gentians' must come very close to
rediscovering in Lawrence's own soul the mysteries celebrated at Eleusis. Here
Lawrence holds back from describing the wedding of Persephone and Pluto
which takes place on the other side of his own death. In the rituals at Eleusis
there was, apparently, no description, only a showing, perhaps the showing of
a single ear of corn, but a showing which, given the receptive spiritual state of
the participants, was at that moment a hierophany. Yet even in the magnificent
spiritual and poetic achievement of 'The Ship of Death', Lawrence found
himself betrayed back (partly by the Orphic myths and esoteric oriental doctrines he was studying) to the world of that which we can presume to understand. Here he undertook to describe and invest with attributes whatever lies
beyond the life of the body, and that, he realized, is to violate the tabernacle:

But anyone who shall ascribe attributes to God or oblivion
let him be cast out, for blasphemy.
For God is a deeper forgetting far than sleep
and all description is a blasphemy.   ['Tabernacle']

Can we imagine poems which would eschew all description? They would
indeed be 'new, strange flowers'.

           *   *   *

It seems that in the buoyant optimism of the first months of his relationship
with Frieda Lawrence thought he could reconcile in himself Apollo and Dionysus, Christ and Pan:

I worship Christ, I worship Jehovah, I worship Pan, I worship
Aphrodite. . . . I want them all, all the gods. They are all God. But I must
serve in real love. If I take my whole, passionate, spiritual and physical
love to the woman who in return loves me, that is how I serve God. And
my hymn and my game of joy is my work.   [*Phoenix* 307]

By 1915 he felt he would have to make a choice. In 'The Crown' Lawrence
discusses the two eternities, the Christian eternity, which is ahead, and the
pagan eternity:

291

If I look at the eternity behind, back to the source, then there is for me
one eternity, one only. And this is the pagan eternity, the eternity of Pan,
of Dionysos, of the sensualist, and the scientist, and the mystic. This is
the eternity we have veered round to, in private life, during the past few
years.   [*Reflections*, 300]

This is perhaps Lawrence's first use of Pan in this large sense, not as specific
local god, nor the sinister, rather Gothic and literary figure of some of his
short stories, nor as a way of idealizing the virility of some of his heroes, but
as all the pagan gods rolled into one, the Pan of Pantheism: 'Pan, All: what
you see when you see in full' [*St. Mawr* 65]. Why Lawrence's dissatisfaction
with the present should have caused him to veer round towards the pagan
eternity of Pan is explained by Jung:

The unsatisfied yearning of the artist reaches back to the primordial
image in the unconscious which is best fitted to compensate the
inadequacy and one-sidedness of the present.   [*The Spirit in Man*, 82, 3]

Jung sees the reactivation of such images as the most valuable task the artist
can perform: 'He has plunged into the healing and redeeming depths of the
collective psyche' [105].

Whenever the collective unconscious becomes a living experience and is
brought to bear upon the conscious outlook of an age, this event is a
creative act which is of importance for a whole epoch.   [ibid 98]

Lawrence's mature pantheism is very far from Wordsworth's. Lawrence certainly believed in impulses from woods and mountains, but not that
they took the form of personal lessons about moral good and evil. Though
there is a good deal that is mawkish and overblown and anthropomorphic in
Lawrence's very early writings about nature, as early as *The White Peacock*
we find a striking awareness of nature's impersonality and harshness. Annable,
the first Pan figure, is no noble savage. His rejection of the insulation society
offers against nature costs him his life.

Later, as soon as he was able, Lawrence took himself to some of
the least comfortable and processed environments on earth and exposed his
pantheism to the spirit of those places – to the lava-streaked slopes of Etna,
the steaming jungles of Ceylon, the Australian outback, the mountains and
deserts of the American South-West. These places are inimical to man, the
intruder. His attempts to import a human scale of values seem both ridiculous
and doomed. Man can live in these places, but only man racially and religiously
adapted, and with the aid of rituals and consciousness evolved over thousands
of years. The wilderness does not need man. Wordsworth's world loses all meaning without man, whose mind invests it with meaning, virtually creates it.

The challenge was now to find a way to write about people, in fiction, without surrendering the newly won biocentric vision. And what, more than anything else, enabled Lawrence to do this, was his closeness, from 1922 to 1925, to the Indians of the American South-West. Here Lawrence found, for the first time, a human life which seemed to him truly religious:

> To the Indian there is no conception of a defined God. Creation is a great flood, for ever flowing, in lovely and terrible waves. In everything, the shimmer of creation, and never the finality of the created. Never the distinction between God and God's creation, or between Spirit and Matter. Everything, everything is the wonderful shimmer of creation, it may be a deadly shimmer like lightning or the anger in the little eyes of the bear, it may be the beautiful shimmer of the moving deer, or the pine-boughs softly swaying under snow.
>
> [*Mornings* 61]

'Indians and Entertainment' was written in 1923. 'Dance of the Sprouting Corn' and 'The Hopi Snake Dance' are also fine essays, but it was not until 1928, three years after his return to Europe, that Lawrence was able to express fully what the New Mexico Indians had meant to him:

> It was a vast old religion, greater than anything we know: more starkly and nakedly religious. There is no God, no conception of a god. All is god. But it is not the pantheism we are accustomed to, which expresses itself as 'God is everywhere, God is in everything'. In the oldest religion, everything was alive, not supernaturally but naturally alive. There were only deeper and deeper streams of life, vibrations of life more and more vast. So rocks were alive, but a mountain had a deeper, vaster life than a rock, and it was much harder for a man to bring his spirit, or his energy, into contact with the life of the mountain, and so draw strength from the mountain, as from a great standing well of life, than it was to come into contact with the rock. And he had to put forth a great religious effort. For the whole life-effort of man was to get his life into direct contact with the elemental life of the cosmos, mountain-life, cloud-life, thunder-life, air-life, earth-life, sun-life. To come into immediate *felt* contact, and so derive energy, power, and a dark sort of joy. This effort into sheer naked contact, *without an intermediary or mediator*, is the root meaning of religion, and at the sacred races the runners hurled themselves in a terrible cumulative effort, through the air, which is the life of the clouds, and so of the rain. It was a vast and pure religion, without idols or images, even mental ones. It is the oldest religion, a cosmic religion the same for all peoples, not broken up into specific gods or saviours or systems. It is the religion which precedes the god-concept, and is therefore greater and deeper than any god-religion.
>
> [*Phoenix* 146–7]

In New Mexico two of Lawrence's greatest needs, the need for bodily fulfilment, symbolized by the horse, and the need for spiritual fulfilment, symbolized by the monk, which had, since their reconciliation in the tenuous rainbow symbol of early 1915, run strangely parallel paths, spontaneously met. His search for god and his search for a vivid life of the body here on earth both led him to Pan. The first thing Lawrence wrote at the new ranch was an essay called 'Pan in America', where he defines pantheism as 'a vivid relatedness between the man and the living universe that surrounds him' [*Phoenix* 27]. It is not simply nature-worship, for Pan is fierce and bristling, sometimes malevolent, with the power to blast; and among the creatures of Pan there is an eternal struggle for life, between lives' [29]. There was indeed real danger up there. Three of the Hawks' horses from the Del Monte ranch below were killed by lightning. The very pine tree in front of Lawrence's cabin that much of 'Pan in America' is about, was terribly scarred by it.

It seemed to Lawrence as much a violation of Nature to idealize, sentimentalize or humanize it as to reject or exploit it. He mocks Wordsworth for dressing up Pan as Lucy Gray, the sweet and pure child of nature, and for refusing to allow the primrose a soul of its own. On the other hand he admired Cézanne whose 'great effort was, as it were, to shove the apple away from him, and let it live of itself' [*Phoenix* 567]. A vernal wood becomes part of the furniture of Wordsworth's mind, teaching him only what he already knows. A true relationship must change us, and is therefore possible only with things which are wholly themselves. Lawrence does not have to shove the pine tree away. It keeps its distance, its resistance, 'a strong-willed powerful thing-in-itself', while at the same time, since it is 'within the allness of Pan', it serves to put him in touch with the many other lives which are part of its life:

The chipmunks skelter a little way up it, the little black-and-white birds, tree-creepers, walk quick as mice on its rough perpendicular, tapping; the bluejays throng on its branches, high up, at dawn, and in the afternoon you hear the faintest rustle of many little wild doves alighting in its upper remoteness. [*Phoenix* 25]

And the tree includes more than that:

The tree gathers up earth-power from the dark bowels of the earth, and a roaming sky-glitter from above. . . . It vibrates its presence into my soul, and I am with Pan. . . . I am even conscious that shivers of energy cross my living plasm, from the tree, and I become a degree more like unto the tree, more bristling and turpentiney, in Pan. [25]

At the beginning of 'Pan in America', Lawrence places the death of Pan at the beginning of the Christian era. But earlier than that civilization itself had proved inimical to Pan:

Gradually men moved into cities. And they loved the display of people better than the display of a tree. They liked the glory they got of overpowering one another in war. And, above all, they loved the vainglory of their own words, the pomp of argument and the vanity of ideas. [23]

Lawrence is not suggesting here that all words and ideas are hubristic, simply those which set the mind of man apart from the rest of creation. An imaginative work is 'a new venture towards God': 'A book is a holy thing, and must be made so again'.

Lawrence finds that the God we have left out of our God-concept in the Christian era is the common element in all three mythologies – Greek, Celtic and American Indian. He calls this God Pan: 'And still, in America, among the Indians, the oldest Pan is alive' [31]. The Indians had rituals to enable them to handle the potent, potentially destructive, energies of Pan. For the white man there must be a death to the old false consciousness followed by a resurrection, equally painful, to a new and deeper reality – the stark, sordid, beautiful, awe-inspiring reality of Pan, which Lawrence himself was now wrestling with on his pack-rat infested, lightning-scarred, but certainly not god-forsaken ranch.

The first fictional fruit of this experience was *St. Mawr*, where Cartwright, who is based on Frederick Carter, defines Pan in terms identical with Lawrence's:

I should say he was the God that is hidden in everything . . . Pan was the hidden mystery – the hidden cause. That's how it was a great God; Pan wasn't *he* at all: not even a great God. He was Pan, All: what you see when you see in full. In the daytime you see the thing. But if your third eye is open, which sees only the things that can't be seen, you may see Pan within the thing, hidden: you may see with your third eye, which is darkness. [65]

'The third eye' is another way of expressing what Blake calls 'fourfold vision' – the vision with which we perceive that everything that lives is holy. Lawrence uses the term again in *Apocalypse* in describing the resurrection or second birth which takes place at the end of the ritual of the Mysteries of Isis:

The initiate is dead, and alive again in a new body. He is sealed in the forehead, like a Buddhist monk, as a sign that he has died the death, and that his seventh self is fulfilled, he is twice-born, his mystic eye or 'third eye' is now open. He sees in two worlds. [*Apocalypse* 107]

It is a dangerous world to enter, full of raw energies like lightning, without insulation or supports or orientations. It was this danger the ancients warned of in the story that to look upon Pan was to be blasted or driven mad. In 1924 Lawrence was to send three fictional women out into this world. The woman who rode away never returned; the princess returned, but without her sanity; Lou, in *St. Mawr*, survives in it, but whether Pan will have any use for her service is an open question.

The female protagonists of so many of Lawrence's fictions are perhaps projections of his own distressed anima, the subjugated feminine component in his psyche, which he is seeking to release from the male hegemony, or rather to reconcile with a chastened animus. James Hillman argues that the successful introjection of the anima in a man

> does not mean acquiring the characteristics of the other gender: rather it means a double-consciousness, mercurial, true and untrue, action and inaction, sight and blindness, living the impossible oxymoron, more like an animal who is at once superbly conscious in its actions and utterly unconscious of them.   [125]

So, in *St. Mawr*, Lou imagines a regenerate man:

> A pure animal man would be as lovely as a deer or a leopard, burning like a flame fed straight from underneath. And he'd be part of the unseen, like a mouse is, even. And he'd never cease to wonder, he'd breathe silence and unseen wonder, as the partridges do, running in the stubble. He'd be all the animals in turn, instead of one, fixed, automatic thing, which he is now, grinding on the nerves.   [62]

The bored heroine Lou is persuaded by a stallion as Evangelist to flee the City of Destruction, to renounce Vanity Fair in favour of another, spiritually vibrant world in the Delectable Mountains of New Mexico, there to become a priestess of Pan. Lou is not, however, to be identified with Lawrence. Some of the finest pages Lawrence ever wrote describe the attempts of the nameless New England woman to tame the New Mexico Rockies, to impose New England plumbing and idealism, an attempt as doomed as that of Pentheus to tame the mountains of Cithaeron. Pentheus does not heed the fate of his predecessor Actaeon; not does Lou learn enough from the failure of the New England woman before her. Her romantic expectations compel her to blind herself to the packrats and the squalor and to cast a glamour over the universe. Lou sees the need to look to pagan gods, but it is not as a priestess of the 'Apollo mysteries' that she will find atonement at Las Chivas (which means 'the goats'). The goats are sacred to the goat-god Pan, who, in his splendour and savagery is very similar to the horned god Dionysus in *The Bacchae*. Lou has not yet reached at the end, and may never reach, Lawrence's own perception that the god in man and the goat in man cannot be separated.

It seemed to Lawrence, however, that the religion of the American Indians had specifically evolved in forms suitable for their race and place. The European, with his very different culture and consciousness, could find invaluable clues there, but would need a different life mode. The attempt to resurrect Pan in Mexico in *The Plumed Serpent* had been a failure. Pan had been too closely delimited by the spirit of place of a harsh and bloodthirsty land. As Lawrence began to long for the softer, greener, more feminine spirit of Europe, Pan came to seem atavistic and too oppressively male. Pan's world came to seem like an ending rather than a new beginning. Of his heroine Kate Lawrence says:

> Her world could end in many ways, and this was one of them. Back to the twilight of the ancient Pan world, where the soul of the woman was dumb, to be forever unspoken. [*The Plumed Serpent*, 312]

＊   ＊   ＊

In February 1925 Lawrence nearly died in Mexico. But that spring at the ranch he experienced his own resurrection. As his health returned everything, in Frieda's words 'assumed the radiance of new life'. Just being alive in the phenomenal world seemed so miraculous to him that his recent preoccupation with power and with saving the world came to seem almost blasphemous to him. He realized, as if for the first time, his own limits. The life of his self-importance was over. His belief that human life 'consists in a relation with all things: stone, earth, trees, flowers, water, insects, fishes, birds, creatures, sun, rainbow, children, woman, other men' [*Reflections* 374] was confirmed, since that new life visibly flowed into him from these sources, from the pine tree (itself resurrected after a lightning blast) and all its associated life, from the four horses, Azul, Prince, Aaron and Ambrose, black-eyed Susan the cow, Timsy Wemyss the marmalade cat, and Moses the white cock:

> And as the white cock calls in the doorway, who calls? Merely a barnyard rooster, worth a dollar-and-a-half. But listen! Under the old dawns of creation the Holy Ghost, the Mediator, shouts aloud in the twilight. And every time I hear him, a fountain of vitality gushes up in my body. It is life. . . . When the white cock crows, I do not hear myself or some anthropomorphic conceit, crowing. I hear the not-me, the voice of the Holy Ghost. And when I see the hard, solid, longish green cones thrusting up at blue heaven from the high bluish tips of the balsam pine, I say : Behold! Look at the strong, fertile silence of the thrusting tree! God is in the bush like a clenched dark fist or a thrust phallus'. [481]

In the light of all this, the leadership principle came to seem obsolete. What was needed was a tender, sensitive, delicate awareness. His next novel (ultimately *Lady Chatterley's Lover*) was to be called *Tenderness*.

＊   ＊   ＊

Lawrence returned to Europe in 1925 to continue his quest, and in the spring of 1927 embarked on a tour of the Etruscan sites with his American Buddhist friend Earl Brewster. There, in the flaked and faded frescos of the underground tombs of the Etruscans, Lawrence found what he had been seeking, evidence that it had been possible, if only for a century or two before Etruria came under the heel of the Romans, for a European people to get themselves into a right relation with nature. His long pilgrimage had brought him at last to these tombs, and in them he found the vivid human life he had been seeking, a life of perfect awareness and relatedness, without the crippling dualism of mind versus body, male versus female, human versus non-human, physical versus metaphysical, life versus death. Here he found a different Pan, with no malice toward men whose activities respected him:

> The intensive culture of vine and olive and wheat by the ceaseless
> industry of naked human hands and winter-shod feet, and slow-stepping,
> soft-eyed oxen does not devastate a country, does not denude it, does not
> lay it bare, does not uncover its nakedness, does not drive away either
> Pan or his children.   [*Phoenix* 45]

The Etruscan vision was like the openness of the child to the world:

> The ancients saw, consciously, as children now see unconsciously, the
> everlasting *wonder* in things . . . They were like children: but they had
> the force, the power and the sensual *knowledge* of true adults. They had
> a world of valuable knowledge, which is utterly lost to us. Where they
> were true adults, we are children, and vice versa.   [*Mornings* 168]

Lawrence was right in sensing that the Etruscans had preserved a lost secret. His description of their art is interchangeable with Groenewegen-Frankfort's description of Cretan art of a thousand years earlier:

> Here and here alone (in contrast to Egypt and the Near East) the human
> bid for timelessness was disregarded in the most complete acceptance of
> the grace of life the world has ever known. For life means movement and
> the beauty of movement was woven into the intricate web of living forms
> which we call 'scenes of nature'; was revealed in human bodies acting
> their serious games, inspired by a transcendent presence, acting in
> freedom and restraint, unpurposeful as cyclic time itself.
>   [quoted by Kerenyi, *Dionysos*, 10]

Blake used Newton and Locke as representatives of single vision. Lawrence uses Socrates:

> Later, when scepticism came over all the civilized world, as it did after
> Socrates, the Etruscan religion began to die, Greeks and Greek
> rationalism flooded in, and Greek stories more or less took the place of
> the old Etruscan symbolic thought.   [*Mornings* 150]

298

To allow one's being to be reduced to single vision is to live in bad faith, or, in Lawrence's phrase, with impure heart:

> But all attempt at divination, even prayer and reason and research itself, lapses into jugglery when the heart loses its purity. In the impurity of his heart, Socrates often juggled logic unpleasantly.   [154]

This murder of 'symbolic thought' was fatal not only for the Etruscans, but condemned Western civilization to over two thousand years of increasingly blasphemous living:

> The old religion of the profound attempt of man to harmonize himself with nature, and hold his own and come to flower in the great seething of life, changed with the Greeks and Romans into a desire to resist nature, to produce a mental cunning and a mechanical force that would outwit Nature and chain her down completely, completely, till at last there should be nothing free in nature at all, all should be controlled, domesticated, put to man's meaner uses.   [174]

Aldous Huxley was one of Lawrence's most sympathetic critics, but in his review of *Etruscan Places* he completely misunderstood what the Etruscans meant to Lawrence:

> For the sake of the double flute and all that it stands for, he [Lawrence] was prepared to sacrifice most of the activities upon which, for the last two thousand years or thereabouts, humanity, at any rate in the West, has set the highest value. The philosophy and the practice of non-acceptance have made it possible for man to become, in some respects, more than human. But in the process he has had to sacrifice much of his former happiness; and while he has become spiritually and intellectually more, emotionally and physically he has, too often, degenerated and become less than human.   [*Spectator* 4 November 1932]

This would be an accurate enough account of Lawrence's position in, say, 1913. But it is a travesty of his position in 1927. The crude choice between the spiritual and intellectual on the one side and the emotional and physical on the other is no longer to be found in Lawrence's writings at this date. Nor is he searching for happiness – that is a desirable but not inevitable by-product of what he is seeking, which is wholeness. He wishes to reinstate the body and its emotions not because he values it higher than the life of the spirit and of consciousness, but because he now knows that to pursue the life of the spirit or of the mind in opposition to the life of the body and to Nature, is to alienate, stultify or pervert the spirit and to turn the mind into a sterile mechanism or juggling act. It is because they had a rich physical life that the Etruscans were able to have a rich spiritual life, or vice versa, since to distinguish between them at all is part of the Socratic sickness. The Etruscans confirmed for him what he had always known, that it is futile hubristic perversity to seek the life of the spirit apart from the given world; for God is in everything that lives and nowhere else.

According to Charles Olson Lawrence resisted the 'high temptation' to complete knowledge, intellectual perfection, which led, in Plato, Christ, Schopenhauer and Ortega y Gasset, to a kind of death. Lawrence belongs rather with Homer (and his 'unchristened heart', in Yeats' phrase) and with Euripides. In defining belief as 'a profound emotion that has the mind's connivance' Lawrence achieved, says Olson, 'a combination both archaic and prospective, which gives man, in his preoccupation with life, the proper instrumentation for its understanding and use'. It is the same high temptation to which Stephen Dedalus succumbs in *Portrait of the Artist as a Young Man* when he propounds a view of art at the opposite pole from Lawrence's:

> The feelings excited by improper art are kinetic, desire or loathing. Desire urges us to possess, to go to something; loathing urges us to abandon, to go from something. The arts which excite them, pornographical or didactic, are therefore improper arts. The esthetic emotion (I use the general term) is therefore static. The mind is arrested and raised above desire and loathing. . . . To speak of these things and to try to understand their nature, and having understood it, to try slowly and humbly and constantly to express, to press out again, from the gross earth or what it brings forth, from sound and shape and colour which are the prison gates of our soul, an image of the beauty we have come to understand – that is art.   [186–7]

All this has the 'true scholastic stink' as Joyce is well aware, and Stephen's pride, his spurning of the gross earth, brings its appropriate Icarus-fall. Lawrence's art is always and avowedly in this sense 'improper'. He valued all art, but particularly the novel, only insofar as it was kinetic:

> It is the way our sympathy flows and recoils that really determines our lives. And here lies the vast importance of the novel, properly handled. It can inform and lead into new places the flow of our sympathetic consciousness, and it can lead our sympathy away in recoil from things gone dead.   [*Lady Chatterley's Lover*, 101]

✳   ✳   ✳

When Lawrence returned from his Etruscan tour in the spring of 1927 he found among his accumulated mail Koteliansky's translation of extracts from Rozanov's *The Apocalypse of Our Times*. Lawrence was very excited:

> Rozanov has more or less recovered the genuine pagan vision, the phallic vision, and with those eyes he looks, in amazement and consternation, on

the mess of Christianity. . . . He is the first Russian . . . to see that immortality is in the vividness of life, not in the loss of life. The butterfly becomes a whole revelation to him: and to us.   [*Phoenix* 369]

Rozanov is discussing with two friends, Kapterev, a naturalist, and Florensky, a priest, the question 'in a caterpillar, chrysalis, and butterfly – which is the "I"?':

Then it became suddenly clear to me . . . that the 'butterfly' is *really*, mysteriously, and metaphysically, the soul of the caterpillar and chrysalis. Thus happened this, cosmogonically overwhelming, discovery. . . . Kapterev mused for a while and said: Observations show that in a caterpillar wrapped up in a cocoon and appearing as though dead, there actually begins after this a reconstruction of the tissues of the body. So that it does not only appear dead, but actually dies. . . . And if you were to pierce the caterpillar, say, with a pin, then no butterfly will come out of it, nothing will come out of it, and the grave will remain a grave, and the body will not 'come to life again'.   [Zytaruk]

It is, of course, not a discovery but a rediscovery of ancient wisdom. On the Mycenean Ring of Nestor two butterflies flutter above the Minoan goddess. Sir Arthur Evans commented:

The symbolic significance of these, moreover, is emphasized by the appearance above them of two small objects showing traces of heads at the tip and with hook-like projections at the side, in which we may reasonably recognize the two corresponding chrysalises. . . . It can hardly be doubted, moreover, that they apply to the two youthful figures who appear beside them on the ring, and must be taken to be symbolic of their reanimation with new life. . . . We see here, reunited by the life-giving power of the Goddess and symbolized by the chrysalises and butterflies, a young couple whom Death had parted.   [Baring 128]

Immediately Lawrence began *The Escaped Cock*. Easter 1927 represented a confluence of several streams in Lawrence's life and thought. His own change of life and nearness of death forced him towards a less metaphorical concept of resurrection than hitherto, a concept which would allow him to reconcile within himself the figures of Christ and Pan. His memories of the white cock Moses at the ranch, symbol of assertive life with the voice of the Holy Ghost, merged with the symbolism of the cock escaping from an egg which he had seen in a shop window in Volterra and the egg of resurrection held up by the man who had died in the Tomb of the Lionesses at Tarquinia. Lawrence was well aware of the pagan symbolism behind the Easter egg. Robert Graves tells us that 'the creation of the world, according to the Orphics, resulted from the sexual act performed between the Great Goddess and the World-Snake Ophion':

> The Goddess then laid the world-egg, which contained infinite potentiality but which was nothing in itself until it was split open by the Demiurge. The Demiurge was Helios, the Sun, with whom the Orphics identified the God Apollo. . . . Since the cock was the Orphic bird of resurrection, sacred to Apollo's son Aesculapius the healer, hens' eggs took the place of snakes' in the later Druidic mysteries and were coloured scarlet in the Sun's honour; and become Easter eggs. [*White Goddess* 248–9]

The snake was also sacred to Aesculapius, who was a fertility and resurrection god as well as a healer (since the snake's ability to shed its skin was mistaken in the ancient world for an ability, like the phoenix, to regenerate itself). In Part I of *The Escaped Cock* the man who had died becomes a healer with a cock under his arm, an avatar of Aesculapius; and the phallic associations of the Aesculapian snake lead naturally towards his transformation into Osiris in Part II.

At the beginning of the story the cock-crow wakes the man who had died back into the life of the body and the natural world from which he had died. He learns from the cock how to re-establish his connection with the phenomenal world, to ride 'the wave of life of which the cock was the crest' [109]. The story ends with his affirmation that the world is 'a vast complexity of wonders', and with a question which implies a the repudiation of his former mission in Part II: 'From what, and to what, could this infinite whirl be saved?' [120].

In *Etruscan Places* Lawrence had coupled Christ and Buddha:

> and before Buddha or Jesus spoke the nightingale sang, and long after the words of Jesus and Buddha are gone into oblivion the nightingale still will sing. Because it is neither preaching nor teaching nor commanding nor urging. It is just singing. And in the beginning was not a Word, but a chirrup. [*Mornings* 126]

In *The Escaped Cock*, as in *Etruscan Places*, the villains are the Romans, who understand nothing but power, who trample on everything they do not understand, and burden the earth with their monuments:

> Because a fool kills a nightingale with a stone, is he therefore greater than the nightingale? Because the Roman took the life out of the Etruscan, was he therefore greater than the Etruscan? Not he! Rome fell, and the Roman phenomenon with it. Italy today is far more Etruscan in its pulse than Roman; and will always be so. [ibid 126]

The Etruscans, according to Lawrence, were a people who 'lived their own lives without wanting to dominate the lives of others' [Nehls III 137]. Both

Jesus and Buddha had wanted to do that as much as the Romans, since saving is as much a form of domination as conquering. Both sought to lift man above greed and desire, yet themselves fell into the greed of the saviour. Lawrence had to rewrite 'The Escaped Cock' to make his resurrected man recognize and reject this form of greed also. He added this passage:

> I have outlived my mission, and know no more of it. It is my triumph. I
> have survived the day and the death of my interference, and am still a
> man . . . The teacher and the saviour are dead in me; mow I can go about
> my own business, into my own single life . . . My public life is over, the life
> of my conviction and my mission, the life of my self-importance . . . Now I
> can live without striving to sway others any more. For my reach ends in
> my finger-tips and my stride is no longer than the ends of my toes. Yet I
> would embrace multitudes, I who have never truly embraced even one
> woman, or one man.   [*Escaped Cock* 24]

He is discovering the Etruscan insouciance, as Lawrence had discovered it. The Etruscans knew the gods 'in their very finger-tips'; they entered into the flow of touch which comes not from pawing and laying hold, but 'from the middle of the human being' [*Mornings* 143–4]. In the revised version the man is much more aware that his earlier denial of the world, including the world of men, was a denial of the life-issue, leading to betrayal and crucifixion as inevitably as, in 'The Man Who Loved Islands', Cathcart's loathing 'with profound revulsion the whole of the animal creation' had led to his physical and spiritual dissolution. *The Escaped Cock* is the story of how Christ became an Etruscan.

Rozanov's challenge had been to 'remove' Christ, with all the accretions of the centuries, from human consciousness. Knowing the impossibility of this, Lawrence sought rather to transform a caterpillar Christ into a butterfly Osiris, to detach Christ from the life-denying Christianity of St Paul or St Augustine and to restore him to the company of the torn and resurrected fertility gods. Rundle Clark speaks of Osiris as

> the most vivid achievement of the Egyptian imagination . . . the
> completely helpless one, the essential victim . . . the sufferer with all
> mortality but at the same time . . . the power of revival and fertility in the
> world. He is the power of growth in plants and of reproduction in animals
> and human beings. He is both dead and the source of all living. Hence to
> become Osiris is to become one with the cosmic cycles of death and
> rebirth.   [97]

The priestess of Isis is able to draw the man back into the unfallen state, 'nakedly breast to breast with the cosmos' [*Apocalypse* 181]. Frazer speaks of Osiris 'diffusing the blessings of civilization and agriculture wherever he went'.

But agriculture is impossible and civilization is not a blessing unless grounded in the fecundity of the goddess.

The story ends:

> The man who had died rowed slowly on, with the current, and laughed to himself: I have sowed the seed of my life and my resurrection, and put my touch forever upon the choice woman of this day, and I carry her perfume in my flesh like essence of roses. She is dear to me in the middle of my being. But the gold and flowing serpent is coiling up again, to sleep at the root of my tree. So let the boat carry me. Tomorrow is another day.
>
> [61]

This clear and serene prose brings together many strands. The sun sinks into the sea each day, but rises refreshed on the morrow. 'The suns come back in their seasons. And I shall come again.' The seed is 'the eternal quick of all things, which yet divides and sub-divides, so that it becomes the sun of the firmament and the lotus of the waters under the earth, and the rose of all existence upon the earth' [*Mornings* 127]. So the man, who is sun-god and corn-god, as he commits himself once more to the waters of potentiality, takes with him in the perfume of the woman the 'essence' of all existence upon the earth, and leaves her pregnant with himself, as Horus was believed to be the resurrected Osiris.

We find now a willingness new in Lawrence to associate resurrection with procreation. This was very much the emphasis of Rozanov's phallic vision:

> It means then the 'World of the future age' is pre-eminently determined by 'copulation'; and then light is thrown on its irresistibility, on its insatiability . . . on its 'sacredness,' and that it is a 'mystery' (the mystery of marriage). . . . But it is obvious that in insects, cows, everywhere in the animal and vegetable world, and not only in man alone, it is a 'mystery, heavenly and sacred.' . . . Then we understand 'the shame that attaches to sexual organs'; it is the 'life of the future age,' through which we enter into 'life beyond the grave,' into 'life of the future age.'
>
> [Zytaruk]

The serpent had gradually accumulated more and more meanings for Lawrence. For the Etruscans 'the serpent represented the vivid powers of the inner earth, not only such powers as volcanic and earthquake, but the quick powers that run up the roots of plants and establish the great body of the tree, the tree of life, and run up the feet and legs of man, to establish the heart'[*Mornings* 207]. Lawrence knew that in yoga this power is called *kundalini*:

> A hero was a hero, in the great past, when he had conquered the hostile dragon, when he had the power of the dragon *with him* in his limbs and breast . . . the liberation within the self of the gleaming bright serpent of

gold, golden fluid life within the body . . . For in his good aspect, the dragon is the great vivifier, the great enhancer of the whole universe . . . It is the same dragon which, according to the Hindus, coils quiescent at the base of the spine of a man, and unfolds sometimes lashing along the spinal way.

[*Apocalypse* 124–5]

The serpent is also central to some versions of the Osiris myth. The star-son (also called Lucifer) is reborn every year, grows with the seasons, and destroys the Serpent-lover of the mother-goddess to become himself her lover. Her love kills him but another serpent is born from his ashes, which, at Easter, lays the *glain* or red egg which she eats, then gives birth to the son once again. Osiris was a Star-son, and though after his death he looped himself around the world like a serpent, yet when his fifty-yard long phallus was carried in procession it was topped with a golden star; this stood for himself renewed as the Child Horus, son of Isis, who had been both his bride and his layer-out and was now his mother once again.

Lawrence knew all this from his reading of such books as Petrie's *The Religions of Egypt,* Pryse's *The Apocalypse Unsealed,* and Madame Blavatsky's *Isis Unveiled.* But he was not interested in displaying his knowledge of mythology, anthropology and Oriental religions, nor in quarrying them for fragments to shore against his ruins. The last paragraph of *The Escaped Cock* needs no notes. What we happen to know of its sources and antecedents and parallels will make fertile connections for us. Words such as 'boat', 'current', 'night', 'seed', 'resurrection', 'roses', 'serpent' and 'tree' are bound to make such connections without our being aware of it, independently of any mythic context. The passage works as simple poetic prose, creating a sense of atonement between the innermost needs and powers of the man and the woman of his choice, his unborn child, the currents and seasons of life itself, the larger world of the distance and the future for him to adventure into, even the Romans, against whom he sharpens his wits and his weapons. The scene in its wholeness is the very opposite of a crucifixion. We imagine this Christ escaping into the Greater Day with the enigmatic Etruscan smile on his lips.

Did Lawrence know an already famous poem also written on Lake Leman just seven years earlier – 'The Waste Land'. There, at the end, Eliot also uses a boat to express the poem's strongest affirmation, that control which is the opposite of death by water:

> *Damyata*: The boat responded
> Gaily, to the hand expert with sail and oar.
> The sea was calm, your heart would have responded
> Gaily, when invited, beating obedient
> To controlling hands

The image is, surely, not very satisfactory. Those 'controlling hands' are too reminiscent of the assured 'young man carbuncular' whose 'exploring hands encounter no defence'. The woman's heart, like the sea, is supposed to respond to and obey the expert handling of the man. Control, in this sense, becomes the imposition of one man's will upon woman and nature, a variant of Plato's chariot driver. Lawrence calls this greed. The man who had died's boat is controlled partly by him and partly by the current: 'So let the boat carry me'.

Eliot reprimanded Lawrence for 'using the terminology of Christian faith to set forth some philosophy or religion which is fundamentally non-Christian or anti-Christian' [Draper 361]. Lawrence might have responded, with Blake, that he was seeking to rescue Christ from the Christians. It was a daring undertaking in 1928, and caused much outrage at the time. Lawrence was called a traitor to the human race. But such is the tact and sensitivity with which he carried it through that many Christians have subsequently responded warmly to it as a corrective to the tendency of orthodox Christianity to be life-denying, and to evade the implications of the phrase 'the resurrection of the body'.

One might wish that Lawrence had been able to follow his regenerate man still further, and imagine a life for him wherever he is heading. We can get a hint of that from 'The Risen Lord', an essay Lawrence wrote in August 1929, which might almost be regarded as an outline for a third part to *The Escaped Cock*:

> If Jesus rose in the full flesh, He rose to know the tenderness of a woman, and the great pleasure of her, and to have children by her. He rose to know the responsibility and the peculiar delight of children, and also the exasperation and nuisance of them. If Jesus rose as a full man, in the flesh, He rose to have friends, to have a man-friend who He would hold sometimes to His breast, in strong affection, and who would be dearer to Him than a brother, just out of the sheer mystery and sympathy. And how much more wonderful this, than having disciples! If Jesus rose a full man in the flesh, He rose to do his share in the world's work, something he really liked doing. And if He remembered His first life, it would be neither teaching nor preaching, but probably carpentering again, with joy, among the shavings. If Jesus rose a full man in the flesh, He rose to continue His fight with money-makers of every sort. But this time, it would no longer be the fight of self-sacrifice that would end in crucifixion. This time it would be a freed man fighting to shelter the rose of life from being trampled on by the pigs.   [*Phoenix* II, 575]

*   *   *

Of *Lady Chatterley's Lover* Lawrence wrote:

> As I say, it's a novel of the phallic Consciousness: or the phallic Consciousness versus the mental-spiritual Consciousness: and of course you know which side I take. The *versus* is not my fault: there should be

no *versus*. The two things must be reconciled in us. But now they're daggers drawn.

[*Letters* VI 340]

In letter after letter Lawrence insisted to his friends that *Lady Chatterley's Lover* was a phallic, not a sexual novel. Few of them, I imagine, could see any difference. What Lawrence was trying to draw attention to was the religious symbolism, for a phallus is the male organ in its function as fertility symbol. The *Oxford English Dictionary* defines it as 'symbolical of the generative power of nature'. Lawrence at this time frequently used the term 'phallic consciousness' to mean simply the opposite of mental consciousness – that is any instinct or intuition or desire or knowledge which bypassed the tyranny of the intellect. 'Phallic consciousness' is the opposite of 'sex in the head', but it also signifies any pre-mental consciousness, not only sexual. In *A Propos of Lady Chatterley's Lover* Lawrence tried to explain the distinction:

> If England is to be regenerated . . . then it will be by the arising of a new blood-contact, a new touch, and a new marriage. It will be a phallic rather than a sexual regeneration. For the phallus is only the great old symbol of godly vitality in a man, and of immediate contact. It will also be a renewal of marriage: the true phallic marriage. And still further, it will be marriage set again in relationship to the rhythmic cosmos. . . . For the truth is, we are perishing for lack of fulfilment of our greater needs, we are cut off from the great sources of our inward nourishment and renewal, sources which flow eternally in the universe. Vitally, the human race is dying. It is like a great uprooted tree, with its roots in the air. We must plant ourselves again in the universe. . . . But the two great ways of knowing, for man, are knowing in terms of apartness, which is mental, rational, scientific, and knowing in terms of togetherness, which is religious and poetic. The Christian religion lost, in Protestantism finally, the togetherness with the universe, the togetherness of the body, the sex, the emotions, the passions, with the earth and sun and stars.

[*Lady Chatterley's Lover* 328–31]

Since these words were written science has changed a good deal and is now almost as concerned as pagan religion or poetry with systems and relationships.

Thus, when Lawrence speaks of sex he is also necessarily speaking of what we have come to call ecology, the relationship between people and the natural environment, which he called the cosmos or circumambient universe. Ecology was not, for Lawrence, a matter simply of the conservation of natural resources, but the deeper ecology of a different consciousness, a wholeness, an atonement, a being in touch. And of all the ways of being in touch which our civilization has almost killed off, perhaps the one which can still give us an inkling of that consciousness is sex.

Any form of regeneration must be preceded by a death – the death of

the old false consciousness, an ego-death. The Elizabethans called orgasm the
'little death', because it seemed to them the only experience short of death
where the soul escaped from the hard shell of self to meet and touch the other,
the not-self. The phallus is in this sense a bridge not only between man and
woman but between self and cosmos. This, then, is what Lawrence meant
when he wrote, in 1927, 'the phallus is a great sacred image: it represents a
deep, deep life which has been denied in us, and still is denied' [V 648], and
in his last work *Apocalypse*: 'The phallos is the point at which man is broken
off from his context, and at which he can be re-joined' [181]

❖   ❖   ❖

The most lasting and central value of Lawrence's work lies in the degree to
which it can help us in this matter of life and death. Even as he neared death
he poured his life into everything he wrote. Into wonderful fictions such as
The Escaped Cock, where the risen Christ repudiates his former mission and
sacrifice in favour of 'the greater life of the body' in the phenomenal world:
'From what, and to what, could this infinite whirl be saved?'

Lawrence's later fiction contains some of the most wonderful descriptions of the natural world in our literature, but the late poems are perhaps
even more charged with his sacramental vision:

> They say that reality exists only in the spirit
> that corporeal existence is a kind of death
> that pure being is bodiless
> that the idea of the form precedes the form substantial.
>
> But what nonsense it is!
> as if any Mind could have imagined a lobster
> dozing in the under-deeps, then reaching out a savage and iron claw!
>
> Even the mind of God can only imagine
> those things that have become themselves:
> bodies and presences, here and now, creatures with a foothold in
>   creation
> even if it is only a lobster on tip-toe.
>
> Religion knows better than philosophy.
> Religion knows that Jesus was never Jesus
> till he was born from a womb, and ate soup and bread
> and grew up, and became, in the wonder of creation, Jesus,
> with a body and with needs, and a lovely spirit.   ['Demiurge']

Lawrence continued to develop these ideas to the end of his life, and
their fullest theoretical expression is in his last work *Apocalypse*. In an early
draft his vision is bleak:

The triumph of Mind over the cosmos progresses in small spasms: aeroplanes, radio, motor-traffic. It is high time for the Millennium. And alas, everything has gone wrong. The destruction of the world seems not very far off, but the happiness of mankind has never been so remote. . . . How they long for the destruction of the cosmos, secretly, these men of mind and spirit! How they work for its domination and final annihilation! But alas, they only succeed in spoiling the earth, spoiling life, and in the end destroying mankind, instead of the cosmos. Man cannot destroy the cosmos: that is obvious. But it is obvious that the cosmos can destroy man. Man must inevitably destroy himself, in conflict with the cosmos. It is perhaps his fate.   [199–200]

In the final version Lawrence managed to rekindle a spark of hope. Here are the last words of his last work:

What man most passionately wants is his living wholeness and his living unison, not his own isolate salvation of his 'soul'. Man wants his physical fulfilment first and foremost, since now, once and once only, he is in the flesh and potent. For man, the vast marvel is to be alive. For man, as for flower and beast and bird, the supreme triumph is to be most vividly, most perfectly alive. Whatever the unborn and the dead man know, they cannot know the beauty, the marvel, of being alive in the flesh. The dead may look after the afterwards. But the magnificent here and now of life in the flesh is ours, and ours alone, and ours only for a time. We ought to dance with rapture that we should be alive and in the flesh, and part of the living, incarnate cosmos. I am part of the sun as my eye is part of me. That I am part of the earth my feet know perfectly, and my blood is part of the sea. My soul knows that I am part of the human race, my soul is an organic part of the great human soul, as my spirit is part of my nation. In my own very self, I am part of my family. There is nothing of me that is alone and absolute except my mind, and we shall find that the mind has no existence by itself, it is only the glitter of the sun on the surface of the waters. So that my individualism is really an illusion. I am part of the great whole, and I can never escape. But I *can* deny my connections, break them, and become a fragment. Then I am wretched. What we want is to destroy our false, inorganic connections, especially those related to money, and re-establish the living organic connections, with the cosmos, the sun and earth, with mankind and nation and family. Start with the sun, and the rest will slowly, slowly happen.   [149]

Here Lawrence both repudiates the 'Immortality Ode' and anticipates Ted Hughes' poem 'The sole of a foot', where Adam resists the high temptation of the 'religion of the diamond body' and the Icarus flight, and accepts that for man the essential connection is that between the sole of his foot and the rock, to which he says:

I am no wing
To tread emptiness.
I was made

For you.

✻   ✻   ✻

Wordsworth himself was unable to sustain his pantheism against his adulation of 'the mind of man'. In the very year of Wordsworth's death, 1850, Tennyson published *In Memoriam*, with its prophetic rejection of Darwinian nature:

> Arise and fly
> The reeling Faun, the sensual feast;
> Move upward, working out the beast,
> And let the ape and tiger die.
>
> [CXVIII]

Had Earl Brewster quoted these lines to Lawrence when he replied:

> But the point is I don't *want* the tiger superseded. Oh, may each she-tigress have seventy-seven whelps, and may they all grow in strength and shine in stripes like day and night, and may each one eat at least seventy miserable featherless human birds, and lick red chops of gusto after it. Leave me my tigers, leave me spangled leopards, leave me bright cobra snakes, and I wish I had poison fangs and talons as good. I *believe* in wrath and gnashing of teeth and crunching of cowards' bones.
>
> [*Letters* III, 719]

Lawrence was pushed to such shrillness by his sense that both religion and rationalism were ranged against him. In the year before Lawrence was born T.H. Huxley had published *Evolution and Ethics*, where he claimed that the purpose of education was 'the application of [man's] intelligence to the adaptation of the conditions of life to his higher needs'. To this end he must be 'perpetually on guard against the cosmic forces, whose ends are not his ends, without and within himself'. He concluded: 'That which lies before the human race is a constant struggle to maintain and improve, in opposition to the State of Nature, the State of Art'. In Lawrence's adulthood that was still the received wisdom, and had become the basis of our entire urban industrial society. Pantheism meant either something archaic or something to do with the Wordsworthian pieties. It had nothing to do with the realities of modern life. It was certainly not a serious option as a religion for the twentieth century. Lawrence took it upon himself to make it so. It was a Herculean task at a time when nature seemed to be disappearing under the 'century-deep deposits of layer upon layer of refuse' [*St. Mawr*], when the machine seemed to have triumphed utterly, when H.G. Wells and the majority for whom he spoke

310

complacently assumed that history was the story of man's progress towards the triumph of mind over both nature and human nature. In the year before Lawrence wrote *St. Mawr* Wells had published *Men Like Gods* in which he argued that man should 'bring to trial' every other creature, from the rhinoceros to the tubercle bacillus, and either bring it into line with his requirements or get rid of it.

In the 1950s Kingsley Amis was expressing a preference for 'woods devoid of beasts' ['Against Romanticism'] and echoing, in poems like 'Here is Where', Socrates' view that 'it is not fields and trees which will teach me anything, it is men in the city' [Plato's *Phaedrus*]. Perhaps this was still the received wisdom as recently as 1969, when Patricia Merivale ended her book *Pan the Goat-God: His Myth in Modern Times* with the statement that 'later writers [than Lawrence] have taken no interest in the Pan-Christ dialectic, or the closely related theme of the death of Pan, or the Romantic transcendental Pan' [218] and that 'Pan is unlikely to become a literary fashion or a public myth again' [228]. Lawrence is assumed to be the last Romantic in this respect, the last writer to try to take Pan seriously. Yet within a year Ted Hughes, reviewing a book on ecology, was invoking Pan in exactly Lawrence's sense:

> When something abandons Nature, or is abandoned by Nature, it has lost touch with its creator, and is called an evolutionary dead-end. According to this, our Civilization is an evolutionary error. Sure enough, when the modern mediumistic artist looks into his crystal, he sees always the same thing. He sees the last nightmare of mental disintegration and spiritual emptiness. . . . But he may see something else. He may see a vision of the real Eden, 'excellent as at the first day', the draughty radiant Paradise of the animals, which is the actual earth, in the actual Universe: he may see Pan, . . . the vital, somewhat terrible spirit of natural life, which is new in every second. Even when it is poisoned to the point of death, its efforts to be itself are new in every second. This is what will survive, if anything can. And this is the soul-state of the new world. But while the mice in the field are listening to the Universe, and moving in the body of nature, where every living cell is sacred to every other, and all are interdependent, the housing speculator is peering at the field through a visor, and behind him stands the whole army of madmen's ideas.
>
> [Faas 186–7]

Though the madmen are still at the helm, Gaia is now a public myth, or a public reality again: 'because this is what we are seeing: something that was unthinkable only ten years ago, except as a poetic dream: the re-emergence of Nature as the Great Goddess of mankind, and the Mother of all life'. (The name 'Gaia' was given to Lovelock by William Golding.)

Developments in the decades since then have confirmed that Lawrence was at the beginning, not the end of an era; and what is now called deep ecology is but the latest name for Pan.

18 GOLDING AND THE CRIME OF BEING HUMAN

Golding's primary motivation as a novelist was indicated by one of his favourite quotations: 'Where there is no vision, the people perish' [*Proverbs* xxix 18]. Not people, but *the* people. Golding wrote for the race. The fates of individuals are of interest to him mainly in so far as they are representative of the fate of the race. And he was fully aware how close to perishing the race now is. The question Golding continually asked himself, and strained all the resources of his art to answer, was, surely, the largest and most urgent of all questions: What is the essential nature of man, and what is his proper relationship with this terrifying and beautiful universe in which he finds himself obliged to attempt not only to survive, but also to achieve his fullest humanity. Thus we can say of Golding what Lawrence said of Hardy, that he 'shares with the great writers, Shakespeare or Sophocles or Tolstoi, 'this setting behind the small action of his protagonists the terrific action of unfathomed nature, setting a smaller system of morality, the one grasped and formulated by the human consciousness within the vast, uncomprehended and incomprehensible morality of nature or of life itself, surpassing human consciousness' [*Phoenix* 419].

The writer who attempts this is obliged to substantiate his vision with an even deeper understanding of the human individual than is required in the predominantly social or psychological writer. He must peer into the dark heart of man's nature, far deeper than the level at which psychoanalysis operates, to the level where that small inner darkness is either dammed against or flooded by the Great Outer Darkness which is God.

Golding had, at the outset of his career, all the required errors waiting to be corrected by his imagination. His father was 'a Wellsian rationalist' – the science master Nick in *Free Fall* is a portrait of him. For a long time William half convinced himself that he too was a rationalist and an atheist. He was aware of himself as 'always having been pretty masculine . . . I never have had a large component of the female in me' [176], and one way in which this manifested itself was in a burning desire to 'know'. Once convinced that science and rationalism could not explain the nature and condition of man, Golding found himself living in two worlds: 'There is this physical one, which is coherent, and there is a spiritual one. . . . This experience of having two worlds to live in all the time . . . is a vital one and is what living is like' [Carey 87]. The interrogator in *Free Fall* could be speaking of Golding himself when he says to Sammy Mountjoy: 'And between the poles of belief, I mean the belief in material things and the belief in a world made and supported by a supreme being, you oscillate jerkily from day to day, from hour to hour' [144]. All Golding's novels were attempts to resolve this dualism, to establish that the spiritual dimension is not always, after all, elsewhere.

✻   ✻   ✻

Ralph, our representative in *Lord of the Flies*, faces a triple challenge: to survive; to confront, understand and come to terms with the Beast (which is a projection from that dark centre of human nature); and to bring his life into a viable relationship with outer nature in its most inhuman manifestations – the island and its surrounding sea. The island is a boat, the isolated and exposed human community, on which the boys must attempt to navigate this sea, with Ralph as captain. He receives conflicting advice and example from three quarters, from Piggy, Jack and Simon. These are, of course, very real, very believable boys; but they also function as externalizations of aspects of Ralph's own being, his highly-conditioned, highly-socialized common-sense materialism (Piggy), his primitive murderous selfishness (Jack), and his sensitive, imaginative openness (Simon).

It is in their contrasting attitudes to the natural world, its flora and fauna, that the boys are first distinguished. There is the conch, for example. Ralph's spontaneous response is to be fascinated by its beauty and strangeness. Piggy immediately tries to draw his attention to its monetary worth and its social usefulness: it becomes for him a symbol of order and civilization. It is of no interest to Jack. When Piggy and Ralph think his raiding party is after their precious conch, in fact it is after Piggy's glasses with their power of making fire. Simon, too, has little interest, presumably because his interest would have been in the creature which originally made and inhabited it. He does not, like the others, automatically appropriate things for human purposes.

Each boy has a different attitude to the island itself. For Ralph it is a 'good' island – 'the imagined but never fully realized place leaping into real life' [21]. But such a place has been imagined with the help of such falsifications of reality as *Coral Island, Treasure Island* or *Swallows and Amazons*. It leaps into life with the arrival of the boys because it is entirely a projection of their daydreams. Piggy, like Crusoe, is only interested in transforming the island into a replica of the familiar adult world he has left behind, though he falsifies that too by assuming it to have been a world of order and goodwill and reason when it was in fact a world of nuclear war. For Jack it is a hunting-ground and potential kingdom. Only Simon responds to it openly, sensitively, for what it is:

> He not only registers the heat, the urgency, the riot, the dampness and
> decay; he also registers the cool and mysterious submergence of the forest
> in darkness, the pure beauty and fragrance of starlight and nightflower,
> the peace. Finally he not only registers both, but accepts them equally, as
> two parts of the same reality. It is these qualities of acceptance and
> inclusion that give us the 'Simon-ness' of Simon.   [Kinkead-Weekes 30–1]

The island presents the boys with the opportunity for a clean start. Here the crime against nature has not yet been committed and need not be. The island has the paradisal abundance of Marvell's 'The Garden':

> Flower and fruit grew together on the same tree and everywhere was the
> scent of ripeness and the booming of a million bees at pasture.   [71]

Simon passes down to the littluns 'double handfuls of ripe fruit'. But all the
boys except Simon assume that the island is there for them to do as they like
with. One of the first decisions is that Jack's choir shall be hunters. The first
exploration of the island begins with the unbalancing of a great rock:

> The great rock loitered, poised on one toe, decided not to return, moved
> through the air, fell, struck, turned over, leapt droning through the air
> and smashed a deep hole in the canopy of the forest. Echoes and birds
> flew, white and pink dust floated, the forest further down shook as with
> the passage of an enraged monster: and then the island was still.
> 'Wacco!'
> 'Like a bomb!'
> 'Whee-aa-oo!'
> Not for five minutes could they drag themselves away from this
> triumph.   [37]

They leave a trail of destruction behind them. The culmination of this first
expedition is the opportunity to kill an entangled piglet. Jack raises his knife,
but does not bring it down:

> They knew very well why he hadn't: because of the enormity of the knife
> descending and cutting into living flesh; because of the unbearable
> blood. . . . Next time there would be no mercy.   [41]

Next time there is not.

Piggy's glasses provide the gift of fire. The first time a fire is lit, it is
allowed to get out of hand and swallow a whole swathe of forest. One of the
littluns is never seen again. Fire is energy without vision, power without
responsibility.

Jack is by no means the only boy with a compulsion to hurt and kill.
Henry pokes with a stick among the tiny transparent creatures which lived
in the last fling of the sea: 'He became absorbed beyond mere happiness as
he felt himself exercising control over living things' [77]. (After the death of
Simon it is these same creatures which exercise control, officiate like angels
over the disposal of the body, receiving and reducing it back into the source.)
Shortly Henry himself becomes the potential victim. Roger throws stones at
him, but dare not hit him: 'Round the squatting child was the protection of
parents and school and policemen and the law' [78]. What finally severs their
bond with that civilization is their discovery of the liberating power of the
mask and the chant. When a ship comes in sight, Jack's hunters, who were
responsible for keeping the fire smoking, are killing their first pig, with a
gratifying amount of blood. They are intoxicated with a new knowledge –

314

a knowledge that had come to them when they closed in on the struggling pig, knowledge that they had outwitted a living thing, imposed their will upon it, taken away its life like a long satisfying drink. [88]

Perhaps the most important difference between the boys is in their reaction to the Beast.

'You have doctors for everything, even the inside of your mind. You don't really mean that we got to be frightened all the time of nothing? Life,' said Piggy expansively, 'is scientific, that's what it is. In a year or two when the war's over they'll be travelling to Mars and back. I know there isn't no beast – not with claws and all that, I mean – but I know there isn't no fear, either.' [105]

Piggy goes some way towards an understanding of the Beast in that he knows it is no more than a projection of fear from the inside of their own minds; but that, for him, is to say that it is simply unreal, does not exist. It is for Simon to discover that it is no less than a projection of 'mankind's essential illness'. Jack wants to propitiate the Beast, offer sacrifices to it. Ralph denies the Beast as long as he can, but is finally confronted by it:

The skull regarded Ralph like one who knows all the answers and won't tell. A sick fear and rage swept him. Fiercely he hit out at the filthy thing in front of him that bobbed like a toy and came back, still grinning into his face, so that he lashed and cried out in loathing. [228]

He splits the skull in two, like Hughes' Crow:

Crow split his enemy's skull to the pineal gland.
Where is the Black Beast?   ['The Black Beast']

Crow is himself the Black Beast. All such monsters are projections from our own inner darkness. What we do not understand we fear, and what we fear we convert, psychically, into external monsters we can strike at and attempt to kill. The Beast speaks to Simon: 'Fancy thinking the Beast was something you could hunt and kill! . . . I'm part of you. . . . I'm the reason why it's no go' [177]. What the children have converted into a Black Beast, an external locus of all evil and obscenity is in fact the goddess, one of whose avatars is the sow as Great Mother. Before the 'dreadful eruption' of the hunters into her paradise she had lain suckling, 'sunk in maternal bliss'. She runs terrified into a sanctuary, 'an open space where bright flowers grew and butterflies danced round each other' [167]; there she is in every way including the sexual, violated: 'The sow collapsed under them and they were heavy and fulfilled upon her'. When they have finished with her she is an image only of their ugliness.

315

We are no longer concerned with debunking children's books. Golding is accounting for all the failures, fiascos often, which have followed the persistent efforts of men, often the best men of their generation, to escape from a sick civilization to some unspoiled place in order to regain Paradise: the New World, the South Seas, Coleridge's Pantisocracy on the banks of the Susquehanna, Lawrence's Rananim . . . None of these has succeeded or ever will succeed because the Black Beast cannot be left behind, cannot be exterminated without exterminating man. Golding as a boy had been attracted by such utopias as Wells' *Men Like Gods*, had wondered why the world was not like that:

> The cruel fact is that had that boy walked into the perfected society, to him would have come out of his blood the hates and loves – no, on a less epic scale, the antipathies and greeds, the jealousies and ambitions, the misdirected energies and deadening sloths; and not just his but those of other people all working with, through and against each other.
>
> [*Moving Target* 19]

It is not because we are dealing with irresponsible children that the island is destroyed. Had Pincher Martin and the crew of his ship been wrecked on the same island, the result would have been the same. In any group of men, the crew in *Rites of Passage*, for example, or Matthew Paris' utopia in Barry Unsworth's *Sacred Hunger*, there will emerge cruelties, perversions, evil. A ship or an island is only the world in little. We are in the process of doing to the world what the boys do to their island and for the same reasons.

Simon attempts to understand nature not in order to control or manipulate it, but in order to be atoned with it, to heal the split within himself and bring his healing wisdom, his clear-sightedness, back for the race. But Simon, like so many of his kind, is ignored, then persecuted, then used as scapegoat. The blows fall on the one place where the Black Beast is not to be found. But there is a strong contrast between the deaths of Simon and Piggy. Each is equally violent and purposeless. But the death of Piggy is recorded in single vision (as through the one lens of Piggy's broken glasses):

> His head opened and stuff came out and turned red. Piggy's arms and legs twitched a bit, like a pig's after it has been killed. Then the sea breathed again in a long, slow sigh, the water boiled white and pink over the rock; and when it went, sucking back again, the body of Piggy was gone. [222–3]

Single vision reduces the human mind to 'stuff', and a dead man is no more than his own corpse. Death obliterates life. The death of Simon is not the end of Simon, any more than the death of Cordelia is the obliteration of all that she had been. Rather, the death affirms, validates, sets the seal on all she had embodied and stood for. In death as in life she remains part of sustaining and redemptive nature.

316

External nature at its most inhuman and intimidating is most evident in *Lord of the Flies*, as in other Golding novels, as the sea. Ralph is troubled by this 'sleeping Leviathan', which reduces and alienates him, threatens to swamp his sense of his own reality and centrality:

> Down here, almost on a level with the sea, you could follow with your eye the ceaseless, bulging passage of the deep sea waves. They were miles wide, apparently not breakers or the banked ridges of shallow water. They travelled the length of the island with an air of disregarding it and being set on other business; they were less a progress than a momentous rise and fall of the whole ocean . . . Wave after wave, Ralph followed the rise and fall until something of the remoteness of the sea numbed his brain. Then gradually the almost infinite size of this water forced itself on his attention. This was the divider, the barrier. On the other side of the island, swathed at midday with mirage, defended by the shield of the quiet lagoon, one might dream of rescue; but here, faced with the brute obtuseness of the ocean, the miles of division, one was clamped down, one was helpless, one was condemned, one was – [136–7]

The continuation of that sentence would have been *Pincher Martin*.

Only Simon's vision is wide enough to include the sea, and with it his own not extinction but transfiguration, his own minute but indestructible participation in the vast and mysterious processes of the world:

> Somewhere over the darkened curve of the world the sun and moon were pulling; and the film of water on the earth planet was held, bulging slightly on one side while the solid core turned. The great wave of the tide moved further along the island and the water lifted. Softly, surrounded by a fringe of inquisitive bright creatures, itself a silver shape beneath the steadfast constellations, Simon's dead body moved out towards the open sea. [190]

In spite of this, *Lord of the Flies* is a bleak book. Golding seems to have little hope that man is redeemable, unless he happens to be born with the equipment of a saint or seer. None of the boys, not even Simon, seems to have much free choice. We are, it seems, in Golding's words, 'born to sorrow as the sparks fly upward' [Carey 173]. The novel ends with Ralph weeping 'for the end of innocence' and 'the darkness of man's heart'. Golding has recorded that he wrote the book in 'sheer grief': 'It was like lamenting the lost childhood of the world' [*A Moving Target* 163]. The loss of innocence seems to be our biological inheritance as a species. Indeed, the next novel, *The Inheritors*, is about the moment in our evolutionary history when, it seemed to Golding, this fall took place.

* * *

H.G. Wells' *Outline of History* was published in 1919. It presented the evolution of man as a steady progress from Neanderthal men (repulsive 'gorilla-like monsters') to ourselves. The few known facts about Neanderthal man were distorted and augmented to fit this preconception. Wells had studied biology with T.H. Huxley, and shared Huxley's belief that the human race was involved in 'a constant struggle to maintain and improve, in opposition to the State of Nature, the State of Art' [*Evolution* 44–5]. Lawrence had a different idea of what constituted progress: 'Hadn't somebody better write Mr Wells' History backwards, to prove how we've degenerated, in our stupid visionlessness, since the cave-men?' [*Phoenix 2*, 434]. Thirty years later somebody did. The result was *The Inheritors*.

Golding has described himself as 'a propagandist for Neanderthal man'. Golding had more facts to go on. His imaginative reconstruction of their lives (like Lawrence's of the Etruscans) was so sensitive to those clues that subsequent evidence has shown that he could safely have gone even further in his claims for their kindness and gentleness. It is now known, for example, that they looked after their cripples and that they buried their dead in flowers. Golding sees them as the last men who could lay claim to innocence. They did not attempt to impose their will on the world: they could not, since they did not differentiate between themselves and the world created and maintained by Oa. It is perhaps Golding's greatest single achievement as a novelist to enable us to share this form of consciousness, without dualism, without conceptual thought, without our sense of the separate and overriding importance of the individual.

Like Jakob Boehme Golding sees the fall as a fall into selfhood, which Norman O. Brown describes as 'a vain project of the part to become independent of the totality conceived as a mother-principle'. Brown quotes Boehme:

Every will which enters into self-hood and seeks the ground of its
life-form breaks itself off from the mystery and enters into a
capriciousness. It cannot do otherwise for its fellow members stir up
dying and death. It lies, and denies union with the Will of God and sets
self-hood in its place, so that it goes out from unity into a desire for self. If
it knew that all things have brought it forth and are its mothers, and if it
did not hold its mother's substance for its own, but in common, then
greed, envy, strife and a contrary will would not arise.   [130]

The Neanderthals are a People. A person is as useless as a severed limb. They are incapable of invention, and are consequently without tools and weapons. Such language as they have is pictorial (wonderfully conveyed in their exchange of 'pictures'). It is poetic, highly metaphorical speech in which metaphor is not comparison but identity. The language Golding invents for the Neanderthals has attracted the attention of linguists interested in 'mind-style', a term coined by Fowler to indicate the way in which linguistic choices made by characters in novels reflect their world-view. For example, as Mike Short points out:

Grammatically, Lok tends to choose intransitive structures where we would normally use transitives, and does not reserve the subject slot of dynamic (often intentional) verbs for animates. Hence 'the stick began to grow shorter at both ends' is used where we might normally say 'the man drew back the bow', thus making it seem as if the way in which Lok categorizes the world does not take proper account of agency and the process of cause and effect, crucial matters in the inability of Lok's tribe to withstand the intruders.   [31]

Fowler concentrates on Lok's 'conceptual deficiencies', but Short points out that

it is possible to see some aspects of the linguistic behaviour pointed to, not as deficiencies, but as positive qualities we have lost. For example, the use of animates and inanimates in the same grammatical positions could be seen as correlates of a sense of oneness with inanimate nature which we no longer have.   [32]

The People live largely through their senses, but Golding is at pains to establish that this is not mere deprivation or savagery. Their rich physical life is inseparable from their rich spiritual life. Their highly developed senses enable them to relate fully to all other life animistically, sacramentally.

The new people, Cro-Magnon, are both immeasurably inferior and immeasurably superior to the Neanderthals. They are superior in that the Neanderthals are a stagnant species, unable to adapt or progress. The People have no spirit of adventure. All they need is a summer home and a winter home and a trail between them, fire, and enough to eat. They ask no more than that tomorrow should be like today and yesterday. They do not fear death as something separate from and inimical to life. Oa means to them life as it is, including death. Therefore they fear change, and, however long they had survived, they would have had no history. The New Men are individualists who do fear death and attempt to defeat it by responding aggressively to the world as it is, attempting to change it so as to acquire both personal and cultural immortality. Their raid on the future is the rape of Oa and the beginning of history.

They are inferior in many ways. Their sensory equipment is crude in comparison. They are characterized by possessiveness, rivalry and guilt. The baby is specifically Vivani's, not the race's New One. Tuami cannot share Vivani with Marlan, as the People share their women. The fight for unequal shares of wine results in the bursting of the wineskin. Marlan uses his power to satisfy his own lust and greed, and buys his safety with atrocity. There is no sanction against killing the Old Man. The New Men, unlike the People, seek to destroy what they fear and cannot understand. This invariably leads to the replacement of sympathetic magic and the worship of the stag as horned god by human sacrifice and the concept of Nature as external devil or ogre to be killed if possible, otherwise placated with the sacrifice of scapegoats. The red devil they flee from is poor uncomprehending, loving Lok, cut off, isolated, dying.

They are prepared to use their own innocent child as offering:

> The religion is a death-religion, which gives man the power to impose his will on nature, at the cost of blood-sacrifice. It contains reverence, but born of fear not dread; and because its whole business is with results, it must succeed or bring rebellion from devotees who have sacrificed in vain.
>
> [Kinkead-Weekes 98]

What reverence they have is not for living things or nature's resources. The New Men do not husband resources, since they do not regard this place as home. Therefore each stopping place is merely a place to be exploited, stripped of its resources, before moving on. They have no responsibility for it. They do not use trails, but blunder through the vegetation leaving swathes of wreckage. They even destroy existing trails by removing log bridges for their fires. They build fires far larger than are needed for warmth. Marlan kills the cave-bear not for meat or self-protection, but to impress Vivani with his bravery and procure her a fur-coat as a love-token and to set her above other women. The New Men have utensils, but they also have weapons. It is but a short step to the Trojan War. The theft of Vivani prefigures

> The broken wall, the burning roof and towers
> And Agamemnon dead.
>> [Yeats, 'Leda and the Swan']

Tuami fashions a beautiful ivory haft, but he intends to use the dagger to kill his rival in love, and his descendents will massacre elephants and human beings for more and more ivory.

The New Men are recognizably ourselves. Golding is encapsulating here the evolutionary moment when humanity as we know it – intelligent, articulate, inventive, adventurous, aggressive, greedy, individualistic, split, fear and guilt-ridden humanity – came into existence and took over. It is not just a tour-de-force. It is his attempt to locate the origin of original sin, the source of our inherited predisposition to wickedness and guilt, to find an organic and historical basis for the theories of the psychologists and for the myths of the fall.

Golding is not simply making another myth. It would be valuable as such even if its scientific content were fanciful. But in fact it is scientifically impeccable. In the popular mind the evolution of man was simply a matter of the brain getting gradually bigger and bigger; but this was not the case. Man has three distinct brains, which Paul MacLean has named the archicortex, the mesocortex and the neocortex. The archicortex, or old brain is the brain we have in common with all vertebrates. We have brought it with us all the long evolutionary journey from the reptilian stage. It is very like the brain of a crocodile. Its function is to control all instinctive and involuntary behaviour. The mesocortex is the brain we share with all other mammals. It is similar to the brain of a horse. (In St Mawr Lawrence dramatizes the rehabilitation of that brain in the relationship between a woman and her horse). In MacLean's words, this brain 'plays a fundamental role in emotional behaviour... It has a greater capacity than the reptilian brain for learning new approaches and solutions to problems on the basis of immediate experience. But like the reptilian brain, it does not have the ability to put its feelings into words.'

The neocortex, which distinguishes man from the other primates, developed, in evolutionary terms, suddenly. According to MacLean:

> During the phylogeny of the mammal, one of the most striking events of all evolution occurs. This is the great ballooning out of the neocortex. In the process, the archicortex and the greater part of the mesocortex are folded like two concentric rings into the limbic lobe and are relegated, as it were, to the cellar of the brain. [quoted by Koestler, 80]

That cellar, in all Golding's works, is the source of all our terrors, the lair of the Black Beast.

The limbic cortex and the neocortex have each retained a high degree of autonomy, and each has a completely different mode of functioning which might well produce different, indeed opposite, responses to the same situation. This would have led to the rapid extinction of the species had not the neocortex been able to push the limbic cortex into the cellar, the unconscious, and lock the door. The neocortex is able to jam the signals coming from the limbic cortex except in sleep, under drugs, in moments of crisis, in mental breakdown, and perhaps, in moments of fourfold vision achieved by poets and seers. If we think of the limbic cortex as the home not of the Black Beast but of our innermost demon which gives us our vitality and our contact with the powers of the world, then what we are doing is disowning, exiling, torturing and trying to kill that demon, and that is the cause of our obscure guilt.

More recently we have come to speak of the duality of the human brain in terms of the different functioning of the left and right sides. As Ted Hughes puts it:

> The limbic system, which is the old mammalian brain governing the basic emotion and monitoring internal conditions, tends to associate itself with the language of sensuous images, intuitive assessments, total patterns. The activity of the cortex, the 'new' brain, which supervises all activities, refines interpretations and controls the behaviour according to 'reason', tends to associate itself with the analytical language of words. This tends to ally the deep subjective life of the animal with the right side, and the objective self-control of the animal with the left side. These are only broad and general tendencies – where 'left' and 'right' are not the

physically different two halves of the brain, but simply the modes of communication (abstract, conceptual, verbal symbols versus sensuous or concrete, image-patterned symbols) favoured by left side and right side respectively, according to research. [*Shakespeare* 158]

Hughes concedes that 'lifting the left side into dominance literally by suppressing the right, seems desirable in some situations'. But where it becomes habitual and automatic 'it removes the individual from the "inner life" of the right side, which produces the sensation of living removed from oneself . . . In some enclaves (particularly familiar in Western Protestant society) where the cultural incentives promoting the rational tendencies of language are extreme, the activity of the right side can be discredited and suppressed almost to extinction' [157–8]. Wells' *Outline of History* is an extreme symptom of this process. And the extinction of the Neanderthals in *The Inheritors* is Golding's mythic dramatization of it.

The feature of the New Men which most amazes Lok is their grotesquely enlarged heads. That enlargement could more properly be regarded as an evolutionary disaster. The new brain was an unwanted present, like giving a child or a tribesman the latest computer without an instruction book. It was too big and complex. It came too quickly. It was impossible to coordinate it with the old brain. We are still living with and still failing to cope with the consequences. Hughes calls *The Inheritors* 'a visionary dream projected from a calamity which is happening at this moment, in the inner life of the reader, before and during and after his reading' [Carey 162]. He describes the New Men as 'a totally new kind of creature: born outside the laws, detached from them and with no direct means of learning them: the first animal to be out of phase with life on earth' [167]. Arthur Koestler says:

When one contemplates the streak of insanity running through human history, it appears highly probable that *homo sapiens* is a biological freak, the result of some remarkable mistake in the evolutionary process. The ancient doctrine of original sin, variants of which occur independently in the mythologies of diverse cultures, could be a reflection of man's awareness of his own inadequacy, of the intuitive hunch that somewhere along the line of his ascent something has gone wrong. [267]

Perhaps the first scientist to address this problem direct, to follow up that hunch systematically, was the South African zoologist Eugène Marais, who spent several years living with baboons in the second decade of this century. Out of this field research came his revolutionary book *The Soul of the Ape*. Marais demonstrated that sense degeneration had reached an extreme point in man, but that this was not an organic change, since it could to a large extent be reversed under hypnosis. He found that intelligence developed at the expense of instinct, so that the most intelligent baboons had the least idea of how to live as baboons. Hughes comments:

In Marais' definition, the 'subconscious' became the contained but for the most part inaccessible world not only of the 'brute' components of instinct but of instinct's positive attributes as well – those superior senses, superior intuitions, and that superior grasp of reality. . . . He had really defined the subconscious as the lost, natural Paradise, where the lack of intellectual enquiry and adaptive ingenuity coincided with a perfect awareness of being alive in the moment, and in reality, (an awareness approaching, maybe, a state of blessedness), and an inborn understanding of 'how to live'. He had explained, in a sense, man's perplexed feeling of being everywhere an exile, everywhere separated from his true being. And without saying that his smarter baboons had suffered something like The Fall, he had brought zoological evidence to the argument that the free intelligence is man's original enemy.

[Carey 164]

But Golding is not simply wailing for our lost innocence, or advocating universal lobotomy. There can be no going back. Even without the New Men to exterminate them, we feel that the People are doomed. The Ice Age is ending. They are helpless against water, lacking boats. Energy, agility, daring, free intelligence and fear superior to theirs is needed to get the new men *up* the fall, in defiance of brute nature. The new men need the fall, in both senses, to provide them with their greatest challenge. It is the price they must pay for their achievement of freedom and consciousness. They are embarking on the great adventure in consciousness, into the dark. Aeons are telescoped into that final chapter as man leaps forward to the Ulyssean adventure with hungry heart. It is all there in the sentence in which the drunken Lok expresses his sense of what it must be like to be a New Man: 'There is nothing he could not do'. Here is the glory and the crime of Homo sapiens, the dangerous freedom and power, the fatal hubris.

Hughes concludes his essay on this novel:

The Cro-Magnons begin to look less like demons of original depravity, more like helplessly processed and forlorn castaways, who are full of plans and plots and enterprise, but do not know 'how to live'. Figures who are, by their very nature, tragic. Subjects, maybe, for Golding's later books.

[168]

The challenge for us, the latest inheritors, is to pass through experience, and in full consciousness recover our vision and wholeness. But the decision that the world was to be ruled by man rather than Oa was disastrous. Oa *is* the world. Never again will it be possible for man to relate to Oa with the unselfconscious innocence of the Neanderthals. But the Neanderthals had an inadequate conception of Oa, inadequate for their survival and for ours. It is not the rejection of Oa that evolution demands, but a more inclusive perception of her. Oa is neither beneficent, a loving mother, nor invulnerable. She is not only in the fire and the ice and the People. She is in everything they most fear and hate: the hyenas, the fanged wolves, the big cats, the cave bears, the mire and deep water, the face and the dead eyes under the water. She is in Behemoth and Leviathan, the hawk which sucks up blood, the vulture which tears Prometheus, the lightning and cactus spines and pack-rats of the New Mexico Rockies.

The Inheritors is not entirely tragic or defeatist. The New Men take with them the Neanderthal baby, as we have brought with us our old brains. Already, before the end of the book, they are beginning to see that baby not as red devil to be feared or infant Caliban to be persecuted, but as something they need to recognize and accept as an essential part of themselves. It is their only hope.

❉   ❉   ❉

All Golding's subsequent heroes are victims of this split, this schizophysiology as MacLean calls it. It is the price we have had to pay for freedom and consciousness. But freedom easily degenerates into being 'at sea' or in free fall, that is, utterly without bearings, ties or supports.

Pincher Martin embodies the very worst symptoms of the disease. He assumes the purpose of evolution has been to produce him. He is the inheritor of everything. If the rule is survival of the fittest, then his capacity to survive is proof of his fitness to do so. He is totally solipsistic. That is, his universe is, literally, self-centred. He is determined to be the biggest maggot in the box, which is to say the last and only maggot in the box. Golding's fable, like Lawrence's 'The Man Who Loved Islands', finds a perfect objective correlative for solipsism: the man who thinks he is an island unto himself is consigned to an uninhabited island, a mere rock, where he undergoes a spiritual death.

Hell is everlasting life without God; and God is relatedness, interdependence, one's vital connection with the not-self, the whole. He compares himself with Prometheus, but is more like Faust, not only claiming independence from God, but arrogating to himself many of the prerogatives of God, including the right to be immortal and the right to create his own universe to go on living in. The universe he creates has to fulfil two requirements – it has to be rational, to satisfy his own intelligence as a place he might have escaped to and a *real* place which is why the rock and its flora and fauna have to be so laboriously and rigorously and concretely realized, and why the few mistakes he makes, the red lobsters and the soluble guano for example, are so devastating – glaring rips in the trompe-l'oeil backcloth; and it has to be a projection of his own inner, psychic and physiological world, since he has nothing else out of which to make it.

Thus we recognize that his world must always have been essentially what it is on the rock. His life has been, like Odysseus', a continual struggle to make the universe recognize his own centrality and permanence. He has been surrounded by inimical beings daring to refuse to conform to his needs and wishes. These he clambers over, ruthlessly reshapes for his purposes, destroys if necessary. Pincher is defined by his name: 'He was born with his mouth and his flies open and both hands out to grab'. Those grabbing hands lead him into his first mistake in creating his island by suggesting to his imagination the claws of a red lobster (forgetting that they become red only when boiled). Lok, as we saw, was a unified being, both within himself and in relation to the not-self. When the last string broke which connected him to his world, he died. To have survived alone would have been inconceivable to him. He folds himself back into Oa. Pincher is exactly the opposite, a fragmented being: 'I was always two things, mind and body'. Being both split and cut off he can live only by extreme self-assertion, a constant struggle to maintain identity at all costs, crucified upon his own body. We are reminded of Eliot's Prufrock, impaled by his own self-consciousness like an insect writhing on a pin. Prufrock's last cry before he gives up the struggle for selfhood is: 'I should have been a pair of ragged claws / Scuttling across the floors of silent seas'. Pincher is a pair of ragged claws which, as his rock dissolves, have nothing left to close on but each other – 'And appetite, an universal wolf, at last eats up himself'.

Yet Pincher's effort to hold on to such a pitiful corrupt identity at such cost becomes at length heroic, like the 'senseless trial of strength' of 'The Contender' in Hughes' poem of that name:

He gritted his teeth like a cliff.
Though his body was sweeling away like a torrent on a cliff
Smoking towards dark gorges
There he nailed himself with nails of nothing.

There is no possible redemption in mere resistance. Hughes and Golding both know that if a man cannot open himself, he must be broken. He must die to the old corrupt self before he can be reborn to a new wholeness. Only thus can pain be converted into vision, as it is with Hughes' Prometheus and the hero of *Cave Birds*, and as it is to be with Sammy Mountjoy and Jocelin. Pincher Martin stops just short of being a tragic figure because we do not see him broken. The last we see of him, though reduced to a pair of ragged claws, he is still resisting. Also, he lacks full existential responsibility. To have acted differently he would have to have *been* different – been someone else. We feel that he was born Pincher Martin rather than that he earned his name by freely taken moral acts or decisions at some earlier stage of his life. There is nothing in the novel to suggest that he ever had any innocence to lose. Hence the invitation to him at the end to 'consider' is somewhat empty. There is nothing for him to consider but whether he has yet had enough of being Pincher Martin. It is not suggested that at that late stage he is capable of becoming someone else.

Pincher Martin is, like *Lord of the Flies*, a static, fatalistic novel, revealing the sickness at the heart of man, but offering no hope of any cure.

*   *   *

Sammy Mountjoy in *Free Fall* is a very similar character to Pincher Martin but different questions are asked about him, both by himself and by his creator. The free fall of the title is the condition in which Sammy, in middle life, finds himself, the condition described so graphically by Lawrence in the poem 'Only Man':

> . . . self-consciousness wriggling
>> writhing deeper and deeper in all the minutiae of
> self-knowledge, downwards, exhaustive,
> yet never, never coming to the bottom, for there is no bottom;
> . . . so it wriggles its way even further down, further down
> at last in sheer horror of not being able to leave off
> knowing itself, knowing itself apart from God, falling.

But it is not assumed that Sammy merely inherited this fallen state. Perhaps the individual recapitulates the history of the race and has to re-enact the loss of innocence at some early stage of his life. Mountjoy spends much of the novel seeking to locate such a moment. He eventually succeeds.

The moment he closes in on was the moment when, at about the time he left school, he had been granted a vision of the divine Beatrice flanked by two of her fellows. The rest of Dante's life – *La Vita Nuova* – was determined by his decision to devote himself henceforth to the spiritual service of his Beatrice. He achieves Paradise, in the *Divine Comedy* through her intercession. Sammy sees his Beatrice as 'divine' only in the slang sense (since he has already rejected spirit as a good rationalist). His decision is to devote himself henceforth, at all costs, to the attainment of Beatrice's body. His name again tells all. He seeks to mount Joy, to attain paradise, not by spiritual aspiration but by fucking. He destroys Beatrice's innocence and, ultimately, her sanity.

But if Golding now thinks of innocence as something which may be lost afresh within each individual life, perhaps it may also be regained. The first stage is to become aware of the equal reality of the world of spirit, equal, that is, with the world of matter, the world mediated to Sammy by his materialistic Science master Nick (it is also the world of Piggy). But the second, much more difficult stage is to unify these two apparently alternative worlds.

> All day long the trains run on rails. Eclipses are predictable. Penicillin cures pneumonia and the atom splits to order. All day long, year in, year out, the daylight explanation drives back the mystery and reveals a reality usable, understandable and detached. The scalpel and the microscope fail, the oscilloscope moves closer to behaviour. The gorgeous dance is self-contained, then; does not need the music which in my mad moments I have heard. Nick's universe is real.
> All day long action is weighed in the balance and found not opportune nor fortunate or ill-advised, but good or evil. For this mode which we

must call the spirit breathes through the universe and does not touch it; touches only the dark things, held prisoner, incommunicado, touches, judges, sentences and passes on.

Her world was real, both worlds are real. There is no bridge.   [252–3]

Between *Free Fall* and *The Spire* Golding wrote:

Any man who claims to have found a bridge between the world of the physical sciences and the world of the spirit is sure of a hearing. Is this not because most of us have an unexpressed faith that the bridge exists?
['All or Nothing']

After his breakdown in the cell, where Sammy has been forced to admit his deepest fears and his inadequacy, he is, in his own words, 'visited by a flake of fire, miraculous and pentecostal'. In his 'complete and luminous sanity', he sees everything as related to everything else, transfigured, glorified, in a 'shining, singing cosmos'. In 1799 Blake wrote to Trussler: 'A tree which moves some to tears of joy is in the Eyes of others only a Green thing that stands in the way'. Sammy has suddenly acquired this fourfold vision:

Those crowded shapes extending up into the air and down into the rich earth, those deeds of far space and deep earth were aflame at the surface and daunting by right of their own natures though a day before I should have disguised them as trees.   [186]

Though this section of the book, chapter ten, is well enough written, it does not seem to be a necessary consequence of what has gone before. It seems theoretical and arbitrary, and only deepens our confusion in our attempts to understand a character who never manages to grip our imagination as Pincher Martin and Jocelin do, who remains, in the last analysis, rather boring.

*   *   *

In essays and interviews Golding frequently testified to his belief in original sin and the fallen condition of man; to his sense of living in two worlds, the physical and the metaphysical. This led others, if not Golding himself, to claim that he was a Christian. But if we trust the tales rather than the artist, we shall find that the fall, as it appears in all of them, could be seen as a fall from the physical into the metaphysical as easily as the contrary. Or rather, that the fallen state of his protagonists expresses itself as a desacralization of the physical world and of their own bodies, such as is encouraged not only by the egotistical sensuality of a Pincher Martin, but equally by the kind of world-rejecting transcendental religion which fires Jocelin in *The Spire*.

Jocelin is the opposite of Pincher Martin and Sammy Mountjoy in that he has chosen the life of the spirit rather than that of the body; but he is a victim of the same split. Unable to find the bridge, he can only maintain his dedication to spirit by denying the world of matter and people and his own body. His determination to build the impossible spire is a perfect image of his repudiation of the earth and its limitations. He is like Hughes' Adam:

> Too little lifted from mud
> He dreamed the tower of light . . .

> Wrapped in peach-skin and bruise
> He dreamed the religion of the diamond body . . .

> Open as a leafless bush to wind and rain
> He shook and he wept, he creaked and shivered.

['Adam']

Jocelin builds his crazy dream – but at what cost?

He believes in the reality of prayer, but not in the reality of stone or flesh. He would exclude from his cathedral, if he could, everything that is not pure spirit. Even the gargoyles he interprets as spewing out all impurities, the opposite interpretation from Lawrence's:

> There was, however, in the Cathedrals, already the denial of the Monism which the Whole uttered. All the little figures, the gargoyles, the imps, the human faces, whilst subordinated within the Great Conclusion of the Whole, still, from their obscurity, jeered their mockery of the Absolute, and declared for multiplicity, polygeny.   [*Phoenix* 454]

To Jocelin it seems that 'the renewing life of the world was a filthy thing, a rising tide of muck'. What seethes where the firm foundations of his church and his faith should be he interprets as

> Doomsday coming up; or the roof of hell down there. Perhaps the damned stirring, or the noseless men turning over and thrusting up; or the living, pagan earth, unbound at last and waking, Dia Mater.   [80]

He has refused to acknowledge Oa, the Dia Mater, thrust her into the darkness of the pit, both as woman and as nature, so that she becomes the devil gnawing at the foundations of his life and troubling his libidinous dreams. His own motives are impure, half faith and prayer and humility, half unacknowledged pride and lust and callousness. Though he abominates the human sacrifices still practised in the pagan temples (including nearby Stonehenge), he blindly sacrifices four human lives to his own spire.

He makes, also, impossible demands upon himself, trying to support the whole enterprise on his own back. His tubercular spine breaks. His spire must fall, founded, as it is, in sin. Yet it does not fall; it stands to this day. Out of Jocelin's pain comes true humility and illumination: 'There is no innocent work. God knows where God may be.' God may be in the sinner, in the pagan earth itself and its creatures. An appletree is not only the source of all our sin, a reminder of the fall; it is also, in bloom, a cloud of angels, a miracle. Christ is not only in holy nails, but plays in ten thousand places. In Hopkins' words, God's smile's 'not wrung' but revealed at 'unforeseen times'. And mortal beauty

> . . . keeps warm
> Men's wits to the things that are; what good means – where a glance
> Master more may than gaze, gaze out of countenance.
> ['To what serves Mortal Beauty']

Jocelin glimpses a kingfisher:

> He saw all the blue of the sky condensed to a winged sapphire, that flashed once.
> > He cried out.
> > 'Come back!'
> But the bird was gone, an arrow shot once. It will never come back, he thought, not if I sat here all day. He began to play with the thought that the bird might return, to sit on a post only a few yards away in all its splendour, but his heart knew better.
> > 'No kingfisher will return for me.'
> > All the same, he said to himself, I was lucky to see it.   [205]

We could not believe in Sammy Mountjoy's sudden access of vision, since it seemed to be not fully paid for, a product of mere panic. But we feel that Jocelin's suffering necessarily releases a vision which had got itself separated off from love, and is now at last reunified. The last thing he sees is the spire through the window, not seen now as a one-way ladder out of the filth, but as a bridge between two worlds, an atonement, redeeming the world of substance and substantiating the world of spirit:

> It was the window, bright and open. Something divided it. Round the division was the blue of the sky. The division was still and silent, but rushing upward to some point at the sky's end, and with a silent cry. It was slim as a girl, translucent. It had grown from some seed of rosecoloured substance that glittered like a waterfall, an upward waterfall. The substance was one thing, that broke all the way to infinity in cascades of exultation that nothing could trammel.   [223]

In *The Spire*, Golding demonstrated the possibility of recovering the vision and reversing the fall.

19 FROM WORLD OF BLOOD TO WORLD OF LIGHT

Early in his career Hughes spoke of 'the terrible, suffocating, maternal octopus of the English poetic tradition' [*WP* 213]. But Hughes himself, despite his deep early involvement with the natural world, was never in much danger of being remade in the image of Wordsworth. The boy who was taken to a nearby pub to watch Billy Red catch and kill rats with his teeth, whose pet fox cubs were torn apart by dogs before his eyes, who dreamed of being a wolf, was not likely to see Nature as Lucy Gray, rather as the sow that eats her own farrow. Nor did poetry first make its impact as mediated by Palgrave and his successors among schoolbook anthologizers, but with the unmediated violence of an Indian war song chanted to him by his brother:

> I am the woodpecker,
> My head is red,
> To those that I kill,
> With my little red bill,
> Come wolf, come bear and eat your fill,
> Mine's not the only head that's red.

The nine-year-old Hughes felt he could do something like that.

Wordsworth sealed his spirit to the inevitability of decay and death. Hughes is determined from the beginning to take a full look at the worst and accept it as nature's norm:

> Drinking the sea and eating the rock
> A tree struggles to make leaves –
> An old woman fallen from space
> Unprepared for these conditions.
> She hangs on, because her mind's gone completely.
>
> Minute after minute, aeon after aeon,
> Nothing lets up or develops.
> And this is neither a bad variant nor a tryout.
> This is where the staring angels go through.
> This is where all the stars bow down.   ['Pibroch']

The sound that haunted Hughes like a passion was

> That cry for milk
> From the breast
> Of the mother
> Of the God

Of the world
Made of Blood.
　　['Karma']

The first lines of the first poem in Hughes' first book *The Hawk in the Rain*
plunge us into a world which is soon to become familiar:

I drown in the drumming ploughland, I drag up
Heel after heel from the swallowing of the earth's mouth,
From clay that clutches my each step to the ankle
With the habit of the dogged grave . . .
　　　　　　　　　　　　　['The Hawk in the Rain']

The last lines of the last poem in his 1982 *Selected Poems* are a world away:

So we found the end of our journey.

So we stood, alive in the river of light
Among creatures of light, creatures of light.
　　　　　　　　['That Morning']

What I want to do in this chapter is to follow that journey, and look
at some of the crucial stations in it.

　　　　　　　*　　　*　　　*

The Hawk in the Rain is about man, imprisoned in single vision as in his own
body, looking out through the windows of his eyes at the surrounding energies,
the 'wandering elementals'. He makes no effort to come to terms with them,
as though that were unthinkable, but cowers, hides, peeps through his fingers,
grips his own heart, runs for dear life. His only defence is poetry, where he
can sit inside his own head and defend his ego with word-patterns.

'The Hawk in the Rain' pitches us into the thick of the battle between
vitality and death which Hughes claimed was his only subject. It is, in this
poem as in many, a one-sided battle. Three of the four elements seem to be
in alliance with death. Earth, even the earth of ploughland, is not fertile but a
mass grave. Water drowns. Rain falls not to engender new life but to convert
earth to down-dragging mud and to hack to the bone any head which presumes
to raise itself. Air manifests itself only as wind which kills any stubborn attempts
at life. The very language is a series of blows pounding life down. What hope
amidst all this for the fire of vitality or spirit? It is located only in the eye of
the hawk, which seems effortlessly, by an act of will, to master it all, to be the
exact centre, the eye of the storm, the 'master-Fulcrum of violence'.

The hawk is as close to the inviolability of an angel as a living creature
can be, yet the 'angelic eye' is doomed to be smashed, the hawk to 'mix his

heart's blood with the mire of the land'. The extinguishing of the hawk's fire, this mingling of mud and blood, as in the trenches and bomb-craters of the First World War which his uncles by their stories and his father by his aching silence had made the landscape of the young Hughes' mind, is what death wants and invariably gets in Hughes' poetry of the fifties and sixties. It is what shoulders out 'One's own body from its instant and heat' ['Six Young Men']. It is 'the dead man behind the mirror' [WP 214]. Yet the powerful ending of this poem comes to seem somewhat histrionic when we compare it with the death of the buzzard in *What Is the Truth?*:

> Finally, he just lets the sky
> Bend and hold him aloft by his wing-tips.
>
> There he hangs, dozing off in his hammock.
>
> Mother earth reaches up for him gently.
> [44]

Also the effect of 'The Hawk in the Rain' on the reader is far from depressing. If the man trying to cross a ploughed field in a cloudburst cannot be the 'master-Fulcrum of violence', the same man later sitting at his desk making a poem of the experience can.

> I turn every combatant into a bit of music, then resolve the whole uproar
> into as formal and balanced a figure of melody and rhythm as I can. When
> all the words are hearing each other clearly, and every stress is feeling
> every other stress, and all are contented – the poem is finished.
> [Faas 163]

This conception of art was very much in tune with the New Criticism fashionable in the fifties, and Hughes' early poems lent themselves to that kind of analysis. But it is an attitude to art he would soon have to modify radically. It is of a piece with the dualistic idea of creation by a sole male god. The goddess *was* heaven and earth, and cannot stand apart from nature. But the god who succeeded her makes nature out of inert materials, like an artist:

> In this way the essential identity between creator and creation was
> broken, and a fundamental dualism was born from their separation, the
> dualism that we know as spirit and nature. In the myth of the goddess
> these two terms have no meaning in separation from each other: nature is
> spiritual and spirit is natural, because the divine is immanent as creation.
> In the myth of the god, nature is no longer 'spiritual' and spirit is no
> longer 'natural', because the divine is transcendent to creation. Spirit is
> not inherent in nature, but outside it or beyond it; it even becomes the
> source of nature. So a new meaning enters the language: spirit becomes

creative and nature becomes created. In this new kind of myth, creation
is the result of a divine act that brings order out of chaos.   [Baring 274]

And within that metaphysic, art is man's effort to bring further order out of
chaos, to transform into music what would otherwise be uproar. Art becomes
a contest against nature.

This is true of even the best poems in *the Hawk in the Rain* such as
'Wind'. Here Hughes brilliantly mimes the distorting and levelling power of a
gale, seeking to find words, like those of the Border ballads, 'that live in the
same dimension as life at its most severe, words that cannot be outflanked by
experience' [*WP* 68]. His wind is real enough, and also carries much the same
larger meaning as the wind Castaneda's Don Juan calls the 'nagual', a wind
which threatens to obliterate the 'tonal' – 'everything we know and do as men'
(or in Hughes' words 'book, thought, or each other'):

> Everyone's obsession is to arrange the world according to the *tonal's*
> rules; so every time we are confronted with the *nagual*, we go out of our
> way to make our eyes stiff and intransigent . . . The point is to convince
> the *tonal* that there are other worlds that can pass in front of the same
> windows . . . The eyes can be the windows to peer into boredom or peek
> into that infinity . . .
>
> As long as his *tonal* is unchallenged and his eyes are tuned only for the
> *tonal's* world, the warrior is on the safe side of the fence. He's on familiar
> ground and knows all the rules. But when his *tonal* shrinks, he is on the
> windy side, and that opening must be shut tight immediately, or he would
> be swept away. And this is not just a way of talking. Beyond the gate of
> the *tonal's* eyes the wind rages. I mean a real wind. No metaphor. A wind
> that can blow one's life away. In fact, that is the wind that blows all living
> things on this earth.   [*Tales of Power*, 172–6]

Insofar as he has the courage to 'peek into that infinity', Hughes displays the
courage of what Castaneda calls a sorcerer:

> A leaf's otherness,
> The whaled monstered sea-bottom, eagled peaks
> And stars that hang over hurtling endlessness,
>   With manslaughtering shocks
>   Are let in on his sense:
> So many one has dared to be struck dead
> Peeping though his fingers at the world's ends,
>   Or at an ant's head.
>
>   ['Egg-Head']

But the very skill Hughes exhibits in the control of language reinforces the
tonal and keeps the wind out. The man who 'cannot entertain book, thought, /

Or each other', can still write a splendid poem, with such finely crafted lines as: 'The wind flung a magpie away and a black- / Back gull bent like an iron bar slowly'.

The later Hughes will no longer erect such verbal barricades:

And we go

Into the wind. The flame-wind – a red wind
And a black wind. The red wind comes
To empty you. And the black wind, the longest wind
The headwind

To scour you.   ['The guide']

Given the landscape of mud and blood, the vast no-man's land, which is the world of Hughes' early poems, it is not easy for him to say how men should try to live in such a world. It is easier to say how they should not. What Hughes pours his most vehement scorn on is the egg-head's pride and 'braggart-browed complacency in most calm / Collusion with his own / Dew-drop frailty'; his spurning of the earth as 'muck under / His foot-clutch'; his willingness to oppose his own eye to 'the whelm of the sun' ['Egg-Head']. Pride and complacency are man's commonest defences against receiving the full impact of the otherness and endlessness of the natural world. What Hughes is trying to say in this poem is, I take it, that the egg-head, in defending his *tonal*, his single vision, at all costs, is resisting birth, which requires the breaking of the ego-shell, because the wisdom which would then flood in would be accounted madness in our world of single vision. In *Moby Dick*, when the Negro boy Pip fell overboard, thought he had been abandoned, and was then rescued, he went about an idiot:

The sea had jeeringly kept his finite body up, but drowned the infinite of his soul. Not drowned entirely, though. Rather carried down alive to wondrous depths, where strange shapes of the unwarped primal world glided to and fro before his passive eyes; and the miser-merman, Wisdom, revealed his hoarded heaps; Pip saw the multitudinous, God-omnipresent, coral insects, that out of the firmament of waters heaved the colossal orbs. He saw God's foot upon the treadle of the loom, and spoke it; and therefore his shipmates called him mad. So man's insanity is heaven's sense; and wandering from all mortal reason, man comes at last to that celestial thought, which, to reason, is absurd and frantic; and weal or woe, feels then uncompromised, indifferent as his God.   [Ch.93]

The tone of the poet's voice in 'Egg-head', however, is at the opposite pole from any divine indifference. The superiority of the poet manifests itself with just as much fervency and trumpeting as the egg-head is accused of. The style is confident and masculine and aggressive to the point of 'braggart-browed complacency'.

Such stylistic overkill is of a piece with the moral and sexual insensibility of some of the worst poems of the nineteen-fifties such as 'Secretary', 'Bawdry Embraced', 'Macaw and Little Miss' and 'The Ancient Heroes and the Bomber Pilot' (a poem glorifying the patriarchal savagery of the Bronze Age).

* * *

In *Lupercal* we are again in a world of 'oozing craters' and 'sodden moors', but this time with an awed acknowledgement that life is possible 'between the weather and the rock', that death and vitality are manifestations of the same forces, generating as well as extinguishing life:

> What humbles these hills has raised
> The arrogance of blood and bone,
> And thrown the hawk upon the wind,
> And lit the fox in the dripping ground.
> > ['Crow Hill']

Nor are these forces now felt as exclusively a downward pull and pressure:

> Those barrellings of strength are heaving slowly and heave
> To your feet and surf upwards
> In a still, fiery air, hauling the imagination,
> Carrying the larks upward.   ['Pennines in April']

(Though, as we are to see in 'Skylarks', to be flung upward is not necessarily an easier life than to be dragged down.)

Given such conditions, how to live? There is the example of the horses patiently outwaiting the darkness of a 'world cast in frost' and rewarded by a glorious sunrise. But that is a portion of eternity too great for the eye of the narrator, who stumbles away from it 'in the fever of a dream'.

Again, in 'November', he admires the 'strong trust' of a tramp asleep in a ditch in the drilling rain and the welding cold, but this patience is as hopeless as that of the corpses on the gibbet:

> Patient to outwait these worst days that beat
> Their crowns bare and dripped from their feet.

At the opposite extreme are the ancient heroes, the big-hearted, 'huge-chested braggarts' who spent their lives in war, rape and pillage, as if the answer were to try to beat ravenous Nature at her own bloody game. They are like the 'Warriors of the North', spilling blood

To no end
But this timely expenditure of themselves,
A cash-down, beforehand revenge, with extra,
For the gruelling relapse and prolongeur of their blood

Into the iron arteries of Calvin.

Some heroes and geniuses are able to live as single-mindedly as thrushes or sharks, but the normal human condition is to be forever distracted from day-to-day living by the opposite pulls of heaven and hell, hope and despair, the dream of an 'unearthly access of grace, / Of ease: freer firmer world found' and the rude awakening from that dream

bearing
Plunge of that high risk without
That flight; with only a dread
Crouching to get away from these
On its hands and knees.
['Acrobats']

Here, in a few lines, Hughes takes in the fall of Hopkins from the spiritual acrobatics of 'Hurrahing in Harvest' to the terrible sonnets; the fall of modernist vision from Wordsworth's egotistical sublime to Beckett's spiritual void.

There is, however, again some discrepancy between style and content. The style has all the necessary weight and strength to mime the pressure of the huge forces of the natural world upon the living organism. But the energies are invoked (often in the form of predatory beasts) with an occasionally overweening masculine confidence that they can be controlled by the imposed form of the poem itself. Were the poems really, as he thought at the time, containing the energies, or were they shutting out by their tightly closed forms energies which, had they come in, would have overwhelmed all pretence at art?

The style of *Lupercal* is confident of its ability both to evoke and control the energies, to plug in to the 'elemental power-circuit of the universe'. Hughes' imagination, purged of the poetic cult of beauty and the Wordsworthian sentimentalities, becomes a great intestine rejecting nothing:

This mute eater, biting through the mind's
Nursery floor, with eel and hyena and vulture,
With creepy-crawly and the root,
With the sea-worm, entering its birthright.
['Mayday on Holderness']

Thus the poet can clamp himself well onto the world like a wolf-mask, and speak with the voice of the glutted crow, the stoat, the expressionless leopard, the sleeping anaconda, the frenzied shrew, the roosting hawk – which is 'Nature herself speaking'. Yet again there is some discrepancy. We are told that the stoat 'bit through grammar and corset', that its 'red unmanageable life . . . licked the stylist out of [the] skulls' of Walpole and his set ('Strawberry Hill'). But the poem which tells us so is a triumph of intelligence and style, in a volume of great stylistic achievement, orthodox grammar, corseted stanzas and even rhyming verse.

This discrepancy is also apparent in 'To Paint a Water Lily' with its elegant rhyming couplets. The poem is a verse exemplum of Carlyle's observations on Nature in 'Characteristics':

> Boundless as is the domain of man, it is but a small fractional proportion of it that he rules with Consciousness and Forethought: what he can contrive, nay, what he can altogether know and comprehend, is essentially the mechanical, small; the great is ever, in one sense or other, the vital; it is essentially the mysterious, and only the surface of it can be understood. But Nature, it might seem, strives, like a kind mother, to hide from us even this, that she is a mystery. . . . Under all Nature's works, chiefly under her noblest work, Life, lies a basis of Darkness, which she benignantly conceals; in Life, too, the roots and inward circulations which stretch down fearfully to the regions of Death and Night, shall not hint of their existence, and only the fair stem with its leaves and flowers, shone on by the sun, shall disclose itself and joyfully grow.

Hughes' example is the water lily, whose leaves are simultaneously the floor of the sunny, conscious world, accessible (visually) to any Sunday painter, and the roof of another, less colourful and 'aesthetic' world, the unconscious, inaccessible to all the senses, accessible only to the imagination. Hughes refuses merely to praise the rainbow colours of nature (for which the painterly style of the poem is well suited), but strives to escape the tyranny of the eye and listen rather to the inaudible 'battle-shouts / And death-cries everywhere hereabouts'. He refuses to paint only the dragonfly alighting on the water lily if his imagination can see into the life of the pond and the horror nudging her root. However, in this poem at least, it can only gesture in that direction – 'Prehistoric bedragonned times / Crawl that darkness with Latin names'. The underwater world, the unconscious mind, is a closed book to the poet. There is no hint of the wisdom of Pip, of the shamanic journey into the 'regions of Death and Night' which Hughes' poems are later to become. In the later poem 'Photostomias' for example, this primitive deep-sea fish, also known as the dragon-fish, could well be described as having 'jaws for heads', but Hughes is there about deeper business than mere description of nature's horrors, about the business of revealing that those horrors are also miracles, are also God:

> Jehova – mucous and phosphorescence
> In the camera's glare –

A decalogue
A rainbow.

In his 1977 interview with Ekbert Faas Hughes described writing 'To Paint a Water Lily': 'I felt very constricted fiddling around with it. It was somehow like writing through a long winding tube, like squeezing language out at the end of this long, remote process'. He found in 'View of a Pig' 'a whole way of writing that was obviously much more natural for me than that water-lily-style'. Faas objected that 'To Paint a Water Lily' was 'one of the most beautiful poems in *Lupercal*'. Hughes replied:

Maybe, but it isn't as interesting to me. And my follow-up to 'View of a Pig' was 'Pike'. But that poem immediately became much more charged with particular memories and a specific obsession. And my sense of 'Hawk Roosting' was that somehow or other it had picked up the prototype style behind 'View of a Pig' and 'Pike' without that overlay of a heavier, thicker, figurative language. . . . All three were written in a mood of impatience, deliberately trying to destroy the ways in which I had written before, trying to write in a way that had nothing to do with the way in which I thought I ought to be writing. But then, that too became deliberate and a dead end.   [Faas 208–9]

'Pike' is a much better poem than 'To Paint a Water Lily', moving from the descriptive and narrative modes of total authorial command in the first nine stanzas into a more open dramatic mode, where what is being dramatized is precisely the fear arising from the speaker's ignorance of what is rising towards him out of the 'Darkness beneath night's darkness'. As Gaston Bachelard writes (not in relation to this poem):

Night alone would give a less physical fear. Water alone would give clearer obsessions. Water at night gives a penetrating fear . . . If the fear that comes at night beside a pond is a special fear, it is because it is a fear that enjoys a certain range. It is very different from the fear experienced in a grotto or a forest. It is not so near, so concentrated, or so localized; it is more flowing. Shadows that fall on water are more mobile than shadows on earth.   [*Water and Dreams*, 101–2]

It is also the fear that what is rising towards him might be too monstrous, too alien, too ego-destroying for the poetry he is yet able to write to deal with. Fishing in deep water at night is the perfect image for the kind of poetry Hughes really wants to write, poetry which projects the most naked and unconditional part of the self into the nightmare darkness, not with the intention of bringing back trophies into the daylight world, but of confronting, being, if necessary, supplanted by, whatever happens to be out there. The poems about fishing and water tend to be those in which this is to be most fully achieved, culminating in 'Go Fishing'.

Hughes knew that the horror with which we view Nature 'red in tooth and claw' was in part a product of our own preconceptions ('What you find in the outside world is what has escaped from your own inner world'), and our tendency to take 'portions of existence' (Blake) for the whole. He knew that not until we begin to understand Nature in its own terms will it show us any other face. Many of the poems in *Lupercal* are strategies for evoking, confronting and negotiating with the Powers. He forces himself and us to confront Nature at its most ugly, savage and apparently pointless, to look into 'the shark's mouth / That hungers down the blood-smell even to a leak of its own / Side and devouring of itself' ['Thrushes']. Perhaps Hughes was again remembering *Moby Dick*:

> They viciously snapped, not only at each other's disbowelments, but like flexible bows, bent round, and bit their own; till those entrails seemed swallowed over and over again by the same mouth, to be oppositely voided by the gaping wound. Nor was this all. It was unsafe to meddle with the corpses and ghosts of these creatures. A sort of generic or Pantheistic vitality seemed to lurk in their very joints and bones, after what might be called the individual life had departed. Killed and hoisted on deck for the sake of his skin, one of these sharks almost took poor Queequeg's hand off, when he tried to shut down the dead lid of his murderous jaw.
>
>   'Queequeg no care what god made him shark,' said the savage, agonisingly lifting his hand up and down; 'wedder Fejee god or Nantucket god; but de god wat made shark must be one dam Ingin'.   [Chapter 66]

Blake felt much the same about the god who made the tiger.

One of the strategies Hughes adopted was his attempt to let Nature speak for herself through the mouth of a hawk in the most famous of his early poems, 'Hawk Roosting':

> Actually what I had in mind was that in this hawk Nature is thinking. Simply Nature. It's not so simple maybe because Nature is no longer so simple. I intended some Creator like the Jehovah in Job but more feminine. When Christianity kicked the devil out of Job what they actually kicked out was Nature . . . and Nature became the devil. He doesn't sound like Isis, mother of the gods, which he is. He sounds like Hitler's familiar spirit.   [Faas 199]

The strategy does not work because Hughes cannot yet get behind the fallen nature of our tradition, and therefore cannot render the hawk's vision other than in terms of deranged human vision – the vision of Canute or Richard of Gloucester or Hitler.

There are, of course, a great many animals in all Hughes' collections. It goes without saying that Hughes is a great animal poet. But we must distinguish between the use he makes of animals in the early poems and in the later. Most of the earlier animals are conscripted as cannon-fodder in the doomed battle of vitality against death. They are in the same trap as man, but Hughes prefers to write about them because they bellow the evidence which man, except in moments of extremity, tries to hide. Norman O. Brown takes Freud to task for what he calls his 'metaphysical vision of all life sick with the struggle between Life and Death':

> We need, in fine, a metaphysic which recognizes both the continuity
> between man and animals and also the discontinuity. We need, instead of
> an instinctual dualism, an instinctual dialectic. We shall have to say that
> whatever the basic polarity in human life may be . . . this polarity exists
> in animals but does not exist in a condition of ambivalence. Man is
> distinguished from animals by having separated, ultimately into a state of
> mutual conflict, aspects of life (instincts) which in animals exist in some
> condition of undifferentiated unity or harmony.   [83]

Thus, as he gradually struggled free from his fatalistic dualism, Hughes began to see the animal world as offering not primarily images of sickness and struggle, but rather images of harmony even between predators and their victims. Hughes' last hawk is no murderous egomaniac; and the relaxed style takes off him the pressure to serve as a symbol of a savage god:

> And maybe you find him
>
> Materialized by twilight and dew
> Still as a listener –
> The warrior
>
> Blue shoulder-cloak wrapped about him
> Leaning, hunched,
> Among the oaks of the harp.
>   ['A Sparrow Hawk']

As late as 1963, in a British Council interview, Hughes was still able to speak of his interest in poetry as 'really a musical interest' and of his desire to produce in his poems 'something final . . . something that won't break down, like an animal'. Later he sought only to listen to and transcribe the music of that harp.

*   *   *

The early sixties was a period of intense experimentation in search of a poetry able to grope its way through that darkness without the map-grid of imposed

340

form or the flash-light of rationality which would have scared away all its creatures. The most significant breakthrough at this time was 'Wodwo', first published in 1961. The success of the poem depends partly on the choice of persona, a 'little larval being' which might have just emerged from an egg or chrysalis, with human intelligence and curiosity, the human temptation to simply appropriate whatever it encounters, yet still naked and open, exposed and tentative; but mainly on finding the right voice for such a creature.

Rhymes, stanzas, 'poetic' effects of all kinds, rhetoric, have gone. And with them has gone the imposition of personality which those techniques had largely served. What we are left with is a very free verse, close to colloquial prose, flexible, responsive at every moment to the demands of the sense and to nothing else. It is a totally unforced utterance, a world away from the bludgeoning verse of 'The Hawk in the Rain'. The wodwo is no 'diamond point of will', no 'eye' or 'I' determined to keep things as they are: his 'I suppose I am the exact centre / but there's all this what is it . . . very queer but I'll go on looking' denies the desirability of being a 'master-Fulcrum of violence' and at the same time the desirability of using the formal elements of poetry, its melody and rhythm, as a means of resolving the uproar, thereby sealing off the poem from the real world. No possible pattern is final or definitive or at the 'exact centre'. How can it be when 'there's all this'?

The language is reduced to a functional minimum from which, like the wodwo itself, it is now free to move out into new, less manipulative forms of expression: 'The nearest we can come to rational thinking is to stand respectfully, hat in hand, before this Creation, exceedingly alert for a new word' [Faas, 172].

This freedom seems to be related to a more inclusive, more holistic vision. 'Still Life', for example, begins as uncompromisingly as 'Pibroch', but we gradually realize that the bleak vision is not this time that of the poet himself, but that of 'outcrop rock' taking itself to be the exact centre, the one permanent exclusive reality. The poet stands to one side, saying 'but there's all this'. The less insistent style allows for a play of humour undercutting the claims of outcrop stone to be all there is, 'being ignorant of this other, this harebell'

> That trembles, as under threats of death,
> In the summer turf's heat-rise,
> And in which – filling veins
> Any known name of blue would bruise
> Out of existence – sleeps, recovering,
> The maker of the sea.

And in 'Full Moon and Little Frieda' we have balance instead of intolerable pressure, fullness instead of lack, unspilled milk instead of spilled blood, and a human being, albeit a child, in a reciprocal and rewarding relationship with a human world and a natural world at one with each other. The poetry here does not impose the momentary resolution, but mirrors it while remaining itself transparent, like water in a brimming pail.

The tragic events of February 1963, the suicide of his wife Sylvia Plath, put an abrupt end to this atonement. Hughes was thrown back at a stroke into a much more deeply felt despair than ever before. It was as though he had seen the face of the goddess, who had blighted him and struck him dumb. It is the bloodiest of all the goddesses, Cybele, a Homeric hymn speaks of as she who 'loves the howling of wolves'. Before his three-year silence descended he wrote 'The Howling of Wolves' and 'Song of a Rat'. The style here has gone very cold, metallic, each line the sharp tooth of a steel trap. The diction is a succession of blank monosyllables forced between teeth:

> The eyes that never learn how it has come about
> That they must live like this,
>
> That they must live

or

> The rat is in the trap, it is in the trap.

To dress such testimony up as 'poetry', (with the association of that word with 'pleasure' relentlessly insisted on by the B.B.C.), would clearly be absurd, almost obscene. Great poetry is truth-telling, and the truth must be in the telling as much as in the authenticity of the vision. Pain, which otherwise is condemned to express itself in silence or inarticulate cries, has, in poetry, its only speech.

That speech will not be the speech of ordinary rational discourse. It searches for the buried world under the world, and for a speech beneath words. The poet opens himself to be 'pierced afresh by the tree's cry':

> And the incomprehensible cry
> From the boughs, in the wind
> Sets us listening for below words,
> Meanings that will not part from the rock.
>   ['A Wind Flashes the Grass']

Meanings emerge from silence, from the blank unprinted page, sparely, one syllable for a line, in a voice which is not the commanding voice of the poet, but the faceless voice which issues the imperatives of living and dying to tree, gnat, skylark and man alike:

> A towered bird, shot through the crested head
> With the command, Not die
>
> But climb

342

Climb

Sing

Obedient as to death a dead thing.
                    ['Skylarks']

Hughes described *Wodwo* as 'a descent into destruction'. He placed
the most up-beat poems at the end; but both 'Wodwo' and 'Full Moon and
Little Frieda' predate the death of Sylvia Plath. If we look at the later poems
in *Wodwo* and *Recklings* we are in a wasteland, a dark intestine, pointless
cycles of recurrence, a dark night of the soul, a world very like that of Samuel
Beckett:

> Having taken her slowly by surprise
> For eighty years
> The hills have won, their ring is closed.
>
> The field-walls float their pattern
> Over her eye
> Whether she looks outward or inward.
> . . .
>
> But with the stone agony growing in her joints
> And eyes, dimming with losses, widening for losses.
>   ['On the Slope']

Now the window has come in, the wind of the *nagual* sweeps away
order and ordinary, and terrible energies are released.

In *New Lines* John Holloway had warned his guest not to go down to
the sea at night: 'It makes no place for those . . . who, to sustain our pose, /
Need wine and conversation, colour and light':

> [I] know, from knowing myself, that you will be
> Quick to people the shore, the fog, the sea,
>   With all the fabulous
> Things of the moon's dark side.
>   ['Warning to a Guest']

Hughes did go down to the sea, and what he found there were ghost crabs:

> All night, around us or through us,
> They stalk each other, they fasten on to each other,
> They mount each other, they tear each other to pieces,
> They utterly exhaust each other.
> They are the powers of this world.

> We are their bacteria,
> Dying their lives and living their deaths.
> ['Ghost Crabs']

The energies no longer need to be invoked. But when they come they are far too inhuman and overwhelming to handle. They supplant his normal consciousness, leaving him stripped of all defences and taken over by them. The 'elemental power-circuit of the universe' jams through him, blowing every fuse. Blake's symbol for the energies is the serpent or dragon. This is the face Hughes now sees on his god or not-god; the serpent as swallower of everything ('this is the dark intestine'), the dragon waiting with open mouth for the woman to deliver her child. Nature is 'all one smouldering annihilation', unmaking and remaking, remaking in order to unmake again. How could such a god be worshipped?

*　　*　　*

It is hard to say just when Hughes arrived at his spiritual nadir. Perhaps it came, poetically, about 1967, when he (or his protagonist) at last refuses to make yet another doomed bid to live within or even rebel against a nightmarish creation, to cling 'with madman's grip / To the great wheel of woe':

> Once upon a time
> There was a person
> Wretched in every vein –
> His heart pumped woe.
> . . .
> So he abandoned himself, his body, his blood –
> He left it all lying on the earth
> And held himself resolute
> As the earth rolled slowly away
> Smaller and smaller away
> Into non-being.
> ['Song of Woe']

But the attempt to say goodbye to earth, to become light and shadowless is also doomed, like Crow's attempt to destroy his mother, the tree of which he is the topmost twig ['Revenge Fable']. Being itself is cruciform, yet the atoms in deep space are praying for incarnation, for life at any cost, as though it were better to be a man on a cross than not to be a man at all ['I said goodbye to earth']. Hughes may have remembered the passage from Blake's *Vala* where the Human Odors arising from the blood of the terrible wine presses of Luvah are driven by 'desire of Being':

> They plunge into the Elements; the Elements cast them forth
> Or else consume their shadowy semblance. Yet they, obstinate

Tho' pained to distraction, cry, 'O let us Exist! for
This dreadful Non Existence is worse than pains of Eternal Birth'.
[Night the Ninth, 736–9]

This acceptance of suffering, powerfully expressed at the end of the
essay on Popa in 1968, suggests the way out of total blackness which the
post-war Eastern European poets had found, and which Crow was intended to
find:

The infinite terrible circumstances that seem to destroy man's
importance, appear as the very terms of his importance. Man is the face,
arms, legs, etc. grown over the infinite, terrible All'.   [WP227]

The style or non-style of *Crow* is another new departure. At the end
of his 1970 interview, Ekbert Faas asked Hughes why he had 'abandoned such
formal devices as rhyme, metre and stanza'. Hughes conceded that

formal patterning of the actual movement of verse somehow includes a
mathematical and musically deeper world than free verse can easily hope
to enter. . . . But it only works . . . if the writer has a perfectly pure grasp
of his real feeling . . . and the very sound of metre calls up the ghosts of
the past and it is difficult to sing one's own tune against that choir. It is
easier to speak a language that raises no ghosts.   [Faas, p.208]

What he did not say, and may not yet have become conscious of in theory,
though it is clear enough in his practice, is that the mathematical and musical
accomplishments of formal verse might actually prevent the poet's language
becoming 'totally alive and pure', and deny him access to the deepest levels
of his own psyche. He went on:

The first idea of *Crow* was really an idea of a style. In folktales the prince
going on the adventure comes to the stable full of beautiful horses and he
needs a horse for the next stage and the king's daughter advises him to
take none of the beautiful horses that he'll be offered but to choose the
dirty, scabby little foal. I throw out the eagles and choose the Crow. The
idea was originally just to write his songs, the songs that a Crow would
sing. In other words, songs with no music whatsoever, in a super-simple
and a super-ugly language which would in a way shed everything except
just what he wanted to say without any other consideration and that's the
basis of the style of the whole thing.

But Hughes does not explain what, in the folktale, is the advantage of choosing
'the dirty, scabby little foal', the advantage of crows over eagles, or of super-
ugly language over the beautiful musical language of our poetic tradition. In a
letter to me, Hughes expanded a little:

345

I tried to shed everything that the average Pavlovian critic knows how to respond to. It was quite an effort to get there – as much of an effort to stay there – every day I had to find it again. My idea was to reduce my style to the simplest clear cell – then regrow a wholeness and richness organically from that point. I didn't get that far.

But again Hughes does not explain the need for this stylistic asceticism. For that explanation we must turn to his writings on the Eastern European poets, who seemed to Hughes to have discovered a universal poetic language, independent of surface sound and texture and therefore translatable, an ABC of what counts. In his essay on Popa he wrote:

> No poetry could carry less luggage than his, or be freer of predisposition and preconception. No poetry is more difficult to outflank, yet it is in no sense defensive. His poems are trying to find out what does exist, and what the conditions really are. The movement of his verse is part of his method of investigating something fearfully apprehended, fearfully discovered. but he will not be frightened into awe. He never loses his deeply ingrained humour and irony: that is his way of hanging on to his human wholeness. And he never loses his intense absorption in what he is talking about, either. His words test their way forward, sensitive to their own errors, dramatically and intimately alive, like the antennae of some rock-shore creature feeling out the presence of the sea and the huge powers in it. This analogy is not so random. There is a primitive pre-creation atmosphere about his work, as if he were present where all the dynamisms and formulae were ready and charged, but nothing created – or only a few fragments. . . . [There is an] air of trial and error exploration, of an improvised language, the attempt to get near something for which he is almost having to invent the words in a total disregard for poetry or the normal conventions of discourse.   [WP 223,226]

What first attracted Hughes to Pilinszky's poems was, he says, 'their air of simple, helpless accuracy'. Pilinszky described his own poetic language as 'a sort of linguistic poverty'. He takes 'the most naked and helpless of all confrontations' and asks 'what speech is adequate for this moment?' His vision is desolate; his language as close as he can get to silence. In his Introduction to Pilinszky's *The Desert of Love*, Hughes writes: 'We come to this Truth only on the simplest terms: through what has been suffered, what is being suffered, and the objects that participate in the suffering' [WP233]. The more affirmative, the more radiant with meaning, a work is going to be, the more essential that its starting point is Nothing, the silence of Cordelia, so that it cannot be said that the affirmative meanings have been smuggled in with the loaded language, that anything has been left unquestioned, that the negatives have not been fully acknowledged. Pilinszky has taken the route Hughes started out on in *Crow*. His images reveal a place where every cultural support has been torn away, where the ultimate brutality of total war has become natural law, and where man has been reduced to the mere mechanism of his mutilated body. All words seem obsolete or inadequate. Yet out of this apparently final reality rise the poems whose language seems to redeem it, a language in which the symbols of the horror become the sacred symbols of a kind of worship.

These symbols are not redeemed in an unworldly sense. They are redeemed, precariously, in some all-too-human sense, somewhere in the pulsing mammalian nervous system, by a feat of homely consecration: a provisional, last-ditch 'miracle' achieved by means which seem to be never other than 'poetic'. [233–4]

Hughes did not get that far in *Crow*. The intention had been to use the figure of Crow as a means of recapitulating and correcting both his own errors and those of Western man. Crow tries out or witnesses all the techniques of single vision – words and numbers, scripture and physics – the result is war, murder, suicide, madness. He confronts the Energies always as something to be fought and killed – dragon, serpent, ogress – obstacles on his blind quest. Crow's mistaken quest, his flight from the female, his search for the Black Beast, was to have become, after many adventures in which he is completely dismembered and reconstituted, a painful reintegration and a shamanic initiation ordeal. But at the very moment when this upward process should have begun, Hughes was knocked back into the pit by another personal tragedy. He refused, in his work for adults, to posit a resolution he had not lived through. Crow was abandoned. The best poems from the first, the negative stage of the story, were salvaged to make *Crow*.

* * *

Hughes is, of all contemporary writers in English, the one most qualified by experience to feel and by intelligence to '*think* adequately about the behaviour that is at the annihilating edge' [R.D. Laing, *The Politics of Experience*]. *Prometheus on his Crag* begins at the point of numbness which had characterized the later poems in *Wodwo* and much of *Crow*. Crow had already contemplated a Prometheus figure in 'The Contender':

He lay crucified with all his strength
On the earth
Grinning towards the sun
Through the tiny holes of his eyes
And towards the moon
And towards the whole paraphernalia of the heavens
Through the seams of his face
With the strings of his lips
Grinning through his atoms and decay

> Grinning into the black
> Into the ringing nothing
> Through the bones of his teeth
>
> Sometimes with eyes closed
>
> In his senseless trial of strength.

Hughes, at that point in his life, had come close to rejecting nature as a 'cortege of mourning and lament'. This left him in a limbo in which the only alternative to suicide or despair seemed to be absurdist revolt, as advocated by Camus:

> The absurd man can only drain everything to the bitter end, and deplete himself. The absurd is his extreme tension which he maintains constantly by solitary effort, for he knows that in that consciousness and in that day-to-day revolt he gives proof of his only truth which is defiance.
>
> [*The Myth of Sisyphus*]

But Hughes was not content to remain crucified on that rock. It was his study in 1971 of the fate of another Titan, in *Prometheus on his Crag*, which revealed to him the possibility that the agony and depletion might actually release the flow of *mana*.

Speaking of the etchings of Leonard Baskin, particularly his many versions of the hanged man, Hughes refers to the mythological motif 'that the wound, if it is to be healed, needs laid in it the blade that made it':

> As if the blade might cut to a depth where blood and cries no longer come – only *mana* comes. Baskin writes, somewhere, that his subject is the wound. One could as truly say that his subject is *mana*. His real subject is the healing of the wound. [WP95]

Such healing is, Hughes claims, 'redemption incarnate' which 'is purchased by suffering':

> Like those Indian gods who play deaf to the mortifications and ordeals and cries of the suppliant, till they can't stand it any longer – the stones of their heaven begin to sweat, their thrones begin to tremble – whereupon they descend and grant everything. And the suppliant becomes Holy, and a Healer. [93]

Like Lorca's *duende*, such *mana* is 'the goddess of the source of terrible life', perhaps of all blossoming and beauty:

> Blossoms
> Pushing from under blossoms –

From the one wound's
Depth of congealments and healing.
['Photostomias']

It is also 'the real substance of any art that has substance, in spite of what we might prefer' [17]. We may speak of this healing and rebirth as a divine gift, but we may equally speak of it in biological terms, as demonstrating 'the biological inevitability of art, as the psychological component of the body's own system of immunity and self-repair'[98].

Joseph Campbell discusses the power of mythology and all creative art in similarly biological terms:

Mythological symbols touch and exhilarate centers of life beyond the reach of vocabularies of reason and coercion. The light-world modes of experience and thought were late, very late, developments on the biological prehistory of our species. Even in the life-course of the individual, the opening of the eyes to light occurs only after all the main miracles have been accomplished of the building of a living body of already functioning organs, each with its inherent aim, none of these aims either educed from, or as yet even known to, reason; while in the larger course and context of the evolution of life itself from the silence of primordial seas, of which the taste still runs in our blood, the opening of the eyes occurred only after the first principle of all organic being ('Now I'll eat you; now you eat me!') had been operative for so many hundreds of millions of centuries that it could not then, and cannot now, be undone – though our eyes and what they witness may persuade us to regret the monstrous game.

The first function of a mythology is to reconcile waking consciousness to the *mysterium tremendum et fascinans* of this universe *as it is*: the second being to render an interpretive total image of the same, as known to contemporary consciousness.   [*Creative Mythology*, 4]

The function of all art is 'the revelation to waking consciousness of the powers of its own sustaining source'.

In the Prometheus sequence, the blade is the beak of the vulture, which gorges itself every day on Prometheus' liver. Prometheus knows that the vulture holds the key. Prometheus, the prototype of the human condition, also hangs weighing the cost, but for a long time can find nothing to set against it, the weight of the whole earth. The first clue comes when a lizard whispers to him 'Even as the vulture buried its head – / "Lucky, you are so lucky to be human!"'. The only advantage Prometheus has over the lizard is consciousness, which opens the possibility of understanding the situation, and thereby converting pain into payment. In poem 20 he permutates the possible meanings of the vulture, starting with all the mistaken meanings, such as Crow might have entertained; for example, that the vulture might be 'some lump of his mother'. But at last he begins to get warmer:

> Or was it, after all, the Helper
> Coming again to pick at the crucial knot
> Of all his bonds . . . ?

In the final poem he correctly identifies the vulture as the midwife attending his own necessarily painful rebirth. That realization *is* his rebirth. And it lifts the weight of the world from him:

> And Prometheus eases free.
> He sways to his stature.
> And balances. And treads

> On the dusty peacock film where the world floats.

There is a beautiful line about the vulture in every draft of the final poem except the published version; (Hughes saved it for the vulture in *Cave Birds*):

> That never harmed any living thing.

Eight thousand years ago the goddess was painted as vulture in the shrines of Catal Hüyük:

> For the vulture, feeding on carrion, does not so much 'bring' death as transform what is already dead back into life, beginning a new cycle by assimilating the end of the old one. In this way the goddess of death and the goddess of birth are inseparable.   [Baring 87–8]

*   *   *

That Hughes, at this moment in his life (the moment also of that 'seismic event' [*Shakespeare* 330] the death of his mother), should have married a farmer's daughter and shortly afterwards become a farmer, may have been a lucky accident or an attempt, conscious or unconscious, to correct the psychic imbalance which had driven him (in the terms he himself uses of Shakespeare) to suppress the right side of the brain. This dominance of the left side produces the feeling of living in a state of Prometheus-like alienation from real things. Nowhere is it more necessary to adapt to the chaos of real things than on a farm. Hughes abandoned his aloofness from tangible reality, even from the mud. As he learned the feel of farming, the hard disciplines of stewardship and husbandry, Moortown farm became for him, in Craig Robinson's words, 'a working laboratory of co-operation between man and nature' [*Achievement* 262].

In his marginalia on Wordsworth's poems Blake wrote: 'Natural Objects always did & now do Weaken deaden & obliterate imagination in Me'. He spurns the corporeal, vegetable world as having no more to do with him than 'the Dirt upon my feet' [*A Vision of the Last Judgement*, 95]. Coleridge agreed with him:

> The further I ascend from men and cattle, and the common birds of the woods and fields, the greater becomes in me the intensity of the feelings of life. Life seems to me there a universal spirit that neither has nor can have an opposite.

Hughes' experience was exactly the reverse. It was by descending again from the far limits of pain and consciousness into woods and fields among men and cattle that he recovered his sense of the universal spirit of life. 'The field and its grass', which he had flung away in 'Song of Woe', Beckett's 'absurdity of pastures', is now recovered, with the practical responsibility, as a farmer, of tending the earth and its flora and fauna. His imagination flourished on this daily input of its proper food. As Robert Bly says:

> Imagination requires food, as a horse does, and contrary to many Jungian speculations, the food of the imagination is not archetypes, but the actual energy given off by old tree roots, mountains, rocks, glaciers, fields of barley, crows.   [Interview in Housden]

What happened to Hughes is recapitulated in *Adam and the Sacred Nine*. Adam lies inert in Eden. Great things are expected of him, but he feels helpless and exposed. His dreams of technological achievements and immortality are so incongruous with his bruised body 'too little lifted from mud' that they merely bewilder him. He is visited by nine birds. Each offers him an image of how to live. The Falcon could not be more different from his weeping and shivering self, with its unfaltering gunmetal feathers, mountain-diving and world-hurling wing-knuckles, bullet-brow, grasping talons, tooled bill. Then the Skylark, living and dying in the service of its crest, cresting the earth, trying to crest the sun, with bird-joy. Then the Wild Duck getting up out of cold and dark and ooze, and spanking across water quacking Wake Wake to the world. Then comes the Swift wholeheartedly hurling itself against and beyond the limits. Then the Wren who lives only to be more and more Wren – Wren of Wrens! Then the Owl, who floats, the moving centre of everything, holding the balance of life and death, heaven and earth. Then the Dove, the perpetual victim, but rainbow-breasted among thorns. Then the Crow comes to Adam and whispers in his ear a waking, reject-nothing truth. Finally comes the Phoenix, which offers itself up again and again and laughs in the blaze. Each bird has found what Adam lacks, its own distinctive mode of living fully within the given conditions. It is not for Adam to imitate any of them. He is defined precisely by his lack of wings. His business is with the earth. He stands, and it is the first meeting of the body of man with the body of the earth. The sole of Adam's foot is grateful to the rock, saying:

> I am no wing
> To tread emptiness.
> I was made
> For you.

These are the first and only words Adam speaks, and they embody the simplicity, humility and acceptance that Boehme had in mind when he said that men must attempt to recover 'the language of Adam'.

Thus it is fitting that the volume, *Moortown*, which begins with cattle knee-deep in mud in the poor fields, should end with Adam's affirmation of his total dependence on nature, a nature whose only god is a god of mud, but with miracles enough. As Whitman wrote: 'The press of my foot to the earth springs a hundred affections' ['Song of Myself' 14]. Instead of dreaming of technological dominion ('flying echelons of steel ... advancement of bull-dozers and cranes' – the dreams of Prometheus) or of everlasting life ('the religion of the diamond body'), Adam must now set out on his quest for what is actually given, Eve, his mother and intended bride.

Lawrence wrote:

> You cannot dig the ground with the spirit. . . . The very act of stooping and thrusting the heavy earth calls into play the dark sensual centres in a man, at last, that old Adam which is the eternal opposite of the spiritual or ideal being. Brute labour, the brute struggle with the beast and herd, must rouse into activity the primary centres, darken the mind, induce a state of animal mindlessness, and pivot a man in his own heavy-blooded isolation.
> [*Symbolic Meaning* 169]

Lawrence imagined his St Matthew as experiencing much the same dilemma as Hughes' Adam. The Saviour would have him live 'like a lark at heaven's gate singing', but he is suspicious of too much Uplift in this life, and insists that as a living man he must maintain his contact with the vitalizing earth:

> So I will be lifted up, Saviour,
> But put me down again in time, Master,
> Before my heart stops beating, and I become what I am not.
> Put me down again on the earth, Jesus, on the brown soil
> Where flowers sprout in the acrid humus, and fade into humus again.
> Where beasts drop their unlicked young, and pasture, and drop their
>   droppings among the turf.
> Where the adder darts horizontal.
> Down on the damp, unceasing ground, where my feet belong

And even my heart, Lord, forever, after all uplifting:
The crumbling, damp, fresh land, life horizontal and ceaseless.

['St Matthew']

Lawrence and Hughes are both in the tradition of Meister Eckhart, who claimed that 'humility' derived from 'humus'. Jung wrote: 'Every renewal of life needs the muddy as well as the clear. This was evidently perceived by the great relativist Meister Eckhart' [*Psychological Types* 244].

This humility clearly must have implications for style. Again it seemed to be almost a matter of accident (Parzival letting the reins lie loose on his horse's neck) that Hughes had not the time or energy after a day's farming to write fully-fledged poems, only to make a few purely factual notes of the more interesting things which had happened:

In making a note about anything, if I wish to look closely I find I can move closer and stay closer, if I phrase my observations about it in rough lines. So these improvised verses are nothing more than this: my own way of getting reasonably close to what is going on, and staying close, and of excluding everything else that might be pressing to interfere with the watching eye. In a sense, the method excludes the poetic process as well.

[*Moortown Diary*, x]

It largely excludes the selective, interpreting, abstracting, ambitious ego, and all our preconceptions about what constitutes the poetic. When Hughes later tried to process the notes into 'real poems', he found that he lost much more than he gained, lost the integrity of the original raw experience. (Lawrence admired Etruscan art because it was not 'cooked in the artistic consciousness'.) So he resisted the high temptation of the mind and the meddling intellect and left well alone.

The new humility requires also that Hughes should no longer 'relegate Nature to a function of human perception' [Scigaj 1991, 180]. On the contrary, it is now recognized as the only reality, into which we are granted an occasional privileged glimpse:

... And so for some lasting seconds
I could think the deer were waiting for me
To remember the password and sign

That the curtain had blown aside for a moment
And there where the trees were no longer trees, nor the road a road

The deer had come for me.   ['Roe-deer']

On the farm miracles so clearly issued out of the dirt and the body's jellies. Farming is a far from romantic undertaking. Hughes' affirmations are fully paid for. He indulges in none of the distortions which make traditional nature worship so vulnerable to the attacks of any clear-eyed realist such as Samuel Beckett. There is no denying that farming is as much to do with deaths and misbirths (astride of a grave) as with happier miracles:

> The deepest fascination of stock rearing is this participation in the precarious birth of these tough and yet over-delicate beasts, and nursing them against what often seem to be the odds. [*Moortown Diary*, 65]

In 'Ravens' Hughes will not deny even to the three-year-old child that the lamb which died being born cried. But what the ravens have done to its body – 'its insides, the various jellies and crimsons and transparencies / And threads and tissues pulled out' – does not cancel the miracle that this mess and spillage so nearly added up to a new life, and that the same strange substances did so only a few yards away, where a ewe investigates her new lamb 'while the tattered banners of her triumph swing and drip from her rear-end'.

What had so disgusted Beckett, 'the pastures red with uneaten sheep's placentas', what he had reduced to 'the whole bloody business', 'a turd', 'a cat's flux', what Eliot had reduced to 'dung and death', Hughes redeems. In the unfallen vision of *Moortown Diary*, *Season Songs* and *What is the Truth?* even death has its atonement, (the lamb's hacked-off head has 'all earth for a body'), and even the worm, even the dirt is god.

Hughes will not isolate the single death from its larger context:

> Though this one was lucky insofar
> As it made the attempt into a warm wind
> And its first day of death was blue and warm
> The magpies gone quiet with domestic happiness
> And skylarks not worrying about anything
> And the blackthorn budding confidently
> And the skyline of hills, after millions of hard years,
> Sitting soft. ['Ravens']

One might have thought that there was little new to say about the countryside and the seasons. Hughes writes of them as if he were the only one of us who is really awake:

> Over the whole land
> Spring thunders down in brilliant silence.

Every April is our real birthday, when the world bombards us with gifts:

> And the trees
> Stagger, they stronger
> Brace their boles and biceps under
> The load of gift. And the hills float

Light as bubble glass
On the smoke-blue evening

And rabbits are bobbing everywhere, and a thrush
Rings coolly in a far corner. A shiver of green
Strokes the darkening slope as the land
Begins her labour.

Season Songs tells us, and what amazing news it is, what it is like to be
alive in this world, with five senses and normal feelings. They embody what
Lawrence called 'a man in his wholeness wholly attending'. Hughes' earlier
books record the hard struggle towards this wholeness. When it is achieved,
life's charge flows freely again, and can be communicated to others through
poems. The agony of Prometheus is behind the apparently spontaneous and
joyful balance of these poems and the humility of their thanksgiving.

*   *   *

The value of nature to Hughes is not aesthetic. He has now got well beyond
the aversion to beauty as something irreversibly compromised. The larger
beauty of his later work has nothing to do with the charming and the picturesque, or with the Wordsworthian pieties still trundled out by sentimental
preservationists. Nature is of supreme value not in spite of, but, in a mysterious
way because of the elements of ugliness, pain and death:

> For that's the paradox of the poetry, as if poetry were a biological healing
> process. It seizes on what is depressing and destructive, and lifts it into a
> realm where it becomes healing and energizing. . . . And to reach that
> final mood of release and elation is the whole driving force of writing at
> all. [Norwich Tape]

It is the absence of this final stage which distinguishes the work of Samuel
Beckett from that of the Eastern European poets:

> At bottom, their vision, like Beckett's is of the struggle of animal cells and
> of the torments of spirit in a world reduced to that vision [of disaster], but
> theirs contains far more elements than his. It contains all the substance
> and feeling of ordinary life. And one can argue that it is a step or two
> beyond his in imaginative truth, in that whatever terrible things happen
> in their work happen within a containing passion – Job-like – for the
> elemental final beauty of the created world. [WP221]

Imaginative truth-tellings demands that both the disaster and the
beauty be fully presented. To select the benevolent, comforting aspects of
nature is to cast her in the role of the green mother. The green mother in
Cave Birds is Nature in its Lucy Gray aspect, Blake's threefold vision, Beulah,

'a soft Moony Universe, feminine, lovely, / Pure, mild & Gentle' [*Vala* I,95–6], which appears to its inhabitants 'as the beloved infant in his mother's bosom round incircled' [*Milton* 30:11]. She seeks with 'songs and loving blandishments' to wipe Enion's tears. But her beauty is delusive. Beulah may be valued as a retreat for temporary solace and refreshment. As a permanent residence it becomes a Lotus Land where the soul dies:

> Where the impressions of Despair & Hope for ever vegetate
> In flowers, in fruits, in fishes, birds & beasts & clouds & waters,
> The land of doubts & shadows, sweet delusions, unform'd hopes.
> They saw no more the terrible confusion of the wracking universe.
> They heard not, saw not, felt not all the terrible confusion,
> For in their orbed senses, within clos'd up, they wander'd at will.
> And those upon the Couches view'd them, in the dreams of Beulah,
> As they repos'd from the terrible wide universal harvest.
>
> [*Vala* IX,377–84]

In *Cave Birds* the green mother offers the hero a return to the womb, not for rebirth but for perfect security, the everlasting holiday promised by all the religions, without contraries or suffering or consciousness:

> This earth is heaven's sweetness.
>
> It is heaven's mother.
> The grave is her breast
> And her milk is endless life.
> You shall see
> How tenderly she has wiped her child's face clean
>
> Of the bitumen of blood and the smoke of tears.
>
> ['A green mother']

In a wood the protagonist sees all the animals move 'in the glow of fur which is their absolution in sanctity'. But they have never fallen. Their 'state of steady bliss' [*Moortown Diary*, 65] is not available to or ultimately desirable for man: 'And time was not present they never stopped / Or left anything old or reached any new thing' ['As I came, I saw a wood']. The only religion the hero's deepest humanity sanctions for him is communion with a world whose gods are perpetually crucified and eaten and resurrected, and men move not in perpetual sanctity, but in the bitumen of blood and smoke of tears. There and only there is the ground of his striving towards an earned atonement. His task, like Blake's Milton, is 'to redeem the Female Shade' which is his own Emanation, his anima, mother, bride and vision.

Hughes' intention, had the *Life and Songs of the Crow* been completed, was to bring Crow at last to a river he must cross. But his way is barred by a huge foul ogress who demands to be carried over on his shoulders. On the way her weight increases to the point where Crow cannot move. Then she asks him a riddle which he must answer before her weight will decrease to allow him to stagger a few more steps. This happens seven times. The first two questions are 'Who paid most, him or her?' and 'Was it an animal, a bird, or a fish?' Crow's answers, 'Lovesong' and 'The Lovepet', are about as wrong as they could be. But he comes to realize that these riddles are all about love, and are, in fact, recapitulations of his previous mistaken encounters with the female, onto whom he had projected the ugly and threatening contents of his own psyche, whom he had tried to kill or otherwise victimize. His answers gradually improve until, in his answer to the final question, 'Who gave most, him or her?', he gets it right. His answer is 'Bride and Groom', where the broken hero and his former victim begin 'with fearfulness and astonishment' tenderly to reassemble each other:

> So, gasping with joy, with cries of wonderment
> Like two gods of mud
> Sprawling in the dirt, but with infinite care
>
> They bring each other to perfection.

Crow reaches the far bank, and the ogress leaps lightly from his back transformed into a beautiful maiden, his intended bride.

The green mother offers a world without goblins. The overweening male ego is the criminal throughout the sequence. But the unselving process is not an end in itself. There can hardly be life without self. The process of individuation must begin again, hoping to avoid some of the mistakes. The alchemical marriage, or coniunctio, is not only a marriage of male and female but of all the polarized elements of the divided self. It is a marriage of heaven and hell. It must be the opposite of the submerging of one in the other, a perpetual creative struggle of contraries. The goblin is the offspring. The couple must not attempt to kill or tame or disown the goblin. They must acknowledge this thing of darkness and attempt to accommodate its energies so that it does not turn ugly and destructive. Without the goblin there would be nothing for the married couple to do but lie in perpetual inertia, in a religious daze.

✻   ✻   ✻

It is hard to decide which poems are the more wonderful, those written out of fourfold vision, or those which re-enact the painful process by which that vision is achieved and renewed. For the former we would go to *River*, for the latter to the Epilogue poems in *Gaudete*.

Here the Anglican clergyman Nicholas Lumb has undergone a terrifying ordeal in the underworld, which is the spirit world and the animal world, the world under the world, the depths of his own unconscious. The experience has destroyed his old split self and enabled him to be reborn of the goddess who is simultaneously reborn of him. Lumb is returned to the surface world by a loch in the west of Ireland. We can imagine him surviving only on the fringe of the modern world, for he returns as a holy idiot, stripped of everything but his new sacramental vision which enables him to perform small miracles such as whistling an otter from the loch and triggering a shattering vision of the creation in an Irish priest, and to write these little poems, some confused memories of his ordeal, some hymns to the goddess. Lumb corresponds exactly (as does the nameless hero of *Cave Birds*) to Hughes' description of the doubling and subsequent correction of the tragic hero in *Shakespeare and the Goddess of Complete Being*:

> Then follows his correction: his 'madness' against the Goddess, the Puritan crime . . . which leads directly to his own tragic self-destruction, from which he can escape only after the destruction of his ego – being reborn through the Flower rebirth, becoming a holy idiot, renouncing his secular independence, and surrendering once again to the Goddess. From the human point of view, obviously the whole business is monstrous: tragic on a cosmic scale, where the only easements are in the possibilities of a temporary blessing from the Goddess (an erotic fracture in the carapace of the tragic hero) or of becoming a saint. [393]

Here Hughes tries to imagine what it might be like to make the apparently impossible choice and accept, even worship, the Goddess in her totality, including her role as Queen of Hell. To accept life, that is, unconditionally, with all its inevitable cargo of pain and death.

These Epilogue poems contain as much pain as poems can, pain which is felt to be essential to the ultimate exultation, the release of mana. Hughes now sees the 'drama of organic life', no longer simply as a battle between vitality and death:

> life itself is what terrifies living things and possesses them with their various forms of madness, and exhausts them with their struggles to control and contain it and to secure its subjective essence of joy.
>
> [*Shakespeare* 326]

These are poems about atonement, what it would be like to be, in Lawrence's terminology, reconnected with the cosmos, or in Hughes' to become once again 'participants in the business of living in this universe' [*Children as Writers* 2, p.5]. A poem about the death of a baited badger ends:

> Me too,
> Let me be one of your warriors.

Let your home
Be my home. Your people
My people.

         *   *   *

In *Remains of Elmet* Hughes turned to look at what had actually been done to his home and people in the Calder Valley. Hughes cannot regret that the moors, into which so many lives were ploughed like manure, are now breaking loose from the harness of men.

It is not only the chimneys, chapels and dry-stone walls of the Calder Valley which must collapse before there can be any new building. The image of stone returning to the earth is one of many images in Hughes for the restoration to Nature of her own, the healing and rededication of the holy elements before man can approach them again with clean hands, with respect and humility, and for purposes more natural, sane and worthily human than the enslavement of body and spirit which has characterized Protestantism and industrialism in England.

Most of the poems are bleak. The *duende* of the Calder Valley is a spirit of disaster and mourning. You can hear it in the 'dark sounds' of the moors – 'the peculiar sad desolate spirit that cries in telegraph wires on moor roads, in the dry and so similar voices of grouse and sheep, and the moist voices of curlews' ['The Rock']. But in spite of this, 'the mood of moorland is exultant'. Many of the finest poems in *Remains of Elmet* celebrate the exhilaration which is the recognition that out of these uncompromising and unpromising materials, this graveyard, this vacancy of scruffy hills and stagnant pools and bone-chilling winds, life is continually renewing itself and making miracles:

And now this whole scene, like a mother,
Lifts a cry
Right to the source of it all.

A solitary cry.

She has made a curlew. ['Long Screams']

Such mothers are not, in our sense, maternal. They have no concern to make life easy for plants or animals, let alone humans. The miracle is that 'out of a mica sterility' comes the harebell's blueness, the heather's nectar.

An indicator of the distance Hughes has now travelled from the world of blood is the extensive use he makes in *Remains of Elmet* of light. Imagery of light is common throughout Hughes, but in his earlier work light is often merely the polar opposite of blood, what you are left with when you have got rid of blood by getting rid of substance, as in 'I said goodbye to earth': 'I arrived at light / Where I was shadowless'. Light without shadow is not only bloodless, it is cold, empty, uncreative, associated with the moon rather than the sun.

Since imagination means wholeness, dualism is the disease it exists to cure. The poet can have no use for the word 'supernatural', not because he disbelieves in spirit, but because, seeing nature whole at last, he sees that everything commonly called supernatural is part of nature, the very essence of nature. All Hughes' work of the seventies was an effort to resolve that dualism of blood and light, to become capable of seeing that light which is nature replete with spirit, the radiance of spirit, creative energy, within all creation, streaming continually from it. In *Gaudete* such vision is granted only to a priest in a moment of exceptional visionary receptiveness:

> He seemed to be flying into an endless, blazing sunrise, and he described the first coming of Creation, as it rose from the abyss, an infinite creature of miracles, made of miracles and teeming miracles. And he went on, describing this creature, giving it more and more dazzlingly-shining eyes, and more and more glorious limbs, and heaping it with greater and more extraordinary beauties, till his heart was pounding and he was pacing the room talking about God himself, and the tears pouring from his eyes fell shattering and glittering down the front of his cassock.

In *Remains of Elmet* every dawn was such a blazing sunrise (at least for those who were out before 'the sun climbed into its wet sack / For the day's work') as the cocks kindled the valley with their crows – 'bubble-glistenings flung up and bursting to light':

> Till the whole valley brimmed with cockcrows,
> A magical soft mixture boiling over,
> Spilling and sparkling into other valleys.

Remains of Elmet is entirely about the crime against nature, which here takes the form of the enslavement of a people conscripted into the mills, the chapels, the trenches, conscripted also into the human attempt to conscript in turn the mothers, the sustaining elements of earth, air, fire and water, to degraded, spiritless purposes. Like Blake Hughes seeks to renew the fallen light. The poems and photographs which are set in the valley bottom are harsh and gloomy – mills, chimneys and bridges reflected in the dull canal. What light there is seems trapped by the surrounding darkness, as the human spirit was trapped in the mills and chapels: 'The fallen sun / Is in the hands of water'. ('It Is All') Water, too, is fallen, conscripted into gulleys, drained of all promise of fertility in the 'worn-out water of women' and the 'lost rivers of men'.

But on the high moors the elements seem to revel and gleam in their freedom. The same wind which had so threatened the embattled ego in 'Wind', now blows great holes in the sky opening it to the huge light of spirit; it frees the hills from their harness of walls. The Methodists had built their foursquare chapels in an attempt to imprison spirit and keep out nature, even a single cricket. Nature is now reclaiming them. The happiest men are those at play, the roofless, wall-less, pitifully buffeted men trying to play football on the highest, most exposed ridge for miles. Though their only spectator is that wild god leaning through a fiery hole in heaven, they are not overawed:

> And the valleys blued unthinkable
> Under depth of Atlantic depression –
>
> But the wingers leapt, they bicycled in air
> And the goalie flew horizontal
>
> And once again a golden holocaust
> Lifted the cloud's edge, to watch them.
> ['Football at Slack']

The comedy is part of the feeling of release from that intolerable 'weight of Atlantic depression' which had characterized the earlier poems about the Yorkshire Pennines. The style, out from under that pressure, plays like the wind. So far has Hughes now travelled since 'The Hawk in the Rain' that Scigaj can speak of 'the ethereal lightness of his poetic line' in *Remains of Elmet*.

✳   ✳   ✳

Scigaj has noted the accumulation of images of light in *River*:

> Most often Hughes portrays the spiritual component of the river's animistic energy through light imagery. Light imagery coalesces with river water regularly to imbue riverscapes with a numinous aura, a sense of the sacredness of the hydrological cycle. Cock minnows gathering in a pool at Easter work together solemnly in the 'lit water', an image Hughes expands at the poem's conclusion to convey brightness from the Source blessing their labour 'In the wheel of light – / Ghostly rinsings / A struggle of spirits' [23]. On the island of Skye an encounter with a salmon leaves the fisherman with a sense of being momentarily absorbed into the spirit world after miles of hiking towards the river's source while staring at the pool tail's 'superabundance of spirit' [31]. Under water, the mystical sea-trout 'Hang in a near emptiness of light' [40]; the West Dart River 'spills from the Milky Way, pronged with light' [39]; and the river's 'Unending' sustenance, a wine distilled from the harvest it helped to fertilize, is squeezed from hills packed 'Tight with golden light' [45]. An abundance of visual and auditory similes and metaphors revive in the reader a sense of participation in an ecosystem that fulfils much more than one's craving for facts and analysis. [*Ted Hughes*, 136–7]

Nature here is not clothed in celestial light, has no need of any borrowed glory. It is wholly constituted of earthly light. All life is matter radiant with spirit. 'In the marriage of these two is a bliss of making and unmaking, all matter spiritualized, all spirit materialized, in the divine harmony of Light' [Smith 93]. This is very close to the vision Nietzsche calls Dionysian:

> The word 'Dionysian' expresses . . . an ecstatic saying of yea to the collective character of existence, as that which remains the same, and equally mighty and blissful throughout all change; the great pantheistic sympathy with pleasure and pain, which declares even the most terrible and questionable qualities of existence good, and sanctifies them; the eternal will to procreation, to fruitfulness, and to recurrence; the feeling of unity in regard to the necessity of creating and annihilating.
>
> [*Will to Power* Sect. 1050]

In accordance with this spirit of acceptance, Hughes looks again at the previously unacceptable face of the goddess, the bloody face of the predator, and declares it good. Nature is indeed perfecting her killers; but if it were only that, the prey species would collapse and the perfect killers would soon have nothing left to kill. Nature must simultaneously perfect the survival skills of the prey. Neither species could have evolved without the other. They bring each other to perfection.

The 'religious daze, the state of steady bliss' which Hughes observed in new-born calves, can also be seen in the dying:

> The spider clamps the bluefly – whose death panic
> Becomes sudden soulful absorption.
>
> A stoat throbs at the nape of the lumped rabbit
> Who watches the skylines fixedly.
>
> [*Gaudete* 177]

Predation is a form of holy communion:

> And already the White Hare crouches at the sacrifice,
> Already the Fawn stumbles to offer itself up
> And the Wolf-Cub weeps to be chosen.   ['Eagle']

'Tiger-psalm' was originally conceived as a dialogue between Socrates and Buddha. Gradually Buddha's side of the argument resolved itself into a tiger and Socrates' into the principle of machine-guns, 'as if the whole abstraction of Socrates' discourse must inevitably, given enough time and enough applied intelligence, result in machine guns'. It is an argument between single vision and fourfold vision. The tiger, unlike the machine-gunners, is carrying out a perfectly rational, restrained and sacred activity:

The tiger
Kills expertly, with anaesthetic hand.

. . .

The tiger
Kills frugally, after close inspection of the map.

. . .

The tiger
Kills like a fall of cliff, one-sinewed with the earth,
Himalayas under eyelid, Ganges under fur –

Does not kill.

Does not kill. The tiger blesses with a fang.
The tiger does not kill but opens a path
Neither of Life nor of Death

In his report on visions seen by thirty-five subjects after taking the hallucinogenic drug harmaline in Chile, Claudio Naranjo tells us that seven of them saw big cats, usually tigers, though there are no big cats in Chile and no tigers in the New World. One woman had a tiger guide throughout her journey. Another actually became a tiger:

I walked, though, feeling the same freedom I had experienced as a bird
and a fish, freedom of movement, flexibility, grace. I moved as a tiger in
the jungle, joyously, feeling the ground under my feet, feeling my power;
my chest grew larger. I then approached an animal, any animal. I only
saw its neck, and then experienced what a tiger feels when looking at its
prey.
[Harner 185]

Naranjo comments: 'This may be enough to show how the tiger by no means stands for mere hostility, but for a fluid synthesis of aggression and grace and a full acceptance of the life-impulse beyond moral judgement'. A vision of such a synthesis occurs frequently in the oral poetry of 'primitive' peoples. Here is a Yoruba poem called 'Leopard':

Gentle hunter
His tail plays on the ground
While he crushes the skull.

Beautiful death
Who puts on a spotted robe
When he goes to his victim.

Playful killer
Whose loving embrace
Splits the antelope's heart.
[Finnegan 163]

Half Naranjo's subjects had ecstatic feelings of a religious nature: 'The sea was in myself. There was a continuity of the external with the internal. . . . The sand and the plants were myself or something of mine. The idea of God was in everything' [188]. But this atonement must always be preceded by a descent into destruction:

> The complex of images discussed first as portraying the polarity of being and becoming, freedom and necessity, spirit and matter, only set up the stage for the human drama. This involves the battle of opposites and eventually their reconciliation or fusion, after giving way to death and destruction, be this by fire, tigers, drowning, or devouring snakes. The beauty of fluid fire, the graceful tiger, or the subtle and wise reptile, these seem most expressive for the synthetic experience of accepting life as a whole, or, better, accepting existence as a whole, life and death included; evil included too, though from a given spiritual perspective it is not experienced as evil any more. Needless to say, the process is essentially religious, and it could even be suspected that every myth presents us one particular aspect of the same experience.   [189–90]

This, certainly, is the controlling myth of Hughes' whole career. Only thus can Tennyson's agonized question be answered. God and Nature are not at strife, and to let the tiger die is to let God die.

Hughes agrees with Eliot that the river is a god. But Eliot's river, 'with its cargo of dead negroes, cows and chicken coops' is purely destructive, sweeping everything as wastage into the sea. Hughes' river is source not sink, it 'will go on issuing from heaven / In dumbness issuing spirit brightness / Through its broken mouth'. It 'will wash itself of all deaths' ['River']. 'Peering into that superabundance of spirit', the human intruder is humbled, feels ghostly, loses all sense of his own centrality and omnipotence as a lord of language. The waters wash away his sense of identity, cause him to 'be supplanted by mud and leaves and pebbles'. After such an experience, 'new and nameless', he can only

> Let the world come back, like a white hospital
> Busy with emergency words
>
> Try to speak and nearly succeed
> Heal into time and other people ('Go Fishing')

Here, as Nicholas Bishop points out 'the personal pronoun is absolutely eliminated from the poem as the protagonist becomes "translucent" to the processes of both the entire surrounding river-scape and those of the explored inner world' [248]. Here Hughes fulfils the hope for poetry expressed in 1952 by the French poet Francis Ponge:

When man becomes proud to be not just the site where ideas and feelings
are produced, but also the crossroad where they divide and mingle, he
will be ready to be saved. Hope therefore lies in a poetry through which
the world so invades the spirit of man that he becomes almost speechless,
and later reinvents a language.   ['The Silent World is Our Only Homeland']

Pilinszky castigates that narcissistic art which 'places the stylistic certainty of
appearances before the self-forgetful incarnating of the world' [Bishop 144].
To return to *River*, the language of all these poems is a rich weave of relationships. A poem may be ostensibly about a single creature, but that creature is
defined by its relationships with other creatures, with weather and season and
landscape. Since 'all things draw to the river' it is therefore the language of
atonement.

In his note to 'Rain-Charm for the Duchy' Hughes describes in detail
the astonishing breeding behaviour of salmon. He concludes:

This is how salmon come to be such sensitive glands in the vast,
dishevelled body of nature. Their moody behaviour, so unpredictable and
mysterious, is attuned, with the urgency of survival, to every slightest
hint of the weather – marvellous instruments, recording every
moment-by-moment microchange as the moving air and shifting light
manipulate the electronics of the water-molecules.   [*Rain-Charm* 52]

The life of the salmon is also the life of the living waters, which is also the life
of earth and sky. The salmon is part of a flow which 'will not let up for a
minute'.

The bliss of unmaking is the theme of, for example, 'October Salmon'.
The spent salmon is the defeated, torn and sacrificed hero whose acquiescence
is a form of worship. The bliss of making is the theme of 'Salmon Eggs':

Something else is going on in the river
More vital than death –

. . .

– these toilings of plasm –
The melt of mouthing silence, the charge of light
Dumb with immensity.
The river goes on
Sliding through its place, undergoing itself
In its wheel.

The wheel, karma, the 'cycles of recurrence', were formerly for Hughes, as for
most religions, images of horror and absurdity. The pressure was to get off the
intolerable wheel. Now it seems that that horror was a product of defective
vision and of the hubristic attempt to redeem nature. Hughes now echoes

Lawrence's risen Christ (in *The Escaped Cock*): 'From what, and to what, could this infinite whirl be saved?'

Like Shakespeare in *A Midsummer Night's Dream*, Hughes seeks to rescue the language of spirit and the sacred from transcendental religion. The early church arrogated to itself many of the most powerful symbols, festivals, rituals, of pagan religion. Now it is time for them to be restored. And if the only language now available to us to express sacredness is the language of Christian worship, then the church's monopoly of that language must be broken. In 'Salmon Eggs' Hughes appropriates the language of the church, its 'liturgy' and 'mass'; the river, the 'round of unending water', the wheel itself, is his 'crypt', 'altar' and 'font'. His eucharist gives thanks for 'earth's tidings' and the 'blessed issue' of salmon eggs. He translates the river's annunciation as *'Only birth matters'*. The Great Mother's only obligation is fecundity.

The influence on Hughes of Buddhism in the sixties was largely replaced in the seventies by the influence of Alchemy, as he strove to find poetic equivalents (overtly in *Cave Birds: an alchemical cave drama*) for the Great Work of Alchemy:

> The 'Great Work' of Alchemy aimed to discover the nature of 'spirit' and to see face to face the 'body of light' that was the foundation of the human body as well as the 'matter' of the universe. The alchemical marriage between sun and moon, king and queen, spirit and soul (including body), expressed the essential identity of spirit and nature, so healing the split that had developed in human consciousness between these two aspects of life. Whoever this secret revealed itself to had penetrated to the mystery of creation and knew there was no death, for he or she understood how life continuously regenerated itself; how the manifest emanated from the unmanifest and 'dissolved' again into the unmanifest.   [Baring 649–50]

This vision of the 'body of light' expressing the divine harmony of matter and spirit is evident in most of the poems in *River*, but most clearly in 'That Morning', the poem with which Hughes chose to end his 1982 *Selected Poems*. Here two awe-struck human beings are allowed to re-enter Paradise, not as trespassers or intruders or voyeurs, but as long exiles being welcomed home. The place, a remote valley in Alaska, and its creatures demanded a sacramental response. The sheer profusion of salmon was a sign and a blessing, the body a 'spirit beacon lit by the power of the salmon', as if this were no longer a fallen world:

> Then for a sign that we were where we were
> Two gold bears came down and swam like men
>
> Beside us. And dived like children.
> And stood in deep water as on a throne
> Eating pierced salmon off their talons.

So we found the end of our journey.

So we stood, alive in the river of light
Among the creatures of light, creatures of light.

It is no derogation of the sacredness of the salmon that they should be also
food, for both man and bear. Campbell writes:

The affect of the successful adventure of the hero is the unlocking and
release again of the flow of life into the body of the world. The miracle of
this flow may be represented in physical terms as a circulation of food
substance, dynamically as a streaming of energy, or spiritually as a
manifestation of grace. Such varieties of image alternate easily,
representing three degrees of condensation of the one life force. An
abundant harvest is the sign of God's grace; God's grace is the food of the
soul; the lightning bolt is the harbinger of fertilizing rain, and at the same
time the manifestation of the released energy of God. Grace, food
substance, energy: these pour into the living world, and wherever they
fail, life decomposes into death.   [*Hero* 40]

This moment out of time is of course precarious. The journey resumes next
day, or that afternoon, to recapture it.
      A more typical hero is the October salmon, worn-out with his two
thousand mile journey, earth's 'insatiable quest', who, despite the 'covenant
of Polar Light' ends as a 'shroud in a gutter' – 'this chamber of horrors is also
home'. And even if the covenant held, and man had the option of life 'among
creatures of light', would he choose the Goddess for his bride and nature for
his home?

The ego's extreme alternatives are either to reject her and attempt to live
an independent, rational, secular life or to abnegate the ego and embrace
her love with 'total, unconditional love', which means to become a saint, a
holy idiot, possessed by the Divine Love. . . . Man will always choose the
former, simply because once he is free of a natural, creaturely awareness
of the divine indulgence which permits him to exist at all, he wants to live
his own life, and he has never invented a society of saints that was
tolerable.   [*Shakespeare* 392–3]

Hughes is doubtful that any man could long sustain the salmon's 'epic poise'

That holds him so steady in his wounds, so loyal to his doom, so
      patient
In the machinery of heaven.
                                                  ['October Salmon']

367

Perhaps the best we can hope for is that our civilization will pass like the others, seeming no more than the nightmare of a stranded immortal who will eventually awake:

> The dream streamed from him. He blinked away
> The bloody matter of the Cross
> And the death's-head after-image of 'Poor'.
>
> Chapels, chimneys, roofs in the mist – scattered.
>
> Hills with raised wings were standing on hills.
> They rode the waves of light
> That rocked the conch of whispers
>
> And washed and washed at his eye.
>
> > Washed from his ear
>
> All but the laughter of foxes.
> > ['A Chinese History of Colden Water']

AFTERWORD

Readers who have found these chapters valid and helpful on specific authors or texts, will, I hope, be drawn towards certain generalizations about literature and criticism, the creative imagination and its relevance to the present ecological crisis. I shall now allow myself the luxury of setting out, for what they are worth, some of the generalizations to which I have been driven.

As we embark on the third millennium, one question rightly dominates the thinking of the sane: is there any reasonable hope of reversing, halting, or even slowing, the destruction of the environment on which we totally depend. Nature has been ill-treated in many ways, spurned, despiritualized, exploited, polluted. Man's systematic attack on Nature has been, in effect, hacking at the tree of which he is himself a leaf, and therefore suicidal madness. Man's attempt to destroy the ecosystem is now so close to succeeding that the belated attempt to stop and heal the damage dwarfs all other human concerns.

> The story of the mind exiled from Nature is the story of Western Man. It is the story of his progressively more desperate search for mechanical and rational and symbolic securities, which will substitute for the spirit-confidence of the Nature he has lost. . . . It is the story of spiritual romanticism and heroic technological progress. It is a story of decline. When something abandons Nature, or is abandoned by Nature, it has lost touch with its creator, and is called an evolutionary dead-end.
>
> [Ted Hughes, *WP* 129.]

The history of Western civilization has been the history of man's increasingly devastating crimes against Nature, Nature defined not only as the earth and its life forms, powers and processes, but also as the female in all its manifestations, and as the 'natural man' within the individual psyche. It is the story of man's mutilation of Nature in his attempt to make it conform to the Procrustean bed of his own patriarchal, anthropocentric and rectilinear thinking. We are all familiar with protests against the dehumanization and blighting of the earth by the industrial revolution. But the industrial revolution was possible only because of changes which had been taking place for thousands of years in the human mind, and when Lawrence realistically describes a pit-bank, 'flames like red sores licking its ashy sides', in the language of symbolism he is describing something no different from the plagues of ancient Thebes or the dumping of nuclear waste. In Lovelock's words man himself has become a plague ravaging the earth.

There is nothing new about ecology except its terminology, and the fact that what is now a rare kind of consciousness (holistic, biocentric) which a minority is trying to recapture, may once have been the universal consciousness of the race. Or perhaps it was lost as early as the evolution of the divided brain in Cro-Magnon man. This is the argument of Jean Marais in *The Soul of the Ape*, of William Golding in *The Inheritors*, in the writings of Paul MacLean taken up by Arthur Koestler in *The Ghost in the Machine*, and in Ted Hughes' essay 'Baboons and Neanderthals' (in Carey, *William Golding: The Man and his Books*). Joseph Campbell, Marija Gimbutas, Baring and Cashford, argue that it was still characteristic of Neolithic man, and came to an end only with the inauguration of the terrible Age of Bronze. John A. Philips claims that it lasted until the beginning of civilization 'which seems to require a seizure of religious power by male gods, in order to break the ties of humanity to blood, soil and nature'. Robert Graves and D.H. Lawrence followed Nietzsche in dating the 'fall' to the sixth century B.C. Socrates and Plato presided over the crucifixion of the old consciousness. At the birth of Christ the spirits wailed round the Mediterranean 'Great Pan is dead'. The Renaissance, the Age of Reason, the Industrial Revolution, the Age of Technology and the Multi-nationals, have all mutilated the body, which will not quite die.

There is now widespread agreement that we must try to recapture something of that earlier vision. This can be attempted in two ways, through deep ecology and through imaginative art. It is my argument that these are, and need to be recognized as, essentially the same. Perhaps our greatest hope lies in a marriage of deep ecology, the life-sciences and the imaginative arts. George Sessions distinguishes between deep and shallow ecology, and Fritjof Capra comments:

> Whereas shallow environmentalism is concerned with more efficient control and management of the natural environment for the benefit of 'man', the deep ecology movement recognizes that ecological balance will require profound changes in our perception of the role of human beings in the planetary ecosystem. In short, it will require a new philosophical and religious basis. Deep ecology is supported by modern science, and in particular by the new systems approach, but it is rooted in a perception of reality that goes beyond the scientific framework to an intuitive awareness of the oneness of all life, the interdependence of its multiple manifestations and its cycles of change and transformation. When the concept of the human spirit is understood in this sense, as the mode of consciousness in which the individual feels connected to the cosmos as a whole, it becomes clear that ecological awareness is truly spiritual.
>
> [Capra, 458]

The shallow ecologist sees only the symptoms in the material environment. The deep ecologist uses imagination to search for the hidden, deeply-rooted causes within:

> What, after all, is the ecological crisis that now captures so much belated attention but the inevitable extroversion of a blighted psyche? Like inside, like outside. In the eleventh hour, the very physical environment

suddenly looms up before us as the outward mirror of our inner
condition, for many the first discernible symptom of advanced disease
within.

[Roszac, xvii]

Deep ecology seeks to respiritualize Nature, to heal the split in the
human psyche, replacing anthropocentric with biocentric consciousness, to
provide the only viable religion for the third millennium. Capra goes on to
claim that such a framework has been 'set forth many times throughout human
history', citing Taoism, Christian mystics, and philosophers from Heraclitus
to Heidegger. He concludes:

It is found throughout Native American culture, and has been expressed
by poets ranging from Whitman to Gary Snyder. It has even been argued
that the world's greatest pieces of literature . . . are structured according
to the ecological principles observed in nature.

[458–9]

For this vast enterprise ecology needs imagination, and imagination's
most articulate expression, literature. What has kept the old consciousness
alive through the thousands of years of its gradual rejection and persecution,
in spite of the obliteration of the beliefs and rituals of nature religions and the
total desacralization of modern life in the West, has been art, myth, and,
especially, poetic literature. The literary imagination connects all the severed
halves – inner and outer, self and other, male and female, life and death, man
and Nature. Every metaphor is a stitch in the suture.

Imaginative speech is essentially metaphorical. For the process of
making metaphors Wordsworth made the astonishing claim:

This principle is the great spring of the activity of our minds and their
chief feeder. From this principle the direction of the sexual appetite and
all the passions connected with it, take their origin: it is the life of our
ordinary conversation; and upon the accuracy with which similitude in
dissimilitude and dissimilitude in similitude are perceived, depend our
taste and moral feelings.

['Preface to the *Lyrical Ballads*', 1800]

Metaphor is the linguistic equivalent of touch. It is the link, the bridge, the
meeting, the marriage, the atonement, bit by bit reconstructing the world as
a unity, blissfully skipping over the supposed chasms of dualism. Hughes
speaks of it as 'a sudden flinging open of the door into the world of the right
side, the world where the animal is not separated from either the spirit of
the real world or itself' [*Shakespeare* 159]. Lawrence speaks of poetry as a
'magical linking up':

The religious way of knowledge means that we accept our
sense-impressions, our perceptions, in the full sense of the word,

complete, and we tend instinctively to link them up with other impressions, working towards a whole. The process is a process of association, linking up, binding back (religio) or referring back towards a centre and a wholeness. This is the way of poetic and religious consciousness, the instinctive act of synthesis. [*Apocalypse*, 190]

Imagery is the body of our imaginative life, and our imaginative life is a great joy and fulfilment to us, for the imagination is a more powerful and more comprehensive flow of consciousness than our ordinary flow. In the flow of true imagination we know in full, mentally and physically at once, in a greater, enkindled awareness. At the maximum of our imagination we are religious. And if we deny our imagination, and have no imaginative life, we are poor worms who have never lived. [*Phoenix*, 559]

The images, which most consistently achieve this magic, are symbols. Jung valued the symbol highly as providing the necessary third ground on which the otherwise polarized halves of the psyche could meet:

What the separation of the two psychic halves means, the psychiatrist knows only too well. He knows it as the dissociation of personality, the root of all neuroses; the conscious goes to the right and the unconscious to the left. As opposites never unite at their own level, a supraordinate 'third' is always required, in which the two parts can come together. And since the symbol derives as much from the conscious as the unconscious, it is able to unite them both, reconciling their conceptual polarity through its form and their emotional polarity through its numinosity. [*Aion*, 180]

Imaginative art would be in a privileged position to lead the way in our time if there were a large enough readership capable of responding appropriately to it. But the capacity for such a response had already in Lawrence's day become rare:

The man who has lost his religious response *cannot* respond to literature or to any form of art, fully: because the call of every work of art, spiritual or physical, is religious, and demands a religious response. The people who, having lost their religious connection, turn to literature and art, find there a great deal of pleasure, aesthetic, intellectual, many kinds of pleasure, even curiously sensual. But it is the pleasure of entertainment, not of experience. . . . They cannot give to literature the one thing it really requires – if it be important at all – and that is the religious response; and they cannot take from it the one thing it gives, the religious experience of linking up or making a new connection [*Apocalypse*, 155–6]

The greatest challenge to literature, education and literary criticism is to try to help readers to recover this faculty. As Lawrence writes:

The great range of responses that have fallen dead in us have to come to life again. It has taken two thousand years to kill them. Who knows how long it will take to bring them to life.   [78]

That ancient vision of atonement is preserved in myth, and both preserved and perennially recreated in art. The purpose of art is to preserve it, and imaginative art cannot do otherwise, since the very nature of the creative imagination is holistic; its primary function is to make connections, discover relationships, patterns, systems and wholes.

Imagination is not a separate faculty which some are born with. It is what happens when the faculties we all have are freed from their usual bonds and divisions, resist the process of training and indoctrination, and speak out with the voice of nature – the voice of human nature of course, but not a human nature which defines itself in contradistinction to the rest of life, the voice of a man or woman, but not one who represses the anima or animus which is their continuity in consciousness. The language of the imagination is necessarily holistic and biocentric. It is grounded simultaneously in the depths of the artist's being and in the external universe. It breaks down the walls of egotism, sexism, nationalism, racism, anthropocentrism. It expresses relationships and wholes. Its language is metaphor and symbol.

A work of imagination shares with a living creature or the ecosystem itself the characteristic of not being reducible to its parts, or explicable in terms of the technique of its manufacture. It cannot be exhausted by analysis. It is a system of interrelationships which, since it extends far beyond the words on the page, engages with everything else in the reader's conscious and unconscious experience, and is therefore virtually infinite. It is a microcosm, a model of the universe.

The living poem is the opposite of a well-wrought urn (or billiard-ball in Lawrence's comic terminology) complete in itself; it sends out countless roots and tendrils, ripples, shock-waves, shrapnel, grapnels, to touch, engage, disturb, grapple with the world, and with a different matrix of experiences in each reader.

Imagination's goal is atonement, the healing of the split between the mind and the rest of our faculties which has brought us to our present chronic, perhaps terminal condition. The analytic reason, operating in a void, is absurd. It has no validating or vitalizing contact with either inner or outer realities. If thought were a matter of mind only, man would be a windowless monad, an ego-bound obscenity, a clever imbecile.

The imagination is by no means the enemy of intelligence or civilization. Its function is to correct any imbalance, which has come about in the psyche, to reconcile and harmonize the warring, artificially polarized elements. What we call intelligence is often merely the analytical and manipulative aspects of intelligence developed to the exclusion of, at the cost of, all other aspects – intelligence cut off from its sustaining and validating connections with the rest of the psyche, with the body, and with everything outside itself. Yeats said 'God save me from thoughts men think in the mind alone'. Such thinking is what Blake called 'single vision and Newton's sleep'.

At a reading Hughes explained how it had come about that a poem ('Tiger-psalm') which had begun life (in the sixties) as a dialogue between Socrates and Buddha had ended up as a dialogue between machine-guns and a tiger:

> the whole abstraction of Socrates' discourse must inevitably, given enough time and enough applied intelligence, result in machine-guns . . . machine-guns descending directly from a mechanical, mechanistic development of logicality which grows from the abstraction of dialectical debate.

The ultimate in 'applied intelligence' and 'mechanistic development of logicality' was perhaps the computer-based systems-analysis of the Rand Corporation which largely directed American foreign policy in the nineteen-sixties – perhaps the apogee of disembodied reason in our history, when the computerized dialectical debate focussed on what figure of American losses in a nuclear war, between fifteen and a hundred million, would be 'acceptable' or 'sustainable'. Dean Acheson said of American policies and actions at that time: 'The criteria should be hard-headed in the extreme. Decisions are not helped by considering them in terms of sharing, brotherly love, the Golden Rule, or inducing our citizens into the Kingdom of Heaven' [quoted in Stein, *Peace on Earth*, 281]. Of the brinkmanship of the Cuban missile crisis Acheson said: 'Moral talk did not bear on the problem'. Nor did it bear on American action in Vietnam. In 1964 the analysts assured the U.S. government that a war in Vietnam could be quickly won. When in 1967 the Rand Corporation's computer was asked when the war would end, it replied that America had in fact won it in 1964. Perhaps the most realistic literature of the sixties was the so-called 'absurd' fiction of Heller and Vonnegut.

What is normally thought of as thinking, all those methods of 'thinking' which have been developed over the centuries in Western civilization, whose dualistic assumptions have been built into the very structure of our language, has specialized in separating things from each other, then separating the parts, analyzing, vivisecting, compartmentalizing, until it has drastically weakened our capacity for thinking in a way that puts things together, makes connections, perceives patterns and wholes. For most of the history of the human race the language of myth and folk-tale was to some extent generally understood, and understood to have a relevance not only to metaphysical truths, but to the health of the race and to the practical business of living. This has largely gone.

Starting from the narrow world we all inhabit, with its hubristic human perspectives and habitual complacencies, the imagination reaches inward towards the roots of our being and outward towards the powers of the non-human world. We know that all mirrors held up to nature, even by scientists, are distorting mirrors. All descriptions of nature are coloured by attitudes, are partly descriptions of the contents of the observer's own psyche projected onto the receptive face of nature. For the scientist this might be a problem, but for the artist it is the whole point of his art. Ted Hughes develops the case:

> The character of great works is exactly this: that in them the full presence of the inner world combines with and is reconciled to the full presence of the outer world. And in them we see that the laws of these two worlds are not contradictory at all; they are one all-inclusive system; they are laws that somehow we find it all but impossible to keep, laws that only the greatest artists are able to restate. They are the laws, simply, of human nature. And men have recognized all through history that the restating of these laws, in one medium or another, in great works of art, are the greatest human acts. . . . So it comes about that once we recognize their terms, these works seem to heal us. More important, it is in these works that humanity is truly formed. And it has to be done again and again, as circumstances change, and the balance of power between outer and inner world shifts, showing everybody the gulf. The inner world, separated from the outer world, is a place of demons. The outer world, separated from the inner world, is a place of meaningless objects and machines. The faculty that makes the human being out of these two worlds is called divine. That is only a way of saying that it is the faculty without which humanity cannot really exist. It can be called religious or visionary. More essentially, it is imagination, which embraces both outer and inner worlds in a creative spirit.   [*WP* 150–1]

But before imagination can operate in this way upon the outer world, it must make the necessary inner and outer connections to allow creative energy to flow through the body and all its faculties. The artist as physician must first heal himself.

Imagination can be defined as a mode of access to and control of the contents of the unconscious. According to Jung

> if the conscious psyche of individuals or of groups (such as nations or even the human race as a species) has become distorted, then the unconscious psyche will, apparently intentionally, compensate for this distortion by insisting on an opposite point of view in order to restore the balance.   [Baring 554]

Thus imagination is subversive, and the imaginative writer of sufficient courage says, in Melville's phrase, 'No, in thunder!' to the prevailing orthodoxies, unquestioned assumptions and shibboleths of his time. The dramatic festivals of ancient Greece virtually came into being in order to testify to the crime against Nature and warn of its inevitable consequences – consequences for the individual, for the state, and for the race. Those protests and warnings have not hitherto been heeded. The truth is too uncomfortable, the implications too radically revolutionary.

*   *   *

It is unfortunate that the word 'hero' with its inevitable associations with bravery, nobility and greatness of soul, should have come to be used to describe the chief male character in any story, for we shall see that many of the so-called heroes of myth, epic and drama are in fact criminals against Nature who should be viewed with horror as exemplars not of heroism but of hubris, or rather of hubris in their very heroism. Vaclav Havel writes:

> The natural world, in virtue of its very being, bears within it the presupposition of the absolute which grounds, delimits, animates and directs it, without which it would be unthinkable, absurd and superfluous, and which we can only quietly respect. Any attempt to spurn it, master it or replace it with something else, appears, within the framework of the natural world, as an expression of *hubris* for which humans must pay a heavy price, as did Don Juan and Faust.   [*Living in Truth*]

Perhaps the most damaging perversity in our response to great literature has been our insistence on treating as heroes the anti-heroes, the criminals. Prometheus has been celebrated as winning man his freedom from the tyranny of the gods. What Prometheus did was to teach man to regard himself as autonomous, to regard nothing as sacred, to 'strike wounds in the divine environment' (Kerenyi), to relegate nature to a heap of raw materials, to regard technology as the highest achievement, to probe nature's deepest secrets and not hesitate to play with fire. In other words, Prometheus set the feet of the race on the road to where we now have to live. Odysseus in *The Odyssey* has been universally praised for similar cleverness and independence, for unscrupulousness, for sacking cities, for butchering young women, subjecting all other considerations to his own name and fame.

We meet hubris in many of the protagonists of Greek tragedy – Agamemnon, Creon, Oedipus and Pentheus for example; in Sir Gawain; in several of Shakespeare's most fascinating characters – Adonis, Theseus, Angelo, Hamlet, Macbeth, Prospero; in Gulliver, and the Man Who Loved Islands, and Pincher Martin; in the poets themselves as well as in their alter egos from the Ancient Mariner to Crow.

It is common for critics to assume that the greatest writers are deficient in basic moral perceptions, that, for example, Homer identifies himself completely with Odysseus, Euripides with Pentheus, the Gawain poet with Gawain, Shakespeare with Prospero, or Swift with the Houyhnhnms. Nearly all the protagonists discussed in this book are simultaneously heroes and villains. In acting out their particular fates they suffer the tragi-comic human condition in all its glory and horror.

Hughes once said at a reading that he was always astonished by 'the extraordinary assumption by critics that they are the judges of literature, rather than criminals merely reporting on the judgements passed upon them by literature'. This is not to say that critics must hold back from passing any kind of judgement, only that such judgement must not be made on the assumption of the superiority of the analytical critic to the imaginative artist. There are other ways in which judgements can be made. Artists frequently pass severe judgements upon themselves: no-one knew more deeply than Coleridge himself how desperately he had mismanaged his talent. Even when the artist is, outside his work, less aware or less honest than Coleridge, his best work can pass judgement on him, in accordance with Lawrence's formulation 'Never trust the artist, trust the tale'. The artist can be, both outside his art and in his conscious intentions in his art, a 'dribbling liar', yet still reveal the truth of the imagination.

The great writers are far from being exempt from the criminality of their species and culture. The difference is that the writer recognizes his own guilt, puts himself in the dock, submits to correction by his own deepest self, the voice of nature within him. Thus in *The Odyssey* Homer makes reparations for the false values of *The Iliad*. And *The Bacchae* is as much a repudiation of Euripides' own former values as of those of Athens. It is the central problem for the Romantics and remained so for the moderns. Eliot found Nature unthinkable (when unredeemed from beyond itself), Beckett absurd, and Sartre superfluous.

The creative writer is not a privileged being, a born judge or infallible seer. I am less interested in writers who are concerned simply to castigate others for failing to live by their own superior values than in writers whose imaginative depth and honesty leads them to reveal, even when they are about quite other business, their own complicity in the crime against nature and their own natures. Such writers earn an authenticity and universality lacking in propagandists for however good a cause. The great imaginative writer may be one who has achieved a measure of fourfold vision – early Wordsworth, early Coleridge, Whitman, early Hopkins, later Yeats, later Lawrence, later Hughes. But that achievement is made at great cost. He is also likely to be the opposite, for much of his life, or in his more normal state – a cursed sufferer from single vision, from egotism, materialism, dualism, who differs from the rest of us in lacking our complacency, in knowing that he is sick and striving in his art to diagnose that sickness, to punish and to heal himself. The artist is a criminal like the rest, but differs from us in that his loyalty to his imagination forces him to acknowledge his guilt and seek correction. Rarely, he manages to get himself, to a degree, corrected.

We are all criminals in the sense that we have all persecuted, exploited or denied essential parts of ourselves, particularly that part which Jung called, in men, the anima. And that innermost self is representative of all that we persecute, exploit or deny in the outer world – women, 'undeveloped' peoples, animals, Nature herself. Imagination is the faculty which enables us to locate and release the violated prisoner, or at least to give her a voice. Those who are most successful in this we call poets. Initially, that voice may well be embittered, revengeful, destructive. It passes a harsh judgement on the poet, our representative. The punishment may be terrifying, as in 'The Ancient Mariner' or bloody as in *Gaudete*. But the pain and the fear, which may be real enough in some cases, are also symbolic of a process which is simultaneously destructive and creative, the breaking of the complacent, self-sufficient ego, which is the locus of guilt. Subsequently the voice becomes gentler, and the healing process can begin.

The 'Nightingale' and 'Grecian Urn' odes are great poems because in them Keats accepts defeat in his fervent attempts to transcend nature. That acceptance opens the way for an even greater poem 'To Autumn', which, with phenomenal courage, transforms to beauty the very flux and transience of nature which, he knew, was shortly to claim his life. The ode 'Intimations of Immortality' is another fervent but failed attempt, of great value to the reader as such, but of none to Wordsworth, since he was unable to acknowledge the failure, which therefore opened the way to nothing but the long decline. Yeats' journey to Byzantium, on the other hand, another magnificent failure, led to the chastened return and acceptance of his greatest poems.

Joseph Campbell claims that with any writer whose realization of his own experience has been 'of a certain depth and import, his communication will have the value and force of living myth' [*Creative Mythology*, 4]. Jung had said the same in *The Spirit of Man*:

> The unsatisfied yearning of the artist reaches back to the primordial image in the unconscious, which is best fitted to compensate the inadequacy and one-sidedness of the present. [82] Whenever the collective unconscious becomes a living experience and is brought to bear upon the conscious outlook of an age, this event is a creative act, which is of importance for a whole epoch. [98] He [the artist] has plunged into the healing and redeeming depths of the collective psyche. [105]

Beyond that the artist must, of course, have the ability to communicate the whole experience through language in a way, which produces an authentic miracle – that some sounds, or marks on a page, should transmit a healing and fertilizing power.

Yet the very act of transforming experience into art through the 'poetic' mastery of language itself exposes the artist to a new dimension of temptation, a new disguised form of criminality. The temptation is to process experience, in Lawrence's terms to cook it in the artistic consciousness, until it loses its savour, its very life and truth, and becomes another form of egotism. There is the temptation to succumb to the embrace of what Hughes called the 'maternal octopus' of the English poetic tradition, to produce your own version of what has been done so beautifully, so expressively, so powerfully, in the past; the temptation to write the sort of poetry that is currently valued, that critics and publishers seem to want; the temptation to put on display one's talents, as the young Yeats put all his circus animals on show in the full confidence that words obeyed his call; the temptation, having achieved some success, a readership, to repeat the same effects and write what Hopkins called Parnassian. Both Yeats and Lawrence at the time of the First World War were arguing that at such a time the poet could earn the right to be noticed only by going naked: 'Everything can go, but this stark, bare, rocky directness of statement, this alone makes poetry, today' Lawrence wrote in 1916. When Eliot read that fifteen years later he responded with rare fervour:

> This speaks to me of that at which I have long aimed, in writing poetry; to write poetry which should be essentially poetry, with nothing poetic about it, poetry standing naked in its bare bones, or poetry so transparent that we should not see the poetry, but that which we are meant to see through the poetry, poetry so transparent that in reading it we are intent on what the poem *points at*, and not on the poetry, this seems to me the thing to try for. To get *beyond poetry*, as Beethoven, in his later works, strove to get *beyond music*. We never succeed, perhaps, but Lawrence's words mean this to me, that they express to me what I think that the forty or fifty original lines that I have written strive towards.
>
> [Mattheissen 1958, 90]

A few years later, at the beginning of another World War, Eliot wrote the line: 'The poetry does not matter' ['East Coker'].

Ted Hughes had the same lesson to learn, the need for the self-abnegation by a famous poet of the pyrotechnics, the 'old heroic bang' on which his fame depended. He admired a generation of Eastern European poets such as Popa and Pilinszky whose work was purged of rhetoric, deliberately impoverished, 'a strategy of making audible meanings without disturbing the silence' [WP 223]. He sought a simplicity not of retreat or exclusion but on the far side of experience and complexity:

> This other rare type has the simplicity of an inclusion of everything in a clear solution. We recognise the difference, because we recognise in this latter kind that the observer has paid in full for what he records, and that has earned him a superior stake in reality, which is not common. Good folk rhymes have this kind of simplicity – experience itself seems to have produced them. . . . To succeed in any degree in producing it, a writer needs . . . a touch of that martial/ascetic brand of temperament – usually alien and even hostile to aesthetic sensibility – to provide the reckless drive towards essentials, and the readiness to abandon the verbal charms of conventional poetry.   [Introduction to *The Reef*]

The achievement of such nakedness is a shedding of what Lawrence called 'the full armour of their own idea of themselves', a form of ego-death. It is also a shedding of the husk, which must split before the seed can germinate. From such humble beginnings whole new myths might grow.

*   *   *

It could be argued that a 'living myth' is not a new myth but a rediscovery and release of the power of the oldest myths. In *The Myth of the Goddess* Baring and Cashford write:

> Nature is no longer experienced as source but as adversary, and darkness is no longer a mode of divine being, as it was in the lunar cycles, but a mode of being devoid of divinity and actively hostile, devouring of light, clarity and order. The only place where the voice of the old order breaks through, though so disguised as to be barely recognizable, is where the inspiration of poetry re-animates the old mythic images.   [298]

It was my first dim realization of this twenty-five years ago which set me out on a quest which revealed that the old order breaks through, either by reanimating the old mythic images or by other means, in a surprisingly high proportion of the greatest imaginative writers of our tradition, and that it is 'barely recognizable' only because we have been conditioned not to recognize what is staring us in the face. So Auden looked at the great body of mythic imagery within and behind Yeats and called it mere silliness. And Philip Larkin gazed blankly at the 'common myth-kitty' and dismissed it as irrelevant to his own or any other poet's concerns, thus castrating his own poetry and criticism. His best poems are about his desperate need for the spiritual healing he allowed his lesser self to spurn.

The distinctive energies of modernism were centrifugal – 'Things fall apart, the centre cannot hold'; now, quite suddenly, as if some world-wide chemical reaction had taken place, these energies have swung round and become centripetal. Fiction has blossomed world-wide as a healing force, with women (who had little to do with modernism) now playing their proper role. Poetry always was a healing force, and this has been strongly reaffirmed by such contemporary poets as Robert Bly, Wendell Berry, Gary Snyder, Ted Hughes, Peter Redgrove and Seamus Heaney. More and more disciplines, formerly aligned against Nature or attempting to function independently of it are now gravitating to a common centre which is the recognition of the interdependence of all life.

*   *   *

It is precisely the periods of greatest national growth and confidence which have produced, in reaction, the dark imaginative vision – Periclean Athens, Elizabethan England, the Age of Reason, the Industrial Revolution, the age of Victorian expansionism, and our own century of technological wizardry. But the situation is different now. Perhaps at last, at this eleventh hour, with so many other voices raised in support, the great writer might gain some serious attention. And the contemporary writer has a different challenge. We no longer need visionary artists to give us warnings; we are bombarded with warnings from every side. The role of the artist now is, more than ever before, to heal, to discover and embody possibilities of regeneration.

The status of the imaginative writer in our own society and in relation to our own impending disaster is very different. In 1970 Ted Hughes wrote of the call to the shaman to go to the spirit world 'to get something badly needed, a cure, an answer, some sort of divine intervention in the community's affairs. . . . Poets usually refuse the call. How are they to accept it? How can a poet become a medicine man and fly to the source and come back and heal or pronounce oracles? Everything among us is against it' [Faas, 206]. Perhaps since then it has become a little less unthinkable. Art, science, philosophy, religion, converge towards a common centre which we are now in a position to recognize as holistic, sacramental, a rapidly growing awareness that, in Coleridge's words, 'we are all one life'. No longer are poetic visionaries voices in the wilderness. Their vision, formerly seen as idiosyncratic and eccentric, is coming to be seen as the essential vision of the nascent world-age.

WORKS CITED

Abrams, Mark, *Natural Supernaturalism*, Oxford U.P. 1971.

Aeschylus, *Oresteia*, trans. Vellacott, Penguin 1956.
    Prometheus Bound, trans. Vallacott, Penguin 1961.

Aristophanes, *The Wasps, The Poet and the Women, The Frogs*, trans.
    Barrett, Penguin 1964.

Auden, W.H., *W.H. Auden*, Penguin 1958.

Bachelard, Gaston, *Water and Dreams*, Dallas 1983.

Barber, C.L. *Shakespeare's Festive Comedy*, Princeton 1972.

Baring, Anne, and Jules Cashford, *The Myth of the Goddess*, Viking 1991.

Bate, Jonathan, *The Song of the Earth,* Picador 2000.

Beckett, Samuel, *Endgame*, Faber 1958.
    Watt, Calder 1963.

Bishop, Nicholas, *Re-Making Poetry: Ted Hughes and a New Critical
    Psychology*, Harvester 1991.

Blake, William, *Complete Writings*, ed. Geoffrey Keynes, Oxford U.P. 1971.

Bradshaw, Graham, *Shakespeare's Scepticism*, Harvester 1987.

Brontë, Emily, *Wuthering Heights*, ed. David Daiches, Penguin 1965.
    The Complete Poems, ed. C.W. Hatfield, Oxford U.P. 1941.

Brown, Norman O., *Life Against Death,* Wesleyan University Press, 1959.

Byatt, A.S., *Possession,* Chatto and Windus, 1990.

Campbell, Joseph, *The Hero with a Thousand Faces*, Princeton U.P. 1972.
    *The Masks of God, 4 vols. (Primitive Mythology, Occidental Mythology,
    Oriental Mythology, Creative Mythology)*, Souvenir Press 1973–4.

Capra, Fritjof, *The Turning Point*, Flamingo 1983.

Carey, John, ed., *William Golding: The Man and his Books*, Faber and
    Faber 1986.

Carlyle, Thomas, 'Characteristics' and the relevant sections of *Sartor
    Resartus* are reprinted in
    The Norton Anthology of English Literature.

Castaneda, Carlos, *Tales of Power*, Hodder and Stoughton 1974.

Chambers, Jessie, *D.H. Lawrence: A Personal Record*, ed. J.D. Chambers,
    Frank Cass 1965.

Coleridge, S. T., *Biographia Literaria*, ed. J. Shawcross, Oxford 1907.
    Poetical Works, ed. E.H. Coleridge, Oxford U.P. 1912.
    Collected Letters, ed. E.L. Griggs, Oxford U.P. 1956–71.
    The Notebooks, ed. Kathleen Coburn, Routledge 1957–73.
    The Friend, ed. Barbara E. Rooke, Bollingen 1969.

Conrad, Joseph, *Heart of Darkness*, Penguin 1973.

Conquest, Robert, ed., *New Lines*, Macmillan 1956.

Cowley, Malcolm, 'Introduction' to *Walt Whitman's Leaves of Grass:
    The First (1855) Edition*, Secker and Warburg 1960.

Darwin, Charles, *The Origin of Species*, Oxford 1951.

Davenport, W.A., *The Art & the Gawain-poet*, Athlone, 1978.

Davies, Stevie, *Emily Brontë*, Harvester 1988.

Dodds, E.R. *The Greeks and the Irrational*, California U.P. 1951.

Donoghue, Denis, ed. *Jonathan Swift*, Penguin 1971.

Draper, R.P. *D.H. Lawrence: The Critical Heritage*, Routledge 1970.

Ehrenpreis, Irvin, 'The Meaning of Gulliver's Last Voyage', *Review of English Literature*, July 1962; reprinted in Tuveson.

Eliot, T.S., *Collected Poems*, Faber 1963.

Emerson, R.W. 'Nature' and 'The Poet' are both reprinted in *The Norton Anthology of American Literature*.

Euripides, *The Bacchae and Other Plays,* trans. Vellacott, Penguin 1954.

Faas, Ekbert, *Ted Hughes: The Unaccomodated Universe*, Black Sparrow Press 1980.

Fiedler, Leslie, *No! in Thunder,* Eyre and Spottiswood, 1963.

Finnegan, Ruth, ed. *The Penguin Book of Oral Poetry*, 1978.

Fowler, R. *Linguistics and the Novel,* Methuen 1977.

    Linguistic Criticism, Oxford U.P., 1986.

Frazer, J.G. *The Golden Bough*, St, Martin's Library, Macmillan 1957.

Freud, Sigmund, *Moses and Monotheism,*

Fruman, Norman, 'Coleridge's Rejection of Nature' in Gravil, Newlyn and Roe.

Golding, William, *Lord of the Flies*, Faber and Faber 1958.

    The Inheritors, Faber and Faber 1961.

    Pincher Martin, Penguin 1962.

    Free Fall, Faber and Faber 1959.

    'All or Nothing', *Spectator*, 24 March 1961.

    The Spire, Faber and Faber 1965.

    A Moving Target, Faber and Faber 198

Graves, Robert, *The Greek Myths*, 2 vols. Penguin 1960.

    The White Goddess, Faber 1961.

Gravil, Newlyn and Roe, eds. *Coleridge's Imagination*, Cambridge U.P. 1985.

Groenewegen-Frankfort, H.A., *Arrest and Movement: An Essay on Space and Time in the Representational Art of the Near East*, London 1951.

Harner, Michael J., *Hallucinogens and Shamanism*, Oxford U.P. 1973.

Harrison, Tony, *The Trackers of Oxyrhynchus*, Faber and Faber 1990.

Hawthorne, Nathaniel, *The Scarlet Letter and Selected Tales*, Penguin 1970.

    The Blithedale Romance, Norton, 1958.

Homer, *The Odyssey*, trans. Rieu, Penguin 1946.

Hopkins, G.M. *Poems*, 3rd. edition, eds. Robert Bridges and W.H. Gardner, Oxford U.P. 1948.

    The Journals and Papers, ed. Humphrey House, Oxford U.P. 1959.

    The Sermons and Devotional Writings, ed. Christopher Devlin, Oxford U.P. 1959.

The Correspondence of G.M.H. and Richard Watson Dixon, ed. C. C. Abbott, Oxford U.P. 1955.

The Letters of G.M.H. to Robert Bridges, ed. C. C. Abbott, Oxford U.P. 1955.

Further Letters of G.M.H., ed. C. C. Abbott, Oxford U.P. 1956.

Hughes, Ted, 'The Rock', *Writers on Themselves,* BBC 1964.

Seneca's Oedipus, Faber and Faber 1969.

'Myth and Education' I, *Children's Literature in Education,* March 1970.

'Foreword' to *Children as Writers 2*, Heinemann 1975.

Gaudete, Faber and Faber 1977.

Ted Hughes and R.S. Thomas, Norwich Tapes 1978.

What is the Truth?, Faber and Faber 1984.

Shakespeare and the Goddess of Complete Being, Faber 1992.

Winter Pollen, ed. Scammell, Faber 1994.

Collected Poems, Faber 2003.

Hume, David, *Dialogues Concerning Natural Religion*, ed. Bell, Penguin 1990.

Huxley, Aldous, 'Wordsworth in the Tropics' in *Do What You Will*, Chatto & Windus 1929.

'Lawrence in Etruria' in *D.H. Lawrence: A Critical Anthology*, ed. H. Coombes, Penguin 1973.

Huxley, T.H *Evolution and Ethics*, Macmillan 1894.

Joyce, James, *Portrait of the Artist as a Young Man*, Penguin 1960.

Ulysses, Bodley Head 1937.

Jung, C.G. Jung's *Collected Works* are published by Routledge and Kegan Paul.

Psychology and the Unconscious was collected as *Symbols of Transformation* (vol. 5).

Psychological Types, (vol.6).

The Archetypes of the Collective Unconscious (vol. 9, part i).

Aion, (vol. 9, part ii).

Civilization in Transition (vol. 10).

The Spirit of Man (vol.15).

Kerényi, C. *Prometheus*, Pantheon 1963.

Kinkead-Weekes, Mark, and Gregor, Ian, *William Golding: A Critical Study*, Faber and Faber 1970.

Knight, G. Wilson, *The Wheel of Fire*, Methuen 1954.

The Imperial Theme, Methuen 1968.

The Starlit Dome, Oxford U.P. 1971.

Shakespearean Dimensions, Harvester 1984.

Koestler, Arthur, *The Ghost in the Machine*, Picador 1975.

Laing, R.D. *The Politics of Experience*, Penguin 1967.

Lawlor, John, '*Pandosto* and the Nature of Dramatic Romance', *Philological Quarterly* 41, 1962; reprinted in Palmer.

Lawrence, D.H., *Apocalypse*, ed. Mara Kalnins, Cambridge U.P. 1980.
　　Complete Poems, ed. Vivian de Sola Pinto and F. Warren Roberts, Penguin 1977.
　　The Escaped Cock, ed. Gerald M. Lacy, Black Sparrow Press 1973.
　　Lady Chatterley's Lover, ed. Michael Squires, Cambridge U.P. 1993.
　　Letters I, ed. James T. Boulton, Cambridge U.P. 1979.
　　Letters II, eds. George J. Zytaruk and James T, Boulton, Cambridge U.P. 1981.
　　Letters III, eds. James T. Boulton and Andrew Robertson, Cambridge U.P. 1984.
　　Letters VI, eds. James T. and Margaret H. Boulton, Cambridge U.P. 1991.
　　Mornings in Mexico and *Etruscan Places*, Penguin 1960.
　　Phoenix, Penguin 1978.
　　Phoenix II, Heinemann 1968.
　　The Plumed Serpent, ed. L.D. Clark, Cambridge U.P. 1987.
　　The Prussian Officer, ed. John Worthen, Cambridge U.P. 1983.
　　The Rainbow, ed. Mark Kinkead-Weekes, Cambridge U.P. 1989.
　　Reflections on the Death of a Porcupine, ed. Michael Herbert, Cambridge U.P. 1988.
　　St. Mawr and Other Stories, ed. Brian Finney, Cambridge U.P. 1983.
　　Studies in Classic American Literature, ed. Ezra Greenspan, Lindeth Vasey and John Worthen, Cambridge U.P. 2003.
　　Study of Thomas Hardy, ed. Bruce Steele, Cambridge U.P. 1985.
　　Women in Love, ed. David Farmer, John Worthen and Lindeth Vasey, Cambridge U.P. 1987.
Leavis, F.R. *The Common Pursuit*, Penguin 1962.
　　New Bearings in English Poetry, Chatto and Windus 1950.
　　Revaluation, Chatto and Windus, 1956.
Lewis, R.W.B. *Trials of the Word*, 1965.
Lorca, Federico Garcia, 'The Theory and Function of the Duende' in *Lorca*, ed. J.L. Gili, Penguin 1960.
McMaster, Graham, ed., *William Wordsworth*, Penguin 1972.
Mahood, M.M., 'Wordplay in *The Winter's Tale*', *Shakespeare's Wordplay*, Methuen 1957; reprinted in Palmer.
Marais, Eugene N. *The Soul of the Ape*, Penguin 1973.
Massey, Irving, *The Uncreating Word: Romanticism and the Object*, Indiana 1970.
Matthiessen, F.O., *American Renaissance*, Oxford U.P. 1941.
　　The Achievement of T.S.Eliot, Oxford U.P. 1958.
Merivale, Patricia, *Pan the Goat-God: His Myth in Modern Times*, Harvard U.P. 1969.
Merleau-Ponty, Maurice, 'Eye and Mind' in *Aesthetics*, ed. Harold Osborn, Oxford U.P. 1972.

Midgley, Mary, *Beast and Man*, Harvester 1978.

Moorman, Mary, *William Wordsworth: A Biography*, 2 vols., Oxford U.P. 1968.

Murray, Margaret, *The God of the Witches*, Sampson Low, Marston & Co., n.d.

Naranjo, Claudio, 'Psychological Aspects of the *Yagé* Experience in an Experimental Setting', in Harner.

Nehls, Edward, ed. *D.H. Lawrence: A Composite Biography*, 3 vols., Nebraska 1957–9.

Nietzsche, Friedrich, *The Birth of Tragedy*, Anchor, 1956.
>   *A Nietzsche Reader*, ed. R.J. Hollindale, Penguin 1977.
>   *Thus Spoke Zarathustra*, trans. Hollindale, Penguin, 1961.

Olson, Charles, *D.H. Lawrence and the High Temptation of the Mind*, Black Sparrow Press 1979.

Palmer, D.J., ed., *Shakespeare's Later Comedies*, Penguin 1971.

Perera, Sylvia B., *Descent to the Goddess*, Inner City Books, 1981.

Petit, Jean-Pierre, ed., *Emily Brontë*, Penguin 1973.

Plato, *Phaedrus*, Penguin 1973.

Ponge, 'The Silent World is Our Only Homeland', in Beth Archer, *The Voice of Things*, McGraw-Hill 1974.

Radner, John B. 'The Struldbruggs, the Houyhnhnms and the Good Life', *Studies in English Literature* 17, 1977.

Redgrove, Peter *The Black Goddess*, Bloomsbury 1987.
>   *The Moon Disposes: Poems 1954–1987*, Secker and Warburg 1987.

Reynolds, David S. *Beneath the American Renaissance*, Knopf 1988.

Robinson, Craig, 'The Good Shepherd' in Sagar, ed. *The Achievement of Ted Hughes*, Manchester U.P. 1983.

Ross, E.C., 'Whitman's Verse', *Modern Language Notes*, vol. 45.

Roszak, Theodore, *Where the Wasteland Ends*, Anchor Books 1973.

Sagar, Keith, *The Reef*, Proem Pamphlets, Yorkshire Arts Association 1980.

Scigaj, Leonard M., *The Poetry of Ted Hughes*, Iowa 1986.
>   *Ted Hughes*, Twayne 1991.

Segal, C. *Tragedy and Civilization*, Cambridge Ma., 1981.
>   *Dionysiac Poetics and Euripides' Bacchae*, Princeton, 1982.

Seneca, *Four Tragedies and Octavia*, trans. Watling, Penguin 1966.
>   *Oedipus*, trans. Ted Hughes, Faber and Faber 1969.

Shakespeare, William. All texts used are the New Arden edition.

Sherry, Norman, *Conrad*, Thames and Hudson 1972.

Short, Mick, 'Mind-Style', *European English Messenger*, vol.1, iii, 1992.

Shuttle, Penelope and Redgrove, Peter, *The Wise Wound*, Gollancz 1978.

Sir Gawain and the Green Knight, trans. Stone, Penguin 1959.

Slater, Philip, *Glory of Hera*, Boston, 1968.

Smith, A.C.H., *Orghast at Persepolis*, Eyre Methuen 1972.

Sophocles, *The Three Theban Plays*, trans. Fagles, Penguin 1984.
>   *Electra and Other Plays*, trans. Watling, Penguin 1953.

Stein, Walter, *Criticism as Dialogue*, Cambridge U.P. 1969.

Steiner, George and Fagles, Robert, eds., *Homer*, Spectrum Books 1962.

Stephen, Leslie, 'Wordsworth's Ethics', reprinted in McMaster.

Swift, Jonathan, *Gulliver's Travels* and Selected Writings, ed. Hayward, Nonesuch Press 1949.

Tillyard, E.M.W. *The Elizabethan World Picture*, Penguin 1963.

Traubel, Horace, *Conversations with Walt Whitman*, 1953.

Tuveson, Ernest, ed. *Swift*, Spectrum 1964.

Van Ghent, Dorothy, *The English Novel: Form and Function*, New York 1953.

Von Eschenbach, Wolfram, *Parzival*, Vintage Books, 1961.

Wallace, Alfred Russell, *The Malay Archepelago and the Birds of Paradise,*

Weil, Simone, *On Science, Necessity and the Love of God*, Oxford U.P. 1965.

Weston, Jessie L., *From Ritual to Romance*, Doubleday, 1957.

Whitman, Walt, *Complete Poetry and Selected Prose and Letters*, ed. Emory Holloway, Nonesuch Press 1938.

    Complete Poetry and Collected Prose, ed. Justin Kaplan, Library of America 1982.

Wilson, Edmund, *Axel's Castle*, Scribner's Sons, 1954.

Wilson, Mona, *The Life of William Blake*, Paladin, 1978.

Wordsworth, William, *Poetry and Prose*, ed. W.M. Merchant, Rupert Hart-Davis 1955.

Yeats, W.B. *A Vision*, Macmillan 1962.

    Collected Poems, Macmillan 1955.

Zweig, Paul, *Walt Whitman: The Making of the Poet*, Viking 1985.

Zytaruk, George J., *D.H. Lawrence's Response to Russian Literature*, Mouton 1971.

INDEX

OTHER CHAUCER PRESS BOOKS BY KEITH SAGAR

THE LIFE OF D.H.LAWRENCE
KEITH SAGAR
(288 PAGES HARDBACK 270 X 210 MM)

This is a new, revised and updated edition of the book John Carey has described as 'a glowing, richly pictorial biography', Doris Grumbach in the *New York Times* as 'a biography satisfying in every way: readable, informative, authoratative – an altogether lovely book', and John Worthen as 'the best single-volume biography of Lawrence we have'.

Since his death in 1930 at the age of 44, D.H. Lawrence has become a legend as both a writer and a man. In *The Life of D.H. Lawrence*, Keith Sagar has written an authentic, vivid biography, drawing on the five thousand five hundred Lawrence letters now available, and the many accounts of him by his relatives, friends and contemporaries. He tells the story directly and dramatically, revealing the dynamics of Lawrence's worldwide quest (both as traveller and as 'thought-adventurer') for a way of life he could recognize as both fully human and deeply religious. Lawrence's life was not just an endless series of quarrels and crises, persecutions and tirades, but consisted also of steady work, periods of insouciance, and many tension-free relationships.

The book is fully illustrated throughout with 150 pictures, some in colour and others that have never before been published. Included are images of his friends and associates, places he lived in and wrote about, and his paintings.

In *The Life of DH Lawrence*, Keith Sagar has written not only about Lawrence the creator of some of the finest works in every genre of modern literature, but also the creator of 'that piece of supreme art, a man's life'.

£25.00

D H LAWRENCE'S PAINTINGS
DH LAWRENCE
INTRODUCTION BY KEITH SAGAR
(160 PAGES, HARDBACK COLOUR 285 X 230 MM)

A major new book on the art of DH Lawrence.

D.H.Lawrence's fame as a writer has tended to eclipse his paintings, but he was a keen painter all his life, and in his last years painting became almost his favoured activity.

He was well aware of his technical deficiencies, but nevertheless put life into his paintings as into everything he touched. In 1929 his paintings were exhibited at the Warren Gallery in London, and attracted much attention before the police seized thirteen of them, which were eventually released only on the undertaking that they would never again be exhibited. A fine limited edition of reproductions was published by the Mandrake Press to coincide with the exhibition. This immediately became a scarce collector's item, and is now virtually unobtainable. Few people have seen the originals, since they have never been exhibited again, many are lost, and the only collections are in New Mexico and Texas.

DH Lawrence's Paintings contains high-quality colour reproductions of more of his paintings than any previous book, including some previously unpublished. It also brings together for the first time everything he wrote about painting, his three essays, (including his long introduction to the Mandrake edition, which constitutes a major analysis of the creative process in art, especially in relation to Cézanne), and extracts from his letters and poems.

Much has been written about Lawrence's views on art, and the influence of the visual arts on his writings, but very little on his actual paintings. Keith Sagar's comprehensive commentary places the paintings in the context of Lawrence's life and work, and is illustrated by photographs, and reproductions of some of the paintings Lawrence copied or was most influenced by.

£25.00